Armoured Warfare in the British Army, 1945–2022

The Scots Greys patrolling in Sharjah, 1970.

Find, Fix and Strike

Armoured Warfare in the British Army, 1945–2022

Dick Taylor

THE **TANK** MUSEUM
Produced in collaboration
with the Tank Museum,
Bovington

Pen & Sword
MILITARY
AN IMPRINT OF PEN & SWORD BOOKS LTD.
YORKSHIRE – PHILADELPHIA

First published in Great Britain in 2024 by
PEN & SWORD MILITARY
An imprint of
Pen & Sword Books Ltd
Yorkshire – Philadelphia

ISBN 978 1 39908 108 5

A CIP catalogue record for this book is
available from the British Library

Typeset in Ehrhardt 11/13.5
by SJmagic DESIGN SERVICES, India.

Printed and bound in India by
Replika Press Pvt. Ltd.

Pen & Sword Books Ltd incorporates the imprints of Pen & Sword
Archaeology, Atlas, Aviation, Battleground, Discovery, Family History, History,
Maritime, Military, Naval, Politics, Social History, Transport, True Crime, Claymore
Press, Frontline Books, Praetorian Press, Seaforth Publishing and White Owl
For a complete list of Pen & Sword titles please contact

PEN & SWORD BOOKS LTD
George House, Units 12 & 13, Beevor Street, Off Pontefract Road,
Barnsley, South Yorkshire, S71 1HN, England
E-mail: enquiries@pen-and-sword.co.uk
Website: www.pen-and-sword.co.uk

Or

PEN AND SWORD BOOKS
1950 Lawrence Rd, Havertown, PA 19083, USA
E-mail: uspen-and-sword@casematepublishers.com
Website: www.penandswordbooks.com

Contents

Acknowledgements and Thanks

The Archive and Library, Bovington Tank Museum
Jonathan Holt
Stuart Wheeler
David Willey

Archives – RL, KRH, SCOTS DG, HCav, QRH, RTR, RDG, QDG
Lieutenant Colonel Nick Berchem KRH
Jack Bolton
Andy Brend
WO1 Lee Burnie KRH
Dave Clegg
WO1 Pete Cubitt QDG
Louie DeVirgilio
Peter Garbutt
Graeme Green
Seamus Hamilton
Ted Heath
WO2 Symone Hodge RL
Mick Holtby
Hannah Kearns
Charlene Muzzelle
Steve Penkethman
Richard Stewart
Richard Stickland
Major John Stork RTR
Angela Tarnowski
WO2 Mark Woods LD

Abbreviations and Terminology

2Lt	Second Lieutenant
3rd Carbs	3rd Carabiniers (3rd Dragoon Guards)
3H	3rd Hussars
4H	4th Hussars
5DG	5th Royal Inniskilling Dragoon Guards (The Skins)
7H	7th Hussars
8H	8th Hussars
9/12L	9th/12th Royal Lancers
13/18H	13th/18th Royal Hussars
14/20H	14th/20th Kings Hussars
15/19H	15th/19th Royal Hussars
16/5L	16th/5th Queens Royal Lancers
17/21L	17th/21st Lancers
AAC	Army Air Corps
ABTU	Arms Basic Training Unit
AC	Armoured Car
ACI	Army Council Instruction
ACV	Armoured Command Vehicle
Adjt	Adjutant
AFV	Armoured Fighting Vehicle
AG	Adjutant General
ANA	Afghan National Army
AO	Army Order
AP	Armour Piercing
APC	Armoured Personnel Carrier
APC	Armour Piercing Capped
APCBC	Armour Piercing Capped Ballistic Cap
APDS	Armour Piercing Discarding Sabot
APFSDS	Armour Piercing Fin Stabilized Discarding Sabot
AR	Armoured Reconnaissance
ArmCen	Armour Centre
AT	Adventure Training
ATDU	Armour Trials & Development Unit
ATGW	Anti-Tank Guided Weapon

BAOR	British Army of the Rhine
BATUS	British Army Training Unit Suffield
BCT	Brigade Combat Teams
Bde	Brigade
Besa	7.92mm AFV Machine Gun
BG	Battlegroup
Bn	Battalion
Bren	.303in Light Machine Gun
BRF	Brigade Reconnaissance Force
Bty	Battery
BW	Black Watch
Capt	Captain
CGC	Conspicuous Gallantry Cross
CGS	Chief of the General Staff
CIGS	Chief of the Imperial General Staff
CLY	County of London Yeomanry
CMF	Central Mediterranean Forces
CO	Commanding Officer
Coax	Coaxial armament, usually MG
CoH	Corporal of Horse
Coy	Company
Cpl	Corporal
Cpl Maj	Corporal Major
CS	Close Support (and Central Schools)
CTA	Cased Telescopic Ammunition
CY	Cheshire Yeomanry
D&M	Driving & Maintenance
DCM	Distinguished Conduct Medal
DD	Duplex Drive
Div	Division
DoW	Died of Wounds
DPM	Disruptive Pattern Material
DR	Despatch Rider
DRAC	Director/Directorate Royal Armoured Corps
DS/T	Discarding Sabot Tracer
Dstl	Defence Science and Technology Laboratory
DY	Derbyshire Yeomanry
ERY	East Riding of Yorkshire Yeomanry
FFR	Fit For Role/Fitted For Radio
FFY	Fife & Forfar Yeomanry
FOO	Forward Observation Officer
FR	Formation Reconnaissance

FVPE	Fighting Vehicle Proving Establishment
GDP	General Deployment Plan
GMT	General Military Training
GOC	General Officer Commanding
GPMG	General Purpose Machine Gun
GPS	Global Positioning System
Hcav	Household Cavalry
HCR	Household Cavalry Regiment
HCMR	Household Cavalry Mounted Regiment
HE	High Explosive
HEAT	High Explosive Anti-Tank
HESH	High Explosive Squash Head
HF	High Frequency
HQ	Headquarters
IED	Improvised Explosive Device
IoC	Inns of Court Yeomanry (sometimes ICR: Inns of Court Regiment)
IS	Internal Security
ISAF	International Security Assistance Force
ISTAR	Intelligence, Surveillance, Target Acquisition and Reconnaissance
JNBCR	Joint NBC Regiment
JNCO	Junior Non-Commissioned Officer (LCpl, Cpl)
KDG	King's Dragoon Guards
KRH	Kings Royal Hussars
KIA	Killed in Action
KRIH	King's Royal Irish Hussars
LBH	Lothian & Borders Horse
LBY	Lothian & Borders Yeomanry
LCoH	Lance Corporal of Horse
LCpl	Lance Corporal
LSgt	Lance Sergeant
LDY	Leicestershire & Derbyshire Yeomanry
LG	Life Guards
LMG	Light Machine Gun
Lt	Lieutenant
Lt Col	Lieutenant Colonel
Lt Gen	General
Lt Tk	Light Tank
Maj	Major
Maj Gen	Major General
MBT	Main Battle Tank

MC	Military Cross
MERT	Medical Emergency Response Team
MG	Machine Gun
MGC	Machine Gun Corps
MGO	Master General of the Ordnance
MIV	Mechanised Infantry Vehicle
MLRS	Multi-Launch Rocket System
MM	Military Medal
MoD	Ministry of Defence
MPDS	Multi-Purpose Decontamination System
MT	Motor Transport
MTO	Motor Transport Officer
MTP	Multi-Terrain Pattern
NAAFI	Naval, Army and Air Forces Institute
NBC	Nuclear, Biological & Chemical
NCO	Non-Commissioned Officer
NIH	North Irish Horse
NITAT	Northern Ireland Training and Advisory Team
NS	National Service/Serviceman
I	North West Europe
OC	Officer Commanding
OCTU	Officer Cadet Training Unit
OMLT	Operational Monitoring and Liaison Team
OP	Observation Post
OPFOR	Opposing Forces
OPTAG	Operational Training and Advisory Group
OR	Other Ranks
ORBAT	Order of Battle
PBDS	Prototype Biological Detection System
PBI	Poor Bloody Infantry
Pdr	Pounder, a classification of a projectile by the weight of its HE shell
PJHQ	Permanent Joint Headquarters
PO	Potential Officer
POW	Prisoner of War
PRI	President of the Regimental Institute
QDG	Queen's Dragoon Guards
QF	Quick Firing
QM	Quartermaster
QM(T)	Quartermaster Technical
QOH	Queen's Own Hussars
QOY	Queen's Own Yeomanry

QRH	Queen's Royal Hussars
QRIH	Queen's Royal Irish Hussars
QRL	Queen's Royal Lancers
RA	Royal Artillery
RAC	Royal Armoured Corps
RACC	Royal Armoured Corps Centre
RAOC	Royal Army Ordnance Corps
RARO	Regular Army Reserve of Officers
RASC	Royal Army Service Corps
RACTR	Royal Armoured Corps Training Regiment
RCB	Regular Commissions Board
RE	Royal Engineers
Recce	Reconnaissance
Regt	Regiment
RE	Royal Engineers
REME	Royal Electrical and Mechanical Engineers
RGH	Royal Gloucestershire Hussars
RH	Royal Hussars
RHG	Royal Horse Guards
RHG/D	Royal Horse Guards/1st Dragoons
RHQ	Regimental Headquarters
RL	Royal Lancers
RMO	Regimental Medical Officer
ROF	Royal Ordnance Factory
RQMS	Regimental Quartermaster Sergeant
R&R	Rest & Recuperation
RSigs	Royal Signals
RCM	Regimental Corporal Major
RRF	Royal Regiment of Fusiliers
RSM	Regimental Sergeant Major
RSMI	Regimental Sergeant Major Instructor
RSOI	Reception, Staging, Onward Movement and Integration
RTR	Royal Tank Regiment
RTU	Returned to Unit
RUSI	Royal United Services Institute
RWY	Royal Wiltshire Yeomanry
RWxY	Royal Wessex Yeomanry
RY	Royal Yeomanry
SCpl	Staff Corporal
SCM	Squadron Corporal Major
Sect	Section
Sgt	Sergeant

Sgt Maj	Sergeant Major
SHQ	Squadron Headquarters
Sitrep	Situation Report
SLR	Self Loading Rifle
SMG	Sub-Machine Gun
SNCO	Senior Non-Commissioned Officer (Sgt, SSgt)
SNIY	Scottish & North Irish Yeomanry
SPG	Self-Propelled Gun
SQMS	Squadron Quartermaster Sergeant
Sqn	Squadron
SRY	Nottinghamshire Sherwood Rangers Yeomanry
SSgt	Staff Sergeant
SSM	Squadron Sergeant Major
SSR	Security Sector Reform
STT	School of Tank Technology
SY	Staffordshire Yeomanry
TA	Territorial Army
TC	Tank Corps
TES	Theatre Entry Standard
TEWT	Tactical Exercise Without Troops
Tk	Tank
Tp	Troop
Tpr	Trooper
UAV	Unmanned Aerial Vehicle
UEI	Unit Equipment Inspection
UOR	Urgent Operational Requirement
UKLF	United Kingdom Land Forces
USMC	US Marine Corps
VA	Vickers Armstrong
VCP	Vehicle Check Point
VHF	Very High Frequency
Vickers MMG	.303in Vickers Medium Machine Gun
WD, WDgns	Westminster Dragoons
WMIK	Weapons Mount Installation Kit
WO	War Office, Warrant Officer
WOI, II	Warrant Officer Class 1, 2
WOSB	War Office Selection Board
WY	Warwickshire Yeomanry
YD	Yorkshire Dragoons
YH	Yorkshire Hussars

Introduction

Be flexible, but stick to your principles.

Eleanor Roosevelt

The measure of intelligence is the ability to change

Albert Einstein

This third volume concludes what is an attempt to deliver an accurate yet readable account of the history of the British invention and subsequent use of armoured fighting vehicles. It is, of course, in all but name, a history of the Royal Armoured Corps, including its armoured and mechanized antecedents that preceded the formation of the Corps by twenty-three years or so. As I mentioned in the introduction to the first volume in this series, this history has proved to be both fascinating to research and difficult to write. This has been particularly so as I have attempted to cover seventy-seven years of history in a final volume about the same size as that covering the six years of the Second World War. Strangely, the more recent the history, the more difficulty I have had. In part, this is due to the problems inherent in dealing with evolving issues, which range from the almost annual attempts over the previous decade to amend the structure and size of the army, to dealing with unresolved problems such as the increasing uncertainty over the Ajax programme and (hopefully not so uncertain) the introduction of the impressive but unimaginatively named Challenger 3. Despite the sub-title indicating an end in 2022 (the time of writing), I therefore decided to conclude the main part of the volume at the end of the Afghanistan campaign in 2014, whilst attempting to end by briefly summarizing the many and complex issues that have arisen since then – in a period that the army liked to call 'a return to contingency'. It is quite possible that in retrospect this will prove to be a contentious period, and that many current soldiers prefer the demands of a campaign to the uncertainty of a peace. I hope that, in time, another volume will be needed to detail the next part of the story, and I would imagine that 2014 will be the start point for that work.

I will also remind the reader that I have already asked for forgiveness for the necessary brevity of the parts of this work in which I talk about the others, whom I have described with affection as 'the supporting cast': the infantry,

Royal Artillery, REME and the Royal Engineers. I hope that it is clear that I have nothing but the greatest respect for these arms, all of whom need to work together to assure success in battle and in peace, and who, so often, have to make do with less than cutting-edge equipment, especially vehicles.

I have also already mentioned that I wanted this series to be as much a social history of the RAC as an operational one. Fascinating as they are, the campaigns and battles in which tanks and armoured vehicles have fought are only one aspect of the whole, and from the outset I wished to include also those essential but frequently unrecorded aspects of the tank crewman's life: training, recruitment, pay, equipment, both vehicle and personal, and not least, how these have evolved or remained constant through the hundred years under investigation. As Wavell once said to Liddell Hart:

> If I had time and anything like your ability to study war, I think I should concentrate almost entirely on the 'actualities of war' – the effects of tiredness, hunger, fear, lack of sleep, weather…. The principles of strategy and tactics, and the logistics of war are really absurdly simple: it is the actualities that make war so complicated and so difficult, and are usually so neglected by historians.

I hope that I have not completely neglected this aspect, as, if my research and contemplation on the subject have taught me one thing, it is that the human factor remains the key element in all forms of endeavour, and in warfare even more so.

In terms of the description of combat and operational service, it was never my intention to try to present a complete picture of any of the many battles or actions in the campaigns featured in this work; that would be foolhardy and would simply take up too much space as well as to miss my point. In attempting to give some background understanding of the reasons for, and subsequent course of, a particular campaign, I have tried to carefully select incidents and actions which can be used to either give a flavour of the use of armour and the parts they played, or to make a point about their effectiveness – or otherwise. A glance at the Bibliography will give the interested reader a start point for a more detailed investigation into the many topics within this series, and of which I have only been able to scratch the surface.

Finally, I will conclude by thanking everyone – and they are numbered in the dozens – who have helped me put this together. I am the Official Historian of the Royal Armoured Corps and as such I am a resource to be used by anyone wishing to better understand and promote the history of all of the persons and units that are, or have been, part of this marvellous creation called the Royal Armoured Corps.

Chapter 1

Reforming the Peacetime Army

The Missed Opportunity

As inevitably happens, the end of the war was followed by a massive series of missed opportunities, the chance to immediately and formally adopt new organizations, tactics and equipment that would reflect the main lessons learned during the conflict, and where possible, from all theatres. This is not to argue that the army should have become fully armoured and mechanized – this would have repeated the spurious 'all tank army' arguments of some of the Tank Corps officers from the inter-war years, and in any case would not have suited the composition and finances of a smaller post-war army. Even with an imminent reduction in commitments – at a huge scale, something that Montgomery's biographer Nigel Hamilton described as 'the running-down of the largest empire in human history' – there was still a clear need for a large number of conventional infantry battalions, supported by units able to operate with them, and for which heavy tracked vehicles could not always be used.[1] But the chance came – and went – to retain the best components of the highly mechanized army of spring 1945, including better balance in the organization of the divisions to allow improved all-arms co-operation. The field artillery regiments within the armoured divisions could all have been converted to SPG, and the gunner FOOs in the division should have remained mounted in specially equipped OP tanks. Likewise, the regiments operating the Ram Armoured Personnel Carriers should have remained in being within the armoured divisions, allowing the outmoded use of lorried infantry to be confined to the infantry divisions. The Royal Engineers should have retained specialist armoured engineer regiments, rather than passing the reduced 'Special Armour Establishment' over to the RTR to manage as best they could. Individual items of equipment such as the cheap, nasty and unreliable Sten could have been easily succeeded by the much better Patchett/Sterling design, already in existence. But none of these things happened, and for the next few years the RAC, save the slow and by no means universal introduction of the Centurion tank, looked very much as it had in 1944.

The McCreery Report

Only four months after the cessation of hostilities in Europe, the first peacetime RAC Conference was held at Bad Oeynhausen in Germany between 5 and 6 September 1945, involving those units and personalities stationed on the continent. Field Marshal Montgomery both initiated and attended the meeting, and took an active part in the proceedings. Chaired by Major General Lewis Lyne, an infantryman who had unusually been GOC 7th Armoured Division at the end of the war and was now commanding the British sector in Berlin, the meeting was an important milestone in the development of the RAC, in main because it led directly to the McCreery Report. It was also the first time it was proposed that the cavalry should be given exclusive rights to the reconnaissance role, both in the RAC armoured car regiments and to provide the function to infantry divisions, in place of the now-defunct Recce Corps.[2] The RTR, it was mooted, should only ever be used as armoured (meaning tank) regiments, as well as manning the Special Armour Establishment (SAE), the successor to the Funnies of 79th Armoured Division.[3] This proposal did not come to pass as formal policy, but it was seriously discussed, presumably led by the more intransigent cavalry senior officers – and was, de facto if not de jure, in place until the commitments of the mid-1950s and the need to 'arms-plot' units made the continuance of the (non) policy impossible to maintain.[4] Amongst other less contentious topics that were agreed was that only two types of future tank should be developed; these were a Capital or Universal tank, to be used as the basis for all heavy armour roles and specialist versions, and a Light tank for reconnaissance.[5] The conference also led to the creation of the specialist Schools Instructor at the three trade schools.[6] There also came into being a belief that new officers should, post-commissioning, spend a few months with their destination regiment before attending the young officers' (troop leaders') course.[7]

In that strange, disconnected way that the British army sometimes does business, only two months later another RAC Conference was held, this time at the War Office in London, chaired by Major General Briggs, the DRAC. Amongst the topics discussed were the following:

- That the Royal Army Service Corps should in future be responsible for manning the APC regiments.[8]
- Tank regiments should be established with their own bridge-layer and bulldozer tanks.
- There should be seven Colonels Commandant RAC, five from the cavalry and two from the RTR.[9]
- The RAC should be divided into two distinct wings, cavalry and RTR.
- Officers would be posted to a specific regiment, but ORs would be on an overall RAC roll, which would allow easier cross-posting between regiments.
- Cavalry regiments currently in armoured cars should remain in that role, but the cavalry regiments currently operating in tanks or as divisional recce regiments should change roles every five years.

In December 1945, Montgomery tasked Lieutenant General Richard McCreery (late 12th Lancers and now commanding the British forces in Austria) to produce a report on 'The Future of the RAC in the post-war army', although why Montgomery was driving this and not the AG or VCIGS is not clear. McCreery formed a small committee, comprising three major generals: the DRAC Raymond Briggs, Pip Roberts (GOC 11th Armoured Division), both of whom were RTR, and Charles Keightley, the Director of Military Training and a former 5th Dragoon Guard. As Briggs was now involved, he would have been well aware of the discussions from the earlier WO conference and thus could hopefully represent the interests of all the RAC units. For a start point, they reviewed the findings of the pre-war Sergison-Brooke report, and it seems that they sought to reduce the powers of the two (often opposing) blocks of the cavalry and the RTR, seen as being parochial and unhelpful. Covering such administrative areas as the creation of the RAC Benevolent Fund and entirely avoiding the issue of any future downsizing of the corps, the main points from the report, published in March 1946 were as follows:

- Separate regimental identities were to be retained – there was to be no bringing together of the units into a genuinely homogenous corps.
- Due to the widespread unpopularity of the wartime RAC shoulder titles, alternatives were proposed including the introduction of a small RAC badge worn on either the left breast pocket or on the upper arm. In due course all of these measures would be declined, and the regiments would return to the pre-war practice of not wearing any insignia that announced that they were part of the RAC.
- Officers would continue to join a specific regiment, although in the case of the RTR, this would remain as a larger entity with multiple regiments.[10] There was to be as little cross-posting in the cavalry as possible, although it was acknowledged that some movement across regiments would be unavoidable for majors and lieutenant colonels.[11]
- ORs would enlist into the RAC; this was seen as being legally necessary in order to be able to compel soldiers, NCOs and WOs to move between regiments as required, although this would be exceptional, particularly for SNCOs and WOs, as it would be damaging for the regimental system.
- There was an acknowledgement that those regiments posted overseas, typically for three or three-and-a-half years at a time, would struggle to maintain a 'presence' within the UK, and recruiting regulars whilst abroad would therefore be difficult.[12]
- With four RAC training regiments still in existence and producing the required numbers of trained recruits, the old RAC Central Schools and Depot at Bovington was to be closed down, although this would lead to the creation of the RAC Centre at the same location and the continuance of the provision of advanced courses there.

- A suggestion for linking regiments to specific counties and/or regions for recruiting purposes was proposed, but this was firmly rejected by the War Office – only to be accepted as necessary in May 1958 as National Service was coming to an end.

In March 1947 Montgomery, by now the CIGS, had to step in to protect the RTR from the often underhand machinations of some senior cavalry officers who sought to use this opportunity to strengthen their position. He stated that, 'The RAC had originally been formed around the RTR and that cavalry regiments were subsequently embodied in the corps. The original regiment of the corps ought, therefore, to maintain its entity as a regiment.' In fact, on hearing that McCreery, who Montgomery 'considered a polo-playing cavalry man of the very type he wished to remove from a professional modern British Army', was talking about 'breaking up the RTR into eight separate regiments', thereby weakening it fundamentally, Monty wrote to the QMG:

> I will never agree to this. I have not seen the report and I do not know how far you have got in the matter, but as far as I am concerned the RTR will be split up into eight separate regiments *over my dead body*. The RTR must

A well-camouflaged Centurion on exercise in Germany. This tank was to become the backbone of the armoured regiments of the RAC for two decades.

remain a regiment …[its] officers will be posted to units of the RTR from time to time up to the rank of Major … I do not know how far this matter has got [but] if action is in train to implement the report and to 'bust up' the RTR, please stop it at once.

The move to 'bust up' the RTR by splitting it into individual regiments, each of which could be 'picked off' in times of government cuts by virtue of their junior ranking in the RAC hierarchy, was subsequently quashed.[13]

Unfortunately for the RTR, this stance was to be conveniently forgotten during the coming years and particularly when discussing the need for regimental amalgamations, as will be shown. A change that was generally welcomed happened on 18 September 1945 when the RTR dropped the use of 'battalion', generally associated with infantry units; in future they would be known as regiments of the larger RTR, for example, 1st Battalion Royal Tank Regiment became simply 1st Royal Tank Regiment, and known within the RTR as 'The First'.[14]

PYTHON, LIAP, LILOP

Although both the Bad Oeynhausen and War Office conferences as well as the McCreery report avoided talking about down-sizing the corps – and why would they, as it was always the politicians, not the generals, who reduced the size of the army? – the wartime RAC was being concurrently reduced massively and quickly. The intention seems to have been to 're-set' the corps at the pre-1939 level, meaning keeping the twenty line cavalry and eight RTR regiments – the Household Cavalry remained resolutely out of the mainstream RAC loop in manning terms. What was needed was a system that allowed the re-creation of the old regiments, as well as returning the wartime conscripts to 'civvy street' quickly and fairly, as the army reduced in size. Work on this had been going on even as the conflict was coming towards the end. By 1944, the government also recognized the need to devise schemes to get the civilian economy functioning again, as well as discharging the millions of servicemen in a fair and efficient manner, as soon as the war ended. Additionally, there were huge numbers of servicemen who intended to stay in the army, and yet who had served many years overseas in operational theatres without ever having returned home for leave with their families.

Python was the name given to the repatriation scheme for soldiers serving overseas. It was based upon both the continuous length of service overseas and the overseas theatre in which each soldier served, so that, for example, troops serving in the Far East required less service to be eligible than those in the Mediterranean. Generally, the amount of time required to be eligible was between three years six months and four years, and troops were put into a queue on the basis of first in, first out. Each soldier was told their 'Python Group', a number indicating where they were in the system and thus when they were likely to be returned to the UK. Serving in the UK was referred to as being in the 'Home Establishment', and soldiers eligible for Python were moved from their overseas location back to the UK, generally a slow process involving troopships.[15] On arrival they were granted twenty-eight days leave, followed by a home posting of at least eighteen months, at which point they became eligible once more for a posting overseas. Because there were simply not enough posts in the UK, BAOR, the Central Mediterranean forces and Austria were later added to the Home Establishment for Python purposes, as it was recognized that taking home leave from these stations was both possible and desirable. Therefore, in future during an overseas tour, usually meaning in the Middle or Far East, each serviceman was entitled to one home leave of thirty days per three-year tour, available once twelve months had been served.

Starting in about September 1944 and accelerating into 1945, Python led to thousands of experienced troops being sent home in 'group number' batches, dismembering whole units in the process – despite the units still having operational tasks to complete. The effects were still being felt in mid-1947; at one point 1RTR recorded that they were at only 50 per cent of their authorized strength, which was probably typical. They did receive replacements, but these were infantrymen, mainly from the Norfolk regiment, which put yet another burden on the already stretched training system.[16] Many units were forced to reduce the number of squadrons to two, or, even worse, to go to 'cadre strength', although thankfully this was usually a temporary measure and an influx of National Servicemen from 1947 on brought them back up to strength, although rapid turnover now became the major problem. The implications of this on a regiment were huge, and by way of example, the KDG described their experience in detail:

> The regiment was employed on garrison duties in the Middle East after the war and up to the time it left Libya in February 1948, when its strength was some thirty-five officers and 600 other ranks. On arrival in England, demobilization had reduced the other rank strength to 150, of which about forty were members of the Sergeants' Mess. Because of the lack of recruits the regiment was kept in being as a 'Temporary Under-posted Unit', [with a strength of about] one squadron and was nominated as a 'Territorial Army Assistance Unit' – with the role of helping three Yeomanry regiments in any way required. We had the further important role of training ourselves when we could, although this was not easy to do because most of the few other ranks were absorbed by the administrative overheads of daily self-maintenance in a scattered RAF camp … The largest number of troopers who could be put to individual training at one time [and only once the annual summer assistance to the TA was finished] was twenty-seven.[17]

Python continued in a slightly modified form well into the 1950s, with soldiers entitled to return to the UK after they had served three years overseas: in this way, almost the whole of 3RTR turned over during the course of their tour in Hong Kong between August 1949 and March 1952.

Another scheme was LIAP: Leave in Addition to Python. During hostilities, apart from some local leave options, the majority of troops serving in the Far and Middle East, and in North West Europe as well as Italy, could not take any home leave, and LIAP allowed those who had been away for some years but who were not yet eligible for Python to be sent home for a few weeks, often entailing a cold and miserable flight in the belly of a bomber or transport aircraft, before returning the same way in order to finish off the final months of their service.[18] LILOP was another scheme: Leave in Lieu of Python, and allowed those who, for whatever reason (mainly regular soldiers or those who wished to become post-war regulars), declined to take advantage of the home posting element of Python, and instead were given sixty-one days of home leave coupled to a guarantee to return to their original unit. Another scheme was SEWLROM, or Special End of War Leave for Regular Officers and Men. Any pre-war regular still serving on 1 December 1946 was eligible for an additional twenty-eight day's UK leave, which for reasons of administrative efficiency had to be taken alongside Python/ LILOP. This created yet another problem for the regiments, as their most senior officers, warrant officers and NCOs were generally regulars, and the combination of leave accrued could mean that the regiments would lose whole swathes of key individuals, including the commanding officer and RSM, for at least four months due to the shipping element there and back which could be measured in weeks.

There remained within the War Office an aspiration to become a regular army once again. The army was still in the process of trying to reduce its size in early 1950 when the Korean War, allied to the need for additional servicemen in outlying outposts such as Malaya and Hong Kong, meant that more were needed – in 1948–9 the army still stood at 850,000 personnel, with the intention to reduce down to about 550,000 the following year. The extension to the period of National Service – see below – meant that it would not be until well into the 1950s that the army was able to look to a new, smaller, all-professional future.

Although the non-professional wartime army was shrinking rapidly, the War Office also recognized the need to re-form the backbone of the army – a cadre of regular professional soldiers and officers. Even as soldiers were being discharged in their tens of thousands, efforts were made to persuade the best of these to stay – at this time, and before the introduction of National Service, there was a desire to return the army to a wholly regular basis within a few years. In a publication of January 1946 called 'Why Drop Out?', the army stated its case to those who were due to leave. One of these was a revision of the poor rates of pay that had been such a cause for grumbling during the war. As an example, it noted that a typical private soldier on joining would now be better off by about a third, now receiving 28s. per week compared with 21s. previously. Similarly, a sergeant receiving the top rates of pay would get 105s. per week, an increase of nearly 37s. Married corporals and below would also receive a marriage allowance of 35s. per week, and a warrant officer up to 45s. The newly introduced civilian family allowance would also apply, with extra money available for qualifying children. Terms of service included only one option; this was the twelve-year engagement (usually meaning an initial five year's regular service with seven in the reserve), which was extendable so that at the end of the term, after twelve years' satisfactory service, the soldier had the right to sign on for the 'full' twenty-two-year engagement at which point he would become pensionable.[19] Soldiers already serving on wartime engagements were encouraged to becomes regulars; any War Substantive (W/S) or Acting rank held would be retained provided a vacancy existed. A specific appeal for soldiers to join the RAC as regulars included the following inducements:

> Every man in the corps has to learn to drive and maintain a motor vehicle, and there is a wide range of specialist technical jobs, such as vehicle mechanic, electrician, [and] wireless operator … For a man with powers of leadership and the ability to think quickly there are especially good prospects … the close comradeship of the AFV crew and the scope for individual initiative by every member of it are particularly attractive features of life in the RAC … For a man to whom appeals the adventures of long-range reconnaissance and the probability of first contact with the enemy in war, the choice of unit might be an armoured car regiment. For the man attracted to the idea of a great armoured drive and break-out, an armoured regiment would be the ideal choice. For the even more adventurous minded, there are the reconnaissance regiments and the airborne divisions. To sum up: for any man who is active, mechanically minded, requires a trade on leaving the army, and has powers of initiative and leadership, the RAC offers a congenial life and extremely good prospects.[20]

The *Standing Orders of the 7th Hussars*, published in 1948 but written in the language of bygone days, indicated what that regiment thought that its soldiers should aspire to, 'A good soldier has a happy life. He is sure of every indulgence that discipline will allow, of the affection and respect of his equals, and the consideration of his superiors; whereas the drunkard, the idler, and the sloven must ever be in trouble.'

Initially at least, many of the wartime sergeants and corporals, including a large percentage of those who had amassed significant combat experience and had won gallantry medals, elected to stay and become regular soldiers, and it was these men who were frequently to become the SSMs and RSMs of many RAC regiments over the next two decades. But despite such inducements and appeals,

A Squadron of 10th Hussars recorded in late 1946 that turbulence was still very high: in a short period 90 soldiers had left the squadron and another 114 had joined it, many coming from other RAC regiments that had been disbanded, and many of whom were effectively in transit, only staying for a short period before they too were repatriated. One sergeant noted that when he returned to his old regiment after one month's leave, he only knew three members in 'his' Sergeants' Mess. The Derbyshire Yeomanry in Italy complained that this system, if system it was, 'was all rather impersonal'. Regiments frequently received short-notice instructions such as 'All gunner mechanics under age group 28 and all NCOs under age group 30 are posted to 14/20H forthwith', and '52 driver mechanics and 4 officers are posted to you from 2LBH'. 4/7DG, on arrival in Egypt in spring 1946, had to accept, en masse, a draft of 'several hundred' men from the disbanding 1st Recce Regt; there was plenty of potential for disgruntlement and problems, but the new men seemed to have been accepted by the old, and by late June the regiment found itself in Palestine, on operations.[21] Another change starting in late 1946 was that the regimental bands were returned to the regiments. During the Second World War they had existed separately to their parent regiments and mostly remained in the UK; some were attached to RAC Training Regiments or used as central bands, and many consisted mainly of boy musicians, who would later become the core of the revived versions. They retained their instruments and regimental property, and in 1946 were delighted to return to their parent units, as were the regiments.[22]

The Rest of Europe

Outside of Germany, at the end of the war a few RAC units found themselves in Austria, Belgium, Denmark, Italy and Greece, all of which with the exception of Denmark required garrisons for the next couple of years. The following regiments served in Austria up until July 1947, when the last British occupation units departed: 16th/5th Lancers, Derbyshire Yeomanry, 17th/21st Lancers, 4th Hussars, 12th Lancers, 8RTR and 10th Hussars. 6RTR were the last to leave. In northern Italy, again leaving in a similar timeframe, were The Bays, 10th Hussars, 12th Lancers, 9th Lancers, 7th Hussars, 8RTR, 14th/20th Hussars, 4th Hussars, 2RTR, Derbyshire Yeomanry, 4RTR and 6RTR, who again were the last to go.[23] Following the deployment of 23rd Armoured Brigade to Greece in late 1944, a number of RAC regiments stayed in the country after the Second World War ended. The only unit to be deployed into the country after the end of the war was 17th/21st Lancers, who were sent to Salonika in late October 1945, staying there until February 1947 when they were posted via Egypt to Palestine. In some ways the most extraordinary deployment at that time was that of 15th/19th Hussars, who from November 1947 until April 1949 found themselves based in Khartoum, Sudan.

The Reformation of the Territorial Army

On the outbreak of war in 1939 the TA was suspended, with all the units becoming part of the regular order of battle; for most purposes, they were treated as regular units although, as has already been noted, TA and particularly war-raised units were always much more likely to be disbanded than the regular regiments. This fate befell many of the TA regiments between mid-1942 and 1946, but on 1 January 1947 the Territorial Army was officially reconstituted, with the various units being brought back into existence over the next few months; in part this was because it was necessary to have large numbers of TA units all around the country in which National Servicemen could conduct the second part of their obligatory service, and all of the arms and services needed to be represented, at least in part to make use of, and maintain, the vast quantities of war materiel that still existed, much of it virtually brand-new. The RAC benefited – at least initially – from the reconstitution, and at first it appeared that the size of the RAC Yeomanry and Territorial RTR would be huge, with thirty-four units being ordered to form (or re-form) and train; for eight years there were even two TA armoured divisions in the UK, 49th and 56th, along with five TA armoured brigades. However, this happy state was not to last long, and in late 1955 the announcement was made that the TA units in the RAC would reduce to nine tank (one of which had the armoured delivery role) and eleven armoured car regiments, the reduction achieved by amalgamating nine pairs of units and converting four to infantry.[24]

In all honesty, the RAC was in many respects quite glad of this, as the non-regular organization was now too large for comfort, and these TA units placed an enormous administrative burden on the regulars, with at least four regiments being stationed in the UK and reduced to cadre strength (AKA Lower Establishment), in order to provide what were disparagingly referred to as the 'TA Stables'. The tanks used for training the TA were generally parked up in the open, with the crews looking after them accommodated in appalling transit camps or even under canvas for months at a time.[25] As well as being numbered in their hundreds, the vehicles were mostly older types that the crews had no experience of and which they had to be rapidly trained to operate.[26] These roles were not surprisingly seen as unpopular, even thankless tasks; as the lower establishment frequently permitted only two squadrons: a Headquarters Squadron for administration, and one 'sabre' squadron to look after the vehicle maintenance duties … and everything else. One of the tasks one regiment reported having to do for each TA camp was to lay 150 tons of stone to provide hard standing for the tanks, and then to pick it all up again afterwards. When 8th Hussars were stationed in Leicestershire in December 1948, the regimental strength was only 196 men, and they were also vulnerable to the threat of providing drafts for other regiments; the regiment had been told to suddenly provide fifty regular soldiers in August 1948 to go to Malaya with 4th Hussars. Additionally, even when up to strength, these tasks often came with the penalty of a widely dispersed regiment: when The Greys returned to Britain from Libya in summer 1955, RHQ went to Crookham near Aldershot, with A Sqn in Tilshead Camp on Salisbury Plain, B Sqn to Castlemartin in west Wales and C Sqn in Park Camp, Lulworth.

When the TA was re-formed, a system of regimental affiliations was constructed linking regulars and TA units. This had nothing to do with the recruitment aspirations of the regular unit, as regional recruiting areas were still some years in the future. This system was adapted over the years as both regular and TA regiments were amalgamated or dissolved, and in 1967, when the RAC was about 13,000 strong, looked like this:

Table 1: Unit Affiliations, 1967

Regular Unit	TA Unit
Life Guards	Inns of Court and City Yeomanry*
Royal Horse Guards	Inns of Court and City Yeomanry*
QDG	Shropshire Yeomanry, Pembroke Yeomanry
3rd Carbs	Cheshire Yeomanry
4/7DG	Fife & Forfar Yeomanry/Scottish Horse
5DG	North Irish Horse*
Royals	Kent and County of London Yeomanry
Greys	Ayrshire Yeomanry
QOH	QO Warwickshire and Worcestershire Yeomanry
QRIH	North Irish Horse*
9/12L	Leicestershire and Derbyshire Yeomanry
10H	Royal Wiltshire Yeomanry
11H	Royal Gloucestershire Hussars
13/18H	QO Yorkshire Yeomanry
14/20H	Duke of Lancaster's Own Yeomanry
15/19H	Northumberland Hussars
16/5L	Staffordshire Yeomanry
17/21L	Sherwood Rangers Yeomanry
1RTR	40/41RTR
2RTR	Berkshire and Westminster Dragoons
3RTR	North Somerset Yeomanry/44RTR*
4RTR	QO Lowland Yeomanry
5RTR	North Somerset Yeomanry/44RTR*

Note: * denotes shared affiliation.

However, despite Britain being awash with ex-servicemen in the immediate post-war years, many of whom had considerable front-line experience, recruiting for the new territorial units was never easy. By the end of 1947 after nearly one year's existence, 40RTR (based in Park Street, Bootle, Liverpool and equipped with Churchill and Stuart tanks and Dingo Scout Cars) was only able to boast that it had succeeded in recruiting ten officers and eight soldiers. Things improved once new National Servicemen started to fill the gaps after their eighteen-month stint with the regulars, and, as ever, some units did better than others. Not helpful was the increasing lack of serviceable modern equipment, not to mention the frequent disruptions, disbandments, changes of role and name, and general uncertainty that the TA had to suffer. The RAC TA units always had to put up with third best in terms of equipment; the first Centurion (Mk 5) tanks were not received by the four tank units until late 1958, finally replacing their Second World War-vintage Comets.[27]

As one later report noted, the main concerns of the Yeomanry over the decades were the same: survival, finding a useful role, having a decent establishment of personnel and equipment, and not least, being perceived by the regulars as being good soldiers. One of the particular problems that the Yeomanry found, was that their smaller establishments, compared with, for example, TA infantry companies, made recruiting (and internal promotion) more difficult. The seemingly endless rounds of moves of squadrons between regiments affected morale, and every defence White Paper was something to be feared. The Royal Wiltshire Yeomanry spoke for all regiments when they recorded that the year 1950 had included 'the by-now customary change of role, establishment and equipment'. The Shropshire Yeomanry reported one particularly disruptive and frustrating

Comets firing on a wintry range in Germany. Undoubtedly the best tank that Britain made during the Second World War, it was superseded by the larger Centurion but remained in use as late as 1959.

(although not entirely atypical) year, 1956, during which they found themselves with three different roles, and therefore organizations:

> We were converted from a Divisional Regiment RAC to an armoured regiment, so we packed off our M10s without much regret and then sat down and waited for our Comets.[28] We waited for months. Everyone badgered everyone else. But at last, the issue orders arrived, and the great day arrived when we were about to collect the tanks. The very same day we were reorganized into a recce regiment – many other words have been invented for 'reorganized!' We sat down to wait again, this time for armoured cars and scout cars. Again, we waited for months. Eventually we borrowed two armoured cars from a local Ordnance museum, and with these trained for camp.[29]

National Service

During the Second World War, soldiers conscripted into the services were required to serve for an indefinite period – the duration of the war, and were known as conscripts or, occasionally, as W/S: war service. After the war, there were a number of schemes used to repatriate and discharge large numbers of servicemen, but substantial commitments around the world remained or developed: Europe, India, Palestine, Hong Kong, Singapore, Malaya, Cyprus ... the list went on. Politicians recognized the need to continue with some form of conscription in peacetime, in order to fulfil two requirements: the need to meet existing commitments worldwide, plus the creation of a large body of trained reserves who could be quickly mobilized if and when war threatened – exactly the thing that had been lacking in both 1914 and 1939.

In July 1947 the National Service Act was passed, and after revision the following year it officially came into being on 1 January 1949, although recruits had started to be conscripted before that. This allowed for an army of 305,000 – although emergencies meant that this had to be later raised by about another 100,000 – in which the National Serviceman (usually conscripted between the ages of 17 and 21) had to serve with the colours for eighteen months, followed by another four years in the reserve, in a TA unit.[30] This was the result of a compromise; the initial plan was for a period of twelve months 'with the colours' to be used for intensive training, followed by six years in the TA which would provide the nation's reserve. However, this plan was made on the assumption that the regular army would be fully up to strength and able to look after all the worldwide commitments, which it was not. Thus National Servicemen were needed for longer, and in greater numbers, which in turn required a larger portion of the regular army to deliver their training, and this meant that many regulars would be employed in training establishments in the UK whilst their non-volunteer colleagues were sent overseas to fight.

Within the RAC, 1RTR were delighted to receive their first batch of no less than 200 recruits fresh from Catterick in December 1947; this was very welcome as the first step in remanning the much understrength regiment. Likewise, the Fifth Skins in Paderborn recorded their excitement regarding the arrival of their first ever influx of NS soldiers arriving in 1949, with 'troops' of up to forty recruits arriving from Catterick every two months or so thereafter. Each NS intake was allocated a group number, which also allowed each National Serviceman to know where he was in the grand scheme of seniority and closeness to discharge. 'Which group are you?' was a frequent question, often asked with overtones of perceived superiority – the lower the number, the more senior and, more importantly, the earlier the date of discharge.

This turn-around, about 8 per cent of the regimental strength changing every two months, meant massive instability. As recruits arriving from the training regiments were only partially trained, it meant that operational regiments had to adapt their structures and modus operandi to account for this. By way of example, The Skins responded by turning one of the three sabre squadrons into a full-time training organization, and even went so far as to get the newcomers to spend their first five weeks in repeating large elements of GMT. The new soldiers were referred to demi-officially as 'nig-nogs'; this was not a racial slur (how could it be, with the vast majority of the soldiers of white ethnicity?) but reflected a northern English expression for a stupid person. In time this became shortened to just 'nigs' and was used for all new soldiers until they had become accepted by their elders.[31]

On 1 September 1950, largely as a result of the Korean War, National Service with the colours was extended to two years, although the reserve service element was reduced by six months to compensate.[32] Group 255 contained those first to fall foul of the extension, and a trooper serving with The Skins put pen to paper to record how he felt (and, for once, demonstrated that an army poet could produce verse that scanned properly!):

> Six Months To Do (or He Didn't Oughta Done It).
> Now 255 came in one day,
> And very cheery too.
> Little knew they'd have to stay,
> With six months more to do.
>
> They trained at Catterick's well-known camp,
> Went home each forty-eight.
> In time they found that they came in
> Just eleven days too late.
>
> Eleven days decided then,
> Their fate for half a year.

And now they're looking forward to
A month that takes them near …

We've been pushed here; we've been pushed there.
And now Bee Ay Oh Arr.
We'll have another leave – we hope,
With getting six months more.

We get well paid for extra time,
Agreed – but what is more.
There'll be no schemes or work, which means:
Inspections by the score.

So make a note you Ministers,
Of all the cash that's paid.
To us with six months more to do
Just standing on parade!

Group 255 goes out next year,
'Browned off', through to the core.
When will all these inspections cease?
Not 'til we're out, I'm sure.[33]

A sensible initiative from February 1950 was the introduction of a shorter three-year engagement for regular soldiers; this encouraged youngsters to join the regular army rather than be conscripted, allowing better pay and promotion prospects, plus it gave them the choice of which arm or regiment to serve in, at the price of an extra year in uniform.[34] But however hard it was pushed, attempts to persuade conscripted NS soldiers to become regulars during their basic training were wholly unsuccessful; only about 2 per cent of those going through the system during 1955 elected to volunteer to become regulars. The reasons for this were manifold, but included the dreadful state of the accommodation at Catterick, which was below even Second World War standards; on moving to Catterick in 1957, 16th/5th Lancers gloomily recorded that the station was notorious for 'its rigorous climate, and appalling accommodation'.[35] Clearly nothing much had improved since 1948, when 8RTR, taking over the responsibilities as a training unit during an appallingly harsh winter, had commented that, 'It is the fate of most units of the RAC to find themselves at Catterick sooner or later, for better or worse, and for warmer or colder – but mainly colder.'

Pay was another important factor. In 1948 at the start of the scheme, a National Service trooper would earn £1 8s. per week, leaving him about £1 per week after compulsory deductions. At the time, the average basic civilian weekly wage was

£8 8*s*. 6*d*., six times more.[36] From 1950, in an effort to promote regular recruiting, National Servicemen in their last six months of service received the same pay as their regular counterparts. In 1961, when NS was in its last throes, the same trooper would receive £1 10*s*. weekly; but by now, the average civilian weekly wage had risen to £15 10*s*., so the wage differential had increased, our trooper now receiving less than 10 per cent of the average wage of his civilian counterpart. On 1 April 1956 a new pay scale was introduced, partly in preparation for the ending of National Service, in order to make the army seem more attractive when compared with civilian rates of pay. For the officers, increases of around £100 per annum were given, leading to the following (indicative) rates coming into use:

Table 2: Rates of Pay (Officers), 1956

Rank	Daily Rate	Per Annum
Lieutenant (after three years in rank)	36*s*.	£657
Captain (after four years)	50*s*.	£912
Major (after two years)	65*s*.	£1,186
Lieutenant Colonel (after two years)	87*s*.	£1,587

Quartermasters, commissioned from the ranks, were paid on a different scale, with more money up to the rank of major, but less for lieutenant colonels: a captain would receive 58*s*. pd/£1,058 pa, a major 73*s*. pd/£1,332 pa, but a lieutenant colonel 80*s*. pd/£1,460.

On the same day in 1956 Other Ranks received an increase of between 14*s*. and 21*s*. per week. ORs, unlike officers, received a weekly rate of pay, within a complicated system that defies logic – it must have been a nightmare for the pay clerks to administer such a scheme.[37] Nevertheless, indicative rates were as follows:

Table 3: Rates of Pay (Other Ranks), 1956

Rank	Weekly Rate	Per Annum
Boy	38*s*. 6*d*. (on entry) to 59*s*. 6*d*. (after six months, and dependent on qualifications)	£100–155
Trooper	84*s*.–171*s*. 6*d*.	£218–446
Lance Corporal	98*s*.–185*s*.	£255–481
Corporal	112*s*.–210*s*.	£291–546
Sergeant	178*s*. 6*d*.–259*s*.	£464–673
Staff Sergeant	199*s*. 6*d*.–280*s*.	£519–728
Warrant Officer Class 2	231*s*.–301*s*.	£601–783
Regimental Quartermaster Sergeant	238*s*.–308*s*.	£619–801
Warrant Officer Class 1	245*s*.–315*s*.	£637–819

Terms of service were also amended, allowing soldiers to join on a shorter three- or four-year engagement, whereas the twenty-two-year engagement had options to leave at the three-, six- and nine-year points. The logic was the longer the engagement, the higher the pay. At this time, accommodation charges for soldiers living in barracks were not levied, but married soldiers living in quarters had to pay. This cost between 20 and 30*s*. a week, but was 44*s*. for warrant officers. An annual single-payment Marriage Allowance varied from £36 to £73 pa for ORs, and between £73 and £191 pa for officers. This pay increase was later adjudged to have been a major reason for an 8½ per cent increase in regular recruiting that year.

Although a medical test was conducted to weed out the clearly unfit before they reported for duty – and which naturally was the subject of many attempts to fail deliberately – another, more stringent examination was carried out during the first week of training. In the first three years after the end of the war this used the Second World War system and gradings. In 1948 a new medical test was introduced, for both regulars and conscripts; this was the PULHHEEMS system, well-known to generations of soldiers, although the vast majority had no idea why it was called that. In fact, it stood for Physique/Physical capacity, Upper limb function, Lower limb function/Locomotion, Hearing (both), Eyesight (both), Mental function/intelligence and emotional Stability. The requirement for RAC soldiers to be above average in terms of intelligence was well understood by the units, but seemingly less so by the authorities, as will be seen shortly.

In order to deal with the increased requirement for training civilians, the RAC Training Brigade at Catterick was formed. This consisted of four RAC Training Regiments also known as Arms Basic Training Units (ABTU), numbered as 65th to 68th inclusive, with 67th being responsible for armoured car training, the other three for tanks.[38] These relieved the need to have RAC field force units used 'out of role', and replaced 12L, 14/20H, 8RTR and 17/21L between December 1950 and summer 1951. Of course, instructors and many other staff were still needed from the field force units and a steady trickle were posted in and out of the training regiments, each of which was responsible for a group of regiment's recruits. For example, in 1954 65th Training Regiment RAC produced all the soldiers destined for 3rd Carbs, 4/7DG, 3H, 7H, 10H, 14/20H and 16/5L. The Korean War armistice and the desire to end National Service led to the four training regiments being disbanded between January 1954 and January 1957, with the training role returning once again to regular regiments employed out of role.[39] To assist the regiments thrown into an unfamiliar training role, and to provide information on the regiment that the recruits were destined for, a formal system of 'link instructors' was set up in 1961, in which each RAC regiment provided (in theory) three officers plus a number of sergeant and corporal instructors. This simply reflected a practice that had been happening on an informal basis for many years. The quality of these personnel varied: one study into the outputs of the training brigade in late 1955 noted that, 'There is evidence that many of the officers and NCOs posted to Catterick do not wish to go there, and that many of them are not wanted back again by their own regiments'. It was thought that this applied to around 20 per cent of the instructors, some of whom had 'arrived with crime [*sic*] records as long as your arm – and have committed more since arriving'.

During the decade or so that it was in place, the National Service recruiting system was notorious for not matching the conscript's existing skills with the needs of the army; at a time when most people left school at 15 and therefore had acquired a trade or skill-set before being called-up, one estimate was that only about one in eight National Servicemen had been put into a job that matched their existing skills. The *4th/7th Royal Dragoon Guards Journal* of 1955 related the story of a visiting general who was insistent that National Servicemen should be given a job in the army that best suited their civilian experience. During an inspection, the general spoke to one recruit and asked him what was his civilian job? 'Keeper at the zoo', replied the recruit. 'And what are you doing now, my boy?' 'Officer's batman, sir.'

The National Serviceman was to be a large part of all RAC regiments during the late 1940s and throughout the 1950s; across the board, the army as a whole in the mid-1950s saw conscripts slightly outnumbering regulars roughly 51 per cent/49 per cent. However, the RAC and Household Cavalry bucked this trend, and took many fewer NS men than most other arms; in 1954 for example, the RAC comprised 45 per cent NS and the Household Cavalry only 43 per cent, compared with, for example, the Royal Pioneer Corps which was 94 per cent NS, or the infantry, nearly 80 per cent. During that year, of the 106,896 NS men who joined the army, only 2,885 went to the RAC or Household Cavalry, representing just under 3 per cent of the total.[40] Simply getting into the RAC as a National Serviceman was therefore a significant hurdle, but large numbers were still required. In the time that 14th/20th Hussars served as one of the tank training regiments at Catterick from 1948 to 1950, they trained 1,732 regulars, 6,167 National Servicemen and produced 276 Potential Officers. Between 1954 and 1956 the Fifth Skins recorded the following numbers passing through their hands at Catterick:

Table 4: RAC Training Regiment Output by Trade, 1954–6

Rank	1954	1955	1956
Driver AFV	356	339	332
Driver/Signaller	37	35	34
Driver BIV[41]	318	279	215
Technical Storeman	78	69	60
Gunner/Driver	163	133	103
Gunner/Signaller	128	124	123

Rank	1954	1955	1956
Signaller/Driver	84	76	60
Signaller/Gunner	398	362	338
Clerk	140	138	136
Equipment repairer	11	10	7
Carpenter and Joiner	9	8	12
General duties	262	183	65
Bandsmen	19	22	0
Totals	2,003	1,778	1,475

These figures are for the intake numbers only: by no means all passed the official trade tests for their designated trades, and so each year some recruits had to be sent to their regiments having only passed General Military Training. The numbers were substantial: in 1954 no less than 619 recruits fell into this category, the following year 502 and in 1956 it was 299. On average, therefore, each year about one-quarter of all recruits failed to pass out with a trade and thus created an additional burden on their regiments, as they could only be employed in a limited range of jobs if retraining internally was not an option. Additionally, when formally asked in 1955, the field force regiments replied that they were not impressed with the standards of the men who had managed to pass their trade tests, and overall considered that only about half of this category were up to the minimum standard required.[42] What was not always realized – or at least acknowledged – was that the RAC was increasingly becoming the only branch of the army (at that time) that was both technical and combat focused. During enlistment, a recruit's intelligence was assessed and given an SSG grade – their Summed Selection Group. There were six categories: 1 was outstanding, 2 above average, 3+ average, 3- below average, 4 well below average, and 5 … poor, although one report preferred to call category 5 the 'troglodytes'. A study in 1960 recommended that the RAC should raise its minimum intake standard from 3- to 3+, arguing that this would hugely improve the percentage of recruits that were able to pass the trade tests, and pointing out that JLR RAC had already done this with excellent results. The study noted that in trade tests taken in Catterick for Class III Signals, Category 3+ men had only an 8 per cent failure rate, whilst that for 3- was 61 per cent.

Two other points are notable from the training system. Firstly, there were no less than seven different combinations of AFV crew trades that could be awarded, and all of these needed a separate route through the training system. This was an unnecessary complication which clearly required resolving and was to result in the basic RAC trades being reduced to three: gunnery, driving and signals.[43] By 1960 the trade structure was confirmed as being in the 'Group B' standard, and comprised BIII signallers, gunners and drivers, BII indicating a crewman fully qualified in all three trades, and BI an up-graded signaller, gunner or driver. These were later termed Control Signaller, Gunner Mechanic and Driver Mechanic.

Secondly, although National Service still had a few years to run, the numbers being sent for training were gradually reducing; in part this was also in anticipation of the regimental reductions and amalgamations that were to happen between 1957 and 1960 which reduced the total RAC manpower. By 1959 The Skins were able to record that 77 per cent of the regiment were regular soldiers and that only seventy-nine National Servicemen remained.

Initial training (known as GMT or General Military Training) followed by AFV 'trade training' for all soldiers destined for the RAC lasted about thirteen weeks and was conducted at Catterick. In the mid-1950s at any one time there were over 16,000 servicemen stationed there, the majority of them National Servicemen being trained for either the RAC or the Royal Signals; on arriving at the nearby railway station large signs proclaimed, 'Signals to the Right, Armoured Corps to the Left'. As a snapshot of GMT and trade training from the viewpoint of one of these soldiers, the recollections of Lance Corporal Bill Fryer 17/21L, who as part of Army Service Group 272, intake 50/02, was one of the first RAC conscripts to go through Catterick in January 1950, are quoted:

On arrival we embarked in a Bedford, destination Waitwith Camp, where we found that we had been allocated for training to the 17th/21st Lancers. We then proceeded to draw our bedding – four blankets, sheets, a bolster pillow and a palliasse: 'Pile of straw over there mate, help yourself'. We were shown to our barrack room, a brick-built, concrete floored hut for forty men, which contained a stove at each end and in the centre, with two naked light bulbs dangling from the flat roof. The huts had been built rather hastily in 1939, and we later found out had been condemned in 1945. A visit to the cookhouse followed, and we were in receipt or our first taste of army fare, for many not a pleasant experience. Many of the lads had never been away from home before, and the corporal in charge was not exactly a mother substitute.

Next day we were kitted out, and had the intricacies of using an electric iron, shrinking berets and bulling boots demonstrated to us. B Squadron were in charge of the five weeks General Military Training course we were subjected to. After our first five weeks came the passing-out parade, and we all got a 48-hour weekend pass. After the leave, I was allocated to a Squadron for D&M training, a ten-week course consisting of two weeks B vehicles General Principles (theory), two weeks driving on the Bedford 15 cwt truck, two weeks of A vehicle theory, followed by four weeks of driving on Centurions Mk I and II. We all duly passed out as drivers AFV B3 and were sent home for seven days leave.

[On return] there were rumours of trouble in Korea, but I was told that I had done well on my course and that I was earmarked for a unit cadre course lasting 4 weeks following which I was to be a Regimental D&M instructor. At this time, I was the only National Serviceman in the regiment instructing on both wheels and tracks. I was appointed a Local Unpaid Lance Corporal, [with a] stripe on the right arm only, and began to wear the Motto. No more money, but a lot of glory! The regiment went off to Germany [in May 1951] and due to the Korean Emergency, our service was extended by six months. I remained behind ERE with 68th Training Regiment RAC until January 1952. During this final 6 months I was appointed to paid rank, receiving regular rates of pay and wearing a LCpl stripe on both sleeves of my battledress. We then had to face a compulsory 3½ years TA service; however, if one volunteered for four years' service one had a choice of regiment, so I promptly volunteered for the City Of London Yeomanry, then a full-blown armoured regiment, part of 56th (:London) TA Division. Joining as a Trooper, I attained the rank of Sergeant just before my 22nd Birthday. My wireless and gunnery training took place within the TA, and I had seven very happy years as a troop sergeant.[44]

Centurion cross-country driver training at Catterick, 1951. Taking the role as one of the RAC training regiments was a necessary but unpopular posting.

The efforts of the ABTUs and the RAC training regiments did not release the operational regiments from the requirement for them to conduct their own trade training, using their own (dual-hatted) regimental instructors; these were mainly corporal and sergeants whose primary role was as tank commanders. For example, the Training Wing of the 11th Hussars in Osnabrück during 1950 recorded that in a 12-month period, no less than 350 recruits (mainly NS men) had passed through, with 251 passing their trade tests; they recorded that this meant a 71 per cent pass rate, although they could equally have said that 29 per cent failed to reach the required minimum standard. B Squadron 10th Hussars in Iserlohn in the same period was made responsible for taking under their wing the 'half-trained' soldiers received from 14th/20th Hussars in Catterick; every intake was about fifty such men and they arrived regularly, a batch every two months. The timing of arrival at the regiment, particularly if based in Germany, made a difference. Soldiers arriving in about October would have six months of unit training before the spring, whereas those who arrived in March could find themselves thrown straight in at the deep end of summer field training. 4th Hussars put it like this in 1954, 'During the past year we have had the inevitable change of National Service men – returning well-trained soldiers to civilian life on the eve of army manoeuvres in exchange for near raw recruits.' But there is no doubt that such men, on the whole, did well and became exceptionally proud of whichever regiment they joined. As the first batch came to the end of their service, the *10th Hussars Journal* noted that on the whole, 'they were intelligent, keen to learn their trades, did extremely well on training and were in fact, by the time they left, first-class soldiers and keen 10th Hussars'.

Trooper Connor of A Sqn The Skins wrote an intelligent article about his experience as one of the first large drafts to go through the National Service 'conveyor belt' between June 1948 and March 1950, in which the stark contrast between the initial training and regimental life was very clear, and which is worth quoting at length:

> The break from family life was an unpleasant shock for me. Here were a bunch of men, thrown together with no discrimination into a large and bleak barrack room. I was one of them and I did not like it. Officers were faces I only saw at infrequent intervals and then I was expected to look upon them as deities. I spent my first four or five weeks in a daze engendered by the impersonality of my new life. The following weeks passed quickly … mainly because my instructor was a nice fellow who first proved to me that NCOs are not deaf to Christian names. He was sympathetic and, if we were considerate to him, it was because he treated us likewise. [My] draft was bound for the 5th Royal Inniskilling Dragoon Guards, [which] struck no chord in my memory. I was mildly surprised that such picturesquely titled regiments still existed, I thought they had died out when shot replaced

sword. On to Harwich, the Hook, and sometime later, Paderborn, a panorama of skeleton buildings and broken bricks.

I think my amazement was shared by the rest of the lads when we found beds ready-made and awaiting our attention. What luxury and thoughtfulness! The meal, similarly, caused incredulity. At Catterick, meal-time began in hope and ended in disappointment and/or gastronomic anxiety. The next day I had a better opportunity to look around and wished that the British Army could take credit for this ample and comfortable accommodation and these well-designed buildings. In the first few days a commendable effort was made by the squadron leader and his supernumeraries to put us at our ease ... during one of these tours [we] heard the Sergeant's prophetic statement made outside the gym 'You'll see a lot of this place.' We did. PT formed too great a part of the five weeks that followed ... I was disappointed and angry at having to do GMT again. I started on my second trade, D&M, and I found it harder than some of my fellow students. Struggling in a dreary classroom with the intricacies of engines makes it easy to doze off, which I did not infrequently. Driving was better ...

During these three months I found my feet and gained the feeling of comradeship for which the army is supposedly famed. The regiment was small and compact. Names became familiar and I began to feel a sense of community. I began to think of my squadron as a boarding school – strict but fair. The SSM was an outwardly stern but inwardly benevolent headmaster. In early February I became a member of one of the tank crews. At Soltau my appetite for makeshift meals and bedding down on hard ground became satiated, and even the boredom of barracks seemed desirable in comparison. I got drenched once or twice and envied the officers their sleeping bags which would not be a luxury if issued generally.

The SSM had told me I would get a job in administration. I was not sorry ... I stayed in the warmth of the block while many of my friends spent cold winter days scrubbing out engines and washing down turret walls with freezing petrol. Because I was allowed to do a job I liked, I approached much nearer to happiness than I had ever previously done in the army. As I write, I am very near to release, and as I want things out of life that the army can never give me, I shall be glad to get out. To be fair, I don't begrudge the time I have spent in the army, nor do I think that National Service will harm many individuals. [The National Serviceman] will see a complete male cross-section of his own generation, and if he is not absolutely self-centred, he will learn tolerance and will benefit by it.[45]

As the time was nearing for release from service, universally known as 'demob', soldiers serving in BAOR could look forward to a four-week-long course at the College of the Rhine Army in Göttingen which had opened in 1945. Soldiers with pre-service trades such as vehicle fitters, carpentry and building etc. would be revised in that trade in preparation for their return to 'civvy street'. The Trades Wing running such courses boasted of holding ½ million pounds of machine tools, plus a library of 15,000 books. Clerical trade courses were also provided, covering subjects such as shorthand, typewriting and bookkeeping. For those from agricultural backgrounds a branch of the college in Ostinghausen offered courses on pigs and poultry; dairy farming; horticulture; and arable farming. By spring 1949 over 18,000 service leavers had availed themselves of these courses.

In 1949 as the first new drafts of NS men were filling the huge gaps left by the departure of the war-time soldiers, 4th/7th Dragoon Guards reckoned that only 30 per cent of the regiment was regular; this was probably typical. From 1957, in anticipation of the ending of the National Service Act, the numbers of men being conscripted reduced and much more effort was put into regular recruiting; at this point the RAC was some 21,000 strong. Despite this, large numbers of National Servicemen remained: in March 1959 The Royals still contained 289 NS soldiers, meaning that 62 per cent of the corporals and below were National Servicemen. Towards the start of the new decade, as a fully professional army beckoned, the proportions altered, but even in the first half of 1962 QDG still had 15 per cent NS. 4RTR marked the loss of their final National Servicemen in style; Trooper Pearce left the unit on 26 February 1961. He was played out of barracks by the regimental band and taken to the station in the CO's staff car. The very last batch of RAC conscripts started their training at Catterick in November 1960 and the last of them finally left the colours in May 1963.[46] This marked the point at which the standing army became, once again and for the first time since May 1939, an entirely regular undertaking.[47] In total, about 1.24 million youngsters served in the British army as National Servicemen between 1947 and 1963. About 1 in 12 served in a theatre of operations in which a campaign medal was awarded; about 400 were killed in action.

The available literature tends to look at NS through the prism of the conscripts, and relatively little has been recorded about those carrying out the training – the regulars. There was always a tension between the needs of the RAC regiments to maintain high standards at all times, and the requirement for those regiments to constantly train new drafts of National Servicemen who arrived at their units every few weeks, only partly trained at best. Just as the efforts of the regiments were starting to bear fruit, the individuals would leave back into 'civvy street', even affecting the regiments deployed on operations. This relentless cycle meant that even the best units could only ever raise their standards to a certain point and could never improve beyond that. Things were even worse for the regiments who, as part of the Arms Plot, had to take their turn functioning as one of the UK-based ABTUs, based mainly in the dreadful accommodation in Catterick – one regiment referred to is as primitive – but also at Barnard Castle or Carlisle for armoured cars.[48] The ABTU job was not a popular one, being seen as something of a mundane conveyor belt which had little attraction for the regular soldiers who had not joined the army to oversee conscript training in North Yorkshire. The vehicles in the training fleet were high-mileage and difficult to keep roadworthy, and the accommodation was notoriously cold and dirty, particularly for those with experience of barracks in BAOR. The poor standard of the various barracks was notorious, remaining at Second World War standards until a substantial rebuilding programme took place in the 1960s. Other aspects of life in Catterick also grated on the soldiers. After the 4/7DG had arrived in Bourlon Barracks in late 1959, they later recorded that:

> June 1960 proved to be the only period of summer weather we were to be permitted this year and [during it] as is apparently normal practice, the local countryside caught fire. We had the fire all to ourselves for a week while the owner of the moor and the local authorities bickered about who should pay for any more soldiers … if it had not started raining (again) it would probably still be burning.

When 5th Royal Inniskilling Dragoon Guards (who had previously served in Korea and then the Canal Zone) came to the end of their three-year stint at Catterick in 1956, they were able to reflect on the experience and allow some of their frustrations to surface:

> Editor: Our third and final year as an ABTU is now almost over. The role has the reputation of being unpopular and unglamorous and, naturally, we are looking forward to becoming an active regiment again … There has been a natural tendency to become impatient with the inevitable routine and monotony, and the role of schoolmaster does not suit everyone.
>
> A Sqn (GMT): With the coming move to Germany, we hope that the permanent staff will become more settled and also that the percentage of regulars will rise. Intakes come fortnightly.
>
> B Sqn (Gunnery and wireless): Our normal rather monotonous routine continues …
>
> C Sqn (D&M): New methods of pre-trade testing and a superhuman effort to drum information into the heads of disinterested recruits was made by the instructors … our basic role of providing the regimental taxi service and general haulage contractor has remained unaltered. We have been known to carry a donkey as a passenger. Potential Officer exercises take up a lot of our time …
>
> LAD: Our heads are bloody but unbowed, and we look forward to a future of manoeuvres in Germany, or a nice peaceful atomic war …[49]

As the Training Brigade HQ and the individual Training Regiments all required their own CO, 2IC, Adjt, RSM, staff and equipment etc., they created, in effect, four additional RAC regiments. When the size of the RAC was once again under scrutiny in the mid-1950s, it was a case of disband them or lose regular regiments; the answer was clear. Eventually what remained after the end of National Service was a single RAC Training Regiment, based at Cambrai Barracks, Catterick. This was staffed by an 'out of role' regular regiment and which conducted basic (fourteen weeks) and trade training for all RAC regiments; the first regiment to take the role was 4/7DG in June 1960.[50] By the mid-1960s, with the regular army well-established and following a further reduction in the number of recruits needing to be trained annually a pragmatic decision was made that the RAC Training Regiment in Catterick would supply the armoured squadron for the high-profile Berlin role for the duration of their tour.[51] This sensibly maintained operational skills in at least part of the regiment and allowed some rotation of personnel between the two locations. Popular as it was, not all soldiers wanted to stay in Germany and there were many who, after a number of years in BAOR or elsewhere abroad, welcomed the chance to serve in the UK, whatever the job.

Rupert and Rodney – The Officers

In January 1947 Sandhurst – renamed as the Royal Military Academy, and with the Gentlemen-Cadets now known as Officer Cadets – returned to its post-war structure and system for training and commissioning the select volunteers destined to be regular officers.[52] The large numbers of short-term Emergency (National Service) commissioned officers needed were selected and filtered from the hoi polloi during basic training, and then trained at the Mons Officer Cadet Training Unit (Mons OCTU) at Aldershot for about sixteen weeks before being sent to their regiments for the residue of their service. From 1948 the army training regiments had received instructions to keep a look-out for potential officers (PO) from the conscripted recruits undergoing basic training, as there would be insufficient regular officers for the size of the army. Over the course of National Service from 1949 to 1960 about 6.6 per cent of men were graded as POs during their basic training. Of course, not all of these wanted a commission, or were successful at obtaining one. The Fifth Skins carried out a stint at Catterick in the 1950s, at the height of the National Service surge. They noted that what all the POs that were under their tutelage had in common was, 'the ambition to pass their period of National Service as officers, but whilst many were enthusiastic and conscientious, others tended to regard a commission as probably the least uncomfortable way of getting through an inevitable but tiresome chore'.[53]

Education played a big part in pre-selection, even before the conscript had reported for basic training; about two-thirds of those who joined the army with a degree found themselves commissioned. The right accent also helped: over 60 per cent of NS officers came from the south of England, a wildly disproportionate amount. And having had relations who had served in the Officers' Mess of prestigious regiments, having attended the right school or indeed just the ability to play 'rugger' at a high standard: all of these virtually guaranteed the PO his commission, particularly in the cavalry regiments where personal connections still meant a lot – some accounts record the stories of male children who at birth were 'put down' for the family regiment (and probably the MCC as well ...).

The first hurdle to be overcome for the PO was the Unit Selection Board, conducted by the commanding officer of the resident training unit and acting as an initial filter; COs increasingly came under pressure during the 1950s to make the USB tougher, as failure rates were deemed to be too high and therefore wasteful of resources. These failures mostly came during the next step, the three-day War Office Selection Board, or 'WosBee', at Westbury in Wiltshire.[54] Candidates were under scrutiny the whole time and performed a series of structured tests designed to establish whether they had leadership potential and the right characters to become officers. These included problem-solving, practical 'command tasks' acting both as leader and as led, discussion periods, interviews and lecturettes. The latter provided some light relief as well as the opportunity to discuss a wide range of topics, personal to the individual PO. One candidate delivered an outstanding 10-minute talk on the social history of whisky: apparently, it was well-received by a 'conducting officer with a face ravaged by his own research into the topic'.[55]

Having passed WOSB, the next step was sixteen weeks at Mons Officer Training Unit in Aldershot, which many complained was more about foot drill than leadership.[56] The overbearing presence of the fat and bullying RSM Brittain of the Coldstream Guards was for many the defining memory of their time at Mons. Some commented that that the intention of Mons seemed to be to produce the perfect private soldier rather than a competent subaltern. This was slightly unfair; the syllabus devoted a lot of time to map-reading and tactics, but there was still a lot of drill and bullshit. As the officer was not (during the National Service era at least) expected to be the master of the vehicle that he was going to serve on, the training conducted on AFVs was at a basic level.[57] The culmination of Mons was the pass-out parade.[58] Following this, the newly commissioned officer was sent to his unit, where he received more – or less – continuation training, depending on the whim of the CO and of course the role and location of the unit. In 1956 the RAC decided to set the number of NS officers in each regiment as between seven and nine; this still represented the majority of the troop leaders, although not all would get command of a tank or armoured car troop, and some would find themselves as the mess secretary or running the stables. However, the actual number of vacancies also depended on how well (or not) the regiment was doing in recruiting regulars; during 1954, the 4th Hussars only received one regular from Sandhurst, but twelve NS officers.[59]

Some found themselves serving in Korea, or Malaya, or Cyprus. Almost all NS officers remained as second lieutenants, as the opportunity for promotion was much less than for the NS NCOs: of the eighty-four NS officers that 14th/20th Hussars employed over fifteen years, only eight were promoted to lieutenant, and all of these were in the years prior to 1950. Some NS officers, of course, found the army and the mess to their liking and elected to remain, although competition was, naturally, stiff. The Skins recorded one exceptional individual in the shape of PO Patrick Brooking who, having been successful in the mid-1950s, next returned to Catterick with the regiment in 1975, when he took over as the Commanding Officer.

In terms of pay, there had been no pay rises during the war years, and there were clear indications that the perception – reality – of poor officer pay was a definite hindrance to recruiting. In 1945 the daily basic rates of pay were as follows:

Second Lieutenant	11s. (£200 pa)
Lieutenant	13s. to 14s. 6d. (£237–265 pa)
Captain	16s. 6d. to 23s. 6d. (£301–429 pa)
Major	28s. 6d. to 33s. (£520–602 pa)
Lieutenant Colonel	43s. (£785 pa)

In early 1946 these were revised, equalling a minimum of a 30 per cent pay rise so that the new annual rates of pay (shown including allowances) were:

Lieutenant after four years' service	£538
Captain after six years	£648
Major after seventeen years	£940
Lieutenant Colonel after twenty-three years	£1,278

Poor rates of pay remained a huge bone of contention as well as a positive hindrance to both recruiting and retention. In recognition of this, on 1 April 1954, a new pay scale was introduced, which boasted that regimental officers would receive per diem increases of between 4s. (captains) and 6s. (lieutenant colonels). The new pay rates were:

Captain (four years' service in rank)	37s. per diem, or £675 pa
Captain (six years' service in rank)	39s. per diem, or £712 pa
Major (two years' service in rank)	49s. per diem, or £894 pa
Major (four years' service in rank)	51s. per diem, or £931 pa
Major (six years' service in rank)	53s. per diem, or £967 pa
Lieutenant Colonel (on appointment)	61s. 6d. per diem, or £1,122 pa

In June 1948, the Soviets blocked the Western nations' access to West Berlin, leading to the necessity to supply the city by air. This provocative act brought home the fact that any vestiges of the wartime alliance with the USSR were dead, and the Red Army now presented a real threat – this was the true start of the Cold War in Europe. As a result, the British army needed to get its house in order, and repair some of the damage done to the structures since 1945. One result was the creation of the Regular Army Reserve of Officers (RARO) and the Army Officers' Emergency Reserve, both of which aimed to create a trained (or at the minimum, partly trained) pool of volunteers who would be able to reinforce the army at short notice; the only requirement was to attend a single period of fifteen days' training each year.[60] Within the RAC this led to each regiment being entitled to hold a number of officers in each category who would return to the regiment annually and conduct a number of days of paid training, usually nineteen, and timed to coincide with major training exercises where they would be employed in liaison roles and as watchkeepers, even occasionally as troop leaders. For some, the timing was even more fortunate as they were sent skiing or similar for the whole of their attachment.[61] Another group of these reservists was allocated to the non-existent Armour Delivery Regiment, allowing a cadre of (semi) trained men who could form such a regiment should the need arise.

For the regular RAC officer who had graduated from Sandhurst, in the mid-1950s his expected career would look like this: two years as a 2Lt, followed by another four as a Lt – the decision on exactly when to give out the second 'pip' was entirely the CO's. At the age of 26, and having passed the requisite promotion examinations, he could then promote to captain, a rank he would hold for about seven years. When he was 33 and, again, having passed the necessary exams, he was eligible for promotion to major. In order to stay in the army, he must then be selected for promotion to lieutenant colonel before he was 45 years old. In 1956 the average age of the COs of cavalry regiments was 41½, in the RTR which still operated a pool rather than single regiment system, it was slightly older, at 43.

In 1959 a new type of commission, the three-year Short Service Commission (SSC) had been introduced, as there was a sudden shortfall in the numbers of second lieutenants joining the regiments due to the ending of National Service. This commission was designed to bring in 18–24-year-old civilians via Mons, with the hope that a proportion of these would want to stay and become regular officers – for this they would have to successfully complete the Regular Commissions Board, or RCB, the replacement for WOSB. By the mid-1980s there were even more routes for those wishing to commission into the RAC, with Regular, Special Regular, Short Service and Short Service Limited Commissions all available.[62] All less the last category still had to pass RCB. In broad terms, the route depended on two things; whether the candidate was (or was going to be) a university graduate or not, and how long the candidate wished to commit themselves to serve for. For those taking the graduate ('grad') route, the chances of gaining a Regular Commission giving a career up to and beyond the pension point were much higher, and promotion was faster, certainly in the early years. The 'non-grads' tended to enter regimental duty earlier as they went to RMAS straight after their A-Levels, and often proved to be the stronger officers on a practical level, in part because they spent more time as troop leaders rather than being fast-tracked into regimental staff roles. A systemic preference for officers with degrees in the RAC became more marked at about this time, often regardless of the subject studied, leading to some strange characters being commissioned on the basis of a good pass in such areas as horticulture, or ancient Persian, and similar. The bottom line as far as the soldiers were concerned was never to do with education, or ambition, or promotion prospects, but simply reflected how well the officer was liked and how good he was at his job. The worst kind of character was seen to be the overly ambitious, bright but intellectually conceited type, who cared little for the soldiers. Fortunately, such types were quite thin on the ground, but could be hugely damaging to a small family regiment if left unchecked.

A strange anomaly that existed was that of brevet rank. This was a system that allowed officers to be promoted one rank higher than their substantive rank, but without the pay. It was used as a reward for exceptional performance that could not be rewarded in the normal way because there were no vacancies at that time; when a vacancy did come up the holder of the brevet would then promote to the substantive rank. The system was still in use in the mid-1960s before being shelved. It did occasionally throw up some strange anomalies, including instances whereby the Commanding Officer and regimental 2IC might both hold the rank of lieutenant colonel, and which might be awkward depending on the personalities involved.

After the war the system of selecting soldiers (usually sergeants and warrant officers) for commissioning 'in the field' was stopped, with almost all officers coming from either Sandhurst or Mons OCTU. The system reverted to the pre-war days when each regiment had a handful of commissioned officers who had come up through the ranks and had been awarded 'quartermaster commissions'.[63] The small numbers of these normally meant that it would be the outgoing RSM who received this, although occasionally the RQMS would be thus appointed. The jobs available to these officers was very limited, usually to quartermaster appointments at regimental duty or outside, as well as taking the post of range officer. Their lowly status within the units, particularly within certain cavalry regiments, was made plain when the annual regimental journal was produced; this would list all the officers of the regiment in seniority, from those who were generals down to the latest NS officer who was fresh out of

Mons, and only then the quartermaster commissions, even if the senior one of these held the rank of lieutenant colonel.

The overwhelming responsibilities of the sole unit quartermaster led to the creation of the appointment of the quartermaster (technical) in 1956 who took over the responsibilities of the now defunct technical adjutant. For a short time the job was often known as the second quartermaster, before the responsibilities were formally divided up. The QM (sometimes known as QM Admin or, more informally as 'boots and socks') was the senior role and looked after the buildings and estate, accommodation stores, clothing, and ammunition, as well as running the carpenters' and painters' shops. The QM(T) looked after the vehicles and spares, and weapons, and would complete this role before becoming QM(A).[64] In 1963 another post was created, that of Motor Transport Officer, or MTO, and this was usually combined with the role of being 2IC of HQ Sqn. In the 1970s the type of commission was renamed to become a Late Entry commission, and such 'through the ranks' officers became known as LEs. Over the decades the number of LE roles increased within the regiments, in part because of problems with recruiting, and included new jobs such as the Families or Welfare Officer (usually combined with looking after the PRI) and the Career Management Officer who looked after the soldier's promotion and careers. This increasing use of LE officers led to opportunities to command squadrons, and across the RAC two per year were able to achieve lieutenant colonel rank, although a poorly thought-out rule prevented further promotion.

Chapter 2

BAOR

In early May 1945 Operation Overlord – the liberation of North West Europe – was completed and replaced by Operation Eclipse, the disarmament of the German armed forces and the occupation, rehabilitation and de-Nazification of Germany. Amongst the allies, Britain was responsible for north-west Germany, the Ruhr, the Netherlands and Denmark. The British Army of the Rhine, or BAOR, was formed on 25 August 1945, replacing the British Liberation Army/21st Army Group, and echoing the original BAOR that had served in the aftermath of the First World War from 1919–29, and in which the O had stood for occupation. Until BAOR came under NATO command in 1952, the units stationed there were still technically occupation troops, with different rules and privileges to those employed by later generations. As a result of agreements between the wartime allies concluded even before the war ended, much of the northern part of what would become West Germany (The Federal Republic) was placed under British control from May 1945, and this area – about the same size as England and Wales – was sub-divided into three districts, each being administered by one of the three British Corps HQ: I, VIII and XXX.

Many of the places that were soon to become RAC garrison towns had been badly hit by air raids during the war, predominantly Osnabrück and Münster, but also including some of the smaller towns such as Paderborn and Hildesheim. Osnabrück, not only a major transportation hub but also under the flightpath of raids to and from Berlin and other eastern targets, was subject not only to its own raids but also received unused bombs jettisoned by aircraft on the return journey from unsuccessful raids elsewhere. By the end of the war about 90 per cent of the old city centre had been destroyed, and about two-thirds of the wider urban area. Even higher figures applied to Münster, a major rail junction, which was heavily hit in October 1944 destroying nearly all of the historic old city and, again, about two-thirds of the whole urban area.

Under Operation Eclipse, the first tasks of the many RAC regiments that found themselves forming the army of occupation included searching for German war criminals, guarding key installations to prevent looting and assisting with the local governance of the population; the end of the war did not mean an end to the violence and deprivation. Large numbers of the population were homeless, food and fuel was in very short supply and many hundreds of thousands of Wehrmacht former Prisoners of War and Surrendered Enemy Personnel were roaming the area.[1] Some of these were trying to get back home, but this was not always attractive for those whose homes lay in the Russian occupation zone. The situation remained chaotic for a number of years after 1945; even two years after the end of the war, there were still 1.2 million refugees and displaced persons in Schleswig-Holstein alone. Until July 1945 British troops were – officially at least – forbidden even to talk to Germans, and it was not until September that they were allowed to enter a German shop, not that many of them were in business at that time.

For the first five years or so following the cessation of hostilities the RAC regiments in Germany could have been forgiven for wondering whether the War Office had any idea what it was doing with them. Like their comrades in Italy, Austria and in the Middle East, the regiments found themselves constantly changing equipment, roles and locations, often settling in to a new location for a few weeks or months – in which a lot of energy was expended in improving the accommodation – only to suddenly receive orders to move somewhere else. In the first few years, many of the locations used were frequently not barracks, but were simply villages or towns in which the units had to establish themselves as best they could. To be placed in an old Wehrmacht barracks was seen as a godsend, and the availability of tank hangars was almost unheard of, most tank and vehicle parks being simply open ground, exposed to the worst weather that northern Germany could produce.[2]

For example 3RTR celebrated VE Day in Bad Segeberg, before being ordered to move to Eichede on 15 May. Two weeks later, on the 28th, they were on the move again, to Friedrichstadt. After three months there on 28 August the next location to be occupied was Süchteln near Krefeld, with the next move taking place in early February 1946 to Flensburg where they would remain until February 1948 before moving to the UK and settling in at Gosport for seven months. They were then sent to Bovington in mid-September 1948. After ten months, in July 1949 the unit was deployed at very short notice to Hong Kong. In that time the regiment had converted from Comets to Churchill Crocodiles, and then to Sherman Crab flail tanks and DDs. For Hong Kong the regiment needed to convert once more, back to Comets, and some of the tanks they took to the Far East being the same ones they had operated in Germany in 1945. However, by the time the Third were on their way to the Orient, the situation in BAOR had stabilized somewhat and most regiments would find themselves accommodated in proper barracks, universally acclaimed as ten times better than anything available in the UK. Other regiments were luckier; in July 1946, after some fairly typical moving around – the troops referred to it using more fruity language – 1RTR took over an ex-Luftwaffe airfield in Detmold which they renamed as Hobart Barracks, set about repairing and renovating it, and remained there until September 1952. In Osnabrück, a purpose-built barracks named Imphal by the first occupiers, the 3rd Carabiniers, was constructed between June and December 1951, complete with real tank hangars, and the unit stayed there until mid-1959.[3]

It has to be said that for a number of years following the German defeat, there remained a mutual suspicion between the victors and the vanquished. The Germans were beaten and starving, their cities and economy destroyed, and a large percentage of the male population either dead or prisoners of war around the world.[4] The black and grey markets thrived, and many soldiers gave (and sold) their rations, coffee, soap and cigarettes to the locals; not surprisingly, there were many liaisons and although initially marriages were banned, it was clear to most that if the British were going to stay in Germany, then relationships would inevitably be a part of life. The British soldiers were well-fed and under orders not to fraternise with the population, although how that could be enforced in an army of young men away from home is open to question: in spring 1948 the *10th Hussars Journal* congratulated nine of its members on their marriages: seven of these were to German women.

As Reichsmarks were still the official currency but virtually worthless, from August 1946 British personnel were paid in a mixture of sterling and British Armed Forces Special Vouchers (BAFSV); these were the only currency that would be accepted in canteens and NAAFI shops. As they quickly became misused in black-market dealings, and to prevent counterfeiting, in January 1948 a second series was issued to replace the first. In turn, these were replaced by the new currency, the Deutschmark, when it was suddenly introduced in June 1948, although anachronistically they remained in use in Berlin until as late as December 1979; soldiers referred to the currency as 'Dees'. Serving in BAOR meant that service personnel received their normal service pay converted into Deutschmarks at a set rate, known as the Forces Fixed Rate, or FFR; it was not completely fixed as it was amended over time, generally downwards, to reflect the changing power of sterling. Another bonus of living in BAOR – as well as other foreign service stations around the world – was the provision from the late 1940s of the Local Overseas Allowance, or LOA. This was intended to cover additional day-to-day expenses incurred through living outside of the UK. The 'pads' got more, with higher rates for those with larger families, and the amount varied according to rank.

Another benefit enjoyed was easy access to cheap loans, either through local German banks or NAAFI. In 1960 NAAFI started offering Germany-based servicemen the chance to buy new cars on hire purchase, which started to bring car ownership into the range of many, if not the more junior ranks, then certainly members of the Sergeants' Mess. By the 1980s even the lowest paid trooper could afford to run a car, with cheap fuel available through the subsidized petrol coupons scheme. However, because of the perceived threat of a Soviet invasion, this did not mean that it was possible to just pop back to the UK whenever the fancy took them. The units in BAOR were not allowed to have more than a certain

The return to peacetime soldiering demanded an immediate return to pre-war standards of smartness and 'bull'. These three NCOs from 14th/20th King's Hussars are demonstrating just how smart battledress could be. The Daimler Armoured Car behind is, unusually, equipped with a Littlejohn squeeze-bore adaptor on the 2-pounder gun.

percentage of their men away at any one time; although this varied, on average this was about 20 per cent. The Christmas and New Year period was generally split in two, with one group returning on about 27 December in order to allow the second group to depart; priority for home leave was mostly given to the single soldiers. It was a standing joke that this was the period when the Soviets should attack, with a lot of the unit out of station and many of those still in BAOR incapable of duty because of the effects of imbibing. Alcohol was a notable feature of the BAOR lifestyle, and was at times something of a curse. The messes, squadron bars and other clubs operated as British pubs – albeit with a selective membership – and booze was both plentiful and extremely cheap through the NAAFI; units leaving Germany and returning to the UK in the 1960s and 1970s often commented that their drinking habits altered as they simply could not afford British pub prices – their drinking was no longer being subsidized by the NAAFI and LOA. Alcoholism was not exactly endemic, but afflicted a significant minority.[5] Drinking on exercises was sometimes tolerated to a greater or lesser degree; in rare but tragic cases this led directly to avoidable fatal and near-fatal accidents, and the wider car ownership from the early 1960s led to a serious issue with drink-driving. As a result of the problems, the chain of command finally and belatedly started to crack down on alcohol-inspired disciplinary incidents, and slowly the situation improved.[6]

The Pads and the Ankle-Biters

In April 1947, only 36 per cent of the pre-war housing in the whole of Nord-Rhein Westphalia was in a liveable condition. In the city of Münster, in the process of becoming a major British garrison, only just over 1,000 houses remained out of nearly 34,000 pre-war. From 1946 the War Office classified BAOR as a home, rather than as an overseas, posting, meaning that there was a need for married quarters to be provided; the first families began to arrive from the UK in late August 1946 under Operation Union. At this time, the British military government were able to requisition suitable houses for use as married quarters and force the German families to leave at short notice; in some locations even this draconian action was insufficient, and families had to be accommodated within the barracks in converted soldiers' barrack blocks.[7] In some cases, entire German villages were taken over for military use, and these were ringed with barbed wire, more to stop burglaries than to protect the inhabitants. Not surprisingly, such measures created huge tensions between the military and civil powers, and many soldiers and their families were uncomfortable with the situation. When 1RTR first took advantage of the provision of married quarters in Detmold in early 1947, thirty-three wives and thirty children made the journey across the Channel, with the latter aged between 12 years and 6 weeks old.[8] Luckily for them, the small town had not received much damage, and the quality of the married quarters seems to have been fairly high.[9] In the days before air trooping using chartered airlines became the norm in the early 1960s, a regular troop train operated out of Liverpool Street station in London, travelling to Harwich and then over the Channel to the Hook of Holland, and from there on to multiple destinations.

The somewhat isolated nature of the postings, amid a foreign and until recently enemy nation, led to a natural tendency to bring the wives and children together as groups, although the hierarchy of the husband's rank still played a large part in deciding who took charge. The CO's or senior officer's wife was expected to run the obligatory Wives' Club. First-name terms were discouraged between the wives, as their husband's rank was of importance, with the use of titles such as 'Mrs Sgt Smith', or the even less personal 'Wife of Sgt Taylor 815' being in common usage.

Until 1955 troops stationed in Germany came only under British military law, but from 5 May of that year they were also subject to German civil law, meaning they could be tried in a German civil court if they contravened German civil law. By the mid-1950s life in BAOR was in many respects very settled, with a routine of in-barracks training and inspections, duties, border patrols and site-guards, sport and adventure training, leave and 'crash-outs'. For the soldiers this was exciting and often confusing at first, but soon became the norm. For the wives, some aspects of this meant many weeks of each year spent at home in the house or flat – the 'pad' – on the married 'patch' without the hubby, and it could quickly become monotonous.[10] One wife of a soldier in The Royals in 1967 decided to express herself in unscanned verse:

> Pack up your cases, catch a military train
> Nowadays its quicker – you fly by aeroplane
> With luck you might alight in some sort of home
> Be it antiquated, modern, or built for a gnome
>
> Once you're installed, you'll expect to see your man
> But you are utterly mistaken, that's not the plan
> There are exercises, marches, and sometimes even fights
> Conspiring to deprive you of your marital delights
>
> When you're tired of patch-life, there's escape from it all
> In Brunei, Malaysia or far away Nepal
> From Germany to Yorkshire to the southern tip of Spain
> And then – its unavoidable – to Germany again

But when the soldiers were back in camp, life within the various messes – Officers', Warrant Officers' and Sergeants', or, in the majority of regiments, the Corporals' Club – allowed a more relaxed social environment.[11] Welfare provision also came via various civilian and religious charitable organizations, including the WVS (WRVS from 1966), TocH, Red Shield and the Salvation Army, as well as the ubiquitous forces radio; the extremely popular 'two-way Family Favourites' programme, allowing messages to be passed between the UK and service families worldwide, was introduced in 1955. In 1979 the British Forces Broadcasting Service (BFBS) started a TV service to complement its radio output. Forces newspapers covered the local news, including *Union Jack* and, from November 1970, *Sixth Sense* – so-called as it originally served only 6th Armoured Brigade.

Each unit operated their PRI, or the President of the Regimental Institutes, a means of selling regimental-specific items such as side caps and stable belts, and generating income for the regiment; in later years some PRIs went into competition with the NAAFI, offering domestic appliances and the like, and many operated their own coach service for travel to and from the UK. Other means of keeping the soldiers and their families happy proliferated. Thrift clubs, bingo, gardening societies, the AKC/SKC services cinema and the like; all allowed organized recreational activities, and in many units access to sports and travel provided diversions for the often-lonely young housewives, who found themselves saddled with looking after the 'bin lids' and with little chance of employment. In the late 1940s the education of children of school age was initially entrusted to the Royal Army Education Corps, but the British Families Education Service was quickly established along with a large number of exceptionally good primary, middle and secondary schools.[12] It was important to pay close attention to welfare, as if it was mishandled there was potential for political problems. By 1983 there were about 53,000 service personnel serving in Germany, but about 103,000 dependants.

By 1948 eight official leave centres had been established in BAOR plus one in Austria, with adventure training, cinemas, dances and even recitals on offer. The three in the Harz Mountains area were used mainly for winter sports plus canoeing, shooting, hiking etc. The one at Nordeney on the North Sea coast was more of a holiday resort, with beaches and sea fishing plus a golf course; soldiers there could even go seal shooting! The one on the Baltic coast was more Scandinavian in style and was equipped with saunas and steam baths. Others at the Möhnesee, Winterberg, Düsseldorf and at Ehrwald in the Austrian Tyrol provided sailing and water sports, plus winter sports and mountain climbing. All of these were free if visited during a short leave, but if they were used during annual leave then 9s. a day was charged for officers, and 4s. a day for soldiers. Where they could, all of the cavalry regiments – and even some of the RTR – quickly established stables and riding schools, allowing many ORs access to a rich man's sport that they could not have dreamed of when in civvy street. Some of the cavalry units took things one step further, and made officer equitation compulsory. 17th/21st Lancers whilst in Austria were one regiment that did this, 'Mr "Abdul" Beeby, the RSM and a Weedon [army equitation school] trained instructor with a caustic wit, soon started an officers' riding school. Mr Beeby; "Mister ????, Sir! If that's the way that Jesus Christ rode his donkey into Jerusalem, I'm not surprised they crucified him!"'[13] Manpower for the stables was usually easy to come by, as there were many civilians or demobilized enemy soldiers, even POWs, who would work long hours in return for regular meals if little or no actual pay. In time, soldiers from the regiments would be posted to 'stables troop', and some regiments acquired packs of hounds and even pig farms; such activities often provided gainful employment for soldiers who could not pass trade tests to allow them to serve in the mainstream regiment, as well as improving the fare on offer in the messes.[14]

Where BAOR had a fault, it was that, for much of its existence, the very routine became a problem; this was especially the case during the National Service era, as all that could be achieved was a basic and quite low level of competence. In 1957 about one-third of the army strength was committed to BAOR, and the percentage of RAC units serving there was even higher than that. One author described BAOR as becoming 'a by-word for comfortable and mind-numbingly dull postings'.[15] This was somewhat unfair, but there was truth in it. The RAC tank regiments necessarily had to stick to an annual programme of training, starting with individual up-skilling and qualification courses run in barracks, to field training. This began at individual tank and troop level, and then progressed through squadron and regimental training, culminating in Brigade, Division and even Corps field training exercises, or FTXs. This involved visiting the same old training areas year after year, as well as Hohne ranges for a fortnight's live-fire gunnery training. 17th/21st Lancers returned to Germany (Sennelager) in 1962 after a tour in Hong Kong and Aden, and one year later remarked that, 'most of the time has been spent in adapting ourselves to the old routine … there is a danger inherent in service in Germany of becoming a servant of repetitive day to day work'. The armoured car regiments had things slightly better, as their lower 'footprint' allowed them to use alternative training locations, often in neighbouring countries such as Denmark and France.

Exercises

Field exercises at regimental level were often referred to as 'schemes', a word which pre-dated the Second World War and was in common currency during the 1960s, and larger formation sized exercises were often called manoeuvres. Both terms were then largely replaced by the generic 'exercise', with the larger ones – those not using military training areas but operating over temporarily requisitioned '443' farmland – these were the infamous FTXs.[16] The latter were popular as it allowed the troops to train on unfamiliar ground, often close to the areas that they would expect to fight the Soviets over, and breaks in the exercise would allow access to German grocers, pubs and, to the author's certain recollection (although the details may be a little hazy), even discos and night clubs. In some cases, regiments 'fought' each other, although without umpires both sides would naturally claim to have won; in 1960 9th Lancers conducted 'a two-day battle against the 5th Royal Inniskilling Dragoon Guards, during which we chased them for many miles'. If the object of the exercise was to allow The Skins to practise withdrawal in contact, then that might have been the case, but one thing is certain – at the conclusion they would have claimed that in fact it was they who had roundly bested the Lancers. However, much of the routine tactical training was conducted not in open country but on oh-so familiar dedicated training areas, including Achmer (Osnabrück), Dorbaum (Münster), the tiny Goldgrund (Paderborn), Sennelager ('probably the worst lager in the world'), Brilon, Borkenberge, Vogelsang, Putlos and in later years even American facilities further south such as Hohenfels and Grafenwöhr, and, from 1997, at the Drawsko Pomorski area in Poland. But the one place that almost all RAC soldiers who served in BAOR recall is Soltau.

From 1950, Soltau – officially the Soltau-Lüneburg Training Area or SLTA – became the primary BAOR tank training area. It was located on Lüneburg Heath, south-west of the town of the same name and running westwards to the outskirts of the town of Schneverdingen. The HQ for the area and the unloading point for tank trains was the bleak and open Reinsehlen Camp, in the north-west of the area, with the villages of Bispingen and Behringen within the boundaries of the area. To the north was the Forst Langeloh nature sanctuary, a forested area out

17th/21st Lancers on exercise, 1950s. Apart from the Centurion tank, almost all of the uniforms and equipment in use were the same as those used during the Second World War.

of bounds to all military vehicles – not that that stopped many a geographically embarrassed tank commander finding their way in there, despite a clearly defined boundary fence with warning notices. It was a training area primarily for tank, and later mechanized infantry, training, and, unusually, it allowed such training to be conducted within the 'red areas' almost all-year round, although AFV movement was generally not permitted on Sundays. The area was about 40km from west to east, and about 10km deep; one part of it in the east was known as the Lüneburg Extension, and was only used by smaller vehicles, not tanks. Overuse, with no recovery time, quickly turned the heathland into a dustbowl, with a pervading dirty, grey dust – when it wasn't a sea of mud – making life difficult for crews and engines alike.

When B Squadron 3rd Hussars went to 'the all-too-familiar Soltau training area' in summer 1956, they recorded that 'except for the new autobahn, little had altered from last year, and SQMS Johnson MM went as far as saying that Red Annie had not even changed her dress' – the mind boggles as to who she was and what trade she plied, but an educated guess can be made.[17] In 1970 1RTR spoke for all the regiments in saying that, 'Soltau changes little from year to year, apart from minor new restrictions … we camp out in the same bivouac areas and train our troops in the same glutinous mud, or all-pervading dust, dependent upon the weather'. Regimental journals for four decades from the 1950s abound with images of vehicles negotiating the familiar features of the Pylon Line, Strip Wood, the 'Jerrycan' or the area around the Schwindebeck River, and, almost without fail, they show one spectacularly bogged tank – usually belonging to a named and shamed officer. Soltau remained a necessary evil – a decent-sized training area which allowed squadron training (although it was really too small to accommodate a whole regiment), but one which soon became familiar, allowing experienced commanders to navigate for much of the time without referring to the map. The manoeuvre area was partly wooded but much of it remained a desert, devoid of any vegetation and stained with the thousands of gallons of engine oil dropped from ailing tanks. Another feature of life on the training area from 1974 that must be recorded was the blue Mercedes 'bratty-wagon' belong to Herr Wolfgang Meier, who would turn up in the unlikeliest of places, including supposedly well-camouflaged hides, to dispense German fast food, beer and even fish and chips.[18]

Following the fall of the Berlin Wall the need for such tank training was increasingly questioned, and environmental concerns were being expressed as to the impact that the armoured training – with Chieftain being a particular culprit – was having on the area. The end was nigh: the last armoured training on the area finished on 11 February 1994, and on 31 July of that year the long-agreement lapsed, and the area was handed back to the German authorities, ending a link to a small area of Germany that the vast majority of RAC soldiers – certainly those from tank regiments – had come to know better than any other.

Gunnery Training

With the large amounts of RAC units stationed in Germany in the immediate post-war period, it was realized that rather than sending hundreds of students back to the UK for courses, it would be more efficient to create a training centre within BAOR to deliver the same product. The RAC Training Centre BAOR opened at Caen Barracks Hohne – at that time it was generally called Bergen/Belsen or just Belsen – on 1 June 1946, with the first students starting training courses on 19 June. By 1947 the centre was not only training RAC instructors in all three trades, but it was also delivering RAC NCO Crew Commander courses as well as armoured tactics courses for junior officers from all arms; the Tactics Wing responsible for these last two courses had opened on 12 September 1946. During 1947 staff from the centre also began to oversee regimental firing taking place on the nearby range complex, with the first three regiments to shoot there being 1RTR, The Greys and then 2RTR. From this point, regiments could expect to have their firing camps overseen and assessed by the central staff from the Centre, and a system of gradings was awarded to squadrons and, collectively, to regiments; achieving the cherished A grade was everyone's goal, and warranted boasting and recording in regimental journals – although any lesser standard was discreetly ignored.[19]

An enormous amount of time and effort was expended in the run-up to, and delivery of, a regiment's two weeks on the open ranges of Hohne – 'annual firing'. Over the years a range of increasingly sophisticated training devices and simulators were produced to assist. These included the Classroom Instructional Mounting, or CIM, a cut-away turret allowing some weapon drills to be conducted; the more sophisticated of these including a hydraulically recoiling main gun. The Field Miniature Range (FMR) used a .22in rifle to fire at rubber targets, including moving, on a large sand table; although introduced in an air rifle form prior to the Second World War, the system was simple and well-liked and remained in service at least into the late 1980s. The Aquilina Gunnery System (AGS) was a development of the FMR concept, and invented by an instructor from the Gunnery School, Sergeant (later Major MBE) Ron Aquilina 3RTR; this used a laser to replace the .22in bullet. The Gunnery Training System, or GTS, was necessary when Chieftain was retro-fitted with the computer-based Improved Fire Control System (IFCS), and was based on the turret of the tank CIM. When anti-tank guided weapons were introduced, simulators – very advanced for their time – were required to practise GW Controllers before firing the scarce and expensive missiles on the open range, and these were provided by the Invertron company.

Although open-range firing was generally enjoyed by the crews, there were downsides to it, and not only if bad weather intervened. No one really enjoyed having a seasoned 'Schools Instructor Gunnery' sergeant watching every aspect of the firing, knowing that every mistake and omission would be noted, contributing to the overall report. An enormous amount of bullshit was expended by some units in preparation, so that as well as practising the crews in the simulators, every vehicle was repainted, special signs made and minetape abounded; it was not uncommon for the tanks to be lined up on a firing point by the squadron sergeant major using a tape measure to ensure that they were perfectly spaced. The sergeant would be treated like a demi-god, and would be well looked after in the extreme, with senior warrant officers tip-toeing around him and squadron leaders going out of their way to satisfy his every need. There is no doubt that a 'which unit can apply the most bullshit' competition, although unofficial, was alive and well in the 1980s, with reports filtering back to other RAC units as to what the latest showy and time-consuming fad was. Other units, and this became more common over time, preferred to let the firing results speak for themselves, and tried to link the firing exercises with tactical training, including living off of their vehicles under camouflage nets at the rear of the firing points rather than using the transit accommodation at Oerbke, and foregoing the delights of the riotous trips to the Hamburg Reeperbahn.

Tank crews scrubbing the 77mm barrel of a Comet after firing on the ranges, a task familiar to even the modern generation of soldiers.

'Be Not Content with a Single Tour of Inspection'

Although this quote comes from Cato the Elder's *De Agri Cultura* and was written in about 180 BC, it could equally have applied to RAC units in BAOR post–Second World War. Part of the routine of every RAC soldier, wherever he was stationed, and whichever vehicle his regiment was equipped with, was the seemingly endless number of formal inspections. In 1959 the *16th/5th Lancers Journal* complained that, 'inspections seem to predominate in this peacetime army, and we have had our fill in the past twelve months'. They were undoubtedly right – the annual calendar was filled with a whole series of inspections, looking at everything with the regiment from administration and accommodation to the vehicles, weapons and ancillary equipment; nothing was so unimportant that it did not warrant an inspection at least once a year. Possibly the most dreaded was the CIV. The Central Inspectorate of Vehicles was a part-REME, part-Civil Service organization that seemed to have little or no understanding of the problems faced by real crews; a missing bolt or uncompleted/unreported 'A job' would be listed on the report without regard to its effect on the 'fightability' of the whole vehicle, or indeed with no regard for the fact that that particular spare part had been unobtainable for two years.[20] 2RTR probably summed things up for everyone in 1958 when they recorded that, 'the inspectors were met by the usual old mixture of ingratiating smiles and anxious semi-hostile stares'. The somewhat random results of the inspections could baffle the most experienced crews, who had invariably spent weeks if not months beforehand nursing the vehicles and trying to achieve the most sought-after grade of Excellent. C Squadron 3rd Carbiniers, a Centurion unit stationed in the inhospitable climes of Aden in 1961, noted that their CIV was 'a bit of a trial, and after considerable efforts we gained a grading of "Unsatisfactory". Six weeks later the tanks were re-inspected and gained a grading of "Excellent", in spite of little being done in between!'[21] In 1956 HQ Squadron of the 3rd Hussars had this to say:

> The CIV inspection of our vehicles loomed large before us. All day long and, as the fateful day loomed, the drivers toiled. Then it was upon us. For a week we watched as our vehicles were taken apart by that grim team. When the last truck staggered from their clutches the inspectors admitted that they had been unable to find a single fault with any of them. Hard on the heels of the CIV came the annual administrative inspection. Once more the squadron buckled to and we lost count of time as hour followed hour of cleaning, painting and polishing. Trucks filled with bundles of those possessions dear to a soldier's heart, but which must never be seen by a General were observed leaving camp at dead of night. The day dawned and with it came the Divisional Commander, who gave

Inspections, both in barracks and in the field, became a dreaded part of the routine of the soldier in BAOR. Conducted for the right reasons, cumulatively they served to make the life of a National Service trooper a constant round of preparing for the next one. (Courtesy QRH)

us a very thorough inspection and asked many searching questions. But by this time nothing could shake us, and he departed declaring us 'quite excellent'.

The Administrative Inspection was a different type of inspection, but just as onerous. As well as investigating the documentation and clerical side of the regiment, it often involved the general – usually the Brigade or Divisional Commander – looking around the technical and living accommodation of the barracks; nowhere was out of bounds to a nosy VIP. Again, just like the CIV, everything that could be painted generally was, and much was hidden lest it might fall under the gaze of the general or one of his snooping aides. It was almost universally accepted that putting on a parade for the visitor would be a good measure of the regiment's administrative efficiency, and so many more hours were spent toiling over uniforms and bulling boots. (For the officers, of course, in the 1950s and 1960s at least, batmen would be doing that for them, allowing them to criticize the turn-out of their men without having any understanding of what they had gone through to achieve it.) A march-past in front of a saluting dais would be common, and the more ambitions Commanding Officers decreed that a mounted march-past would be more in style, requiring rehearsals for days beforehand. Heaven help the tank commander whose vehicle broke down on the big day, damning his regiment to everlasting shame. And after the parade the general would be entertained to a lavish lunch in the Officers' Mess, so that having admired his martial reflection in the highly polished regimental silver, he could go away and write a glowing report on the ability of the unit to withstand the Russian horde …[22]

In about 1965 the CIV system was replaced by the UEI, or Unit Equipment Inspection, and by the early 1970s it became the PRE, or Periodic REME Examination. Additionally, vehicle servicing – preventative maintenance – was carried out on a scheduled daily, weekly, monthly, quarterly and annual basis, which whilst it kept the vehicles in good condition – spare parts notwithstanding – meant that the crews became slaves to the tank park, and thus had less time when in barracks for other forms of training.

Berlin

Berlin in 1945 had probably suffered more damage, due to both the bombing and the Russian attack, than any other German city; in May 1945 75 per cent of the housing stock had been completely destroyed, and much of that which was left was barely usable. The city had been comprehensively destroyed, with little or no coal, gas, electricity or water. Bodies still littered the streets and would be disinterred for months and years to come as clearance took place and rebuilding commenced. One observer described it as a 'grey city', which included the inhabitants. The amount of rubble was extraordinary: it was estimated that about 500 million cubic meters of rubble needed clearing from bombed cities and towns in Germany, and the artificial Teufelsberg hill, now the highest point in Berlin, was made of rubble and other bombsite debris dumped there over the course of twenty-two years of clearance operations.[23] Many soldiers who thought they had seen it all in London and other cities over the last few years were horrified by the level of destruction they now witnessed. Stationed there in the summer of 1945 as a subaltern with 11th Hussars, Richard Brett-Smith wrote in his extremely well-observed memoir of the time that he was amazed that he could detect 'no apparent resentment among Berliners about our bombing. It was taken as a matter of course, and indeed rather admired for its efficiency.'[24]

One of the greatest problems faced by 11th Hussars and the early occupation troops was the behaviour of drunken and out-of-control Russians, looting, robbing and raping. (This was before the zones of occupation were more strictly enforced, and sixteen years before the erection of the Wall.) Amongst other tasks that the Cherrypickers found themselves conducting was escorting convoys of

German mothers and schoolchildren down the Autobahn, westwards to what would become in 1949 the Federal Republic, or West Germany. The Russian provocation that led to the blockade and Berlin Airlift of June 1948 to May 1949 produced a marked change in the relationships between the Germans and the British, cemented in 1949 by the formation of NATO and the realization that the real job of BAOR was to help prevent the westward expansion of the Soviet Empire. Although most soldiers stationed there did not realize it, the Berlin Brigade/Garrison was never formally part of BAOR or its command structure, albeit the distinction was often tenuous.

By the late 1940s the city was very much back on its feet and it would be possible to state that 'the most glamorous posting in Germany was undoubtedly Berlin'. The military train took the soldiers into Charlottenburg station, which was their introduction to the city, if they were not lucky enough to fly into RAF Gatow. British soldiers wore the Berlin Brigade badge on their sleeves; it was a black circle rimmed with red: to the troops it was known as the 'septic arsehole' or similar. The first RAC units to serve in Berlin were 11th Hussars (from July 1945 to March 1946 on armoured cars), 8th Hussars and 1RTR (from August 1945 until March 1946, on Comet tanks). Over the next few years squadrons from the Life Guards, the Royal Horse Guards, The Royals, 11H (again) and 13/18H were all stationed there. Tanks were once again required as the Cold War got colder, and arrived in mid-November 1951 in the shape of a half squadron of Comets from 3rd Hussars.

From 1948 the resident armoured car squadron was stationed in Smuts Barracks in Charlottenburg; this was a former SS Panzer Kaserne and was shared with the Brigade RE squadron. In 1952 the armoured car squadron was replaced by a tank squadron, initially from the specially created 1st Independent Squadron RTR. When this was disbanded due to defence cuts in 1957, various units took it in turns to detach one squadron for this popular role for about two years at a time; initially this came from the BAOR-based APC regiment, then from another short-lived RTR independent squadron. From 1965 until 1988 the RAC Training Regiment in the UK supplied the squadron, which was a sensible decision as it allowed at least some of the soldiers to maintain tank skills whilst having a break from the monotony of Catterick. Because of the lack of suitable training areas within Berlin, the armoured squadron would be replaced by a temporary (sometimes composite) squadron from one of the Germany-based armoured regiments for a few weeks each year, allowing the Berlin unit to fire on the ranges at Hohne and carry out tactical training. Some specialist urban training was, however, conducted using the bespoke facilities in the city, including the American Ruhleben 'fighting city', as well as the small rural training areas on the Havel and the Grunewald. In late 1972 Chieftains were deployed to Berlin for the first time with A Sqn 4RTR, replacing the ageing Centurions, and they remained there until 1991 when C Sqn 14/20H

3rd Hussars in their Comets arriving in Berlin in 1951, to become the resident armoured unit. (Courtesy QRH)

left, being the final armoured unit stationed in Berlin; their tanks departed on 13 June 1992, still resplendent in their urban camouflage schemes, and the squadron rejoined the regiment shortly afterwards.[25]

Exercise Rocking Horse was the name given to the Berlin Garrison 'crash-out' exercise, and the armoured squadron could move faster than any of the BAOR-based units; partly this was due to having one troop on 4 hours' notice to move, and partly because the tanks were already loaded with their war stocks of ammunition. In BAOR the names of the equivalent exercises were different and changed over the years, being called such things as Quick Train, Rocking Horse and Active Edge, the latter being the same initials as alert exercise, designed as an Operational Readiness Test, or ORT, to deploy the whole regiment into its General Deployment Positions (GDP), and causing many a sleepy orderly officer to have kittens when the codeword was issued without warning. In periods of heightened tension, notably during the Berlin Airlift and the Cuban Missile Crisis, the exercise quickly took on the nature of a real deployment, and during the 1950s and 1960s some married families took to stockpiling additional fuel for their private cars in case their families had to make a quick dash for the Channel ports. Life in the city though was generally good, and the posting was a popular one. Even as late as 1967 Major Inglis of 15/19H was able to record that in Berlin certain perks were available that would be unheard of elsewhere; he noted that because the German government met the full costs of the NATO troops stationed there, all of the married officers and men could employ a German servant, although, – horror! – these would only be part-time for the junior ranks.

Chapter 3

RAC Development Part One

Into the 1950s

The Centurion was introduced from 1945 as a stop-gap tank, the last of the Cruiser line until a genuine Universal Tank could be designed. This was intended to be the FV201, using a standard hull which would be the basis not only of the gun tank but also for a range of specialized AFVs; however, the project ran into difficulties and was cancelled in 1949. This left the way clear for Centurion, which by default became the primary British gun tank until it started to be replaced by Chieftain in the mid-1960s. Centurion initially entered service armed with the wartime 17-pounder gun, and was incrementally improved throughout its service, eventually running to thirteen main marks with no less than twenty-four sub-marks.[1] From the Mk III, introduced in 1950, the 20-pounder was used as the main armament, and the outdated BESA MG was replaced by the Browning .30in from the Mk 5.[2] A lengthened hull allowing more on-board fuel to be carried emerged with the Mk 7, solving the long-standing problem of a limited operational range.[3] At the RAC Conference in 1956 it was stated that 1,048 of the Marks 5, 7 and 8 would remain in service as the standard tank for the next six to eight years, all with increased armour on the glacis plate, as well as the prospect of a large percentage of the fleet being upgunned with a new main armament.

The outstanding L7 105mm gun was introduced from 1960 with the Mk 10, and the stabilizer facility within the electronic gun control equipment was improved to allow a reasonable chance of shooting accurately on the move. Infra-red night equipment was introduced towards the end of its life, not only for driving but also in the form of a removable searchlight mounted on the gun mantlet. A .50in Ranging Gun was added from 1966, assisting greatly with the difficult task of estimating the range to a target, as well as a thermal sleeve on the barrel to aid consistency. The tank finally left service as an RAC equipment in mid-1974, although specialist types remained in the hands of REME, the RE and the RA until after the 1991 Gulf War. Centurion was a popular vehicle, admired by its four-man crews for being practical and reasonably simple, although it did become increasingly complex as it evolved; its performance in action in the hands of the Indians and especially the Israelis gave the crews even more confidence that they could defeat Soviet medium armour using APDS ammunition – but earlier, before the introduction of the 105mm, the appearance of the Soviet Josef Stalin series of heavy tanks gave great concern, leading to the acquisition of a stop-gap tank in the form of the Conqueror.[4]

The Conqueror, almost universally called the 'Conk', was a complex tank, and the largest that the RAC had fielded in service up to that point. It was brought into service from 1956 with its American-designed 120mm L1 gun meant to be able to deal with the heavy Russian tanks at 2,000m leaving the 20-pounder armed Cents to look after the T55 medium tanks. Starting in 1955 nine were allocated to each tank regiment in BAOR; most of them were used as a three-tank troop in each sabre squadron, though some experiments took place in some units with a single Conqueror squadron.[5] Running mixed fleets is never helpful from the logistics point of view, and the introduction of the excellent 105mm L7 gun on Centurion rendered them redundant, and they were withdrawn in about 1966, when the even more powerful 120mm-armed Chieftain was about to enter service.

Within the armoured reconnaissance regiments, the changeover from the Second World War Daimler Armoured Car to the 76mm-armed six-wheeled Saladin started to take place in 1958, with the first Saladin Mk 2 (the service version) coming off the production line at Alvis in December 1957; by April 1959 both armoured car regiments in BAOR had been re-equipped, although the usual lack of money was preventing others being modernized, including the Yeomanry units.[6] The replacement of the antiquated GMC trucks to the Saracen APC had happened earlier, as Saracen production was given priority in order to better

The Conqueror, a tank brought into service purely as a counter to the perceived threat from Soviet heavy tanks. The introduction of Chieftain made it obsolete. (TM1858/B6)

protect the troops conducting convoys in Malaya.[7] As well as being used by the RAC regiments allocated the APC role in BAOR, it was also used as an APC by the Assault Troops of Recce Regiments, and command and ambulance versions were also operated. The Recce Tps in the armoured regiments in BAOR finally had their ancient Dingos replaced by Ferret Scout Cars from 1959, although the Recce Regiments had started to receive theirs a few years earlier. Although scout cars by definition were not intended to be used in the primary reconnaissance role, their small size and weight, plus speed and general 'nippyness', made them useful; within the armoured recce regiments sabre squadrons normally used a mix of Saladins and Ferrets, although those designated as air portable were equipped solely with the latter.

As well as AFVs, there was a whole range of Second World War-era 'B' vehicles, aka softskins, that needed replacing. From 1953 the Bedford RL 3-ton all-wheel drive lorry replaced the various old Second World War-vintage trucks of similar capacity, and was to become the standard logistic load carrier of the RAC for the next twenty-plus years. Also during the early 1950s the 4x4 Austin Champ started to enter service in place of the American Jeep. This proved to be a mistake; in an attempt to produce the perfect utility car, the Champ was expensive – twice the price of the Land Rover which was already a proven vehicle, as well as being unnecessarily heavy and unreliable. Although the Austin design remained in service with the TA until the mid-1960s, the Land Rover was in widespread use in the regular army by the mid-1950s and quickly surpassed the Champ, remaining in service (albeit in much improved forms) throughout the period and is still in service at the time of writing.[8]

From about 1953 the 9mm Patchett machine carbine started to be issued in Malaya on trial in place of the Sten, and which was then developed into the L2 sub-machine gun, or Sterling as it was informally called. It was also referred to even less formally as the SMG, or 'small metal gun', and was taken into widespread RAC service in about 1960 in lieu of the pistol which, since the First World War, had been considered as the standard personal weapon of the AFV crewman.[9] In terms of uniforms, until the early 1960s the RAC soldier looked very similar to his predecessor serving in 1945, in that he wore battledress, the RAC steel helmet (which remained in service until the mid-1980s) and both the denim and 'Pixie suit' coveralls.[10] Webbing remained the 1937 Pattern, and was mandated to be worn in skeleton order (belt, pistol holster, ammunition pouch and cross straps) in vehicles in order to make the extraction of casualties easier. What started to change things was the Korean War effect – this led to the introduction of specialized cold-weather clothing, including parkas and the 'woolly-pully' jumper (officially the Jersey, Mans, Heavy).[11] The decision to allow the rest of the army to wear berets in place of khaki side caps or the hideous Cap GS (never worn within the RAC) was promulgated in AO 54/1947, and with only a few exceptions led to the dark-blue beret being adopted by the majority of

Until the introduction of the Bedford RL in 1953, aka the '3-tonner', the RAC had been relying on Second World War-vintage lorries for its logistic support.

the army, including within the RAC, and replacing the wearing of the black beret that had been allowed in armoured units since 1941. 11th Hussars were allowed to retain their brown beret with crimson band dating to their mechanization, and of course the RTR remained in black.[12]

Officer's Messes increasingly reverted to the use of extravagant and stylish mess kits as these had been suspended on the outbreak of war. In 1948 a new pattern of No. 1 Dress, or 'Blues', was authorized for the army; this was a very dark-blue, almost black uniform with a stand-up collar, the basic design of which was then amended by individual regiments to match their traditions and taste. For example, most cavalry regiments adopted chain-mail epaulettes, and regimental buttons, trouser stripes and collar facings were also used.[13] Soldiers, SNCOs and warrant officers were routinely issued a less-well tailored – and cheaper – version of No. 1 Dress, which, as well as being used by all ranks as the best parade uniform, was worn on formal occasions in the mess until the introduction of senior NCOs' mess dress starting in the early 1960s.[14] From the 1950s coloured stable belts, a privately purchased item, were once more made available through the PRI, another step in reinforcing the regimental identities that were so important to the units and individuals; such extravagances could not be easily forced upon the National Serviceman, but when the army once more became all regular, pre-war practices were resumed.

8th Hussars demonstrating the many orders of dress in use in the regiment in Tidworth, 1950. Battledress was introduced in 1937 and stayed in service until the early 1960s. (Courtesy QRH)

In late 1957, over twelve years after the end of the war, the regiments were finally told which battle honours they had been awarded for the conflict. In total 206 were recognized that could be won by RAC units, and the numbers of honours given to the individual regiments of course varied enormously, depending on where the regiment had served. For example, the RTR won fifty-five, 11th Hussars forty-three, KDG twenty-seven and the 12th Lancers twenty-six. 3rd Carbs, fighting in Burma, received thirteen, and 14th/20th Hussars, who spent much of the war serving in backwaters, three. From 1956 the regiments, including the Yeomanry, were once more authorized to carry regimental guidons and standards, which had not been allowed for many years, and over the next few years a series of impressive parades followed as the new versions were made bearing the up-dated battle honours and presented with much pomp and ceremony.[15]

The 1960s

The 1960s saw more changes, the most important of which was undoubtedly the introduction of Chieftain as the new 'Main Battle Tank' (NATO terminology), to replace both Centurion and Conqueror. Its development started in the early 1950s but the first prototype did not appear until January 1960, and it did not start field trials until 1962, finally entering service with 11th Hussars in November 1966.[16] Revolutionary in many ways, it included such features as a reclining driver's position to reduce overall height, ballistically shaped cast turret and hull fronts, a sophisticated fire-control system, a 120mm gun with three-piece ammunition, night-fighting equipment and careful consideration given to increasing survivability, including the stowage of the ammunition bag charges below the turret ring and an NBC protection system. It also complied with NATO policy in being powered by a complicated multi-fuel engine, and it was this which proved to be its weak point. It quickly developed a reputation for breaking down regularly, and much effort was expended in trying to solve the problems of reliability. It was also a much more complex tank than Centurion, and this led to a greater training burden than previously, something that would only increase as the tank was improved and developed over the next three decades. It eventually ran to eleven main marks, in many ways was the best tank in the world and finally left service in March 1996.

The introduction of the FV432 series of AFVs (originally intended to be called Trojan but the name was dropped for some reason) in 1963 finally gave the infantry a purpose-designed tracked APC, nearly twenty years after the Ram Kangaroo had been developed on the Normandy battlefield. It was also the basis for a range of support vehicles that appeared later in the decade, including command, ambulance, mortar, REME and Swingfire GW launcher versions, as well as being the chassis of the Abbot 105mm SPG. The introduction of the outstanding Stalwart 6x6 logistic load-carrier in 1966 gave the echelons a highly

The FV432, here in its Mk 1 petrol-engined form and mounting an 84mm Carl Gustav anti-tank weapon, was introduced in 1963. As this book is published, it still remains in service in its Mk 3 version, having completed sixty years of service.

The much-admired Stalwart, an amphibious load carrier with an armoured cab that was used as a forward logistic support vehicle. Its excellent cross-country performance allowed it to carry fuel and ammunition forward in order to conduct replenishment close to the front line.

mobile wheeled vehicle – it was also designed to be amphibious – with which to support the tanks; it was based on the Saracen automotive design and even featured a lightly armoured cab.[17]

Improvements also affected uniforms. In late 1957 it was announced that battledress, in use since 1937, was to be withdrawn and be replaced by a new two-piece, olive-green combat suit, the zipped design allegedly based on a 'ski jacket'. A parka would also be issued for extreme cold weather, lessons learned from the Korean War – although it had apparently taken the War Office nearly ten years to turn the lesson into reality.[18] In 1967 rubber soled DMS boots replaced the old, studded ammo boot, so dangerous on AFVs.[19] Second World War-style greatcoats were still issued, and the boy soldiers at the Junior Leader's Regiment (see Annex B) were still wearing the pre- Second World War SD in the late 1950s. The 1958 Pattern webbing equipment was only starting to be issued to the RAC in the late 1960s, priority having gone to the infantry.[20]

No. 2 Dress was introduced into service from 1961; the original intention was to provide each soldier with two 'ginger suits' based on the style of officer's Service Dress and meant to be used as a smart walking-out uniform – in large part to attract more regular soldiers in the post-NS era – but it was quickly decided to only issue one suit, partly as civilian dress was routinely authorized for walking out (for the first time), and partly because of the proposed introduction of a new form of uniform known as Barrack Dress.[21] By the mid-1960s the general issue of ceremonial No. 1 Dress (Blues) was halted, largely for reasons of cost, with warrant officers and sergeants authorized to wear privately purchased mess dress, and No. 2 Dress replaced Blues for most ceremonial parades.[22] At about the same time as No. 2 Dress appeared, the old-style brass badges, buttons and shoulder titles were replaced by new 'Staybrite' versions, which were of a type of glossy plastic that did not require daily cleaning. It was notable that the ending of National Service and the transition to an all-regular army saw a reduction in the petty restrictions in life that the junior ranks found so annoying and which affected retention rates. Many of them were abolished or relaxed and soldiers were allowed to leave camp in civilian clothes without needing any form of official pass to do so; soldiers were allowed to simply 'book out' of camp. 'Lights out' at set times was removed and gradually the standard of living accommodation was improved.[23]

On training exercises, there was much more emphasis on the threat posed by battlefield nuclear weapons, probably as a result of the tensions caused by the 1962 Cuban Missile Crisis, in which it seemed that all-out war was likely and units were ordered to move to their General Deployment Positions, complete with full loads of ammunition. This gradually switched to greater concerns about chemical warfare, and from the late 1960s soldiers were issued with chemically resistant NBC, aka 'Noddy Suits', along with rubber gloves, boots and S6 respirators; by the 1980s it had become de rigeur to conduct most field training in these, and some units took to wearing them for the whole time in a typical two-week exercise period in order to become accustomed to operating in them.[24] However, training exercises in the 1960s were very much less professional than those in the decades to come, as the RAC transitioned from a largely National Service organization in which it was impossible to raise standards much because of the levels of turnover, into a fully regular service. It was still common in the 1960s for units to deploy to Soltau taking an Officers' Mess – and sometimes the WOs' and Sergeants' Mess – marquee with them, allowing all officers to gather together each evening for formal dinner and drinks. It was equally common for the RHQ set-up to include a towed 1-ton Office Trailer, for the exclusive use of the CO as his office and sleeping quarters, complete with pyjamas and sheets. Night training was still something of a rarity, although the introduction of improved night equipment and a general upsurge in professional standards meant that change was coming in this area, and sleep was to become a more precious commodity on exercise.

Another great improvement that was invisible to most soldiers was the authorization and creation of Home Headquarters from February 1962, allowing

By the 1970s the wearing of NBC suits on exercises was the rule rather than the exception. Although they were sometimes worn for the extra warmth they provided, the charcoal linings made them uncomfortable, particularly in the summer.

each regiment to have a permanent footprint in their allocated recruiting area. With a tiny staff and usually headed by a retired field officer, the HHQs quickly justified their existence by assisting with recruiting, and dealing with a plethora of administrative and welfare tasks that otherwise would have fallen on the regiments, or indeed gone undone. (As a larger unit with five regiments, the RTR had opened up its own Regimental headquarters in April 1959.)

Pay improved somewhat as a result of forming an all-regular army. By way of example, in May 1966 the lowest paid Trooper would receive £8 6s. pw, plus free accommodation and food. If married he would receive an additional allowance, and if married and over the age of 21 then he was entitled to a Married Quarter (MQ), although these could not be guaranteed; in a lot of cases younger soldiers occupied 'hirings', not officially MQs but rather local flats or houses, rented by the army to make up the shortfall. Hirings were temporary arrangements; not only were they unpopular with the army as they were generally much more expensive than MQs, but they were often in far flung locations some distance away from the MQ 'patch', leaving newly-wed couples somewhat isolated, particularly if they didn't have a car. In addition to these allowances, all soldiers were entitled to thirty days' leave per year and three free return railway warrants in the UK, or a more generous forty-two days leave plus one free return flight to the UK if stationed in BAOR.

The Yeomanry, as usual, spent the decade wondering when the enhancements to the new regular army might trickle down to them, and nursing the usual concerns about the future: re-roling, amalgamations and disbandment. The announcement that the Territorial Army was to be reorganized once again was made on 20 July 1960, which, anticipating the end of National Service, made a pragmatic decision to cap the peacetime strength at 123,000 (which only represented two-thirds of the mobilization strength, the shortfall being made up by calling up reservists), and which was mainly brought about by reducing the number of major units from 266 to 195.[25] The stated reason for taking this approach was that there were too many units of which many were under-strength, and therefore of questionable effectiveness. A typical example of what this meant within the RAC was that the Westminster Dragoons were amalgamated with the nearby Berkshire Yeomanry (an RA unit) to become the Berkshire and Westminster Dragoons.

The 1970s

The major equipment change in the early 1970s saw the introduction of the Combat Vehicle Reconnaissance Tracked – CVR(T) – family of vehicles, starting with the 76mm-armed Scorpion in 1972, as the tracked replacement for the Saladin Armoured Car, and used by both the reconnaissance regiments and in the recce troops in armoured regiments.[26] Attempts to call it a Light tank were firmly rebuffed, with the RAC emphasizing that its role was to be a 'recce by stealth' vehicle with a main armament for protection only – it was not a tank. Other members of the family subsequently brought into service were the Scimitar (30mm Rarden cannon), Striker (Swingfire GW), Sultan (Command), Samaritan (Ambulance), Spartan (APC) and for the REME, the Samson recovery vehicle.[27]

Entering service in more limited numbers during the mid-1970s was the wheeled member of the family, the CVR(W) Fox Armoured Car, armed with a 30mm Rarden cannon. Quickly gaining a reputation for being easy to roll over if mishandled, the FV721 Fox entered service in 1975 and was withdrawn some eighteen years later. Packing a lot of punch in a small air-portable vehicle, the Fox also saw service in some TA Yeomanry squadrons, primarily as a rear-area security vehicle.[28] From 1977 the new Clansman radio system started to make an appearance, with 'dial in' frequency changing and a much-improved vehicle 'harness' or control system, including live intercom. On the logistics front, the Bedford MK 4 Ton 4x4 Trucks started to replace the older RL from 1970.[29]

Uniforms also changed, with the Disruptive Pattern Material (DPM) combat suit replacing the plain olive-green versions from late 1972, with troops destined for Northern Ireland being the priority for issue. At long last 1958 Pattern webbing completely replaced the old pre-Second World War 1937 Pattern, although RAC troops generally favoured carrying a reduced version, usually limited to the belt with an ammo pouch or two and the respirator haversack. Many of the issued field-uniform items remained woefully inadequate, with waterproof oversuits still not standard issue, cold-weather parkas limited to one or two per crew, dreadful 'socks polyester' and the all-but-useless woollen gloves on which the fingers were only about 3in long.[30] Woollen ankle puttees were introduced in 1975 to replace the 1937 Pattern webbing gaiters used until then, with the RTR dyeing theirs black to match the coveralls, although some units considered that they presented a hazard on the tank park as they could become tangled in rotating machinery, and preferring to wear them only with lightweight trousers and combat uniforms. Precautions against NBC warfare became a constant feature of life, with frequent training in barracks, and which was carried on during field training, with some units (somewhat unrealistically) conducting exercises in which the crews had to remain masked up for 24 hours at a time.

On the social front, Corporals' Messes (based on the WOs' and Sgts' model) became more or less standard, although these did not include separate accommodation. Regimental coloured pullovers became almost universal as part of Barrack Dress, although some soldiers – and particularly the attached personnel from REME etc. – disliked being forced to pay for these non-issued items. Cavalry regiments, led by SCOTS DG on their amalgamation in 1971, began to adopt the wearing of over-the-shoulder pouch belts in place of waist belts with No. 2 Dress; once again, these had to be bought from the PRI by

In 1973 Sir Michael Carver was promoted Field Marshal and shortly thereafter became Chief of the Defence Staff. He is one of three members of the RAC to achieve the highest army rank, the others being Sir Richard Hull (17/21L) and Sir John Stanier (7H).

the soldiers. Squadron bars were a notable feature of life in Germany and Cyprus, although for a number of reasons they were not able to be replicated by UK-based units. A welcome programme called Op Humane made a start on the modernization of antiquated barrack blocks, leading to improved conditions for those lucky enough to be in such a barracks – although this came at the cost of greatly increased charges. The Military Salary was introduced in 1970, in an attempt to both improve pay but also to better relate the complicated pay structure to equivalent jobs in the civilian world. Also introduced at the same time was the X-Factor, in which 14.5 per cent of total pay was allocated on the basis of the unusual and demanding aspects of military life, including restrictions on personal freedom and, if necessary, the need to make the ultimate sacrifice.

Chapter 4

Operations Part One

India, 1945–7

Just prior to the outbreak of the Second World War, over 45,000 British troops had been stationed in India, including 3 cavalry regiments. At the cessation of hostilities, even more were to be found in the sub-continent, although it was clear to many that the stay was likely to be a short one, with partition and independence beckoning. Arriving in the country in 1945 were formations and regiments sent out in anticipation of the need to invade Japan, and many of these were retained in the area until they were either posted elsewhere or disbanded in situ. The units that remained found themselves, along with the rest of the army, engaged in the drawdown to independence, including policing the many acts of inter-communal violence that became a feature of the time; eventually an estimated 4 million civilians would die during the violence. On 18 July 1947 an Act of Parliament conferred independence on India and Pakistan, to come into being on 15 August, an astonishingly short time for withdrawal from the sub-continent. The reality of internecine conflict between Hindus and Muslims left the British units in a role similar to that of an army of occupation for the remaining time, but fortunately there was no second Indian mutiny, and there was no requirement to deploy the RAC units in an armoured role, either to keep the peace or for self-protection. 3rd Carabiniers, who had become outstanding proponents of the use of tanks in jungle operations during the war, had departed just before this development in January 1947. Although some other British units remained into 1948, the final RAC units to leave India were – appropriately bearing in mind the RTC commitment to the country between the wars – both from the Royal Tank Regiment: 7RTR and 43RTR, who departed in late summer 1947.[1]

Palestine, 1945–8

The roots of the British commitment to Palestine came from the Balfour Declaration of November 1917, expressing the desire to make Palestine 'a national home for the Jewish people'. After the war, and with the downfall of the Ottoman Empire that had previously controlled the region, in 1920 the League of Nations made Palestine a British Mandate, following on from the occupation in 1917 by Allenby's armies – which included a few tanks, their first appearance in the region, but not the last. Between the wars tensions were high and sporadic violence between the majority Arabs and minority Jews was frequent, but in 1936 a full-scale rebellion broke out, leading to the whole of Palestine being placed under British military control in 1938. Limitations on Jewish immigration imposed by the British government in 1939 fuelled Jewish grievances, leading to the formation of rival paramilitary groups – meaning Zionist terrorists – such as Palmach, Irgun, Haganah and the Stern Gang. For much of the middle period of the war, until 1944, Palestine was in effect a huge military camp, used for training and recuperation for troops fighting in the Western Desert, as well as having troops on hand should trouble arise in the strategically important Syria or Iraq. Most Jews cooperated with the British war effort; indeed, some were to be found within the army, where the training they received would soon be turned against their former instructors. Headquarters British Troops Palestine was in Jerusalem, in the huge King David Hotel building, shared with many government departments.

When the war in Europe ended, the only British formation in Palestine was 1st Infantry Division, which had arrived there in early 1945 in order to recuperate from a period fighting in Italy. Between September and December three RAC units were sent to the country: the King's Dragoon Guards, 3rd Hussars and 15th/19th Hussars, not initially because of a perceived need for them as security forces, but to form part of the UK Strategic Reserve for the region. The first British soldier was killed on 31 October 1945, when a series of attacks on infrastructure targets shook the country. Continued British insistence on restricting Jewish immigration made further conflict inevitable, and on 14 November the army was asked to come to the assistance of the police, who could not cope. All the units in the country became active in conducting internal security duties – a phrase that would soon become common parlance for RAC soldiers worldwide – with armoured and scout cars being, as ever in these situations, particularly useful, although tanks were available and were used.

During 1946 and 1947 the Life Guards, 12th Lancers, 17th/21st Lancers, 8RTR, 4th/7th Dragoon Guards and 9th Lancers were also sent to the area.[2] Their duties involved manning checkpoints, mounting patrols, supporting infantry operations, protecting railway lines and other important infrastructure, searches and the placing of cordons.[3] Some specialist operations were required: B Squadron 15th/19th Hussars was made responsible for long stretches of the coastline, to prevent illegal immigration and smuggling. As their post-war history made clear, 'the regiment could only play its part in the frustrating business of trying to enforce the unenforceable'.[4] Opportunities for recreation were still taken in the usual style, including the unlikely pastime of Jackal-hunting, although sports matches had to be made secure – sport was played 'always with the attendant bren-gunner to guard the players'.[5]

Unlike later decades when operational tour lengths were generally limited to a maximum of six months, these tours could last for over two years. Breaks could

An unusual type of street patrolling in Jerusalem. A 17/21L Daimler armoured car, the ubiquitous vehicle of the recce regiments until replaced by the Saladin, was small and agile enough to undertake a whole range of tasks that larger vehicles could not.

be taken by moving the unit, or part of it, back to the Canal Zone in Egypt allowing training to take place, but for those at the sharp end, the sheer intensity/ boredom mix of an operational tour could be very wearing. Nonetheless, it was very much an operational theatre and pressure on the units increased. On 22 July 1946 Irgun blew up the King David Hotel, the main British HQ, killing ninety-one people, many of them locals. As a result Operation Shark was mounted eight days later, with house-to-house searches for terrorists and their arms in Tel Aviv and Jaffa; all three RAC regiments in the area were involved in the operation, which stalled further terrorists outrages for a number of months. During the year 49 British soldiers were killed, and well over 100 wounded. In 1947 there was more of the same. Gregory Blaxland described the contribution of the armoured units to the campaign:

> There was an adequate supply of armour. The 1st Kings Dragoon Guards patrolled the northern and north-east frontiers from the end of the war until the early months of 1947, when they handed over to the 17th/21st Lancers. The 4th/7th Dragoon Guards long provided tank support for the 1st Division and Jerusalem Brigade. The 3rd Hussars provided tank support for

the 6th Airborne and had two squadrons of armoured cars. The 12th Royal Lancers patrolled the centre of Palestine for a year between 1946 and 1947. The 9th Queen's Royal Lancers and the 8th Royal Tank Regiment filled a supporting role for shorter periods, and the 15th/19th Royal Hussars were in the southern sector until handing over to the Life Guards in April 1947. Thus harm seldom came to road convoys.[6]

The tanks of the 3rd Hussars (with which one squadron was equipped) entered the arena and patrolled the streets with infantry escort by day and night. Fired at point blank range to ensure accuracy, one round of gunfire was found to be sufficient to silence any fire-spouting strongpoint.[7]

On the afternoon of April 26 [1948] the HLI were ordered to attack a house in a dominating position overlooking the convoy route. They were allotted a troop of Cromwell tanks of the 4th/7th Dragoon Guards [and] two armoured car troops of the Life Guards. It was a real war at last … the attack went in at last light, with searchlights providing artificial moonlight to allow the tanks to strike target. They did so effectively enough, and the HLI stormed the building to take thirty seven prisoners and remove twenty wounded and dead.[8]

A 17/21L vehicle checkpoint outside Jerusalem in what was then known as Palestine, c. 1947. The campaign to contain a hostile population intent on self-determination was an impossible one for the army to win, and all troops withdrew in mid-1948. (Courtesy RL)

The British mandate ended at midnight, 14/15 May 1948 and the withdrawal to Egypt began at 0800 on the 14th; in order to facilitate the withdrawal, as so often, additional troops were needed and in April 4RTR, with two squadrons of Comets, was sent in from Egypt to assist. By 30 June 1948 the British army's evacuation of Palestine was complete, with the Life Guards, 4th/7th Dragoon Guards and 17th/21st Lancers being the final RAC units to depart, with the last of all, the 3rd Hussars – 'the regiment that could claim longest residence of all in Palestine' – taking the rear-guard role before withdrawing on receipt of the codeword 'Scuttle'. During the campaign 223 British soldiers had been killed; as an example, 17/21L lost 16 soldiers during their tour of duty, including the youngest RAC casualty, Boy (bandsman) Dennet who drowned in a swimming accident. An extraordinary incident occurred at the very end, when on 29 June 1948 Trooper Flanagan and Corporal McDonald stole two Cromwell tanks from a depot, driving them out of the base and turning them over to Haganah, to whom they deserted, later joining the newly formed Israeli Armoured Corps.

Egypt, the Canal Zone and the Suez Crisis, 1947–56

In 1947 four RAC regiments were serving in Egypt: The Bays, 9th Lancers, 4RTR and 6RTR. On the disbandment of 2nd Armoured Brigade three of these were redeployed, leaving 4RTR in Shandur as the sole RAC regiment in Egypt, and even then, the unit was liable to be sent as reinforcements into Palestine. Initially equipped with Comet tanks, in mid-1949 the first Centurions were sent to 4RTR for hot-weather trials, and by the end of the year the regiment had been fully converted to the new tanks, a good morale boost as the uncertainties of the post-war period were beginning to bite, and most of the experienced wartime soldiers had departed, their places being made up by increasing numbers of National Servicemen. During the period from then until 1951 a number of other units spent periods in the Canal Zone, including The Royals, 13th/18th Hussars, 15th/19th Hussars, 16th/5th Lancers and 17th/21st Lancers.[9]

By 1951 only 4RTR and The Royals, an armoured car unit, remained; tensions in Egypt had reached the point where British servicemen had to conduct internal security patrols, off-duty servicemen were in danger of being murdered and the large numbers of families had to be returned to the UK for their own safety. During January 1952 some Egyptian police units mutinied and it became clear that it would be necessary to put down the mutiny to prevent it spreading. This was Operation eagle. The infantry role was given to the Lancashire Fusiliers, with a composite troop of five Centurions from A Squadron 4RTR commanded by a young second lieutenant, Tony Godwin, in direct support, plus a Daimler Armoured Car troop of The Royals mainly used on escort and cordon duties.

Three of the Centurions were tasked to support the attack on the Bureau Sanitaire and the remaining two in support of the infantry used against the Caracol police station. Both locations were in Ismailia, in the centre of the Suez Canal, and were in the process of being fortified by the mutineers. In an early example of restraint, no direct action was initially taken, in order to allow the police to stew overnight and, hopefully, come to their senses.

At the Bureau Sanitaire at first light on 25 January 1952, a loudspeaker announcement called for the police to surrender, and in response men were seen moving into positions on rooftops. After a second appeal was likewise ignored, and some small-arms fire was opened from within, a Centurion broke through the main gate and halted – again, hoping that this might induce a surrender. After a few minutes and no sign of a capitulation, the decision was made to fire a round of 20-pounder blank from the tank; someone had obviously had the foresight and imagination to include blank rounds within the tanks' ammunition load for such an eventuality. Unfortunately, this had the opposite effect – the mutineers probably thought that it was a service round – and they opened up on the British troops and in particular the tanks, including one of The Royals' Daimler Armoured Cars parked by the destroyed gate. Still maintaining restraint, the tanks initially responded only with coaxial machine-gun fire, all three tanks now being inside the grounds and lined up three abreast, firing only MG until yet another appeal to give up was ignored, at which point eight rounds of 20-pounder HE were fired, and the infantry then moved in to clear the buildings hand-to-hand and room-by-room. The police fought with surprising grit, even going so far as to try to knock out the tanks using petrol bombs. But it was an unequal contest and they finally surrendered in the late afternoon, having had fifty-six men killed and about eighty injured in the action. The Fusiliers had five men killed and another nine wounded; no RAC personnel were injured. At Caracol the other two tanks under command of the troop sergeant, Sgt Jim Howell, had been giving permission to use main armament but again chose to exercise restraint, using only controlled bursts of MG against observed targets which brought about a surrender around midday. The use of the tanks, both as a show of force and in support of the infantry, doubtless saved British lives and demonstrated the utility of armour in IS operations. However, on the political level the action showed once again just how unpopular the British were in the Canal Zone, being seen as an occupying force that provoked the increasingly strong feelings of Egyptian nationalism, and in October 1954 Britain agreed to withdraw all of its troops from Egypt within twenty months. The final two RAC units to serve in the country before withdrawal in early 1956 were the Life Guards and, last of all, 1RTR, having been sent there on their way back from Korea. It would not be too long before British troops were to return in quite different circumstances, in what is usually known as the Suez Crisis.

Suez, 1956

Only six weeks after the withdrawal, the military chiefs were told by Prime Minister Eden to plan for an immediate reoccupation of the Canal Zone. This was due to the fact that on 26 July 1956, Colonel Nasser, the Egyptian leader, had seized the strategically important canal and declared that it was nationalized, despite it belonging mainly to shareholders in France and the UK.[10] No plans for such an operation existed, and at first it was hoped that the mere threat of force from the UK and France working together would bring Nasser to his senses, using joint military power if required. To that end, all personnel in the process of leaving were 'frozen', and a recall of reservists was authorized to make the point, and about 23,000 (mostly NS and mostly unhappy) ex-soldiers were recalled into the army, which included 55 officers and 710 men for the RAC.[11] Training of units earmarked for the operation, should it become necessary, started in August, but the provision of armoured units for a proposed seaborne invasion was not straightforward. A new armoured division, the 10th, had recently been formed from the armoured units stationed in Libya, but was in fact no more than a large Brigade, and in any case, the treaty with Libya forbade the use of the formation without Libyan agreement, which was scarcely likely.[12] The better equipped and trained units in BAOR could not be released from their NATO commitments, and thus the only source of armour was the six regiments in the UK, which were all understrength in both men and equipment, and heavily committed to TA assistance. 1RTR and 6RTR from Tidworth were the two tank regiments chosen to take part. They were notified on 1 August that Operation Poker, deployment preparation, was to commence, along with a single Daimler Armoured Car regiment, the Life Guards. Also in the frame were The Bays and 5RTR, both stationed in Libya, but in the event, neither was deployed.

Getting these units ready for embarkation was fraught with problems, and was indicative of just how poorly prepared Britain's peacetime army was only eleven years after a world war had ended. Neither of the tank regiments was equipped with their full scales of Centurion tanks (6RTR only holding twenty-six 'old' models), and these were not of the latest marks, still being armed with the BESA MG rather than the Browning.[13] Due to their commitments and the problems caused by a constant refreshing of their National Servicemen, neither unit had been able to fire the required annual gunnery crew tests, with only half of 1RTR and about a quarter of 6RTR being up to date. B Sqn 1RTR were the only part of the regiment in good order, being the Warminster demonstration squadron; the other two sabre squadrons were engaged in TA assistance in Thetford and Tilshead. 6RTR was even worse off, having no official mobilization role allotted to them and needing about 200 reservists to bring them up to strength.[14] Maps for the planning were supplied by the retired

General Sir Percy Hobart from his personal archives. In order to get them ashore landing craft would be required, and again these were sadly lacking, with only enough to allow one squadron of tanks to be landed alongside two battalions of infantry – hardly the stuff of D-Day. In order to meet the intended operation start date of 15 September, shipping would have to leave the UK by the 8th. Although 1RTR was overall in far better order and was meant to have priority, for some reason 6RTR was despatched to Plymouth where they loaded up at the end of August, sailing for Malta on 2 September on four 'Army Department Landing Ship Tank': HMS *Puncher*, *Ravager*, *Salerno* and *Suvla*. 1RTR did not complete their embarkation until 8 September, their tanks being moved to Portland on civilian Pickford's transporters as there were not enough military tank transporters for the job.[15]

Whilst this was happening, Captain Peter Berry of 7RTR was ordered, completely out of the blue, to form a scratch unit with one other officer and thirty-two men. He was to get the personnel from his own regiment as well as some members of both 5th RIDG and 14/20H from 65th Training Regiment at Catterick, and then report to the Amphibious Warfare Experimental Establishment in north Devon. There they discovered that they were to form 'No. 1 Landing Vehicle Tank Troop RAC', and be trained in using LVT Mk III, an unarmoured derivative of the wartime Buffalo and which they had never seen before. This they did in ten days, managing to ram the Appledore lifeboat in the process. The following day they found themselves flying to Malta, to allow them to collect sixteen LVTs and train with their intended cargo, units of the Royal Marines – why they could not operate their vehicles themselves has never been explained. Also complete in Malta by 12 September after an uncomfortable twelve-day voyage in squadron packets was 6RTR, with men and vehicles spread across fourteen different ships. They were to wait there, almost entirely devoid of opportunities to train, for nearly a month; the only place large enough to hold them was No. 2 Polo Ground, and the fourteen tanks of C Squadron were required to be waterproofed for deep wading in true D-Day style. This was done, each tank requiring around 80 man-hours of work to complete the task. And then they waited, during which time the weather caused the waterproofing to deteriorate so that the job had to be done a second time – after laboriously stripping off the previous kits first. Meanwhile, the so-called priority unit, 1RTR, was sent back to Tidworth where they could at least try to fill in some of the gaps in the crew's training. No one was sure whether the operation, now called Musketeer, was going to take place; in mid-October some of the reservists, so hastily called up in August, were granted a week's leave.[16]

An ultimatum was issued by Britain and France on 30 October, and when this was not answered, the air campaign started the following day, which led to Nasser ordering around forty ships to be sunk in the canal, completely blocking it. The 30th also saw the amphibious force leave Malta bound for Egypt, under the pretence that this was just a loading and disembarkation exercise. In fact, within 6RTR only two officers, the CO and adjutant, held the required security classification to have been told that this was in fact going to be the real thing. The majority of Egyptian forces was deployed in the Sinai against the Israelis who had attacked the day before the ultimatum.

The first airborne drops and helicopter assaults by the British were delivered on the morning of 5 November 1956 on El Gamil airfield. The following morning just before dawn, the first Royal Marine commandos came ashore on the beaches of Port Said, transported in Second World War-era landing craft as well as Berry's troop of sixteen LVTs, whilst the navy destroyers laid down a smokescreen on the beaches.[17] There was some opposition on the beaches which was quickly dealt with using on-board Brens and Vickers MMGs, but on entering the town Sergeant Kizlo was killed by fire coming from a building. In another incident, Trooper Cade, an LVT driver, was wounded in the arm and head and his commander, Sergeant Roberts, immediately took over, preventing the column being halted. Disaster was averted when a marine managed to throw a hand grenade that had been dropped into the troop-carrying compartment back out of the vehicle – it landed under the cab of the following LVT where, luckily, there was armour underneath. Later in the day, after the marines had been disembarked, the LVTs were used to move casualties as well as ammunition and other stores, driving with their rear loading ramps down to speed up loading and unloading. Two 14/20H sergeants described their experiences:

> It appeared as if every citizen of Port Said had been issued with rifles and automatics and were gathered on our route, Sgt Baker's Troop, 3rd Troop, had, definitely a very hot time of it. One very brave? man ran into the road and squatted down with an anti-tank rocket launcher, luckily the gunner in the leading tank was on the alert and bounced him off the road with his BESA.

The vehicles were later used to conduct waterborne patrols on the 'evil-smelling' Lake Manzala to the west of the town, and discovered that whilst they were at home on water, they could become bogged in mud just as easily as any other tracked vehicle. Following the ceasefire the crews settled down into a sort of routine, which included the ability to get a daily shower using the RN ships, and on land were administered by 6RTR.[18]

On the morning of the 6th the seaborne landings took place; C Sqn of 6RTR supporting 40 and 42 Commandos RM were the first tanks to land less than half an hour after the LVTs, driving off their LCTs into 6 or 7ft of water about 150yd from the beach. When trying to use the explosive charges to 'blow off' the waterproofing material, six of the fourteen tanks failed to function correctly leading to the ludicrous situation of the crews going 'to work with spanners, sledge hammers, crowbars, matchets and finger nails' to remove the offending articles. Once sorted out, the leading tanks 'used their Brownings stabilised [and] killed the crews of three 57mm anti-tank guns' – this was almost certainly the first ever engagement by British tanks using the Centurion stabilizer gear. During this period even the REME got involved in the fighting, with the ARV commander using his Browning MG to engage snipers occupying a building overlooking the Fishing Harbour. They were later followed by the remainder of the regiment, with A Sqn driving south through the town onto the causeway to link up with 2 Para, and B Sqn supporting 45 Commando in clearing the Arab Quarter; due to lack of space, the echelon had to park on the beach. The Landing Ships Tank carrying the other two squadrons and the echelon came in as close to the beach as possible, meaning the non-waterproofed Centurions and other vehicles only had to wade in about 4ft of water. As only two LSTs could beach at any time, the disembarking of the armour took longer than intended, and it was the overall lack of armour that caused the force commander the most worries, fearing that the Egyptians could appear at any moment with their Russian T34 tanks or SU-100 self-propelled guns.[19] By this point, 1RTR had finally sailed from the UK, but were still at sea on slow-moving ships.[20]

All the 6RTR tanks were quickly in action, the biggest threat initially coming from riflemen and machine-gunners firing onto the tanks from the roofs of buildings; the Centurion Mk 5 did not mount a commander's MG and this proved to be a major disadvantage – as already noted, the Armoured Recovery Vehicles of the REME did have such a weapon, and used it as they were coming ashore. Four anti-tank guns were spotted and knocked out by the Centurions before they could inflict any damage. Some of the action bordered on the bizarre, 'At one moment, Cpl Fowler's tank in 11 Troop was charged by two Coca-Cola lorries full of infantry. One was destroyed by a 20-Pounder HE shell, the other, hit by Browning fire, drove out of control into the canal.'[21] Later, an even stranger incident occurred:

> In the leading tank Sgt Jachnik was helping his radio operator repair the wireless set, while the driver was preparing lunch and the gunner was cleaning the Browning machine-gun ... [the crew failed to notice] the party of twenty five Egyptian infantrymen approaching ... At the sound of voices Jachnik popped his head out of the turret and saw, nearby, a man with a whip who shouted, 'Hands up!'. Jachnik replied 'Fuck off!' and was promptly nicked in the ear by a bullet as the enemy opened fire. He dived into the turret for his Sten gun, but the matter was decided by Sergeant Stebbing, whose tank was in support. He fired a burst of Browning and one HE round close to Jachnik's tank, killing and wounding some of the Egyptians and driving the others off. This was called 'The War of Jachnik's Ear'.[22]

Suez, 1956. Sergeant Jachnik of 6RTR meets up with 'les Paras' shortly after being strafed by friendly aircraft.

Another history of the campaign recorded that:

> The Centurions gave [the Royal Marines] diligent support. They fired belt after belt from their Brownings at located strong points, put down smoke canisters to cover street crossings, and shepherded men across open spaces by use of their hulks [*sic*] ... The 20-Pounders of the Centurions were brought into use and let loose their shells for about ten minutes.[23]

Later that evening, A Sqn were ordered to drive hell for leather to El Tina, carrying French Colonial paratroopers on their engine decks. The reason for the abandonment of caution was a signal from London that, due to world and especially American pressure, there was to be a ceasefire in place by midnight. The ceasefire was applied, although shooting still continued, with grenade-throwing and snipers an ever-present nuisance; on some occasions rockets were also employed against the tanks, and Trooper George Morton of 6RTR died on the 9 November. Scout car and Buffalo patrols became the order of the day for the next few weeks, and it was reported that 6RTR used the time to play a 'tremendous amount' of football, wearing a strip that had earlier belonged to an Egyptian police team. After forty-seven days a UN force took over from the British troops, allowing 6RTR to withdraw on 22 December 1956 into the same LSTs that had disgorged them seven weeks earlier, A Sqn being the last to leave. The Suez Crisis caused the downfall of Eden, and Macmillan's new government

11 Troop C Sqn 6RTR displaying the spoils of war, including a couple of fezzes. The troops involved in the Suez invasion would not be awarded a medal for the campaign, a mark of its unpopularity amongst the public.

included Duncan Sandys as the Minister of Defence, which was to lead to a series of cuts in 1957 as a result of his White Paper, including a further reduction to the size of the RAC by eight regiments.[24]

The Malaya Emergency, 1948–60

About 400 miles from north to south, and only about 200 miles wide, the Malay peninsula was important to Britain because of its wealth of rubber plantations and tin mines, mainly located to the western side on the 50-mile wide coastal strip.[25] The terrain of Malaya was well suited to an insurgency. The majority of the larger settlements were found towards the coast, and with the prosperous and strategically important island of Singapore, an independent Crown Colony, was at its southern tip separated by the Johore Straits.[26] Other than where it had been cleared, jungle dominated the peninsula, covering about 80 per cent of the land and clothing the spine formed by the Titiwangsa Mountains, up to 7,000ft high and which created a watershed mainly to the west with multiple waterfalls and streams. Two types of tropical jungle – known in the local dialect as *ulu* – were found. Firstly, there was primary jungle, which was under the high canopy where little light penetrated and which tended to inhibit undergrowth, with many rivers and streams as well as steaming mangrove swamps and uninhibited bamboo that could seriously hinder progress on foot. Secondary jungle occurred where vegetation grew outside of the canopy, and which could be very dense and, again, an impediment to movement. It was an alien place for European soldiers, the hot and muggy climate with extremely high humidity and frequent tropical rainfall making physical exertion difficult.

The roots of the Malayan conflict lay in the desire of a small, mainly ethnic Chinese minority within Malaya to eject the British 'occupiers' and install a Communist regime. During the Second World War the Japanese had successfully conquered the country, and as part of a plan to evict them, the British had created and equipped the Malayan People's Anti-Japanese Army in 1943, with Force 136, an SOE unit, supplying officers to train them. They were equipped with about 3,500 British light weapons, but it is fair to say that their contribution to the overall course of the war was marginal at best. However, notwithstanding this, by the time of the Japanese surrender the force was large and reasonably well-trained, about 10,000 strong with about 4,000 active trained guerrillas, deployed in 7 groups. As the Japanese surrendered there was a short interregnum period when a determined guerrilla force might have seized control of the country, before the British administrators returned in force, but the opportunity was missed and the resultant war would last for twelve years.

The end of hostilities meant that the MPAJA was disbanded at the end of 1945, and a sweetener was offered for each guerrilla returning his arms – a guaranteed job, a sack of rice and $350 – about £45, which was a substantial sum. Nearly 7,000 did so, and 5,500 weapons were surrendered.[27] However, about 4,000 of the force chose to take to the jungle armed mainly with smalls arms taken from the Japanese under the Communist leadership of Chin Peng and Lau Yew, in order to start an insurgency which began in earnest in 1948; their troops came to be known as CTs, or Communist Terrorists, or more commonly simply as bandits. By that time British forces in the country were limited to a number of understrength Ghurkha battalions, two infantry battalions, plus one regiment of field artillery operating as infantry. A new political construct, the Malayan Federation, came into being on 1 February 1948, and this was the catalyst that sparked the beginning of what was referred to as the Malayan Emergency.

Initially renamed with a singular lack of imagination as the Malayan People's Anti-British Army, Chin Peng's men took to calling themselves the Malayan National Liberation Army, or MNLA, and – taking instructions from Stalin – first struck in April 1948, attacking and killing rubber and tin workers, with foremen a particular target, as well as slashing rubber trees and destroying infrastructure. In June the first European overseers were killed, leading to a State of Emergency being declared on the 16th – it would remain in place for nearly twelve years. Due to the lack of army units in country who could respond, it was quickly decided to deploy 4th Hussars from their barracks in Colchester to Malaya, but as they had been reduced to cadre strength, about 400 regular personnel from other regiments were drafted in before the unit set sail in August. Such reinforcement was a necessary evil of the system forced upon the RAC by manpower shortages, and it meant that the long-held desire to allow other ranks to 'belong' to a particular regiment for their whole service was often unrealistic. An interesting observation is that such cross-unit postings – a very similar thing happened with the units bound for Korea from 1950 – do not seem to have had much of a negative impact on the unit's cohesion, the newcomers quickly settling in and becoming part of the unit.

In late September 1949 the 850-strong 4th Hussars arrived in Malaya. The initial intention was to use them as a quasi-infantry unit, as had happened previously with 26th Field Regiment RA, equipping them with some GMC C15TA vehicles; these were Canadian-built lightly armoured wheeled trucks of Second World War vintage.[28] The vastly experienced Hussars' CO, Lieutenant Colonel George Kidston-Montgomerie, quickly appreciated that much more could be done if the regiment was organized as an armoured car unit with Daimler Armoured Cars as well as Dingo, Lynx and Humber Scout Cars. This was agreed, but equipping the regiment took a painfully long time. Even when the Daimler Armoured and Scout Cars arrived to augment the GMCs, they were not entirely ideal; the armoured cars 2-pounder main armament was not suitable for most types of engagement and so the BESA machine guns became the most used weapon. Many of the scout cars were modified by adding additional armour to raise the sides of the hull, and in some cases, turrets were added giving more protection for the crews. The turretless versions often mounted twin Bren LMGs, as the production of overwhelming firepower in an ambush was seen as a key capability and the best way of suppressing the enemy by driving them off or killing them. These improvements were the result of bitter experience: in the last day of 1948, only two months after arriving 'in-country', an indication of the intent and capability of the enemy manifested itself:

4th Troop A Squadron under the command of the command of Lt Michael Questier and accompanied by 2Lt Jon Sutro, a young officer straight out of Sandhurst, set forth from Ipoh to patrol the twenty miles to Sungei Siput … The Troop was nineteen strong and was carried in two GFMCs and one 15-Cwt truck. Each vehicle mounted a Bren gun and each soldier carried hand grenades and was armed with either a rifle or a Sten sub-machine gun. On one of the smaller roads they were ambushed by a force of over seventy communist terrorists who, it later transpired, had been in position for over two days hoping to engage a softer target … During the furious firefight that followed, Questier and six of his men, including Corporal Finch the acting troop sergeant, were killed and another nine wounded. Sutro took charge and skilfully extracted the remainder of the troop including the wounded.

The open topped GMC was a Second World War armoured troop carrier that saw extensive service in Malaya until replaced by the Saracen. This one is operated by 4th Troop B Squadron 4th Hussars. (Courtesy QRH)

Six dead CTs were later found. For his conduct that day Sutro was awarded the Military Cross and Lance Corporal Smith the Distinguished Conduct Medal.[29]

Another truth quickly evident to the regiment was that there was an awful lot of country to be covered by a single mobile unit, but they made the best of a bad job and deployed the three sabre squadrons to cover as much of the country as they could.[30] Their main role developed from patrolling into convoy escorting, a generally boring but essential task. This was so firstly to protect workers travelling around on buses who had proved to be an easy target for terrorist attacks, and then later, to prevent food supplies falling into the bandit's hands; it had quickly been realized that depriving the terrorists of access to food would be a useful if indirect weapon – and so it proved. In order to spread themselves more effectively across the country, the Hussars were authorized to form a fourth sabre squadron in April 1950, which they managed to do despite not being given any additional manpower. Another task that they were given was VIP escorting – the need for this was brought home when the High Commissioner Sir Henry Gurney was ambushed in his Rolls-Royce car and murdered in early October 1951.[31] Subsequently, 12th Lancers routinely provided his own armoured car (called Birdwood, modified and with a dummy wooden barrel) plus escorts to prevent a repetition, as the nature of the country lent itself to ambushes and hit-and-run tactics.[32] A Squadron 4th Hussars commented that, 'all the squadron vehicles put up a considerable mileage with little tangible result, except that the roads remained open and incidents were few'. The action tended to be reactive, and although some patrolling was conducted on foot, the majority was vehicle mounted. 3rd Troop A Squadron 4th Hussars obtained an 'early success on the notorious Benta – Jerantut Road, when they were fortunate to break up a bandit ambush whilst the bandits were still engaged in looting food lorries ... The troop killed two and wounded others before they fled.'[33]

The deployment of 4th Hussars was in some ways typical of many of the RAC postings of the time, in that although the regiment had an operational role, it was an accompanied posting, with families including children able to be quartered, and the calendar year included regimental days, sports events and sometimes trips to neighbouring countries. The Regimental Headquarters was in Gunong Panjang Camp in Ipoh, north of Kuala Lumpur, with outposts across the country in squadron or sometimes troop strength, including at Raub, Taiping, Kedah, Negri Sembilan, Kuantan and Pahang. Although at about 850 men the regiment was unusually strong in terms of manpower, there was still a requirement to undergo all the routine vehicle and administrative inspections, have troops on leave or sent away on long courses (often to the UK), as well as dealing with the usual influx and outflow of officers and soldiers, and a higher than normal rate of illnesses caused by the tropical conditions. This meant that there was never enough combat power for all the tasks. It became apparent that one regiment, however large or good it was, could not be considered sufficient for the task, and in July 1950 a second armoured car regiment in the shape of 13th/18th Hussars arrived in-country. This allowed Malaya to be divided into two areas, with the in-place 4th Hussars becoming responsible for the North Malaya Sub-District and the new regiment taking on the south.[34] However, from late August 1949, 4th had to detach one of its sabre squadrons to reinforce Hong Kong due to the perception of an increased threat there, once again dissipating the resources. 4th remained in Malaya until early October 1951 being replaced by the 12th Lancers, thus completing an operational tour of three years and two days, probably setting the post-war record.[35] In that time it lost twenty-two killed or died, with a further thirty-two wounded.

Operationally, the appointment of Lieutenant General Sir Harold Briggs as Director of Operations in April 1950 marked a turning point. Briggs was responsible for laying the groundwork for campaign success, including a rigorous programme of food denial and a policy of clearing complete states of their 'resident' terrorists, allowing areas to be declared 'white'; critically this was done from the centre of the peninsula out, with the intention of creating a cleared buffer zone between the terrorists in the north (who often sought refuge within Thailand), and those in the south. The appointment of General Sir Gerald

A patrol of 4th Hussars take a break. Arriving in late 1949, the regiment remained in Malaya, constantly on operations, for three years.

Templer as the new supremo in February 1952 led to an increased focus on the requirements for intelligence and psychological warfare, and although very much based on the successes of the Briggs Plan, led to the campaign becoming regarded as the model on how to conduct a rural counter-insurgency. The first 'white' area was declared in 1953, allowing the local lifting of emergency regulations and clearly showing that the campaign was being won, albeit slowly.

Statistics can help to illustrate how the campaign became increasingly successful. At the end of 1948 terrorist incidents were averaging 50 per week across the country, and since the start of the emergency 149 members of the security forces (which included police) had been killed, with over 200 wounded at little cost to the bandits. During 1951 the tables had turned, and over 1,000 terrorists were killed, with 121 captured and 201 surrendering; however, this came at a high price, with over 500 members of the security forces killed, demonstrating the intensity of the campaign at this, its kinetic high point. In part these high casualty numbers were because initially the MPLA operated in very large units, which allowed them to attack in force but meant that they were unable to break contact easily when the security forces gained the upper hand in a firefight, and which led to high casualties. Learning from their mistakes and forced to by increasing security force success, they broke up into smaller units – in part necessary due to much reduced numbers and lack of weapons – and refined their tactics to concentrate on attacking so-called soft targets – which meant that they tried to avoid contact with the RAC units with their protected vehicles and automatic firepower. During 1954 just over 700 bandits were killed, with 51 captured and

211 surrendering. However, in achieving this 'only' 87 security force soldiers were killed.[36] By the beginning of 1955 nearly one-third of the country was 'white'. Most of the combat was taking place deep in the jungle and this meant that most of the tasks that the RAC units completed became, in the main, routine to the point of becoming boring. As the campaign progressed and the number of terrorists at large diminished, with their supply of weapons severely restricted, the bandits restricted themselves to attacking weakness and learned to stay well clear of convoys and patrols conducted by the armoured car units.

It was difficult for the armoured cars to seize the tactical initiative. More often it was the bandits that sprang ambushes, usually on unescorted vehicles or convoys travelling on roads, although occasionally they became bold enough to take on the armoured cars, particularly if the topography favoured them. In August 1951 a half-troop of C Squadron 13th/18th Hussars were ambushed by an estimated fifty bandits on the Rompin–Bahau road when the armoured cars entered a 20ft-deep cutting covered in jungle. The driver of the lead GMC APC was struck in the hand and was unable to steer, and the vehicle overturned in a ditch throwing the crew out, fatally injuring the local interpreter. A Daimler Armoured Car managed to engage the ambushers using machine-gun fire and forcing them to withdraw as the GMC crew, all wounded, took cover behind their wrecked vehicle. In a tragic incident in September 1951 the same squadron set an ambush in the Seremban area, under command of the OC. A firefight occurred before the ambush was properly set, killing one CT and wounding another, but alerting the whole area in the process. Second Lieutenant Harden, a National Service officer, left his section area in order to pass a report, giving instructions that his section should open fire if any movement to their front was detected. He must have become disoriented on his return, easily done in dense jungle, as he approached his own section in the pouring rain from their front where he was shot and killed. Two months later, Sergeant J.C. Thomas of A Squadron won the Military Medal when his patrol surprised about twenty CTs in the act of holding up a bus. His vehicle came under heavy fire as it stopped, but – possibly a unique event in the history of the RAC – he ordered a bayonet charge up the bank towards the enemy, firing as they charged and scattering the ambushers.

On arrival in late 1951 12th Lancers, taking over from 4th Hussars in the north and operating out of no less than nine separate and widely dispersed locations, commented that:

Our role is chiefly in patrolling roads and in escort duties – but if opportunity occurs and information arrives, we go after the enemy on foot [but] reliable information is scarce and usually supplied first to the police and next to the infantry. We receive, as it were, the crumbs from their table ... We have only had one really good contact that should have resulted in a kill [as] the Bren gun which was the weapon detailed to spring the ambush misfired and the bandits made good their escape … A Squadron [only had] two contacts in its nine months at Ipoh. During the nine months no convoy escorted by us, nor any of our patrols were molested or even shot at by the enemy. Operationally, this was a dull period … The role is inclined to be monotonous since roads are so few and the jungle impenetrable to wheels. Unless the communists choose to chance their arm against us, which we have found them loath to do, we have little opportunity of showing our mettle.[37]

But a shooting war was still being fought and occasionally more exciting actions took place, and one such was recorded by the regiment, on 22 May 1953:

A very successful ambush was pulled off by 1 Troop A Squadron (2Lt R Arkwright) near Taiping. Time has proved that no ambush has much hope of success without good information, luck and fire control. Not everyone who formed an ambush party had the patience, fieldcraft or killer instinct to get the best out of what fortune offered. Too many Brens jammed, something had given the show away early, or just nothing had happened … It was to be half way up a rubber covered hill overlooking a path to a culvert under the main road … The troop dropped off its APC whilst it was in motion about an hour away (a standard tactic) and walked back to the position. Movement through the jungle invited attack by leeches and ferocious ants … It is not impossible to meet a tiger. Much can therefore go wrong but on this night it didn't. Within half an hour of taking up his position the troop leader heard the cracking of twigs and whispering … he saw two figures … at about twenty yards he opened fire with his rifle. This was the signal for a general engagement after which a search of the ground found five food packs, a Japanese rifle and a trail of blood. The next day tracker dogs rapidly located a wounded [terrorist] … The regiment mounted hundreds of ambushes during its time in Malaya and this was one of the very few successful ones.

It is true to say that as the years went by, the RAC regiments saw less and less action, although of course they could not be withdrawn as their mere presence added to campaign success – it was not all about kills. During their nearly three-year tour, 12th Lancers estimated that they covered about 4½ million miles. In that time they had sixty-three small-arms contacts, in which they could only confirm two kills, two bandits wounded and one captured, and suffered eleven wounded of their own in action. Later, from mid-1956 until late 1958, the King's Dragoon Guards calculated that their vehicles had covered 2¾ million miles, but despite undertaking many infantry patrols into the *ulu*, some lasting over ten days and requiring supply by helicopter or parachute, there were only three confirmed contacts with one solitary bandit killed and another wounded. This of course reflected the improving security situation and the ever-decreasing number of active terrorists.[38]

Although it is generally believed that tanks were not – could not – be used during the Malaya campaign, this is not quite correct. Although the six RAC regiments stationed in the country during the emergency were all armoured car and therefore cavalry units, in March 1951 B Sqn 3RTR sent a number of their Comet tanks from Hong Kong to Gurun in the north, as the terrain there allowed them to set up a 2-mile-long AP range and exercise in reasonably tank-friendly terrain, neither of which were available at their base in Hong Kong.[39] Tank troops would rotate through the facility for six weeks at a time, conducting useful tactical training. Additionally, in July 6 Troop was involved in operations against the CT, in which their 77mm HE and BESA MGs were used to suppress the enemy as part of a genuine all-arms operation also involving artillery and infantry, and controlled from a circling aircraft. Their solitary casualty was Lieutenant John Hibbs, killed on 11 November 1951 in an ambush; the detachment closed in February 1952. Hibbs was only one of 350 officers and soldiers killed during the Emergency, as well as 159 Gurkhas, 128 Malayan soldiers and 1,346 policemen. Confirmed bandits killed totalled 6,710, with 1,287 captured and 2,702 surrendered – many more would certainly have perished in the jungle from wounds, disease and malnutrition. Although most campaigns are not decided by body counts, in some ways the Malayan Emergency was, as the CT force diminished over time, with little prospect of reinforcement.[40]

The Emergency was declared over on 31 July 1960, with a victory parade held the following day in Kuala Lumpur and featuring 13th/18th Hussars' armoured cars in pride of place. During the twelve years six cavalry regiments took part in the campaign – one of them twice, with sixty of their officers and soldiers being killed. The deployments were as follows:

- 3 October 1948–5 October 1951: 4H All areas
- June 1950–8 July 1953: 13/18H South
- 1951: Detachment 3RTR (from Hong Kong)
- 6 October 1951–19 August 1954: 12L North
- 8 July 1953–June 1956: 11H South
- 20 August 1954–24 May 57: 15/19H North
- June 1956–early November 1958: KDG All areas
- September 1958–December 1960: 13/18H All areas

At its peak in manpower terms in 1953, the Emergency saw two RAC armoured car regiments supporting twenty-three British infantry battalions stationed around the country.[41] With a total of about 30,000 British troops deployed, it is notable that the majority of these were National Servicemen.[42] In pure numerical terms therefore, the RAC regiments played something of a supporting role, as the brunt of the fighting fell, as usual, to the infantry. However, this should not hide the fact that the role of keeping the lines of communication open, as well as escorting VIPs and convoys of other personnel and civilians, and denial of food to the bandits, were key aspects of the success of the campaign overall. Without the escorts many more lives would have been taken and the Emergency prolonged. Not surprisingly, following the end of the Emergency, British troops continued to be stationed in the country for some time. From 1960 the sole RAC unit in Malaya generally prioritized the detachment of one of its sabre squadrons across the straits to Singapore on Internal Security duties leaving two often under-strength squadrons to deal with 'up country'. These units were: The Royals (from late November 1960 until October 1962), QRIH (to September 1964), 4RTR (to July 1966) and finally the Life Guards until November 1968. It is interesting that tucked away in The Royals' history is the observation that during the early 1960s the attention of the RAC soldiers was sometimes to be focused elsewhere, as 'there was a general feeling that we might find ourselves in the vanguard of a British force joining a Commonwealth Division [fighting] with the Australians and New Zealanders in Vietnam'.[43]

The Korean War, 1950–3

For the majority of the British population in 1950, Korea was a place that most had never even heard of, and even those that had would struggle to place it on a map. British forces had never served there, and it had generally been considered, in geo-political terms, to be of interest mainly to China and Japan. The latter had used it as a colony, annexing it in 1910 and using its (limited) resources and especially its manpower during the Second World War. The US only became involved as the Pacific War came to a close, and reluctantly committed small and poorly equipped forces there subsequently, to assist in training the 'ROKs' – the army of the Republic of Korea. In September 1945 the Americans had come to an agreement with the USSR that they would observe a de facto border using the 38th Parallel, a line of latitude that conveniently divided the peninsula in half. This led to the creation in 1948 of two republics: the hard-line Communist People's Republic (or North Korea) above the parallel, and South Korea, or the Republic of Korea, below. The Russians provided training and equipment, including copious amounts of artillery and a couple of hundred T34-85 tanks, to the North Korean army, whilst the Americans were more parsimonious with their support to the south, which received no tanks, only a token force of M8 Armoured Cars designed for ceremonial escorts for the president.[44]

The Korean peninsula extends southwards from the Asian mainland for nearly 700 miles, a little longer than the British mainland, with the Yellow Sea to the west and the Sea of Japan to the east; at its closest point, Japan is only 30 miles away. Combined, South and North Korea together are slightly smaller in area than the United Kingdom. In terms of terrain, soldiers arriving in the country were amazed how backward it was – in the days long before Samsung and Hyundai – as no real investment had entered the country. The road system was terrible, and much of the eastern side of the country was dominated by steep, scrubby hills and mountains; it has been described as looking like a mixture of the worst features of Dartmoor, the Brecon Beacons and the Highlands of Scotland. Most of the low-lying country had been turned over to rice cultivation, with the paddies making the passage of even smaller and lighter AFVs very challenging. There was very little in the way of forests, as almost all of the wooded areas had been systematically depleted years before for fuel, leading to problems with climactic erosion; the effect of this was that the country seemed to be a sea of mud during the harsh snowy and rainy winters, and a huge dustbowl during the baking summer season. In short, anyone finding themselves unfortunate enough to be sent there to fight was going to find it a miserable experience, even before a shot was fired – and so it proved.

With the permission of Stalin and supported by Mao, both of whom were convinced that the US would not come to South Korea's aid, Kim Il-Sung launched his North Korean army of ten infantry divisions supported by his sole armoured brigade in a surprise attack across the parallel in the early hours on 25 June 1950, sweeping all before them and reaching the capital Seoul in only three days. Continuing southwards, the pace of the advance could have been much speedier had the army not paused after taking Seoul, and even more so had it been more mechanized. Fortunately, this was not the case, and this allowed

7RTR Churchill crews making the best of a bad job in the depths of the hideous Korean winter of 1950/51.

just enough time for the Americans to interdict the invaders using air attacks and naval gunfire support, followed by a cobbled together collection of occupation troops from nearby Japan. The US army in Japan was not configured to be used as a quick reaction force, and was limited to chucking into the fight anything that could be deployed. This included tanks, the only ones available immediately being a few M24 Chaffees, which were quickly found to be totally outclassed by the more powerful Soviet models; Max Hastings noted that there were, 'Four communist spearheads … driving south, led by their almost invulnerable armour'.[45] The South Korean army, such as it was, was unable to stop or even slow the attack. Subsequently though, an improved American armoured force was deployed, and made up of a few battalions of whatever could be moved quickly from the US, with obsolescent M4A3 Shermans as well as more modern M26 Pershings and M46 Pattons. These took part in the only tank-versus-tank engagements of the war, and most of the T34s were destroyed during this phase; by about October – before the RAC units arrived – the role of the tank was mostly confined to providing direct fire support for the infantry. The advance was brought to a halt at the end of July around the perimeter of Pusan port, and with their combat power all but spent, the North Koreans were vulnerable to a counter-offensive. Meanwhile, the still-new United Nations organization had a real conflict to deal with. The Russian envoy at the UN had walked out earlier in the year, and this 'fluke of history' allowed a vote for collective action to take place without it being vetoed, and so a multi-national UN army was brought into being by a UN Resolution passed on 27 June.

In Britain the government was initially not at all certain that it would be able to offer help to the UN, even if it wanted to. The army was spread too thinly around the globe already, and the defence budget had been reducing, with much of the available spending earmarked for the new and very expensive nuclear arsenal. The army was, as always happens, the poor cousin and lacked modern equipment; in most terms, it was still organized and equipped on Second World War lines. The first response from Whitehall was to react as the Americans had, by despatching sea and air power but no ground forces. The nearest RAC unit to the conflict was 3RTR based in Hong Kong, having been sent there at short notice in August 1949 as a response to the threat of Chinese aggression, but it was judged that they could not be spared from the defence of the colony, and, therefore, aside from despatching a paltry two infantry battalions to Korea, any other forces would have to be assembled, trained and then sent from the UK.[46] Adding to the uncertainty was a suspicion that the Korean situation might be a bluff, a diversionary attack intended to draw forces into the theatre before a larger, more dangerous attack was made by, or on behalf of, the Soviets elsewhere. Eventually, it was decided to send 29th Infantry Brigade group from the UK, and which would include an armoured regiment. 8th King's Royal Irish Hussars (8H) was selected.

Being ordered to ready themselves for Korea was a huge surprise to the Hussars. They had spent most of the previous two years based near Oadby in Leicestershire in the unglamorous TA support role, which allowed them little time to do more than service, maintain, clean and un-bog tanks used by the enthusiastic amateurs. Little tactical training had been possible, although since October 1949 B Squadron had been the RAC Demonstration Squadron at Warminster, which meant that they were more up to speed than the rest of the regiment, albeit on Comet. The rest of the regiment had only moved to Mooltan Barracks Tidworth in mid–March 1950 and had started to convert from Comet to Centurion in June; they had no time to settle down before they were warned off for service in early August, mostly as their role was officially that of the UK strategic reserve. The usual British sangfroid and sense of unreality was very much in play as the regiment readied itself for an unexpected deployment. Lieutenant Colonel Jumbo Phillips 'preserved every cliché of the British cavalry going to war. He suggested taking fishing gear, four rolls of lavatory paper, and a shotgun – though not your best gun.'[47]

After the Second World War 8RTR, then 3RTR, then 7RTR had all been given the unglamorous task of maintaining the so-called Special Armour Establishment, the rump equipment and role of 79th Armoured Division, with its squadrons spread across the UK with RHQ in Bovington. In order for 7RTR to deploy a single squadron of Second World War-vintage Churchill Crocodile flamethrowers – 'C' was selected – the whole regiment had to be combed for personnel fit and able to be used, and who met the strict criteria imposed by the War Office. As much training as could be done was undertaken before the unit was given some leave and then embarked for the long voyage east. Unlike 8th Hussars, the unit thus formed was mainly composed of soldiers from the parent regiment who possessed considerable operational experience. In order to make the RAC units destined for Korea up to strength, volunteers had to be sought from across the corps, and it seems that these came forward in somewhat surprising numbers. It is probable that most if not all RAC regiments were represented by individuals who served there over the next three years.[48] The Hussars recorded at the end of their tour that they had been bolstered by fourteen regular officers from other RAC regiments, and seventeen emergency commissioned officers from the reserve; no less than 700 National Servicemen had served in their ranks during the tour. The Fifth Skins, on being told in June 1951 that they would be the relieving unit, had to change around 350 personnel, over half of their strength, with some only joining them just before embarking for the 5-week voyage.

One of the unexpected and most unwelcome aspects of the Korean War was that National Service had to be extended from eighteen months to two years across the whole army. Additionally, batches of ex-servicemen from the Army Emergency Reserve became liable to attend refresher training in case they were needed. These were known as the Z Reserve and in 1951 totalled about

Churchill Crocodiles of C Sqn 7RTR being off-loaded, early November 1950. Although they never used their flamethrowers in action, they were employed as gun tanks and were the first RAC unit to arrive in Korea.

130,000 men; the training plan was for them to attend, where possible, a suitable TA annual summer camp for 15 days, of which no less than 10 were expected to be on exercise – there was no question that the army should take the easy way out and just drill them on the square for a fortnight. But it was also appreciated that there would be many men who would need more specialist or technical training, and this included the RAC reservists, who needed to get back on to a tank – and in most cases a newer, more modern Centurion rather than a Second World War-era model on which they had been trained – for the first time in many years. The TA clearly could not cope with the numbers, and so the regular units in the UK found themselves playing host. This was an unwelcome burden on the few RAC field-force regiments stationed in the UK, already stretched by having to deal with their own National Servicemen as well as supporting the annual TA training. For example, in June 1953 4th/7th Dragoon Guards received a batch of thirty-five such persons, followed two weeks later by a similar sized group. Many of the reservists greatly resented being called back to the colours, rightly questioning why they were required when younger National Servicemen should be bearing the brunt. This was because the War Office had decided that only volunteer National Servicemen would be allowed to serve in Korea, that they had to be able to serve there for a minimum of seven months, and that no one under the age of 19 could be deployed. Many of the recalled reservists were a decade older than that, and 8th Hussars noted that of the 500 or so that were posted in to them on mobilization, none were younger than 25. Some had even been prisoners of war in the previous conflict, including Captain Donald Astley Cooper, a regular 8th Hussar who had spent three years of the Second World War as a POW and who would return to his regiment only to be killed in Korea within a few weeks of his arrival. One hopes that some of the resentment must have gradually dissipated as the reservists were made to feel part of the regimental family, although there was often terrible muddle over pay and scenes of wives demanding the return of their husbands, and some officers reported spending much of the voyage to Korea dealing with complaints from their reservist soldiers.

By the time the two RAC units had arrived towards the end of the year, the course of the war in Korea had changed significantly. Reinforcing the Pusan perimeter, the US were able to bring in enough forces to not only ensure their survival, but to take the offensive by mid-September, advancing back up the peninsula and retaking Seoul on the 27th. Amphibious landings well behind the lines at Inchon on the 15th had unhinged the North Korean attempts to defend the city, and in their retreat northwards, most of the remaining T34s were lost, over 300 in total. The opportunity to cross the 38th Parallel now presented itself, despite the restoration of the territorial integrity of the ROK having been achieved. On 7 October, UN forces followed the lead taken by ROK forces and crossed the parallel, seeking to completely destroy the remnants of the North Korean forces. The northern capital Pyongyang fell on 19 October and the forces pushed up towards the Yalu River, marking the border with China. Stalin was not prepared to send Soviet troops to assist, but Mao was inclined to intervene, and on the same day that Pyongyang was captured, 200,000 Chinese 'volunteers' entered North Korea, preventing North Korean collapse and prolonging the war. By November 1950 US forces were under attack by large Chinese assaults and forced to retreat southwards during December; the newly arrived British forces, caught up in this, were horrified by what was a rout, with American units streaming south with little or no cohesion. Seoul was recaptured on 4 January 1951. Ceasefire negotiations failed and Seoul changed hands once more on 14 March 1951. By July 1951 the front lines had largely been drawn, and the war settled down into a stalemate, with conditions often resembling the First World War. This did not mean that the violence was at an end, and some major actions still had to be fought during 1951.

C Squadron 7RTR were the first British armoured unit to disembark at Pusan with their sixteen Churchill Crocodiles on 5 November 1950, although it quickly became clear that the flame-throwing capability would not be as useful as predicted, and they were to be mostly used as standard infantry support tanks.[49] They were followed ten days later by 8th Hussars with their three squadrons of brand-new Centurions. They had been equipped with the latest Mark III versions, mounting the outstanding 20-pounder gun and propelled by the improved 4B version of the Meteor engine. The mere fact that they went to war in Britain's newest tank was soon to cause problems. Unbelievably, Recce Troop were mounted in Cromwells, the 75mm-armed Cruiser tank that was totally obsolete by 1950; why they did not receive the much better armed and armoured Comet has never been explained, especially as the similarly armed US M24s had been comprehensively outmatched by the opposition's T34, whereas the Comet would have been able to compete with the T34 as well as delivering more HE 'punch' from its 77mm gun.

The British force was not well equipped for the rigours of the Korean winter, with winds coming straight from Siberia to the north; even the much-vaunted Zoot Suit, the blanket-lined tank crewman's overall, could do little to keep out the biting cold, and greatcoats were impractical both for the infantry and the tank crews. The lack of suitable clothing and rations was a scandal, and Max Hastings decried the War Office's declaration that 29th Brigade was 'the best-equipped military force ever to leave Britain' as 'rubbish – the British in Korea in the first year of the war suffered privations of almost Crimean proportions'.[50] This was slightly unfair but it did apply to the first two unfortunate infantry battalions of

7RTR carrying American troops, late 1950. Later in the campaign some excellent winter clothing was provided, but these crews are clearly yet to receive it, and are wearing the standard-issue European clothing: greatcoats, tank overalls and the like. (TM 2310/A5)

27th 'Woolworths' Brigade, sent from Hong Kong, whereas the troops coming from the UK were somewhat better equipped for the conditions, although sleeping bags and other cold-weather items had to come from the Americans.

On arrival, 29th Brigade were moved north to Seoul, a long, cold and dispiriting train journey, with the infantry tasked to locate and destroy remnants of the North Korean army operating as bandits. One battalion moved up as far as Pyongyang only to find themselves in the middle of a headlong retreat by the disintegrating US Eighth Army, which did not end until they were back around the 38th parallel once more. Gregory Blaxland described the situation in these terms:

> Throughout December 29 Brigade saw plenty to gasp at but no-one to fight … The 8th Hussars had to bear the greatest exasperations. Having brought two squadrons of their precious Centurions by train to Pyongyang, they then had to drive them back along ice-packed roads not just across the parallel but through Seoul and far to the south, for it was considered that they would only encumber the withdrawal. For two days without pause the monsters lumbered southwards on what by rights was their running-in journey, leaving behind one broken down and demolished. Then, unbelievably, they were ordered to Pusan, where these two squadrons (but not the third) embarked for Japan, vehicles and crews in separate ships, before recall orders reached them. It was a bewildering and humiliating start to a campaign, and it is a marvel that morale remained high.[51]

In fact, Blaxland only tells part of the story. The Hussars arrived in Pusan, and the unloading was done in a haphazard manner, with A Squadron coming off the boats first, followed by B and then C. As soon as they were complete by squadrons, they were despatched north to Pyongyang, which the US and ROK had captured. In order to get them moving, only a 'nominal load of ammunition' was put onto each tank, before being loaded onto railway flats for a miserable seven-day journey to the North Korean capital – in the depths of winter. No sooner had A Squadron arrived, with B Squadron somewhere behind them, than the order was given to withdraw them to the south, as the Chinese advance had started and the Americans were streaming back across the parallel. C Squadron was able to be halted en route, about 40 miles north of Seoul. In order to de-train, because there were no unloading ramps, the Centurions of B Squadron had to be carefully and slowly turned around on the flats before making the drop to the floor, 'as gently as possible'. Both of the forward squadrons then started the withdrawal southwards on tracks – and the brand-new Centurions started to give trouble. As they had not been run-in in the UK, the retreat became their running-in period, with fuel starvation problems being the main cause of breakdowns. Fortunately, only one tank in A Squadron had to be abandoned, because of a badly thrown track that required oxy-acetylene cutting tools, of which there were none.[52]

8th Hussars Centurions during the retreat south, January 1951. For the Hussars, the initial months of the campaign were a frustrating time, with much confusion caused by the haphazard way in which they were used. (Courtesy QRH)

It was imperative not to allow the brand-new Centurion Mk III with its 20-pounder gun to fall intact into Chinese hands, and the Brigade Commander ordered the unit to destroy it. The breech block, sights, 'certain secret equipment' and all removable items were taken from the Tank. it was then packed with nearly seventy HE shells, eighteen in the engine compartment, and fifty more in the turret, particularly around the stabilizer equipment. The fuel lines were cut, and a petrol-soaked camouflage net stuffed into the engine compartment, with a 50yd-long fuse laid away from the tank. It went up like a torch, the HE shells starting to explode almost immediately; after 90 minutes the tank was nothing more than 'an over-cooked carcass'. In a further attempt to make it useless, American aircraft then attacked the hulk, guided by an 8th Hussars officer.

The regiment managed to escape without being in contact with the enemy, and spent a frustrating and cheerless Christmas in the Suwon area, south of Seoul. Possibly because of the concerns over the destroyed tank, a decision was made to withdraw the Hussars back to Japan. The crews from both A and B Squadrons were sent there, with their tanks still in Pusan awaiting loading, when the inevitable counter-order came. C Squadron alone remained in country, along with HQ Squadron, including Recce Troop. Much worse was to follow for the regiment.

The Battle of 'Happy Valley' (later renamed officially as Koyang) was fought in early January 1951 north of Seoul, and resulted in the single largest loss of life and tanks suffered by the RAC during the war. 29th Infantry Brigade Group was sited north of Seoul and tasked with defending the 'bridgehead line' east of the town of Koyang, on the left flank of, and supporting, the US 24th Infantry Division's positional defence along the rough line of the Han River. 1st Bn Royal Ulster Rifles were forward left, with 1st Bn Royal Northumberland Fusiliers on the right. In the early morning of 3 January, Chinese units attacked the two forward battalions in force, using the cover of darkness to make an undetected approach. Six Churchills of 7RTR acting as gun tanks were sent forward to assist in breaking up the attack on the right flank, where their combined BESA fire was fundamental in repelling the attack on the Fusilier's Y Company. However, the American unit to the left of the British brigade started to withdraw southwards, and the link between the UK and American forces was broken, exposing the British left flank and allowing the gap between the formations to be exploited by the Chinese, experts at infiltration tactics.[53] Making a coordinated withdrawal became impossible, and in any case the British could not start pulling back until late in the evening on the 3rd. The two battalions in the front line were meant to conduct simultaneous but separate withdrawals, thereby fighting their own independent battles during the night. It was hoped to break clean without engaging the enemy.

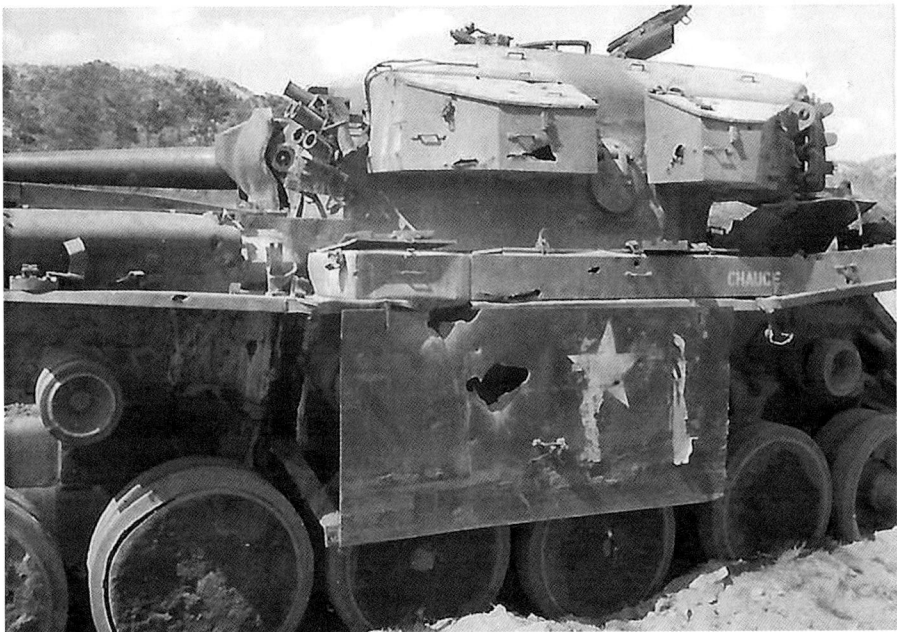

Serious shell damage to CHAUCER of 8th Hussars. The British government were terrified that the latest Centurion III might fall into Korean – and thus Chinese and Russian – hands, and some were destroyed by their own troops. (Courtesy Sergeant Sidney William Sherriff 8KRIH)

The withdrawal of the Fusiliers on the right at 1830 was successfully assisted by the half-dozen Churchills of 7RTR. Fighting the enemy off and almost out of 75mm ammunition, the Churchill crews took to firing Bren guns from the turrets of their tanks and could not understand why the Chinese did not press home their attack on the vulnerable force. As it was, the Churchills were the last ones out, the commanders having to dismount and lead the tanks through the darkness on foot, with the infantry reaching their RV with lorried transport later than night.

With the Ulstermen on the left was a mixed force of Cromwells, mainly from the Hussar's Recce Troop, bolstered by six OP Cromwells from 45 Field Regiment RA.[54] Commanded by the Recce Troop leader, Captain Astley Cooper, this group was known as Cooper Force and was the northernmost part of the Hussars. Why the task was given to these obsolete tanks rather than the more powerful Centurions of C Squadron requires explanation. Two factors seem to have been in play. Firstly, the War Office was insistent that under no circumstances must Britain's latest tank be allowed to fall into Communist hands. Because of this, the Brigade was loathe to commit the Centurions into circumstances where withdrawal was not guaranteed. Secondly, it may be that the decision to commit Cooper Force was partly taken on the grounds that the lighter and smaller Cromwells would be better able to cope with the conditions in the RUR area, and that the OP tanks were not there for their fighting capacity, but in their normal role as OP tanks to provide supporting fire to the battalion, as well as being able to carry infantry on the engine decks should it become necessary.[55] During the afternoon, fierce fighting had erupted, and the Hussars' Cromwells completely expended all their 75mm ammunition, requiring replenishment before night fell and the withdrawal attempted. Astley Cooper tried sensibly but unsuccessfully to be allowed to withdraw before it was dark, but his request was refused for fear that the noise of the tanks moving would alert the Chinese to what was taking place.

Unhappily, the only withdrawal route open to the battalion was a single narrow and icy road, with a steep cliff to one side. The rifle companies of the Ulsters were delayed by the need to move heavy equipment off the snow-covered hill tops, and they only started the withdrawal at about 2100. Initially all went well, and an enemy attack that threatened to interfere with the movement was unaccountably halted, allowing the three rifle companies to continue the withdrawal. At about 2200 S Coy (the Support Company) was about to move off when they were engaged from the flank. The tanks of Cooper Force and the MMGs of the battalion mounted on Oxford Carriers returned fire, allowing the withdrawal to commence. Having only moved about 300yd, it was found that the vehicles could not keep to the narrow track, and were slipping all over the perilous surface and temporarily blocking it, slowing progress down at a crucial moment. The enemy was now attacking in numbers and seemed oblivious to the casualties being taken. Fire was heavy and mostly inaccurate, but more and more carriers became bogged in the waterlogged fields and had to be abandoned. In an effort to clear a village held by the enemy the tanks were called up and charged southwards, taking possession of the burning village – but then the leading tank of Lieutenant Alexander became inextricably bogged and the escape route to the south was blocked for good, trapping all the remaining vehicles on the enemy side; Alexander was killed when a mortar bomb landed on his turret. Some tried their luck in the paddy fields but this was hopeless. The tanks were attacked by hordes of Chinese troops using bundles of hand grenades and pole charges (Bangalore torpedoes), and the tank crews had to abandon the burning and immobilized Cromwells in an attempt to escape. The action was described thus:

> To the open dismay of Astley Cooper, brigade decreed that the tanks were to act as a rear-guard, moving out in darkness with a single platoon for close protection. Twenty-year old Lance Corporal Robert Erricker [was] co-driver of Lieutenant Godfrey Alexander's Cromwell … the track down the valley through which they departed was barely wide enough to carry a tank. Even as the infantry withdrew in front of them, they came under fire from the hills overlooking the road. Astley Cooper saw to his dismay that a village along his line of retreat was already ablaze. The tanks ground and battered their path along it, infantry clinging to the hulls and being shot off as they drove … Chinese mortar bombs began to fall on the hull. Johnnie Healey, their BESA gunner shouted: 'The guvnors hit!' They pulled their officer down into the turret, and found that he had been hit by a mortar fragment in the head. The tank swerved off the road. They had thrown a track. Another tank halted alongside. 'All right, spike your gun and get out of it!' shouted the commander.
>
> Then there were Chinese soldiers all around them, motioning them down. They were put up against a wall, hands in the air. 'This is it' muttered Erricker miserably … Suddenly another tank was upon them, spraying tracer. Captors and captives dived for cover. When the firing stopped and the Chinese began reassembling their prisoners, Healey and Bates, the wireless operator, had vanished. They made good their escape to the British lines … Astley Cooper's tank cast a track on the rough ground. His crew bailed out and escaped. Their commander was never seen again.[56]

As well as the two dead officers and another captured, twenty other Hussars were posted as missing, presumed killed, although in fact many had been taken prisoner. The Gunners lost twenty posted as missing. In late March the regiment was able to send a party to the area to complete the 'grisly' task of recovering bodies. Fifty-three were found, from many units, including that of Astley Cooper, one of the few who could be positively identified. They were buried in a mass grave with due ceremony.

With A and B Squadron's tanks back in Pusan, where they would remain until the order was countermanded allowing them to re-join the action, the only remaining tanks available were the eighteen Centurions belonging to C Squadron 8th Hussars, commanded by Major Henry Huth MC. In ferociously cold conditions in February, a UN counter-offensive was mounted, and the squadron went into action on 11 February, fighting in the most bitterly cold weather. Remarkably, the first target was one of the Cooper Force Cromwells, captured five weeks previously. Although it was about 2½ miles away, well beyond the theoretical range of the 20-pounder, it was hit and destroyed by the second shot fired. The squadron also conducted joint patrols with the infantry, hoping to bring the enemy to battle, but frustratingly they remained out of sight.

C Squadron, generally operating as two half squadrons, was the sole tank unit in support during the famous Imjin River battle in late April 1951. The four battalions in 29th Brigade – having been reinforced by a Belgian battalion – were under command on an American infantry division and in prepared defensive positions along the river line; the nature of the country prevented a continuous line being established, so each battalion occupied tactically important high ground. Overall, the brigade was expected to defend a line some 20km long, a difficult undertaking but critical to prevent a Chinese offensive into Seoul. Unbeknown to the defenders, the Chinese commander was intent on exactly this objective, as a May Day present for Chairman Mao. The battle started on the night of 22 April, and was largely an infantry affair, with C Squadron (reinforced with American M24 light tanks) failing in an attempt to support a Filipino infantry counter-attack to force a passage through to the Gloucesters on the 24th, grimly hanging on top of hill 235. The lead tank was knocked out in a defile which blocked the route and prevented the force from making any more progress, still over a mile from the beleaguered defenders. Two further attempts using tanks also failed. On the 25th a planned withdrawal to a new line further south was made, and was again supported by C Squadron, although the remnants of the Gloucesters could not force their way out. Huth, who was to receive a DSO for his actions, described the withdrawal as 'one long bloody ambush'. One account recorded the part played by the Hussars during the move back:

C Squadron 8th Hussars, on whom so much depended, were early in trouble. Half of them, under Captain Ormrod, set out at dawn from their leaguer to join the forward battalions, dropping off valuable reinforcements for B Company 1st Ulsters, on the pass, in the form of a troop of the 55th Field Squadron RE. There was a shroud of early mist along the valley bed, and it clotted periscope vision, with the result that two Centurions lost direction and were bogged. The Chinese swarmed upon them like angry wasps, and the two tanks sprayed each other with fire to free themselves. Other tanks joined in and scattered Chinese in all directions with point-blank salvoes from their 20-Pounders.[57] The mist lifted, to the advantage of the tanks, and the valley temporarily quietened. One tank was eventually recovered under fire; the other had to be demolished.[58]

Peter Ormrod received an MC for his bravery and leadership. It can be appreciated that boggings in the unsuitable terrain were a frequent occurrence, often under fire, and the need for recovery was paramount. Centurion ARVs were not yet in production, and the task fell to ancient Churchill ARVs, supplemented by RE-crewed Centurions with their turrets removed, and referred to as 'tugs' or 'towers'; these vehicles were not only used as extemporized recovery vehicles, but were also employed in carrying forward supplies and defensive stores (sometimes including Asahi beer), as well as evacuating casualties. (Later in the campaign the Hussars had to surrender a Churchill ARV to the Chinese after it had broken down atop Hill 227 and unable to be recovered.) Despite the rugged terrain, the ability of the Centurions and Churchills to climb steep gradients came as a great but welcome surprise.

During the battle the RAP of the Hussars was unable to extricate itself in time, and the MO was captured. The tank crews could hear the doctor on the radio, giving a running commentary, 'I am about to be captured … I have been captured.' By the end of the fighting six Centurions and five other AFVs had been lost by the regiment. The infantry had become somewhat mixed up during the confusion of the withdrawal:

> The commander of C Squadron, Major Huth, who had rushed back from leave when the battle started, had personally been shepherding the Belgians back with his own Centurion and one other. Warned by air-dropped message that a mass of Chinese was fast coming in between him and the Ulsters, he moved back to confront them. A tense fight followed, with the Chinese going down in scores, but always coming on behind the paddy bunds on the valley's bottom. Slowly the two tanks gave ground, peppered and stalked from every piece of cover and yet giving protection with their turrets to some wounded they carried … although the power traverse in Huth's tank jammed, the Chinese were held at bay until the last soldiers, British and Belgian, had hobbled past the American's positions.[59]

Huth himself was credited with firing the final shot of the Imjin battle.

It should be emphasized that the units sent to Korea were stationed there for a one-year tour, although a form of operational mid-tour leave was introduced and, copied from the Americans, known as Rest & Recuperation (usually referred to by the British soldiers as Rack and Ruin). Usually lasting only five days, R&R could be taken in Japan, a short flight away and seeming like a different planet for the arriving troops. Where this was not possible, national rest camps were operated

Spring 1951 brought a thaw and with it the problems of trying to cross muddy paddy fields, not always successfully.

behind the front line. Other than this, the troops had to make themselves as comfortable as they could, no easy task bearing in mind the extreme climates in winter and summer – in summer tropical kit was issued, as the temperatures soared above 100 degrees.

The arrival of summer also marked an end to the war of movement, with positions taken up on tactical high ground in order to dominate approaches. The tanks were driven up to high points, confounding those who prophesied that they would never make it, and were frequently dug-in to deep pits prepared by the engineers, often using civilian labour provided by the Korean Service Corps. Some positions were assessed to be vital to the defence, requiring the tank to be positioned before the winter weather made movement impossible, and then left in position for the next months; their suspensions and hulls were heavily sandbagged to prevent damage from shellfire. In other locations the tanks were able to be pulled back out of sight of the enemy and moved forward as and when required.[60] The tanks were well protected in hull-down positions, often with overhead cover as the biggest threat during daytime came from shellfire. Alongside the tanks deep crew shelters called 'bashas' (occasionally 'hutchies') were constructed, adding more than a whiff of First World War trench warfare to proceedings.[61] The tank crews made elaborate range maps of all likely positions and approaches, allowing them to be accurately engaged at night using the tank's fire-control equipment, often in support of infantry patrols sent out to dominate no man's land and interrupt the activities of the Chinese who themselves preferred to operate in the dark. The pinpoint accuracy of the 20-pounders was much valued, with corrections from the infantry such as 'right about eighteen inches' being reported. Any observed movement or gun flash was likely to be met by a rapid and highly accurate HE shell fired by the Cents; it was noticeable how seldom movement was seen in the Chinese lines during daylight. During this time the Churchills of 7RTR were detached in support of American units (before departing in October), whilst the three Hussars squadrons were parcelled out to support the three infantry brigades that now made up 1st Commonwealth Division. A near-desperation to engage enemy armour was sometimes apparent, but none materialized; excitement mounted when a vehicle was spotted in the distance during September and thought to be a self-propelled gun, but it was eventually recognized – after being engaged with AP – as nothing more than a 'ox-drawn honey cart at full gallop'. Some deep penetrations were made into Chinese-held territory as part of reconnaissances in force, but unless they were attacking, the Chinese preferred to avoid contact during daylight. Despite the restrictions in movement, 8th Hussars continued to provide important fire support through the autumn and into their second winter, and some localized operations were put into train in order to seize more commanding heights.

A Centurion of 8H occupies a hill-top position. By summer 1951 the war settled down to a more static affair, often resembling First World War trench conditions – but with tanks. The ability of the tank to climb extremely difficult terrain, plus its very accurate firepower, brought it many plaudits. (TM 2510/D4)

After a rapid and efficient handover 5th Royal Inniskilling Dragoon Guards – The Skins – took over at midday on 6 December 1951; that evening the personnel of 8th Hussars came together as a complete regiment for the first time since disembarking thirteen months previously, and sailed for home on the 15th; in fact, they were sent to the UK only for well-deserved leave before being posted to Lüneburg in BAOR, leaving many of their personnel behind and having to form a virtually new regiment from drafts of new National Servicemen.[62]

As they left, it was time for reflection:

Despite the restrictions imposed by precipitous slopes and soggy paddy fields, the 8th had raised the art of close support of infantry to a new pitch of efficacy and had not only pleased their clients but were themselves bubbling with enthusiasm for the Centurion. Five of their officers (including a doctor) and thirteen soldiers had been killed.[63]

The majority of their casualties had come from the ill-fated Cooper Force action, and the unfortunate MO was Captain George Beith RAMC, killed when a shell hit the RAP during Operation Commando in October. Captain Wilfrid St Clair Tisdall MC recorded that, 'we felt a great hatred of being there, of the country'. His comments probably reflected his soldiers' view of how poorly South Korea functioned as a nation, and its backward systems, rather than of their performance during the campaign. As they departed, the regimental journal recorded their memories of the challenging climate and terrain, but it also took time to comment that 'we shall remember the Chinaman, for whom we in our heart of hearts had great respect. He was a brave, dogged fighter who took untold punishment and whom we chased and stropped up unceasingly with the 20-pounder and who, despite all this medicine, counter-attacked with a smile on his face.'[64]

The Skins came from BAOR via England, and were made up to strength by taking drafts from eight cavalry and two RTR regiments in Germany. Their deployment was ordered in early June 1951 and hence preparation was not as rushed as 8th Hussars had been, and they had two weeks on Hohne ranges all to themselves in order to convert to Centurion III. But a problem surfaced because they were stationed in Germany; the question arose, what to do with the wives and families? As well as many German spouses, at least three other European nations were represented. The wives met and decided that they would stick together as a group whilst the men were at war, and in August were shipped off – with the regimental band – to a truly dreadful camp 'awaiting demolition' in Catterick, with no organized welfare or other facilities. Some ended up staying there for eighteen months.

On arrival in Korea the men found themselves fighting a very different campaign to that of their predecessors, with relatively little movement. Inheriting the tanks, equipment and positions from the Hussars, they were supplied with much better winter clothing, the army having learned many lessons from the poor situation of a year previously. Fortunately, in the late 1940s the army had been researching the replacement of battledress, introduced in 1937, with a more modern series of combat uniforms based on a two-piece suit designed around ski wear. This meant that when the war started, it was possible to very rapidly produce a new combat uniform suited to the terribly cold conditions of the Korean winter, including not only an olive-green combat suit but also 'Finnish' ski-boots, a hooded parka, quilted mittens, thick woollen underwear and the like, issued before deploying and described by The Skins as excellent. The very first versions of the 'woolly-pully', the ribbed woollen pullover later to become synonymous with the British army were issued. Petrol space heaters were issued, although careless use of these in confined spaces like bashas caused many a burn, and the opportunity to trade rations with the many different nations in the UN force was not missed. A ration of two bottles of beer a day was very welcome, and much UK media attention was focused on another novelty, the issue of one 24V electric razor issued to each tank.

Aside from four manoeuvre operations, described by the regiment as 'minor', the regiment spent its year in Korea manning positions in the now relatively static front line. Generally, this meant having two squadrons 'up', one with each of the British brigades, with the third in reserve in a camp that the regiment built and subsequently improved; known as Gloucester Valley Camp, this was also occupied by RHQ, HQ squadron and the LAD (because of the recent changes in army organization, for the first time the LAD was completely made up of REME-badged personnel).[65] From the camp operated a number of Korean 'washee-washee' women, content to do all the regiment's laundry in return for three meals a day, with other Korean labourers employed on camp maintenance. Movement around the country was now made much easier as the US army engineers had created a network of roads, and although a ceasefire line had been agreed, the peace negotiations were still ongoing and both sides sought to improve their positions, both tactically and strategically. The Skins, coming towards the end of their tour, noted that over ten months of 'success and failure have been measured in yards, and the Commonwealth Divisional front has not given or gained an inch'.[66]

The positions adopted by the regiment included the two most exposed and therefore dangerous high spots within the Commonwealth divisional area, points 159 and 355. The former was probably the worst, atop a finger of ground jutting out towards the Chinese defences where it served as something of a provocation. During the summer the Chinese attempted to force the Centurions to retire from their commanding positions, and used prodigious amounts of artillery to try to make the positions untenable. The safest place under bombardment was inside the tanks, although crews caught outside at the start of a 'hate' had no choice but to stay where they were. Most shelling was 122mm in calibre which was not sufficient to do substantial damage to a Centurion, and Sergeant Irving's tank from C Squadron sustained seventeen hits during one barrage in July, the crew being unhurt. In total the regiment's tanks received forty-five direct hits over the course of five days. However, tragedy befell one tank on 4 September when, in a thousand to one chance, a shell went under the overhead cover and entered the open hatch of a 4th Troop C Squadron Centurion, killing all four members of the crew inside.[67]

The four manoeuvre operations mounted by the regiment were codenamed Liverpool, Ascot, Jehu and Maindy. The first two were simultaneous tank raids on 16 February, designed to advance about 1,000yd across the front line in order to force the enemy to unmask their gun positions, allowing them to be engaged. Anti-tank mines and sniper fire proved to be the major hazards, as the tank crews found themselves trying to climb 'the roughest and steepest going imaginable'. By midday it was clear that the enemy positions around the tanks required infantry to clear them out, and in the early afternoon the tanks started to withdraw, the enemy fire increasing notably as they did so. The troop sergeant in 2nd Troop C Squadron was hit by what was adjudged to be an anti-tank HEAT shell fired from a recoilless rifle, which made a 3½in hole in the turret but without any real damage to crew or equipment. The OC's tank broke a track which had to be repaired under fire, and by 1400 the operation was over.

Jehu was the next mobile operation, mounted on 17 June. This was another raid, timed to take place before an expected period of heavy rain. As well as attacking a battalion-sized position that occupied a dominating feature, it was hoped to draw any Chinese tanks and SPGs thought to be in the area into battle, and if possible, capture prisoners. Fire support came from the divisional artillery and infantry heavy weapons, as well as from A Squadron augmented by one troop of Canadian Shermans.[68] B Squadron created a diversionary attack to the north, whilst the RE cleared lanes through the Chinese wire and their own defensive minefields. The leading troop leader, Lieutenant Taylor, had previously accompanied an infantry patrol into the enemy location in order to understand better the lie of the land. Although quickly reaching the first objective soon after first light, the movement of the tank force had broken the earth bunds surrounding the paddy fields, quickly turning the area into a morass in which three tanks of the following troop became bogged. Lieutenant Taylor in the leading tank on the objective was hit by an anti-tank weapon starting a fire, which he had to dismount to put out. Sniping increased and when a Chinese mountain gun attempted to engage them at close range it was knocked out by Sergeant Bertrand. The troop was able to engage a system of bunkers that had now become visible, bringing in artillery fire as they did so. In the rear the OC's tank had run over a mine which came close to disabling the tank, but it managed to limp back to safety. As the Chinese had elected not to contest the battle and stayed out of sight, it was clear that nothing more could be gained, and, skirting the bogged area, Taylor's troop returned towards the start line. This prompted the hidden defenders to reappear and engage both the withdrawing tanks and the fire base occupied by A Squadron with both small-arms and accurate artillery fire. However, there was still the matter of three bogged tanks to attend to. An ARV sent forward hit a mine and became bogged itself. The next ARV had its winch cable severed by a shell and the EME, Captain Cuthbert, was wounded whilst trying to direct operations. A medical 'tug' was sent forward to collect him, but itself became bogged. As the regimental journal phlegmatically recounted, 'That made five tanks in a bog being shelled …'.

After 'strenuous work', by the end of the day three had been recovered, leaving the mined ARV and one Centurion still in the paddy field. In order to recover them the sappers had to clear a minefield before bulldozing a track alongside the area, allowing the Technical Adjutant, Captain Cupper, to take forward two 'patched-up' ARVs and a tug to attempt the recovery on the 20th. Immediately engaged by Chinese mortars, the New Zealand artillery laid a smokescreen that they kept up for nearly 3 hours, firing 2,000 shells in order to do so. As the ARV was being recovered to Point 159, Chinese artillery hit the area and Second Lieutenant Albrecht of A Squadron was killed, his tank set on fire and two other officers including the NZ FOO were wounded. The Divisional Commander then stepped in and ordered that no attempts be made to reach the final tank for a while. Sometime later the last Centurion was able to be recovered, although an Australian soldier involved in the operation was killed. Despite the losses, Operation Jehu was assessed to be successful, as many more casualties were inflicted on the Chinese. However, as a result, the defenders started to construct huge anti-tank ditches across the front, thereby limiting future opportunities for such raids.[69]

In the middle of November, 4th Troop B Squadron assisted 1st Bn Black Watch in repelling a 'vicious attack' made on the Hook feature:

> The action began at about 2100 hours, with heavy enemy shelling and reports of enemy movement. 4th Troop was deployed in two halves at either end of the battalion sector. The troop, assisted by a fifth tank firing from east of the river Samichon, brought down vigorous fire on the enemy's forming-up areas and axis of advance. The searchlights (of American origin) mounted on some of our tanks were of help until the smoke and haze of battle rendered observation difficult or they were damaged by enemy fire.[70]
> The forward platoon was overrun, but went to ground and re-emerged to drive the enemy off the Hook feature. At 2308 the enemy were reported to be forming up for a fresh attack, The Black Watch asked for a tank to be sent up on the Hook itself, and at 0110 hours the troop leader himself [Lt Mike Anstice] moved up, covered by the remainder of the troop who were using their searchlights again. The troop leader, after flattening two abandoned

gunner vehicles blocking the track … climbed slowly up on the top of the precipitous feature. At 0134 he made contact with the Black Watch and got into position to start firing, by the light of his searchlight, to considerable effect. At 0317 his tank was penetrated by a hollow charge projectile fired at very close range, and the driver, Tpr Lewis, was wounded. By great skill and care, the tank was driven back by the gunner, LCpl Williamson, [and] the driver evacuated.[71]

At first light an infantry assault by Canadians secured the Hook, allowing the troop to withdraw after offering 9 hours of intimate support; Anstice was awarded an MC. Further support operations continued throughout November, during which time the regiment sustained another eleven direct hits by artillery on their tanks. In a most unusual encounter on the 28th, an A Squadron tank was shot at by an enemy 85mm vehicle (presumably an SU85 self-propelled gun). The advance party of the relieving regiment, 1RTR, arrived on 2 November and the handover was completed by last light on 8 December 1951. The Skins departed Korea on the 14th, bound not for the UK but for another overseas posting, this time to Egypt, where it wasn't possible for leave to be taken until the end of March.

The First Tanks had used the ability of an eight-regiment RTR to fill the unit with veteran officers and senior NCOs, although as ever there were insufficient regular junior soldiers and reservists and National Servicemen made up the numbers. All four of the squadron leaders were Second World War veterans who had once commanded regiments. On taking over they found that half of the two forward squadrons were emplaced in forward positions, with the other half held back out of sight and in reserve. The task was similar to that of The Skins, and over time the troop positions and particularly the bashas had been much improved; although never exactly comfortable, the living conditions were better and the bunkers were more shellproof. It was discovered that if the fuse caps were left on the 20-pounder HE rounds, the shells could be fired through the slit of an enemy bunker where they would explode deep within, making them more effective. In the course of the tour, the regiment recorded having fired 23,800 20-pounder rounds, and the tanks were hit 68 times by artillery; none were destroyed. 1RTR suffered twenty casualties including only one KIA, the unlucky Trooper P. Dixon, killed behind the lines when his scout car was hit by a chance shell. As previously, most of the danger came from Chinese artillery and mortar fire, and it was not unusual for a troop to receive about 200 bombs and shells each day. US Flak jackets were issued in an attempt to reduce casualties from shell splinters.

On 28 May 1952, halfway through the tour, the Chinese dropped a huge artillery barrage on the Commonwealth positions and then attacked using human-wave tactics. One tank in B Squadron was struck by what was thought to be an

85mm solid shot which failed to penetrate, a rare example of the Chinese using direct anti-tank fire against the Centurions. But it was C Squadron who found themselves in the thick of the action, supporting 1st Bn Duke of Wellington's Regiment on the Hook. Managing – just – to defeat the enemy waves with a combination of 20-pounders and BESA MG fire, each tank received an average of 5 hits and they fired over 500 rounds of HE and nearly 30 rounds of MG. This was the last major assault directed against the Commonwealth Division, although B Squadron, taking their turn on the Hook, fought off a heavy attack on 24 July directed against the neighbouring US Marines and which spilled over into their area. An armistice was signed on 27 July 1953, and instructions for the ceasefire were read out personally by officers or transmitted over the radio net. Lance Corporal Fawkes of B Squadron read out the instructions over the wireless at 2200 hours, simply commenting that he was 'glad it is all over'.[72]

When 5RTR was sent out to replace The First at the end of 1953, the uneasy ceasefire was generally observed, although one trooper was killed when he stepped on a mine, but the unit spent a fairly boring year based in Gloucester Valley Camp, with various schemes and exercises used to maintain readiness. Doubtless this led to the usual mixed feelings – a desire for some 'real' action, and a dread that this might become reality. A surprising incident that turned to hilarity came about when propaganda leaflets were suddenly dropped over their camp, promising anyone £1 million if they delivered a Centurion tank to the north; history does not record if anyone seriously considered this lucrative offer. Although some mobile exercises were possible, many of the lower ranks found themselves as a labour force, assisting in strengthening the already strong defensive positions. At the end of the tour in late December 1954 the unit returned home, shipping the Centurions with them and ending the RAC involvement in the peninsula.

Cyprus, 1954–60

Cyprus is a rocky eastern Mediterranean island of some 3,500 square miles, about 140 miles in length and half the size of Wales. It is dominated by two main mountain ranges, the larger and more wooded Troodos in the west, and the long and narrow Kyrenian range in the north, with a large flat central plan in between which houses the capital city of Nicosia. Aside from this and the small port town of Kyrenia on the northern coast, the other major towns are located on the southern and eastern coasts: from the west these are Paphos, Limassol, Larnaca and Famagusta. The climate is subtropical, with a very hot summer season but with snow possible in the higher peaks of the Troodos during winter.

In 1878, at the Congress of Berlin, Britain took control of the island of Cyprus from the Ottoman Empire, formally annexing the territory in 1914 at the outbreak of the First World War. In 1925 it became a British Crown Colony. Cyprus is the third largest island of the Mediterranean and gave Britain a useful base close to, but not dependent on, the other imperial interests in the area, Egypt and Palestine. During the Second World War there had been some concerns that the island might be seized by the Axis (as had happened to Crete), and consequently it was garrisoned, including by a number of RAC units. In the event it was not seriously threatened, and the country became something of a backwater, but had the advantage of allowing troops to live less stressful lives there than they would in other parts of the Middle East, and the time was often used by the RAC units to conduct training and conversions. During the late 1940s Cyprus was an operational leave centre for troops stationed in Palestine and Egypt, with two camps operated near Famagusta, the wonderfully named Golden Sands Camp organized by the NAAFI and the rather more prosaic Number 181 Leave Camp, an army run affair. At this time the civil population was a little over ½ million, of whom about 80 per cent were Greeks, with the majority of the remainder being of Turkish descent.[73] Both sides hoped for a closer political affiliation, even to the extent of unification, with their homelands, and it was this, allied to a desire for full independence from Britain, that set the scene for the outbreak of serious violence in the mid-1950s.

By 1954 it was clear that Britain would be forced to leave Egypt sooner rather than later, and so in June it was decided to transfer HQ Middle East to Cyprus. It was initially based in Wolseley Barracks in Nicosia from 1 December, but with the intention of moving into a new base to be built in the village of Episkopi close to Limassol, along with a new RAF airbase at nearby Akrotiri, designed to relieve the pressure on RAF Nicosia. The timing of this was unfortunate; to the Cypriots, of both stripes, it looked as though the colonial power was strengthening its hold on the island; in fact, there were no plans to increase the amount of active units based on the island. At exactly the same time a strident nationalist movement, headed by the new leader of the Cypriot Greek Orthodox church, Archbishop Makarios III, was calling for Enosis – unification with Greece which of course would mean the end of British rule.[74] The idea of Enosis was not new, as it dated back to when the island was part of the Muslim Ottoman Empire, in which the Greeks were the minority and who naturally turned to their original community for protection.[75] Since the late 1920s there had been regular calls for Enosis, accompanied by outbreaks of violence, but despite an illegal plebiscite being organized by the church – with Greeks only voting – neither Britain nor the United Nations were in favour of self-determination.

In early 1955 the garrison that made up Cyprus District was extremely small, consisting of only two infantry battalions and a gunner regiment, plus some support units, but with no armour. Unbeknown to them, revolutionary elements from within the Greek Cypriot community were – with much help from Athens including the smuggling of arms and explosives – organizing an underground army, named in early 1955 as Ethniki Organosis Kyprion Agoniston, or EOKA for short.[76] The military leader of EOKA throughout the campaign would be Colonel George Grivas, an experienced Greek army officer and fervent supporter of Enosis. Resourceful but utterly ruthless, it would be Grivas who gave the orders or approved of the subsequent operations that killed and injured hundreds of people, including many civilians. The first attacks came with a series of bomb attacks on April Fool's Day 1955; as one historian drily recorded, this was 'an ironic date presaging four year's devoid of laughter'.[77] An indication of things to come occurred the following day, when a grenade was thrown into a bus carrying service wives in Nicosia; fortunately it failed to explode.[78] The small British garrison lacked intelligence sources, and could only do its best to protect vital installations – many more troops would be required for them to be able to undertake offensive operations against the terrorists. The Cypriot police were the targets of many attacks, not only on their stations but also with the assassination of ethnic Greek policemen who supported the rule of law and not the insurgency. The first British soldier to be killed in action died in a grenade attack on 27 October, amid a three-fold reinforcement of the garrison, but which still saw the units spread too far and too thinly. A State of Emergency was declared on 26 November 1955; as a result servicemen were now on active service and would qualify for the Cyprus clasp to the General Service Medal after 120 days' service (later reduced to 90).[79]

The main problem faced by the authorities was a near-complete lack of intelligence. Almost all of the Greek population, egged on by hate-filled rhetoric from Athens, supported the aims of EOKA and were partisan in the extreme. Not only would British troops find themselves having to deal with riots, but they were also frequently stoned by civilians (mostly youths) and when assassinations took place, often in broad daylight in busy streets, no witnesses could be found to come forward and identify the attackers. The guerrillas had a range of options to use as hideaways, from carefully concealed man-made caves and monasteries in the mountains, to elaborately constructed secret areas in supporters' houses, similar to priest holes. This meant that early British tactics amounted to trying to reduce the impact of riots, to carry out hot pursuits following shooting and bombing incidents, and, most likely to succeed but also the most intensive in manpower, cordon and search operations.[80] Infiltration of British camps and residences was to be another real problem in the years to come, and EOKA found it relatively easy to place bombs inside the wire, including by NAAFI employees.

In 1955 the Life Guards, the only RAC armoured car regiment remaining in Egypt, was asked to send a number of armoured cars to provide an escort for the Military Governor in Nicosia – the lesson from Malaya had clearly been learned. Shortly afterwards, the remainder of A Squadron was sent, taking Second World War-era Daimler Armoured and Dingo Scout Cars. Until their replacement by a complete armoured car regiment in the shape of the Royal Horse Guards (The Blues) in late February 1956, this squadron represented the only armoured vehicles on the island, making them much in demand.[81]

The Blues were shortly to be equipped with brand new Ferret Scout Cars and Saracen APCs. As the new Saladin Armoured Cars were still not yet ready for service the venerable Daimler Armoured Cars soldiered on. Despite this threefold increase in armour, they still found themselves with more tasks than they could cover, and had to disperse the three squadrons across the island, in Nicosia (Camp Elizabeth, named in honour of Queen Elizabeth II), Limassol and Famagusta.[82] Further reinforcements were not forthcoming, as the RAC was stretched elsewhere, in Suez, Malaya and increasingly in the Persian Gulf, and a policy remained in place that units in BAOR were not to be sent elsewhere. The solitary RAC unit was there to provide patrols and escorts, road blocks and observation posts, as well as assisting in cordon and search by providing a mobile reserve of firepower. A problem was that the cars could only be used on roads and well-made tracks, and not in the mountain forests nor in the town centres. It appears that EOKA deliberately avoided contact with them where possible, preferring a strategy of going after soft targets, including off-duty soldiers and even their families with many grenade attacks conducted against married quarters and civilian hirings – fortunately many such devices were home-made and failed to explode. The Blues' first casualty in action was on 26 September 1956; their doctor, Surgeon Captain Gordon Wilson, was murdered in his car after treating a Greek-Cypriot woman.[83] In particularly callous incidents marked ambulances and civilian females were deliberately targeted; also in September 1956, Mrs Mary Horton working for the Women's Voluntary Service providing welfare support for service personnel was killed in an ambush, and Mrs Catherine Cutliffe, a gunner's wife, was shot in the back in front of her daughter whilst shopping in Hermes Street, Famagusta in early October 1958, with another wife Mrs Robinson being badly wounded in the same cowardly attack. Another victim was Sergeant Wilfred Jepson of 14th/20th Hussars serving on detachment on the island, who was murdered and his wife injured in front of their young daughter whilst returning from a church service.[84] One commentator noted that almost without exception, British gunshot casualties during the Emergency were shot from behind.

In 1956 there was an upsurge in violence, partly as EOKA became more experienced and confident, but mainly due to the arrest and deportation of the vitriolic Makarios – when his home was searched it contained not only bomb-making materials but also communications with Grivas approving the executions of civilians viewed as opposed to the idea of Enosis. In order to reduce the amount of hate being broadcast on civilian radio from Greece, the broadcasts of Radio Athens were jammed. Despite various attempts at ceasefires – and respected by Grivas only when it suited him – violence continued but despite the enormity of the task, many terrorists were either killed or captured during search operations; the end of the winter of 1956/57 saw EOKA in a parlous state, although Grivas still eluded capture.

The Ferret Scout Car, here in its Mk 1 turretless version, came into its own in Cyprus, being both fast and nippy, carrying a machine gun and being proof against small-arms fire.

With the lack of intelligence, the vigilance of individual soldiers could be key, as The Blues discovered:

> [On 22 October 1957] Trooper Murray, a 19-year old A Squadron scout car driver, observed two boys stuffing something down the lining of the bus seat they occupied ... he extracted two sellotaped paper packets. These contained copies of Grivas' island-wide orders for activity during the celebrations on Oxi day, 29 October ... Entirely owing to Murray's alertness, realistic preventative measures were taken and EOKA's plans misfired.[85]

During late 1956 there was a huge influx of additional troops onto the island as a result of the Suez Crisis and at first some of these were able to be used on operations, but towards the end of the year most of them were focused on the upcoming invasion of Egypt, and other troops then had to be diverted from anti-EOKA tasks to protect these units, thus giving EOKA a much-needed respite.

In spring 1957 the negotiated release of Makarios from exile in the Seychelles (although he could not return to Cyprus) had marked the start of a new phase with some potential for ending the conflict – by this time the number of troops in Cyprus had increased dramatically, with twenty-six major units stationed on the island. Despite this attacks continued and in late November 1957 terrorists succeeded in penetrating the RAF airbase at Akrotiri and destroying one

In early 1956 the Royal Horse Guards deployed as a complete regiment to Cyprus; they continued to use the Daimler Armoured Car as the new Saladins were still not available.

Canberra jet bomber and damaging four other aircraft; once again it proved to be an inside job, and in order to reduce such attacks all 3,000 of the local NAAFI employees were sacked and replaced by volunteers from the UK. Not all of the attacks were directed against the British, and at regular intervals the troops found themselves being asked to prevent often savage inter-community violence between the Greeks and the Turks. On 5 July 1958 the experienced Blues found themselves involved in an incident which in many ways typified their experience:

> In the midst of the heat and madness a patrol of four armoured cars from those widespread peacekeepers, the Blues, visited the village of Avgorou, not far from Famagusta. The subaltern in command [Blake] ordered the arrest of a youth who kept taunting the troops with EOKA symbols. Seven troopers dismounted and grabbed him but were set upon by a group of villagers, men and women, who fired the boy … Three more cars arrived with twenty four men. They tried to enter the house but were forced back by a deluge of bricks and stones. The villagers then charged en masse, and forced the troopers back into their cars. One man hit the officer in the face with a brick and leapt onto his armoured car. The officer carefully elevated

his machine gun so as to hit no-one else and killed the man with a short burst. The Blues then withdrew, leaving one other dead behind them, a woman who had been killed by a stone ... of course the Greeks made the most of the two killings, blaming that of the woman on the 'British murderers'.[86]

Unfortunately revenge was a way of life for the Cypriots and five days later two of The Royals, Cornet Fox-Strangeways and Trooper Proctor, both National Servicemen, were shot in the back in the same street in Famagusta that would shortly witness the murder of Mrs Cunliffe. Less typical but also worth reporting at length was the experience of Cornet Auberon Waugh, son of Evelyn and later to become a famous writer himself. A National Service officer with The Blues, he recounted his story as follows:

On patrol, we always travelled with a belt in the machine guns of the armoured cars, but without a bullet in the breech. The machine guns we had trained on, called Besa, needed two cocking actions to put a bullet in the breech. The Browning which we had in Cyprus needed only one. It is most probable that I cocked the gun in a moment of absent-mindedness ... I had noticed an impediment in the elevation of the machine gun in my armoured car, and used the opportunity of our taking up position to dismount [and] seize the barrel from in front and give it a good wiggle. A split second later I realized that it had started firing ... I had received six bullets – four through the chest and shoulder, one through my arm, one through the left hand. My troop Corporal of Horse, who had been on patrol arrived back at that moment and swore horribly at my driver, whom he imagined to be responsible ... The machine gun had shot nearly the whole belt – about 250 rounds – into the Kyrenia road, before being stopped by Corporal Skinner ... In the silence which followed, Corporal of Horse Chudleigh came back to me, saluted in a rather melodramatic way as I lay on the ground ... He was a tough Bristolian parachutist and pentathlete. On this occasion he looked so solemn that I could not resist the temptation of saying 'Kiss me Chudleigh'. [He] did not spot the historical reference and treated me with some caution thereafter.[87]

Waugh's foolishness in June 1958 probably marked the low point in what was otherwise a most successful tour for The Blues. In late January 1957 an A Squadron patrol, operating with Special Branch, had arrested one of the most notorious terrorists, Nicos Sampson, the self-confessed killer of Captain Wilson and who will appear again much later in the narrative. Showing admirable flexibility, they even returned to an earlier way of life when A Squadron made use of donkeys (and sometimes bicycles) in the Troodos Mountains, which not only gave them improved mobility on the steep mountain tracks, but were also all-but silent – the noise of the armoured cars' engines often gave away their approach, allowing terrorists to flee. The regiment also devised a system of mounting 2in mortars onto the cars, allowing them to fire illumination flares for night operations. Despite such professionalism, tragic incidents still occurred: in October 1958 Cornet Wilson was nearly killed when his Ferret was blown up by an improvised mine in the Kyrenian Mountains; the car was flung 400ft into a valley killing the driver, Trooper Birch, but Wilson somehow managed to grab hold of a ledge which saved his life. In a very different type on incident in December 1958 Trooper (acting Corporal) Jeffrey Marklew won a George Medal attempting to rescue Captain Mulady, the pilot of a burning Auster light aircraft which had struck overhead power cables and crashed near Nicosia.

In early May 1959, just over two months after the declared end of the Emergency on 19 February, 12th Lancers replaced The Blues, allowing them to return to the UK after an operational tour lasting just over three years.[88] The Twelfth were clearly not at all enamoured of their new posting, describing Cyprus as:

> Not a particularly popular station … although parts are outstandingly beautiful [it] gives a general impression of poverty and squalor … [with] little to offer apart from dust, rubbish and empty beer cans … the camp at Nicosia was perhaps the most uncomfortable that the regiment has occupied for many years … Heat, dust and glare in the summer were replaced by gales, rain and deep mud in the winter.

By now patience on all sides was all but exhausted and a series of high-level negotiations took place, and on 19 February 1960 it was announced that Cyprus would be granted independence within the Commonwealth; Makarios was allowed to return on 1 March. Independence as a republic was achieved on 16 August 1960, which suited Makarios but not the embittered Grivas and some of the more hard-line EOKA leaders, who still wanted to become part of Greece, and most definitely did not wish to form an independent state that made significant concessions to its Turkish minority. The weaknesses in the structure of the new state meant that trouble was never far from the surface, and Britain would remain committed to the island, albeit in different forms, for decades to come. As a key part of the independence deal, 99 square miles of territory were retained in order to form two Sovereign Base Areas (SBA): the now completed cantonment at Episkopi plus RAF Akrotiri in the west, and Alexander Barracks in Dhekelia (plus the small RAF station at Pergamos and a Royal Signals outpost at Ayios Nikolaos) in the east.[89] Somewhat fittingly, the final RAC unit to serve in Cyprus before independence was The Blues, who suddenly found themselves sent back to the island in late June 1960 as emergency cover for the last months of British rule, before quietly leaving the day before independence.[90]

Unfortunately for all, independence did not mean the same as lasting peace, and we shall return to the troubled island in due course. In the course of the emergency just over 100 British service personnel were killed in action, with over 600 wounded; including the non-battle casualties, the number of deaths rises to 371.[91] It was a messy, brutal campaign, with the assassinations of service personnel and the deliberate targeting of service dependents making it especially distasteful. However, if there was some good to come out of it, it was that the army built on its experience of conducting counter-insurgency campaigns, and also its understanding of how to deal with internal security problems, both of which would be used in Aden and then Northern Ireland over the next decade.

The Gulf Region, 1954–71

Jordan

The first post-war RAC commitment in the Persian Gulf region was the deployment of an armoured regiment to Aqaba, in southern Jordan, accompanied by families. This began in December 1954 when The Bays were sent to Wessex Camp for a tour lasting just over a year, being replaced at the end of February 1956 by 10th Hussars. One squadron was always on detached duty at Ma'an, in the interior of the country. The unit had been placed on high alert during the Suez Crisis, with the families being sent home or moved to Cyprus. When the tour was completed in mid-April 1957 the regiment was not replaced, and three of their tanks were sent to the Iraqi army which had purchased them, the remainder being shipped home. Tragically, the greatest loss of life suffered by a single RAC unit in peacetime happened then when the Hussars, in the process of pulling out of Aqaba, lost eighteen of their number plus six attached soldiers when the RAF Valetta aircraft they were travelling in crashed on 17 April 1957; three RAF crewmen were also killed.[92] The accident occurred when the aircraft's port wing collapsed in severe weather causing it to crash about 20 miles out from Aqaba. The soldiers were buried at RAF Habbaniya in Iraq.

South Arabia

Aden is an Arabian province at the south-western tip of the Arabian peninsula, close to the entrance of the Red Sea and the sea lanes to the Suez Canal. The city of Aden is to the eastern side of a bay, with Little Aden to the west; the water between the two forms a large natural harbour. (Little Aden was the site of a British Petroleum oil refinery that became the base location for the RAC troops stationed in Aden, known variously as Mareth Lines, Falaise Camp and Balaklava Camp.) Although desperately poor and undeveloped, Aden had become an important coaling station for the Royal Navy from 1839, and became a Crown Colony in 1937. During the Second World War it was a staging point for naval movements between Egypt and India. After the war the RAF re-assumed command of the area, having previously formed four battalions of local troops commanded by British army officers, and called the Aden Protectorate Levies, or APL.[93] This area of south Arabia, with hostile Yemen to the north and friendly Muscat and Oman to the east, was itself divided into two areas, the Western Protectorate which included Aden in the west, and the much larger Eastern Protectorate, the size of France, to the east; each Protectorate consisted of a number of sheikhdoms. Under some pressure from Britain, the Federation of Arab Emirates of the South (later renamed as the Federation of South Arabia) was formed from six of the sheikhdoms in February 1959, with four others joining shortly afterwards and, very grudgingly, Aden joined in January 1963. The country is harsh, rocky desert, with a coastal plain overlooked by steep and often impassable peaks and mountain ridges. Inland temperatures frequently top 100 degrees of dry heat, requiring special provision to be made for logistic supply; on medical advice, British soldiers operating in the region required 2 gallons of drinking water each day. Frequent dust storms could make life extremely difficult, and Aden and the coastal areas could be both hot and humid.

Of greatest security concern was the Republic of Yemen, which considered Aden and the other sheikhdoms in the Protectorates to be part of that country, partly as this would give Yemen control of Aden port and thus better access to the Indian Ocean. Of Marxist leanings and strongly and openly egged on by Nasser's Egypt, Yemeni forces and proxies would be the direct and indirect source of many attacks on British personnel, and families, in Aden. The Imam of Yemen was behind the violence that started in 1955, and he would continue to agitate to remove the British presence from the region, including harbouring, training and supplying those who were prepared to fight the British, and who were generally referred to by the somewhat innocuous-sounding title of dissidents; the troops preferred the slang 'Dizzies'.

When violence erupted against the British in June 1955, with attacks killing two RAF officers and a dozen of the Levies in the up-country state of Upper Aulaqi, the army had to be called upon to step in; once again, the proponents of 'air control' had to concede that there are many occasions when only boots on the ground can have the desired effect. Troops were despatched from the Canal Zone garrison which was in the final process of drawing down, including an armoured car squadron of the Life Guards. Because Ataq, the nearest airfield to the deployment location, was unable to take the heavy Hastings transport aircraft, the squadron had to land at RAF Khormaksar in Aden and then take their new Ferret Scout Cars overland along a circuitous route of nearly 350 miles, where the absence of real roads made the deployment very difficult. Two broken-down scout cars and seven lorries had to be left behind as testament to the hard going; it was to take the squadron a four-day trek into the interior just to marry up with the infantry battalion they were to support. A day or so later an advance was made against a dissident-held area, and with fire support from the machine

An RTR Mk 2 Ferret in the mountainous terrain of South Arabia. Although it was vulnerable to mines, the vehicle once again proved its utility in both Aden and the Radfan.

guns of the Ferrets, relieved the siege of a fortress, the enemy preferring on this occasion to not engage the British army – although this would not always be the case. The squadron remained as the only RAC unit in Aden until April 1956 when they were redeployed. From mid-1957 an armoured car squadron was routinely posted to Aden in order to provide the mobility necessary to support both the British forces and the APL.

Incredibly the first squadron selected for this task – from the whole of the RAC – A Squadron 15/19H, was just coming to the end of a thirty-three-month operational tour of Malaya when it was told that rather than returning to the UK with the rest of the regiment, it was being sent to Aden for six months instead. This was a damning reflection on just how stretched the British army, and the RAC in particular, had become as more and more operational commitments suddenly flared up in the mid-1950s.[94] As well as the standing commitments in BAOR and the Far East, the corps had to find troops to deploy to Suez, Cyprus, Jordan and now south Arabia, and such requirements generally fell heaviest on the armoured car units. On arrival, A Squadron had to be divided into two halves, to look after two separate commitments. One half squadron was something of a political statement and was sent to do very little in Mukalla in the Eastern Protectorate, and the other was based in Aden itself where this small and much busier force of only two sabre troops took on the role of convoy escorts and to generally use their mobility – and if required firepower – to maintain the peace. On arrival in Aden the squadron 2iC, Captain Murray, quickly realized that the existing convoy procedure was far too pedestrian and brought unnecessary risk, and introduced the concept of the fast convoy, which not only reduced the transit time to Dhala from a day to 3 hours, but also led to a complete cessation in ambushes. A different kind of risk then presented itself. Although mainly blazing hot and dry, when rain fell it came down in torrents, turning the passes through the mountains into death traps for the unwary. 'Tidal waves some four feet high' could roar down the routes with little warning, and one patrol commanded by Sergeant Harris only just had time to dismount and take refuge high up on the sides of a pass when such a flash flood carried away their 4-ton Ferrets, causing much damage.[95]

In mid-July 1957 the Sultan of Muscat requested British assistance in suppressing a rebellion, and a troop from the squadron was despatched to support an infantry battalion sent to the region. The ubiquitous Captain Murray was selected to lead the expedition, taking with him one of the troops from Mukalla as none could be spared from Aden.[96] The revolt started in the town of Nizwa and had resulted in the rebels taking possession of the fortress at Firq. The RAF airlifted the five Ferrets of the Hussars to the airstrip at Fahud, where they had to wait for the cooler evening before setting off – daytime temperatures exceeded 130 degrees. This involved a night journey over the desert of some 60 miles, navigating without a map and completed by following the tyre tracks made by the lorries of the infantry battalion that had left a day before. Arriving at Firq, a reconnaissance of the rebel position by Murray the next evening was met by fire and he had to cover the retreat of the patrol with his Browning. The following dawn, a deliberately restrained approach to the enemy position by the scout cars supporting the battalion led to the rebels retreating towards the sanctuary of the Jebel Akhdar, and Sergeant Congreve tore down the rebel flag from the fort. The troop was then stood down (taking a captured cannon with them) and moved across the desert for another 80 miles to Muscat where the vehicles received much-needed maintenance and repairs. Returning to Aden, A Squadron remained there until 4 October 1957 when they were relieved by B Squadron 13/18H, who arrived three weeks after 15/15H had departed, at the start of what would become a one-year tour.[97]

With only four sabre troops, the Lilywhites had to carry out the usual escort duties to and from Dhala in the Western Protectorate, station a troop (sometimes two) in Riyan in the Eastern Protectorate which was over 400 miles from the squadron HQ, as well as have another troop at Nizwa in Oman supporting the Sultan. The impossibility of this was recognized when in January 1958 two additional troops from the regiment's A Squadron were added to the order of battle, and in mid-April half of a Life Guards air-portable squadron further bolstered the force, which was now clearly approaching a regimental commitment.[98] Supporting the isolated detachments was a constant headache, requiring replenishment of fuel and ammunition, as well as spare parts for the vehicles, not to mention the ration and water requirements.

The detachment at Dhala, commanded by a newly commissioned National Service second lieutenant, was probably the busiest place to be stationed. The camp was spartan in the extreme, 5,500ft up in the mountains, and mainly supplied via the adjacent airstrip. As well as convoy escorts, the troop there patrolled the Yemeni border, sometimes being engaged from across it, including by both 75mm artillery fire and 12.7mm heavy machine guns. On a few occasions the troop acted as come-ons, 'trailing their coats' in full view in order to identify enemy firing positions which could then be targeted by artillery or air strikes. In April a large Yemeni cross-border raid besieged a fort that contained a British political officer. A relief column including a four-troop composite squadron (a troop of 13/18H, two from the LG and a troop from the APL squadron) was deployed. Described in the British press as an 'eighty mile running fight', the Hussars' squadron leader was more prosaic, and judged that during the operation they received only seven rounds of hostile fire. The fort and its occupants were relieved successfully. Second Lieutenant Mark Barty-King, the 18-year-old Hussar troop leader at Dhala and on the relief force, was subsequently awarded the MC.

Another troop found itself deployed by air to Ataq in order to assist in suppressing more tribal dissention, taking one day to travel 25 miles over the most appalling going, and sometimes having to use the vehicle jacks to get the Ferrets over boulders. On the return trip they were twice ambushed and one of the drivers was wounded; he was evacuated by helicopter after some spectacular flying through low cloud and along the wadi.[99] The other detached troop at Nizwa also had their share of action. In late March 1958 a two-car patrol commanded by Sergeant Steel was escorting vehicles from the Trucial Oman Scouts when the convoy was attacked on the outskirts of a village. Steel recalled:

> Immediately attacked, directing his scout cars' fire against the ambushers and effecting a successful diversion to cover the deployment of the Scouts … his immediate action saved many casualties. During the initial attack one British officer was shot and fell. Steel manoeuvred his car to shield him. Then, dismounting, he went to his aid, but found that he had been fatally wounded…. returning to his scout car he saw an Arab soldier lying wounded in the open and ran to his assistance. He returned to his vehicle to find the Scouts preparing to launch an attack … deploying his cars he directed covering fire … Firing began again and Steel returned to the wadi in an attempt to draw the dissident's fire. Later in the afternoon an attack was launched and Steel again [supported] the ground troops [when a demolition party] were pinned down. Steel again moved forward and directed covering fire and a diversion to cover the withdrawal. In the early hours of the following day, Sergeant Steel re-entered the area to recover the damaged Land Rover … Steel took over the damaged vehicle and was towed out of the wadi by the third scout car.

Four times during the action Steel dismounted under fire, and was later awarded a (somewhat parsimonious) Military Medal.

During their tour in Oman, an average of twenty British and Omani vehicles a month were blown up by mines using the road between Muscat and Nizwa. Damaged Ferrets often had to be towed over 100 miles across country to allow them to be loaded onto a Landing Craft and then shipped to Aden for workshops repair. At this point in the campaign it can be noted that the majority of the action was taking place in remote desert and mountain locations, far from the HQ element stationed in Aden. This would change. When B Squadron left Aden in early September 1958 – this time to re-join the regiment – it was to deploy to another trouble spot, Malaya, for their second consecutive operational tour.[100] Taking over from them was a regiment, the Life Guards (less one squadron). This also marked the point at which Sharjah, over 1,000 miles away in the north-eastern corner of the Arabian peninsula, became another commitment for the RAC unit in Arabia and which remained in being until 1971. Sharjah was one of the seven Trucial States (which became the United Arab Emirates in 1971) and which were deemed to be important for Britain to support. On a rotation basis, one of the sabre squadrons from the Aden armoured car regiment was detached to support and assist the Trucial Oman Scouts, and was based alongside the RAF airbase.[101] This was more of a training commitment, and the squadrons there took the opportunity to conduct long-range desert patrols, often for many hundreds of miles through the desert wilderness. This commitment came to an end when Britain withdrew from 'east of Suez' and the UAE was formed as an independent state.

Between November 1959, when The Royals relieved the Life Guards, and December 1963, when the Aden Emergency was declared following a grenade attack on the High Commissioner in which two were killed and over fifty wounded, another four regiments took their turns at providing the Aden armoured car unit. These were 11H, QRIH, 9/12L and then 4RTR, who had arrived in August 1963 and were in the process of proving to some critics in the cavalry that the RTR was perfectly capable of operating on armoured cars – meaning those in the cavalry who had somehow forgotten that it was the RTC armoured car companies which had converted them to armoured cars in the first place …[102]

The Royals, arriving in Aden in late 1959, commented that, 'It looked just like a penal settlement … Aden is an odd place; the finest cameras can be bought, probably cheaper than anywhere else in the world, but what is there to photograph? Wirelesses can be bought for next to nothing, but there is virtually nothing to listen to.' Taking over from them, 11th Hussars found Falaise Camp in Little Aden in November 1960 much better than they had expected, and remarked upon the excellent hospitality at the hands of BP who kindly allowed them to use their swimming pool – complete with 'its essential shark net!'. Laundry was rapid and cheap, and even troopers employed a 'boy' to look after their room and bull their boots and prepare their kit to a high standard. However, boredom was an enemy and the attractions of the camp, usually based on the reliably hot weather, would pall after a few weeks, and the Mermaid Club, cinema, NAAFI canteen and the locally run emporium (usually called the Golly Shop or similar) would become repetitive.[103] Many soldiers were surprised to realize that they preferred being 'up-country' on operations or training, although as the 1960s progressed, there was more of the former and less of the latter.

For the first few years of the 1960s the RAC regiments posted to Aden on one-year tours got into the routine of training, supporting operations and enjoying the delights, such as they were, of the station. Some units took the opportunities to mount expeditions into East Africa, and to experience novel sorts of adventure training; sub-aqua was popular, and one group of officers even went tiger hunting in India. This is not to say that life in Aden immediately before the emergency was declared was all sunbathing and swimming, far from it. In fact, the 9/12L history remarked that during a tour in which they had two squadrons stationed in Aden and one in Sharjah, it was noticeable that internal security incidents within Aden itself were becoming more frequent and they often had to deal with 'hostile demonstrations and riots'. In June 1963 a troop of C Squadron had to suppress mortar, machine-gun and field artillery fire in the area of Negd Murd. During the engagement some soldiers from the squadron even helped 3rd RHA with the ammunition supply for their 105mm pack howitzers in order to increase the rate of fire. A few days after this, an estimated sixty enemy personnel crossed the border and occupied a cluster of houses, supported by three artillery pieces, two anti-aircraft guns, three mortars, a heavy machine gun and even two APCs. After a night approach march the troop deployed at dawn, and 'a spirited fire-fight followed during which the Saladin fired forty rounds [of 76mm] and the gunners 180'. With incidents like this, the commanding officer noted that in a tour in which half of his troops had been engaged by enemy fire, he was surprised that no one in the War Office had seen fit to issue a clasp to the General Service Medal for a tour that was operational in everything but name.[104]

One of the biggest problems faced by the unit manning the Aden station was that parts of the regiment were always spread over a wide area, generally with the three sabre squadrons in three very different locations. Although this varied over time, most typically RHQ, the main Headquarters Squadron element, the REME LAD and one sabre squadron would be in Little Aden, and of the other two, they would be either 'up-country', which meant being somewhere up towards the Yemeni border, detached to Sharjah, forming the strategic amphibious reserve and therefore either in Bahrain or afloat somewhere in the Persian Gulf, or even fulfilling the single squadron commitment in Singapore or Hong Kong. As an example, in 1960, the CO of The Royals totted up the amount of time and distance he had spent flying in order to visit his widely dispersed troops that year; it came to 40,450 air miles with 157½ hours of his time spent in the air. As well as the roulement armoured car regiment, Centurion tank squadrons were also sent to Aden where the remote desert locations made excellent training areas; the first unit to do this was C Squadron QOH in March 1960, who also conducted amphibious trials and exercises in the region. From late 1962 a tank regiment was stationed in Aden, alongside the armoured car regiment, in an operational role.[105] Another problem faced by the Aden unit was that as well as keeping the peace in Aden and the Protectorates, the unit was also liable for emergency commitments within the Gulf region if required; in 1961 just such an issue arose, in Kuwait.

Kuwait, 1961

On 19 June 1961 Kuwait, at the time the leading oil producer in the region, became independent from Britain. Six days later the unstable leader of Iraq, Abdul Qasim, announced that Kuwait was going to be 'incorporated' into Iraq, most likely through military action and 'by the full moon'. Kuwait appealed to Britain for urgent military assistance. Operation Vantage was mounted in very short order, Britain having obligations to Kuwait that it felt had to be met swiftly and in force. As well as sending a very strong naval taskforce, Britain quickly deployed ground units including half a squadron (C) of 3rd Carabiniers, who were the amphibious tank unit in the northern Persian Gulf, there for just such an operation and which landed from the Landing Ship Tank HMS *Striker* on 1 July, ahead of the Royal Marines by half an hour. By the end of that day the British had half a brigade group in place and ready for action, a remarkable achievement, the other half of C Squadron having arrived and activated a stockpile of Centurions held in Kuwait for just such an emergency. Only two days later an advance party from A Squadron of The Carbs (stationed in Aliwal Barracks, Tidworth) arrived followed by the remainder of A Squadron and then RHQ, which activated more reserve tanks and brought more combat power to the defence. This force remained in place until 12 August, when B Squadron relieved C in order to allow them to return to Aden and prepare for their scheduled handover. In turn the remaining Carbs were relieved by 17/21L in late September who took over the tank role for the last few weeks until October, when the operation was terminated and the Arab League assumed responsibility for Kuwait's security.

It was also deemed necessary to deploy an armoured car regiment, and so on 3 July RHQ and three troops of A Squadron 11H arrived in Kuwait; over the next few days the remainder of A and all of B arrived, as well as most of HQ Squadron and the LAD, flown in from Aden and taking over vehicles from the reserve stockpile. They would remain there until October in a covering force role on the border.[106] Key to holding Kuwait from any incursion was the dominating feature of the Mutla ridge, north of Kuwait city. Both RAC units reported just how awful the conditions within Kuwait were, as the operation took place in the hottest part of the year, and logistic support was of the ad hoc variety. Within the first five days 10 per cent of the force was out of action needing medical treatment due to the

Centurions of 3rd Carabiniers deploying at speed to the dominating feature of the Mutla ridge in Kuwait, 1961. (Courtesy SCOTS DG)

effects of the heat – there had been no time for acclimatization for those coming from outside the region, and even those from elsewhere in the Gulf found the conditions much more intense. The daytime temperature was 125 degrees, and there was precious little shade to be found up on the ridge; The Carbs estimated that each man was drinking up to 5 gallons of water each day. They also noted that during this period elements from the regiment could be found in no less than eight locations concurrently: Tidworth, Warminster, Ogbourne St George transit camp, Cyprus, Aden, afloat in the Gulf, Bahrain and Kuwait, a span of command that would take some beating.

In 1963 after the fall of Qasim, Iraq finally recognized Kuwait's independence, but that was not the end of the story, and within three decades a much larger British force would find itself coming to the aid of Kuwait in a real shooting war, as will be recounted later.[107]

The Radfan Campaign

Also in 1963, and following the declaration of the Emergency in Aden in December, it was realized that one area of near-total lawlessness now needed to be dealt with. This was the Radfan, a large mountainous area about 70 miles north of Aden bordering Yemen and which was home to many thousands of dissidents, at least some of whom were more than happy to receive weaponry from Yemen and to use it against the British and the FRA. The first attempt to suppress the area started in early January 1964, under the codename Operation

Nutcracker. The main infantry components came from three battalions of the FRA operating for the first time as a brigade. The armoured car unit, now 4RTR, was in command of the armoured component of the operation, for which they were allocated one troop of B Squadron 16th/5th Lancers, equipped with the latest mark of the Centurion tank armed with the L7 105mm gun. It was not, by any stretch of the imagination, tank country, and a great deal of effort was expended in building an improved route up-country in order to make logistic resupply easier. It has been widely reported that it was in the Radfan during 1964 that the 16/5L became the first unit to use 105mm-armed Centurions in action, and claiming as they did so that they were also the first RAC unit to use tank main armament in action since Korea, completely forgetting about Suez in the process![108] The purpose of the tanks was to make a point about Britain's combat power, and the only time that B Squadron troop got to fire their 105mm guns was during a fire-power demonstration designed to make recalcitrant tribesmen think twice about tangling with such a force. Therefore, although the guns were fired within the scope of the operation, they were not used against the enemy … yet.

By the end of January Nutcracker had appeared to achieve its aim, and the locals had mostly decided not to engage the British force, which was then dispersed back to its bases. However, as the Lancers' history concedes, 'this was only a lull before the storm'. By the middle of April the campaign had to be re-opened, as the FRA were unable to cope with the increasing violence in the region, including much use being made of anti-tank mines. Three forward bases were occupied by the RAC units to mount operations from Thumeir, Wadi Taym and Dhala.[109] To increase the combat power of 4RTR, mainly from D Squadron equipped with Saladins and Ferrets, the Recce Tp and one tank troop of C Sqn 16/5L were attached, and remained under command until August. Patrolling and escorting convoys through the high mountain passes was reminiscent of the much earlier experience of fighting in the North-West Frontier of India, with snipers and mining incidents the main dangers; it was noted that, 'the chances of actually spotting a mine were slight and the only way to locate one was to run over it'. It was in this second phase of the campaign that 4th Tp C Sqn 16/5L did get to fire their 105mm guns in action, taking part in an operation to clear Bakri ridge on 19 May and then an advance down Wadi Misrah, 2 miles from the base at Thumeir on 21 May.[110] In August 1964 4RTR handed over the armoured car commitment to 10th Hussars, with the campaign still ongoing. The Hussars, returning to Arabia as an armoured car unit nearly a decade after the tragedy in Jordan, had ten vehicles mined during an Aden tour of thirteen months – seven Ferrets, two Saladins and one Scammel. The success in (mostly) suppressing the dissidents in Radfan had an unintended consequence, which was to shift the focus of the Yemeni-backed insurgency from the border area into the city of Aden itself.[111]

In the middle of December 1964 the Fifth Skins arrived as the resident tank unit, replacing the Lancers. The Skins found themselves detaching their

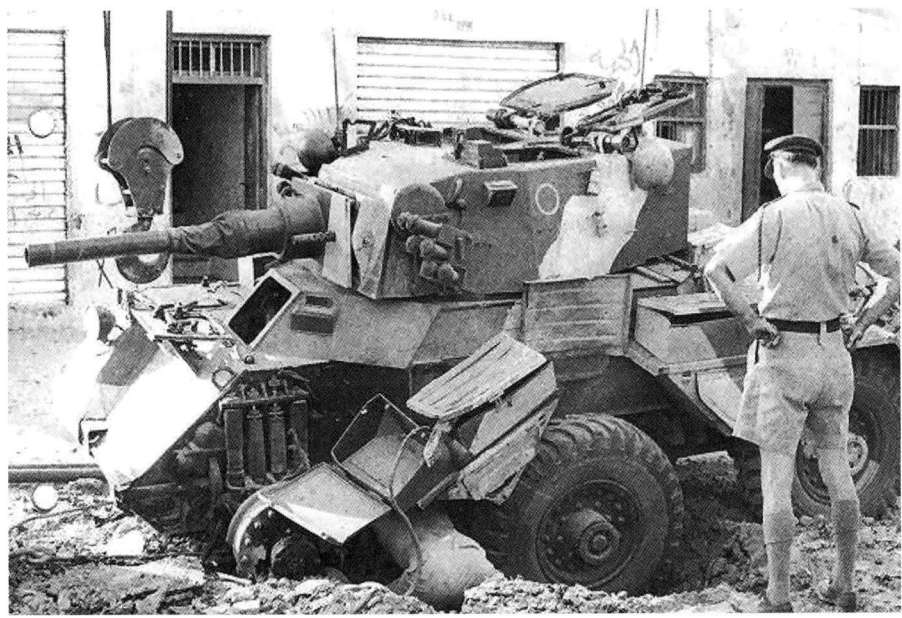

From August 1964 10th Hussars were the resident unit in Aden; mines were a frequent menace during their tour with ten vehicles including this Saladin falling prey to them.

armoured and scout-car elements from Recce Tp for duty in the Radfan with 10th Hussars, where locating the mines again proved to be difficult; both the commander and driver of the scout and armoured cars had to constantly keep a close eye out for tell-tale signs of ground disturbance, although with little chances of success if travelling at speed. The Ferret of Corporal McGinty hit a mine on the last day of 1964, and two days later Sergeant Barter's patrol was ambushed but luckily without casualties. In April 1965 two more Ferrets were mined, with the unlucky Sergeant Barter again one of the victims, this time falling prey to a Mk VII mine laid in a pool of muddy water which seriously injured his driver, Trooper Puckerin.[112] Partly as a result of this attack, all Ferrets were grounded for a period in May whilst the hulls were strengthened to make them more resistant to mine attack. The Saladins with their larger ground clearance proved to be a better vehicle at protecting the crews than the much lower Ferret, and as a result the newly introduced Stalwart load carrier, based on the Saladin/Saracen chassis, was successfully used as a troop carrier to lead wheeled convoys in those areas where mines were a major threat.

Sometimes the attacks were more direct, particularly on the known routes where the rebels often sniped at or attacked patrols and convoys, and occasionally even indulged in frontal attacks against bases, usually at night when it was less likely that they could be targeted by the RAF. Sergeant Binks of C Squadron 4th/7th Dragoon Guards won a splendid Military Medal in the Radfan on the night of 10 March 1966, when the base location he was in came under heavy attack. He sprinted through enemy fire for hundreds of yards from his tent to his Saladin, where he single-handedly loaded and fired the 76mm gun, destroying firstly an enemy rocket launcher and then another position held by riflemen. Two weeks later his Saladin was blown up by a mine whilst he was leading a convoy, and despite the damage coolly reported the situation accurately. His citation read, 'His conduct throughout the operations in the Radfan was an inspiration to all.'

Withdrawal from Arabia

The announcement by Prime Minister Wilson in early 1966 that Britain intended to pull out of 'east of Suez', which included south Arabia, by 1968 was a strategic mistake, as it intensified the campaign against the British in Aden. This was in part because many of the locals, particularly those in the government, police and FRA, either left the country or threw in their lot with the side that was not guaranteed to triumph, the so-called dissidents. Intelligence almost dried up for the same reason, and it became more difficult to involve the FRA in planned operations, as security could easily be compromised. More British infantry was required and additional battalions had to be drafted in to deal with the increasing disorder; a reinforced B Squadron of 5RTR was converted to infantry within three weeks in order to increase the numbers between April and July 1967. The normal RAC commitment however remained the same, and the tank regiment clearly did not have the same utility as the armoured car unit, other than its Recce Tp. At this time, the first issue of the (later to be) famous Yellow (and Blue) Cards was made as part of the IS effort in Aden. These explained the rules for opening fire; previous to these, soldiers were issued an aide-memoire of sorts that was kept in their paybook. The card introduced the concept of the use of minimum force, and explained in outline the circumstances in which lethal force – opening fire – could be considered as reasonable. These early versions allowed the troops to use lethal force in the protection of property, which later versions, for example, in Northern Ireland, removed.[113]

The scale of the internal security issues meant that despite the intention to 'draw-down' and leave the colony, more troops were required, and there had to be a division of responsibilities. 24 Brigade looked after Little Aden and 'up-country', whilst Aden Garrison (later Aden Brigade) took responsibility for the urban sprawl of Aden city, which housed 700,000 mainly hostile inhabitants. The Queen's Dragoon Guards was the second-last RAC armoured car unit to fulfil the Aden role, from September 1966 until 21 July 1967, and extracts from the unit history gives an insight into the situations they found themselves dealing with:

A Squadron spent a quiet time in Sharjah, B Squadron operated on the Plain of Lahej, based in Little Aden, while C Squadron was up in the Radfan. Another detachment was at Beihan on the edge of the empty Quarter. The QDG Air Squadron was based at Falaise airfield in Little

Aden. The squadrons were moved around every three months or so, partly to give the hard-worked operational squadrons in Aden a change and a rest, and also to give everyone varied experience … A detachment in the native town of Sheikh Othman [between Aden and little Aden] supported the resident infantry battalion, and came under regular attack.[114] Corporal Giles and Trooper Mayo were wounded by grenades whilst out on patrols, Mayo seriously when the grenade was lobbed into the turret of the armoured car. B Squadron Headquarters also came under mortar attack.[115]

In Dhala … the Musaymir detachment found two mines outside their front gate. Early in January 1967 the dissidents attacked the camp at Habilayn one night; twenty-eight belts of Browning and forty-six rounds of 76mm were fired and the attack was beaten off. On 12 January the outposts at Musaymir and Dhala were withdrawn, and a few days later the squadron came back to Little Aden.

In Aden there came a series of incidents from 10 to 14 February, during which British troops were attacked sixty-six times. On the 13th a troop had a grenade explode under their Saracen, whereupon a section of the Irish Guards debussed and killed the thrower. On 28 February Sgt Dakin was supporting a platoon of the Northumberland Fusiliers who came under heavy rifle and automatic fire. Dakin burst through a gate and arrested twelve locals, some of whom were caught with 'warm-barrelled' pistols in their hands.

In order to control the flow of arms and ammunition into Aden, a series of searches and checks were carried out in the desert and on the frontier under Operation Band. The regiment searched 4883 vehicles, 23000 individuals, and 449 animals. It was long hours with little reward.

A UN mission arrived on 2 April, and during the five days that it was in Aden the QDG were involved in more than ninety incidents, including three major street fights … 6000 rounds of Browning machine gun and 500 rounds of other small arms were fired to protect the infantry … In Little Aden a crowd of fifty gathered to watch a scout car commander being decapitated by a wire stretched across the street. Fortunately the car's turret broke the wire. The crowd were enormously amused and so the car commander arrested the man who was laughing the most.

In fact it was never a funny place to soldier in. During the five days that the UN mission was in Aden – locking themselves up in a hotel and rarely venturing out – there was a noticeable upsurge in violence and eighteen servicemen were wounded. The unit history again:

Cpl Withycombe had four grenades thrown at his vehicle in ten minutes …
Lt Grounds had a narrow escape [when] a rocket was fired from a building

above him, skimming over one mudguard, flashing across the glacis plate and bouncing off the other mudguard to explode in the road a yard in front of his Saladin.

The Air Squadron were also busy. Sergeant Forde, the son of Sergeant Major Forde of The Bays, an antecedent regiment:

> … was asked to fly his helicopter to retrieve four Fusiliers on picket duty … He flew in and picked up the first pair, landing only for the briefest moment as the area of the picket was under aimed fire. The Fusiliers jumped onto the panniers on each side of the helicopter. He then went back to pick up the second pair, and when they were in the panniers, he lifted off, rose to about fifty feet, then was hit in the knee, and was unable to operate the tail rotor. In spite of this he managed to land the machine, but he couldn't get out. One Fusilier had a leg broken and the other severed, so couldn't move. The other, Duffey, leaped off his pannier, released Sergeant Forde, dragged him out, went back for his friend, dragged him away also, then went back for the wireless set – then the aircraft caught fire and burned out. All three were picked up by another aircraft and taken to safety.[116]

On 27 July 1967 the QDG left Aden, having handed over to the Queen's Own Hussars, who remained there, battling right through their four-month tour before departing in November; their camp, and responsibilities for, Little Aden were handed over on 13 September. During the emergency 68 British soldiers had lost their lives, and over 300 were wounded in action. Aden became independent as the capital of the People's Republic of South Yemen on 30 November 1967; at least some of the departing Hussars probably realized that countries that call themselves People's Republics are invariably neither democratic nor formed for the good of the people, as the subsequent history of the region has reinforced.

The Borneo Confrontation, 1963–6

Fought between April 1963 and August 1966, this conflict was called a 'confrontation', a word taken from the state that initiated it. In fact, it was an undeclared war and was in many ways a part of the wider Cold War, fought by a proxy of both the Soviet Union and China – Indonesia – against the new state of Malaya which was supported by Britain, Australia and New Zealand. In 1957 the Federation of Malaya became independent from Britain; in May 1961 the UK and Malayan governments jointly proposed an enlarged Federation to be called Malaysia, and which would include three states that did not form part of peninsula Malaya – North Borneo, Sarawak and Brunei. These states were located in the northern quarter of the island of Borneo, with Indonesia owning the remainder. Indonesia began to assist the TNKU, a Marxist guerrilla army based on the island. In late December 1962 the TNKU started what would be called the Brunei Revolt, and which led to British forces being mobilized from Singapore in support of the Sultan. The revolt was poorly planned and executed, and was ended five months later by the direct intervention of the British forces, including special forces (22SAS) and Gurkhas. On 15 December 1962 C Squadron Queen's Royal Irish Hussars was hurriedly deployed from mainland Malaya and arrived in early October on what they thought was going to be an accompanied tour.[117]

However, in January 1963 the Indonesian Foreign Minister publicly announced a policy of *konfrontasi*, meaning in effect that it would not recognize Malaya and sending sponsored guerrilla forces into action, with the first overt attack made on a police station in Sarawak in mid–April. The topography and political make-up of Borneo lent itself to a guerrilla campaign. The border between the northern states and Indonesia is over 1,100 miles long, and is difficult to mark on the ground, as it wends its way through deep jungle and mountainous ridges, crossed by numerous rivers and streams. Roads were few and poor. Due to the lack of crime, the police force was weak and possessed no intelligence capacity, and the armed forces of Malaya were still dealing with the Malayan Emergency.

Borneo was in no sense a campaign obviously suited to the involvement of AFVs, at least not in most circumstances. It is probably fair to say that had the armoured car units not previously proved their utility in complex and unforgiving terrain, particularly in Malaya, no one would have thought to despatch armour to the island. However, as soon as trouble flared up it was decided that an armoured car squadron could be useful, and so it proved. Although C Sqn QRIH and its successors only had limited impact during the Brunei Revolt, the small force of Saladins and Ferrets gave the unfolding campaign a dimension that the Indonesians could not match.

The QRIH rotated its three sabre squadrons, plus the associated 'slice' of the HQ logistic and support personnel and equipment, through the commitment; at some points additional sabre troops from Singapore or Malaya reinforced the squadron, meaning that some personnel spent about half of their time in the Far East stationed in Borneo on operations. The main location was at Semengo Camp near Kuching in the west, with many outpost stations, including Simanggang, Bau, Sungei Tenggang and Serian – once again the nature of the campaign meant the dissipation of the squadron, making it very much a troop leader's war. During A Squadron's tour:

> The Saladin troops did a good deal of 76mm shooting at enemy incursions, as a deterrent to them and in support of Gurkhas and other battalions. The Ferret troops patrolled and escorted without ceasing, and also had the task of suppressing Communist subversion and attempts at militant action. In Sabah C Squadron scout cars went to places never visited by such vehicles before and succeeded in both reassuring the friendly and dismaying the dissident … River and foot patrols were as enjoyable and valuable as ever.[118]

A QRIH Saladin, once again a key component of the British ability to deploy armour quickly, on patrol in Borneo following Indonesian incursions. (Courtesy QRH)

One section of the newly founded air troop, using Auster light aircraft, assisted in 'searches, sea patrols and other air reconnaissance tasks'. The only casualty was:

Sgt Thackeray, who was shot at from the other side of the Indonesian border on his first sortie in December 1963. He was badly injured in the arm, and his passenger was mortally wounded. He did extremely well to put his Auster down in a jungle clearing without further injury to himself or his passenger, although the aircraft was smashed. Sgt Thackeray made a full recovery in hospital.[119]

The Hussars handed over to A Sqn 4RTR in September 1964; in the middle of August, Indonesia significantly upped the ante when it began to launch attacks against mainland Malaya, including seaborne landings on the east coast of the peninsula, and which had involved QRIH troops helping to round up the invaders. As each squadron of 4RTR arrived it immediately went on alert and as soon as it completed the takeover it was in effect straight on to active operations. This led to the squadron in Singapore, normally a peaceful posting with only some routine IS duties to perform, being placed on increased readiness in case of another invasion. Another landing was indeed attempted by the Indonesians on 29 October, but this was also a failure and was negated within 36 hours.[120] Back in Borneo, the troops stationed there on six-month tours – with the families either in Malaya or Singapore – found that as well as escort duties, some vehicles were used dug-in to support some of the small jungle outposts, as well as using Saladin 76mm gunnery to engage suspected enemy locations in mountain caves.

> … a company of 1st/10th Gurkhas, however, relied on one of our Saladin troops for some months to give it cover when they moved south for border operations, an Indos could pick them off from the ridge. The troop would move up and put down prophylactic fire along the ridge line at absolute maximum elevation.[121]

Specific difficulties were discovered. Unlike the Yemenis who the regiment had fought in Aden, the guerrillas did not stand and fight. The C13 HF radios they were equipped with for long-range communications were all-but-useless at night, because of tropical conditions, which prevented swift responses to incidents and allowed bandits to melt away before a quick reaction force could arrive. In one case, the enemy covered a road with oil, presumably one of the few with tarmac, so that the scout cars skidded off the road when they arrived. A support troop was founded and acted purely in the infantry role, and other forms of dominating the area were employed. The CO of 42 Commando Royal Marines said of the regiment that 'they drive, march, boat and helicopter in, and there's nothing they won't try'.[122] 4RTR was the first RAC regiment to send its troops to the Jungle Warfare School in Malaya, where the arduous two-week course culminated in a three-day exercise in the *ulu*; this was adjudged to be extremely useful.

In February 1965 B Squadron The Queen's Dragoon Guards took over the Borneo task, handing over to C Squadron after six months. B Sqn moved to the Far East from Northern Ireland, and the regimental history recounts an amusing if probably apocryphal retelling of the events surrounding the deployment:

> QDG was ordered to send an air-portable squadron to Cyprus in ten days' time … On day nine a telephone call from the Ministry of Defence said 'Sorry, a terrible mistake. We meant an armoured car squadron, and we

meant Borneo not Cyprus.' Within six days all of the squadron's vehicles, together with a flight of QDG [Skeeter] helicopters, were loaded at Belfast …

They took over similar tasks to their predecessors, and gave a useful description of the conditions:

[The squadron] base was situated on a small knoll around a police post, with sandbagged bashas for everyone, weapon pits and bunkers. The post was surrounded by barbed wire and panjis (sharpened slivers of bamboo). One night an Indonesian patrol of three men reached the perimeter fence, but were driven off. The rainfall in Borneo measured nearly 200 inches a year, falling mainly in a daily deluge around dusk … other patrols used a [native] long boat fitted with an outboard motor to cruise up and down the rivers. The two Saladins at Batu Lintang were dug in and helped to repel an attack on the 1st/10th Gurkhas soon after their arrival.[123]

From February 1966 H Squadron 5RTR replaced them; they were quickly in action, as the regimental history recounts, 'Within forty-five minutes of taking over, 4 Troop was called out, and within a few days the rest had found out what it was like to lie in ambush for forty hours in the rain'. The final RAC squadron arrived on 23 July 1967 and came from the Life Guards. The confrontation was officially ended on 11 August 1966, with C Sqn The Life Guards being stood down and re-joining the rest of the regiment in Malaysia a month later. The Indonesian attempt to subvert and undermine one of its neighbours had failed completely. Four RAC soldiers, three from QRIH and one from 4RTR, had died during the operation.

Hong Kong

Possibly the most exotic of all the overseas RAC postings, Hong Kong (aka Honkers) was not classed as an operational tour, despite being – a bit like Berlin – surrounded by a potentially hostile Communist enemy. After the Japanese had been removed from the colony at the end of the Second World War, the garrison settled down with a brigade of infantry and an RA field regiment, but with no RAC commitment. However, the ascendancy of Mao in the Chinese civil war of 1948 made plain that a larger British military commitment was required to deter any aggression, and so in May 1949 B Squadron 3RTR was quickly despatched from Bovington in order to provide a Comet tank unit. Within weeks it was decided to increase this to a whole regiment, so the rest of 3RTR followed, arriving in early August 1949 at San Wei Camp; after a year, a new and more permanent camp at Sek Kong was taken over. At about the same time 4th Hussars, serving in Malaya, sent an armoured car squadron to the colony.

Comets of 7th Hussars on parade in Hong Kong, c. 1953. (Courtesy Ted Gregg)

As elsewhere, accidents happened whilst on exercise – some compensation will be due here …

Although it was undoubtedly a very exotic and popular posting, there were downsides. Typhoons, tropical rainstorms, could make life difficult, and the lack of training facilities could reduce a unit's effectiveness quite quickly. And in the days before air trooping became the norm, in the late 1950s, most troops were still shuttled around the world on troopships (including HMT *Empire Windrush*, which found lasting fame in another role), with the voyage to Hong Kong being one of the longest. Although much better than the ones used during the Second World War, the standards of comfort on these ships could be low, and this went lower with rank – or lack of it. 3RTR recorded their impressions when returning to the UK from Hong Kong in 1952, 'If any of our readers have not travelled in a post-war troop ship, they should picture themselves in a largish vibrating oven in which they must make shift to live, eat and sleep for five weeks in company with 129 other lads, all sweating from every pore.' It was noted that the sergeants and warrant officers travelled in comparative comfort initially, there being enough space for them to be accommodated in cabins, officer style. However, when the ship docked in Mombasa the situation changed and they were condemned to the troop decks for the rest of the voyage.

The provision of a tank regiment remained the RAC contribution for some years, and the Comets were finally replaced with Centurions in 1959, when 1RTR was the resident armoured regiment.[124] From September 1961, during the time when 17/21L was posted there, the size of the unit was reduced to a single, detached squadron.[125] The final tank unit in Hong Kong also came from 1RTR, when B Squadron was the last active unit from 1965 until early 1967, the tanks then being put into storage and activated on a regular basis by squadrons coming out from the UK or BAOR for a (very popular) short tour of about six weeks.[126] The armoured car contribution was somewhat patchier, but both Daimlers and then Saladins were used there by squadrons until Scorpion was brought into use, by C Sqn 16/5L, in July 1973. Fittingly, the last RAC squadron to serve in Hong Kong also came from 1RTR, with C Squadron leaving in February 1976, ending RAC involvement in the colony.

Chapter 5

The Professionals

More Reductions and Amalgamations

The April 1957 White Paper on Defence set forth the perceived future of the British military; Duncan Sandys, the new Conservative Minister of Defence, produced the paper. The British army was to be reduced in size and reorganized to reflect the ending of National Service and the change to an all-regular army, and to 'keep the Army abreast of changing circumstances, policies, weapons and techniques of war', political speak heralding large reductions. Over fifty major units and a large number of smaller ones were to be disbanded or amalgamated, with the intention of leaving the army at an overall strength of 165,000. The process was to be carried out in two phases, to be completed by the end of 1962. For the RAC this initially meant losing six regiments through another round of amalgamations (known as Phase 1) which took place as follows:

24 October 1958 QRIH (from 4H and 8H)
3 November 1958 QOH (from 3H and 7H)
20 February 1959 QDG (from KDG and The Bays)
3 April 1959 4RTR (from 4RTR and 7RTR)
31 October 1959 3RTR (from 3RTR and 6RTR)
1 July 1960 5RTR (from 5RTR and 8RTR)

Between 1958 and 1960 the first round of amalgamations took place since 1922. Three new cavalry regiments were created, and six of the RTR regiments became three, leaving five in total. Shown here are the badges of the new cavalry units, in seniority order: QDG, QOH and QRIH.

7th Hussars were given fifteen months' notice of their upcoming amalgamation with 3rd Hussars. The message was delivered whilst they were on a troop ship, returning from Hong Kong to England. The regiment, whilst saddened and noting that the amalgamation would inevitably lead to forced retirement for many of its officers and soldiers, generally took the news positively. 'All Seventh Hussars can rejoice that their partners are to be the Third; we both have similar traditions, interests and high standards.' Likewise, 8th Hussars were told of their amalgamation with 4th Hussars in July 1957. They noted the fact that due to the upcoming amalgamation, no more National Servicemen would be posted to them after June 1958, to allow the two regiments to reduce in size naturally, but, probably more importantly, to allow the resulting Queen's Royal Irish Hussars to become a completely regular regiment as quickly as possible. The running-down of NS men in both amalgamating regiments reduced the number of redundancies needed to be found from within the regular soldiers, although naturally, this positive effect was less pronounced amongst the senior ranks who tended to be almost exclusively regular.

Despite the apparent equality, in that the amalgamations affected six cavalry and six RTR regiments, the axe fell unequally on the smaller RTR and to a lesser extent the line cavalry – the Household Cavalry was untouched, once again – so that the former lost three-eighths of their regimental strength, as well as 1st Independent Squadron RTR in Berlin which was to be disbanded by November 1957.[1] There seems to have been an understanding amongst the cavalry colonels that previous RTR reductions and amalgamations would be conveniently forgotten during each new round, so that proportionally the RTR always lost more, despite Field Marshal Montgomery's order that this would not be so. Just before the amalgamation axe fell, in 1957 the RAC totalled about 21,000 officers and men; the reductions would see about 3,000 of these made redundant or otherwise released.

The amalgamations did not stop there, as (the, at that point secret) Phase 2 was concurrently being planned. Right in the middle of the Phase 1 round of amalgamations taking place, on 21 January 1959, a public announcement was made on the radio 6 o'clock news that 9th and 12th Lancers were also to amalgamate, and this was the first that the two regiments had heard of it. The Commanding Officer of the Twelfth was at a cocktail party in Cyprus when a junior subaltern rushed in to tell him that he had just heard the news on the British Forces Network, and Lieutenant Colonel Laurie of the Ninth in Detmold was told, not by the War Office, but by his children's nanny. It transpired that the War Office had informed the colonels of the two regiments, who were sworn to secrecy, but then omitted to inform the two COs. Despite this dreadful mis-communication, the two regiments took it upon themselves to make it work. The Twelfth sent the following telegram to the Ninth:

Our Hunter the tired has never been gelded
If yours is a mare the twain may be welded
The result of the match when you have a good look
Can't fail to turn out the best in the book.

With equal style the Ninth responded:

Our Hunter is gelded, no foal can we breed
But our Lancer like yours is well-mounted indeed
So we'll ride in half-sections, knee to knee in the line
And show the whole world there is nothing so fine.[2]

When the two regiments came together on 11 September 1960 another unforeseen effect of the amalgamations manifested itself; although overall the numbers from each regiment were equal, the WOs and SNCOs in the Twelfth were generally much older with more seniority than those of the Ninth, meaning that the ex-Twelfth members of the Sergeants' Mess were higher up the respective promotion rolls and therefore dominated the next promotions. Additionally, the Ninth Lancers found themselves at another disadvantage, as, following the amalgamation, they were to be an armoured car unit. The Twelfth had never been anything but since 1928, but the Ninth Lancers were a long-term tank regiment and needed to learn new skills.[3]

The Household Cavalry had manoeuvred themselves cleverly to avoid any threat of amalgamation. They had agreed that in future, and contrary to historical precedent, that one regiment would henceforth be stationed in BAOR and the other in Windsor. Both units would operate armoured cars, the Windsor-based one with a strategic air-portable role, as well running as a training squadron to look after their own recruits, separate to the RAC system being operated in the north of England. This was put into action in autumn 1959 when the Life Guards took over Harewood Barracks in Herford.[4]

9th/12th Lancers was formed in September 1960; the CO of 9th Lancers was told of the impending amalgamation by his children's nanny!

Once the amalgamations and reorganizations were complete, the RAC looked like this:

> The 2 Household Cavalry Regiments (plus the mounted component in London)
> - 1 APC regiment (in BAOR)
> - 12 armoured regiments
> - 8 armoured car regiments
> - At any time one of each of the armoured and armoured car regiments would be out of role in order to man the training and administrative commitments in Catterick and Barnard Castle

Finding the manpower to man this seemingly modest order of battle was a constant headache as the last of the National Servicemen were coming to the end of their service. One wit at the 1959 RAC Conference noted that 'never in the field of national expenditure has so much been maintained by so few'. With a smaller but all-regular army on the cards, a huge change was about to take place.

Forming a Regular Army

As late as 1952 the army was still operating on the promotion system adopted through necessity during the war. This meant the continued use of the War Substantive (W/S) system, in which a rank was held conditional on the war being in progress. On 1 April 1952 – why does the army insist on so many important changes coming into effect on April Fool's Day? – a 'Peacetime Promotion Code for Other Ranks' was brought into us. The main changes this implemented were:

- All W/S ranks were relinquished.
- The rank held on the mysterious 'shadow roll' became the individual's substantive rank.
- Acting ranks (paid) could be used to fill vacancies.
- The system of 'Unpaid Acting' ranks was ended, and replaced by the use of (unpaid) 'Local' rank.[5]
- Commanding Officers had the authority to promote within their unit establishment up to Acting (but not substantive) Sergeant.
- All other promotions had to be agreed by RAC Records.
- Promotion was to be based upon seniority and merit, tempered by the need to hold specified trade and educational qualifications.
- An 'Accelerated promotion roll' was created, to allow outstanding individuals to move through the ranks as fast as possible.

There is no doubt that the end of National Service was not only welcomed by the vast majority of the country, but also led to higher standards within the RAC.[6]

Returning to regimental duty with 3rd Carbs in May 1965, Major P. Maxwell had the following to say:

> During my two years away, National Service had ended, and the squadron is entirely made up of regular soldiers. No-one would attempt to decry the National Serviceman and the valuable service he gave in his two-year military career, but training him was like trying to fill a bath with the plug out; no sooner had one had time to train him in one trade and make him proficient in the field than he was due for demobilisation. The standard of tradesmen [is now] much higher, for with the introduction of the regular army the trade structure in the RAC has been changed, demanding a much higher standard – but regrettably no increase in pay.[7]

In fact, he was wrong on this last point, as the system for regular soldiers' engagement and pay was now much improved. A series of substantial pay increases had come into effect on 1 April 1960, so that captains and below would see an annual increase of £73, majors £91 10s. and a lieutenant colonel £146. Soldiers, who were paid weekly, not annually, also benefitted. Corporals and below saw an increase of 7s. per week, sergeants 10s. 6d. and staff sergeants and above 14s. This was in anticipation of the imminent move to an all-regular establishment, and was designed, in part, to encourage at least some NS men to stay. The complicated and disliked star system of pay increments was also ended.

A lot of thought had gone into working out how best to manage the transition to an all-regular army – 'The Professionals' as they were advertised as – and enormous efforts were made by the regiments, assisted by their new Home Headquarters, in recruiting on their patches, including putting on the Keep the Army in the Public Eye (KAPE) tours, and introducing a Satisfied Soldier scheme.[8] In 1965 a soldier joined on a twenty-two-year engagement, but with the options of terminating service at the six-, nine- or twelve-year points.[9] Taking either of the first two options left a residual reserve liability of six and three years respectively, whereas completion of twelve years' service or more only required one to join the General Reserve, which was only for national emergencies and did not require any form of annual training. In terms of pay, this used a complicated system based on rank, trade, length of engagement and, not least, whether the soldier was single or married. For example, a trooper who was a Class III tradesman and intended to serve for nine years would receive £8 15s. per week, and on promotion to lance corporal the same soldier would receive a pay rise of £1 8s. per week. A Class I corporal on a twenty-two-year engagement would receive £13 2s. 6d., and a staff sergeant on the same engagement £17 10s. A Class I warrant officer received £19 5s. per week, plus an increment of 2s. 6d. per day once he had served over eighteen years. If married, a soldier ranked trooper to corporal received an allowance of £3 17s. per week, and the regimental sergeant major £5 13s. 9d. Other allowances were paid for rations if living out, for travel to and from work, disturbance on posting (£50, but only for married soldiers) and a local overseas allowance had also been introduced, with different rates for each country. In summary, the weekly pay scale in 1965 looked like this:

Unmarried Trooper (Recruit) on joining	£7 16s. 6d.
Married Trooper (Recruit) under 21, on joining	£11 14s. 6d.
Married Trooper (Recruit) over 21, on joining	£12 15s. 6d.
Unmarried Trooper BIII (after six months' training)	£8 15s. 0d.
Married Trooper BIII (after six months' training)	£13 13s. 0d.
Unmarried Trooper BII (qualified full crewman)	£9 5s. 6d.
Married Trooper BII (qualified full crewman)	£14 3s. 6d.
Unmarried Lance Corporal BII (qualified full crewman)	£10 3s. 0d.
Married Lance Corporal BII (qualified full crewman)	£15 1s. 0d.
Unmarried Corporal BI	£11 14s. 6d.
Married Corporal BI	£16 12s. 6d.
Unmarried Sergeant (after nine years' service)	£14 7s. 6d.
Married Sergeant (after nine years' service)	£20 9s. 6d.
Unmarried Warrant Officer Class 2	£17 6s. 6d.
Married Warrant Officer Class 2	£23 7s. 6d.

If married and accompanied, or during leave, a ration allowance of 6s. 10d. per day was paid.[10] A gratuity was payable on leaving, subject to having served between twelve and twenty-one years, and for those with twenty-two years' service, a weekly pension of between £3 6s. (corporal) and £5 10s. (warrant officer Class 2) was payable.

With the end of National Service, the regiments were all faced with the same problem: how to recruit enough regulars to keep the regiment viable, in order to head-off any possibility of amalgamation or disbandment.[11] Although regimental accounts frequently refer to the supposition that well-recruited regiments were not as vulnerable to amalgamation than less fortunate ones, regional politics and pressure from supporters played a big part in the decisions, as will be seen. As an example, 14th/20th Hussars calculated that in the early 1960s, following the ending of National Service, they required no fewer than 540 recruits to fill their gaps, and they mostly had to come from Lancashire. This was because in 1957 it had been decided by the RAC Council (endorsed by the Army Council the following year) to split the UK up into regimental recruiting areas in a manner similar to that historically used by the infantry with their 'county' regiments; this 'Area Recruiting Scheme' came into being in May 1958, with four areas jointly recruited from, the remainder being exclusive to specific regiments.[12] Within the RAC these were initially based upon the affiliations that the regular regiments had been allocated in January 1947, when the suspended animation of the Territorial

Army was lifted, and new TA units formed (or resurrected) nationwide. This led to a policy whereby each Cavalry and RTR regiment 'adopted' (was affiliated to) one or sometimes two TA Yeomanry units. The main effect of this affiliation on the regular regiments was that they had to supply a number of Permanent Staff, or PS, typically the Second in Command, adjutant, quartermaster and RSM, as well as a number of training SNCOs. In addition to expanding the experience and promotion prospects of both officers and other ranks, this greatly assisted the Yeomanry and over time developed a strong bond between the units that was to be exploited when the recruiting areas were apportioned. On 1 October 1960 following the reorganization of the TA the affiliations were realigned so that each regular unit was affiliated to a single Yeomanry unit, and vice versa.

By way of example, in 1947 15th/19th Hussars was allocated the Northumberland Hussars, and by the mid-1960s the regiment, following rigorous and successful recruiting efforts in the North East, had a distinctly 'Geordie' character.[13] Similarly, 16th/5th Lancers was paired with the Staffordshire Yeomanry, and ten years later Staffordshire became the main recruiting area for the regiment. When the various areas were first allocated to the RAC in May 1958, the RTR regiments were given the following areas and affiliations:

Table 5: RAC Recruiting Areas, 1958

Regiment	Area	Affiliated TA Unit	Remarks
1RTR	Lancashire, Cumberland, Westmorland	40/41RTR	Lancashire shared with 14/20H. Cumberland and Westmorland shared with 4/7DG and Greys
2RTR	Middlesex, Hertfordshire, Essex, Kent, London	Westminster Dragoons	London shared with Royals
3RTR	Cornwall, Devon, Dorset, Somerset	NSY/44RTR	Bristol and Cheltenham shared with 11H
4RTR	Scotland	Lowland Yeomanry	Shared with 4/7DG, Greys and 7RTR
5RTR	Yorkshire	NSY/44RTR	Shared with 9L and 13/18H
6RTR	Norfolk, Suffolk, Cambridgeshire, Huntingdonshire, Bedfordshire	NSY/44RTR	On amalgamation this area will be allotted to 3RTR[14]
7RTR	Scotland	Lowland Yeomanry	Shared with 4/7DG, Greys and 4RTR (prior to amalgamation)
8RTR	Cornwall, Devon, Dorset, Somerset	NSY/44RTR	To assist 3RTR in this area whilst stationed in Tidworth (prior to amalgamation)

Recruiting was hard work, and each regiment spent a lot of time working out how best to go about it. An initiative that came from the Secretary of State in 1960 led to the famous KAPE tours – keeping the army in the public eye. For the RAC regiments, this meant taking every opportunity to deploy a team of specially picked men, with armoured vehicles whenever possible, into the main towns and county shows and other large events, in order to drum up interested youngsters of the right quality. Although not directly concerned with the AFV trades, taking the regimental band along proved to be a good draw. As with all such efforts, the results varied. In their first full year of regular recruiting, 1963, The Carbs only managed to attract forty-six recruits. The following year this had dramatically improved to eighty. What surprised them was that in order to generate this number, about 250 potential applicants had to be interviewed by the recruiting sergeants, as the majority would prove to be unacceptable, due to failing the educational and/or medical tests, or because they were not deemed to be of sufficiently good character – the old story of joining the army to avoid jail was becoming less true.[15] The most successful regiments were able to recruit more than they needed, and thus be more selective, although this sometimes led to brakes being applied, creating a boom and bust cycle. Over time, increasingly healthy recruiting figures led to a raising of the educational requirements for the RAC, which had a positive effect on trade-test passes and grades. But even getting an applicant to Catterick was no guarantee, as an average of 16 per cent of each intake left before completing training. The same problems did not seem to occur with recruiting Junior Leaders, with many boys leaving school and joining 'Brats' with the intention of having a full career.[16] Recruiting was often a case of feast or famine, and not through the fault of the units; 15th/19th Hussars put a lot of work into their 'patch', and by 1988 was fully up to strength. As a result, the RAC imposed a recruiting ban on the regiment, preferring to concentrate on and prioritize other regiments that were not doing so well. By the following year the regiment was thirty below strength.

Not all of the original county allocations stood the test of time. When the regimental areas were first allocated, 4th/7th Dragoon Guards was affiliated with the Scottish Horse and therefore expected to recruit only from Scotland. By 1960, with the regiment stationed in Catterick, it was very clear that it was failing to compete with the Scots Greys and 4RTR as well as the large numbers of (well-known) Scottish infantry battalions, and numbers of recruits were dwindling. The regiment persuaded the RAC Council and War Office to change its recruiting area, no mean feat, and as a result they were allocated North and West Yorkshire, the start of a particularly strong bond to the county. The two Irish regiments, the Fifth Skins and the newly formed Queen's Royal Irish Hussars, were of course expected to recruit from Ulster, but the Province provided insufficient recruits, so in time The Skins were also given Cumberland vice 1RTR plus Stockport in Cheshire, and the QRIH received Sussex plus two recruiting offices in central London. 5RTR was originally allocated Yorkshire, but in 1960 this was changed to Lincolnshire; when the regiment disbanded in 1969 Lincolnshire was passed to 17th/21st Lancers.

The same happened in 1971 with 3rd Carabiniers when it was to a great extent absorbed by amalgamation into The (fiercely Scottish) Greys; The Carbs had recruited from Cheshire and North Wales, and these areas went to The Skins and the QDG respectively.[17] As other regiments amalgamated over the coming decades, the recruiting areas themselves were amalgamated and amended, so that by 1990 – just before the next round of reductions – the country was divided up as follows:

Table 6: RAC Recuiting Areas, 1990

Regiment	Area	Remarks
HCav	Countrywide	
QDG	Wales, Shropshire, Herefordshire	
SCOTS DG	Scotland	Shared with 4RTR
4/7DG	North and West Yorkshire	Leeds, Halifax, Wakefield shared with 1RTR
5DG	Ulster, Cumbria, Cheshire	Ulster shared with QRIH
QOH	West Midlands, Warwickshire, Worcestershire	Not Wolverhampton
QRIH	Ulster, The Strand, Acton, Finchley, Surrey, Sussex	Ulster shared with 5DG. Finchley shared with 2RTR
9/12L	Derby, Leicestershire, Northamptonshire, Blackheath	
RH	Gloucestershire, Oxfordshire, Buckinghamshire, Wiltshire, Berkshire, Hampshire, Isle of Wight	
13/18H	North Humberside, South Yorkshire	
14/20H	Lancashire, Manchester, Isle of Man	Manchester shared with 1RTR
15/19H	Northumberland, Tyne and Weir, Durham, Cleveland	
16/5L	Staffordshire, Wolverhampton	
17/21L	South Humberside, Nottinghamshire, Lincolnshire	
1RTR	Merseyside, Manchester	Leeds, Halifax, Wakefield shared with 4/7DG. Manchester shared with 14/20H
2RTR	London (less The Strand, Acton, Blackheath), Essex, Suffolk, Norfolk, Cambridgeshire, Bedfordshire, Hertfordshire, Kent	Finchley shared with QRIH
3RTR	Cornwall, Devon, Dorset, Somerset, Bristol, Avon, Channel Islands	
4RTR	Scotland	Shared with SCOTS DG

Some of these areas would, in short order, themselves amalgamate again following the Options for Change reductions in the early 1990s.

Yet More Amalgamations

In 1966 the Labour government published a Defence White Paper, which announced the decision to concentrate on supporting NATO in Europe and confirmed a reliance on nuclear deterrence rather than conventional strength. However, a worsening economic climate led to the September 1967 announcement that the army was to lose another seventeen major units including another two more amalgamations for the RAC. This time – and for the first time – it included an amalgamation between Household and Line cavalry, by merging the Royal Horse Guards (The Blues) with 1st Royal Dragoons (The Royals) in March 1969, to become the Royal Horse Guards and First Dragoons, known to all as The Blues and Royals.[18] The second merger led to 10th Hussars and 11th Hussars amalgamating in October 1969 to become the Royal Hussars. This was followed two months later by the disbandment of 5RTR (the RTR choosing to disband one regiment, the junior, rather than the option of amalgamating 1RTR with 2RTR, the only two regiments that had not been touched by the reductions of less than a decade previously), and one regular regiment was to be taken out of role to become the RAC Centre Regiment at Bovington, with QRIH taking on the job from August 1968.[19]

A lot of talk surrounding which unit should amalgamate with which centred on the somewhat nebulous concept of the different characters of the regiments, as well as more serious arguments concerning the ability of different regiments to be operationally effective and maintain healthy recruiting figures – which were not always enough to escape the axe, as 3rd Carabiniers was about to find out. On 1 April 1968, a single Colonel Commandant RAC was appointed, to replace the previous system whereby there were two Colonels Commandant, one representing the cavalry and the other the RTR. The first person to take up the appointment was the distinguished cavalryman, Field Marshal Sir Richard Hull,

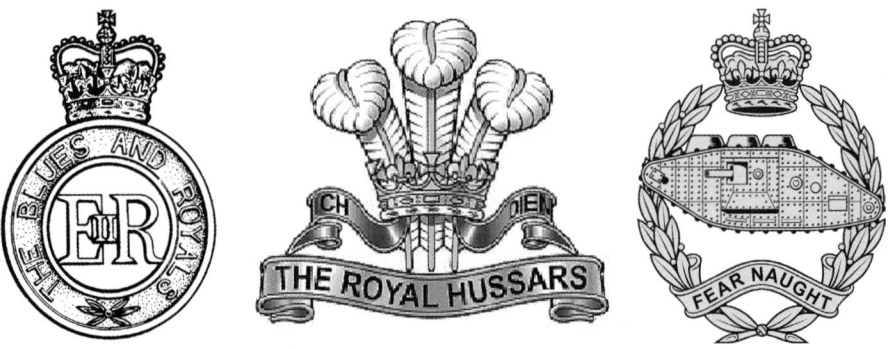

At the end of the 1960s two further amalgamations took place, forming The Blues and Royals and the Royal Hussars. 5RTR also disbanded, the RTR choosing to disband a complete regiment rather than subject two units to the pain of amalgamation.

and he was immediately embroiled in a row regarding the amalgamation of the Royal Scots Greys. The 'Fifth Reduction' as it was known at the time had been announced in the Supplementary Statement on Defence Policy 1968 released in July, simply stating that the RAC would reduce by one regiment, without giving any details of who and when. As before, the choice was stark; either disband one regiment, or amalgamate two. The first option was simpler, and the regiment under the microscope was The Greys, as they were the only unit that had managed to avoid the reductions and amalgamations that had taken place since 1922; they had been told as recently as 23 November 1967 that they would not be amalgamating – at least not immediately, but the threat remained. The Greys of course were a Scottish regiment, and immediately mobilized a similar range of supporters to those used to delay their mechanization in the 1930s. Ideally, they wanted to escape the process completely, but when it became clear that this could not happen, reluctantly started to look around for the most suitable partner. Until then the remainder of the RAC had looked on, assuming that The Royals would be the choice to amalgamate with The Greys, but the selection of The Royals as partners for The Blues threw that assumption up in the air.[20]

The first choices made by The Greys were, for unclear reasons, 15/19H or 14/20H, in that order. Both regiments strongly resisted the proposal, correctly stating that it went against the time-honoured principle of only amalgamating like with like, and that if they were forced into an amalgamation, they would prefer to do it with each other and remain as Hussars. A similar approach to 17/21L was met with the same arguments and a blunt refusal, noting that if they had to amalgamate (again), their choice would be to join with 16/5L – an amalgamation that actually took place much later, in mid-1993. The Fifth Skins was next under the microscope, but as an Irish regiment with over 60 per cent of its ranks from Ulster they were able to play their version of the national card, with senior officers noting the potential for religious problems between Scottish Protestant and Irish Catholic soldiers, especially as inter-factional tensions were rising in the Province at the time.

The next suggestion was the Life Guards; they had reduced from two regiments to one in 1922 but, at least outwardly, looked to have escaped the worst of amalgamations, and had at least retained their title. But when Earl Mountbatten found out about the proposal, he made it 'very clear to Dickie Hull that he was not prepared to consider discussion of an amalgamation'. 4RTR was next, attractive merely as the other Scottish RAC regiment, 4/7DG, having switched from recruiting in Scotland to Yorkshire in 1960. For some of the more forward-thinking soldiers this had the potential for starting the sort of mergers that could result in the formation of a genuine RAC, with the distinctions between the cavalry and the RTR erased at last, but the proposal was so far removed from the like-with-like principle that it was never seriously considered. It is also probable that the RTR saw it for what it was, a blatant attempt to remove the recruiting competition and partner with a regiment that The Greys could dominate, as well as involving a regiment that had only been amalgamated (with 7RTR) in 1959.

Finally, 3rd Carabiniers were brought into the equation in late October 1968, and seem to have been offered the choice between amalgamation with The Greys and disbandment – in fact, this stark choice should have been given to The Greys at the outset, as it was, if truth be told, their turn to bear the pain that every other regiment had gone through in the past fifty years.[21] The Carbs tried to deploy the argument that they were a Welsh unit, but despite their bracketed title (Prince of Wales' Dragoon Guards) and recruiting areas including North Wales, only about 20 per cent of their soldiers came from the principality and this was thus able to be conveniently ignored.[22] Also ignored was the fact that they were going to be the first regiment to be amalgamated twice, having been one of the 'victims' in the 1922 round. After the customary bargaining and manoeuvring for position, the two regimental colonels finally agreed to the plan on 23 January 1969, ending seven months of frantic and often cynical manoeuvring within the RAC. The Army Board approved the compromise, and the announcement of the amalgamation was made in the Defence White Paper of February 1969, although at that stage the new title of the regiment had still to be confirmed. The Royal Scots Dragoon Guards (Carabiniers and Greys) was eventually decided on, with the Welsh element being removed completely; The Greys had the best of the deal, despite being the junior of the two regiments. Formed on 2 July 1971, the new regiment retained the Guards honorific and thus seniority, but overall reflected The Greys much more than it did The Carbs, and quickly acquired a fiercely Scottish character, which it has retained. In an unusual move, the regiment

was allowed to form a detached fourth sabre squadron, stationed in Edinburgh, whilst the remainder of the new regiment started life in Herford, Germany. The members of D Squadron quickly found themselves busy, being sent on operational tours to Cyprus (with the UN) and to Northern Ireland; it was finally disbanded in November 1976.

After a lengthy process of manoeuvring, the Royal Scots Dragoon Guards were formed in 1971 from 3rd Carabiniers and the Royal Scots Greys.

Naturally, regular army reductions also affected the Yeomanry. By way of example, in 1966 the Royal Gloucestershire Hussars, affiliated to 11th Hussars, recorded the impact of yet another TA reorganization on them:

> Possibly the most important thing of 1966 is that this regiment is to continue ... We are to form a Gloucestershire Home Defence Force regiment as part of 71 Regional Group ... the affiliation between the RGH and 11H will continue, although on a much reduced scale. The Training Major, Adjutant and QM go, but the RSM is to remain as the only regular permanent staff.[23]

Only the following year, on 1 April 1967, the RGH found themselves reduced to a 'skeleton regiment', and immediately 'lost two of our drill halls, most of the vehicles, most of the permanent staff, and all the pay'. They even noted that if they wanted to go on exercise in the future, they would have to pay for the petrol themselves out of their budget – desperate times indeed to be in the TA. Eventually, through a lot of lobbying and sheer bloody mindedness, they were permitted in 1969 to retain a cadre of just three officers and five NCOs, based in Cirencester. Two years later there was another reorganization, and the unit became part of the Wessex Yeomanry with an infantry role, which in 1979 became the Royal Wessex Yeomanry, and in 1983 once more became part of the RAC, as a wheeled recce regiment.

Training in Libya

After the Germans and Italians had been ejected from North Africa in 1943, substantial British forces remained in the region, mainly to be ready for the invasions of Sicily and Italy later that year. After the ending of the war, both Egypt and Libya remained garrisoned, although as we have seen, Egypt had to be abandoned by 1956. Fortunately, in 1953, Libya signed a twenty-year treaty with the UK under which the UK was able to operate military bases in the country, in exchange for financial and military assistance. This allowed Libya to be used as an RAC station, and which remained in being until late 1969. In February 1947 Italy, the formal colonial power, formally relinquished control and on Christmas eve 1951 the pro-Western Kingdom of Libya was founded. For most of the next two decades, a single tank regiment was stationed in Libya, including camps at Barce, Homs, Sabratha, Zavia, Benghazi and Tripoli, with accompanied tours of around two years for most. The location was ideal to allow tank training – and ranges – to take place with few restrictions, and the regiments also gained much experience in desert navigation techniques. At times an armoured car regiment was also posted to the country, and had even more opportunities to practise tactical skills in demanding and often featureless terrain – on more than one occasion a vehicle would stray into an uncharted Second World War minefield and lose a wheel, bringing a surprising reality to the exercise. 2RTR were posted to Libya in 1959 and had this to say about their initial experience as an armoured car unit:

> Troop training in the desert started in earnest … the first real penetration of the interior took place when a party, largely composed of officers and other ranks with not long to serve [presumably NS men] set forth on exercise Swansong, which was an expedition some 600 miles southwards into the Fezzan. Rather to everybody's surprise the whole part appeared back on the expected day, having been in wireless contact with base each night. There is no doubt that Homs must be the best station that exists now for the RAC … the whole of Libya is on the doorstep for a training ground.[24]

During the 1960s the use of the country was extended to include exercising troops, with many armoured car squadrons being flown in for a few weeks of outstanding training; the RAF airfield at El Adem was often used as the base, with 'Chatham Camp' used as the desert base, some 65 miles to the west. However, the Gaddafi-led coup of September 1969 ousted the ruling moderate government and Britain was no longer welcome; the last RAC troops, an armoured car unit from B Squadron 17/21L, left in early 1970, and the corps needed to find somewhere else to conduct large-scale armoured training.

Saladin crews of 2RTR on exercise in the Libyan Desert, the RAC's best training ground of the 1960s. (Courtesy Charlie Welchman)

Command Troop 3RTR in a hide on Soltau. Although professionalism in the field increased over the years, much of the routine of training on Soltau in the early 1990s would have been familiar to his counterpart from forty years previously.

An extreme example of an inexperienced troop leader getting into trouble A second lieutenant on a night navigation exercise was using his thermal sight to find the track paralleling the range road, the deep fording pit was frozen over and to him it looked like a road, and this was the result.

A Challenger, fitted with the SIMFICS tactical gunnery simulator, makes its way along the infamous 'pylon line' on the Soltau training area. Pressure from the German government following the end of the Cold War led to the training area being closed in 1994.

The Chieftain had its problems, not least in terms of reliability, but it was an impressive tank designed with a whole range of survivability features that were ahead of its time. Eleven marks were produced, and it remained in service until 1996.

A Scimitar on exercise on Salisbury Plain in the 2000s, by which time it had already been in service for thirty years. The CVR(T) series of vehicles was a rare attempt at successfully developing a family of variants based on a common chassis.

A Saladin in a semi-fortified emplacement, mainly there to protect the wheels. The 76mm gun was a simple but effective weapon, capable of delivering a decent weight of fire with both speed and accuracy.

Second Lieutenant Russell and a Saladin of B Sqn 3RTR in Sharjah, 1969. After the end of the Aden campaign, individual armoured car squadrons continued to be posted there. Deployments to such locations were excellent training for the crews, who were able to practise conducting long-range desert missions,

Sergeant Roy Emery of B Sqn 3RTR on UNFICYP duties, September 1978.

Above: *The author commanding a Saladin of F Sqn 3RTR on patrol in the Sovereign Base Area, 1987. The SBA squadron was the last regular unit to operate Saladin and Saracen, and some spare parts had to be sourced from the Tank Museum.*

Right: *Rural: Richie Elson from 3RTR carrying a GPMG on patrol in South Armagh, late 1990. Troops knew better than to use gates, and had to transit through fields by forcing their way through the blackthorn hedges.*

Left: *Urban: troops from 9/12L 'hard target' through Belfast, 1993.*

Below: *A Scimitar from The Blues and Royals overlooking San Carlos Water; the 30mm Rarden cannon proved to be an effective weapon engaging enemy defensive positions, even though it was not put to the test in an anti-armour role.* (Courtesy HCR Museum)

The CVR(T)s of The Blues and Royals confounded the negativity of those who questioned their place in the Task Force, and once again confirmed the utility – and necessity – of light armour. (Courtesy Robin Innes Ker)

The tank commander's view: the training area at BATUS was largely prairie, a barren, desert-like expanse of wilderness that made navigation for the less than competent something of a nightmare. (Courtesy Bob Jacobs)

The prairie was scorching hot in the summer, and this meant that fires were a frequent problem. Tracer ammunition fired from the machine guns meant that exercising troops could quickly find themselves in the middle of a rapidly spreading conflagration.

Friendly fire? Staff Sergeant Bob Jacobs inspects damage caused to his tank's episcopes by infantry machine-gun fire (accidentally?) hitting his tank. (Courtesy Bob Jacobs)

The introduction of a live enemy (OPFOR) in 1995 added a whole new dimension to the exercises, and made the training at BATUS much more realistic and testing. These crews from QRL are manning the so-called Sturgeon (representing a BMP vehicle) as part of OPFOR, 1997. (Courtesy RL)

An HCR Scimitar advances across the BATUS wilderness. The ability to train at BATUS has undoubtedly played a major part in maintaining and increasing the skills of both armoured and reconnaissance soldiers over five decades. (Courtesy HCR)

As well as moving personnel around to bring the deploying regiments up to strength, there was a shortage of spares for the vehicles, leading to a cannibalization programme. This is a tank of 3RTR who were in South Armagh at the time, and who returned to find their tanks looking like this. (Courtesy Mike Williams)

British tanks at the port of Al Jubail in Saudi Arabia in late 1990, prior to being 'desertized' and up-armoured ready for the conflict.

Now fully modified and up-armoured, Challenger crews 'bombing up' with a full load of ammunition prior to the start of the ground war.

3 Tp A Sqn 16/5L. The regiment was used in a novel and aggressive manner, and led the advance into Iraq.

Both armoured brigade commanders, Brigadiers Patrick Cordingley (7th) and Christopher Hammerbeck (4th), elected to have the option to command their brigades from a tank, allowing them to get forward and influence what was, often, an untidy battlefield. The regimental COs did likewise; this is CHURCHILL, the mount of Lieutenant Colonel Arthur Denaro QRIH.

The result: destroyed Iraqi armour. The TOGS thermal gunnery system gave the British a crucial edge in night fighting.

Each squadron of 16/5L had a guided weapons troop of Strikers. These soldiers, from the C Sqn GW troop, have been doing what almost every servicemen did after the ceasefire, and been collecting souvenirs that they could not take back with them – officially at least.

Going home. Little did the crews realize that many of them would be returning, this time to conduct a full-blown invasion and occupation of Iraq, within twelve years.

SCOTS DG were heavily involved in the fielding – much delayed – of Challenger 2, but became the first regiment to be fully equipped with the new tank in 1998. This tank is on exercise in Poland. (Courtesy SCOTS DG)

B Squadron 9/12L was the first sub-unit of many from the RAC to deploy on Operation Grapple in Bosnia. Arriving in November 1992, they were responsible for escorting humanitarian aid convoys in very trying conditions.

A two-car patrol of Scimitars from the Light Dragoons forcing their way through the Bosnian mountains in the snow.

The deployment of Challengers under IFOR and then SFOR gave the new force much more credibility, and helped greatly to keep the fragile peace. (Courtesy Richard Stickland)

Challenger 2 had its first operational deployment in Bosnia with SCOTS DG. Moving 70-ton tanks around in a civilian setting took a great deal of care …(Courtesy Andrew Totten)

A Challenger from KRH in Pristina during the occupation of Kosovo, June 1999. The commander, Sergeant Glenn Evans, seems delighted to be there.

Chapter 6

Operations Part Two

Cyprus, 1960–2018

Following Cyprus achieving independence as a republic in 1960, British forces remained on the island, mainly in the two Sovereign Base Areas but also operating out of some smaller locations, such as the isolated RAF communications camp on Mount Olympus. At this time there were no RAC units on the island, the last one having withdrawn the day before independence was granted. Over the next three years tensions remained high on the island, and there was sporadic violence between the two main ethnic groups, although it was generally small in scale and was able to be contained by the Cypriot authorities. Just before Christmas 1963 there was a huge upsurge in inter-communal fighting following the deaths of two Turkish Cypriots, and the resulting violence saw over 500 deaths and many more injured. As a result large numbers of people were displaced from their homes, and some Turkish communities began forming their own enclaves for protection – across the whole island they were outnumbered about 4 : 1 and those living within mainly Greek communities were very vulnerable. Cyprus was close to civil war and President Makarios appealed to the British – the nation he had spent much of his adult life trying to evict from the island – to use its troops from the SBAs to restore order. British troops quickly found themselves negotiating ceasefires and putting themselves between potentially warring factions, and as part of the British response, the British army commander drew a 'green line' through the centre of Nicosia from west to east, dividing the Greek communities in the south from the Turks in the north.[1] During this period the Guards Independent Parachute Company was deployed in Ferret Scout Cars, but they were quickly replaced by A and C squadrons from The Royals who took over their vehicles and tasks. Additionally, squadrons from the 14/20H and the Life Guards were also sent as reinforcements. In a microcosm of the madness of the situation, the latter, operating in the Kyrenian Mountains, deployed a troop to rescue Greek schoolchildren who were under fire from Turkish elements, only to be stoned by the same schoolchildren a few days later. The deployment of SBA troops as peacekeepers was a temporary sticking plaster over serious problems, and a longer term solution was required.

Amid a real fear that Turkey might contemplate invading Cyprus in support of its minority kinsmen, the United Nations Force in Cyprus, UNFICYP, was established by UN Resolution 186 of 1964. It had a mandate that was – and is –

renewed on a six-monthly basis; as with all UN missions, the idea is to deploy a force for only as long as it is necessary, and then withdraw it. The UN when it initially deployed from 2 March 1964 comprised troops from Britain – the largest single contributing nation – as well as from Austria, Canada, Denmark, Finland, Ireland and Sweden, and a contingent of Australian civilian police; in total, the force was 6,500 strong.[2] For the next ten years, UNFICYP were to be found in camps and observation posts across the whole of the island. The RAC contribution settled down by the start of 1965 to a single Ferret-equipped scout-car squadron, based for a number of years at Zyyi ('Ziggy') Camp on the southern coast, and then from February 1970 at Gleneagles Camp in Nicosia, largely built – and named – by The Scots Greys. By then the squadron had become known as the Force Reserve, as it not only had routine patrolling tasks to complete, but was also the only on-call component of the force that was both armoured and mobile, the majority of the force being static infantry units. It found itself reacting to incidents around the island, and the six-month tour duration meant that the deployment was unaccompanied, with the squadron coming from one of the RAC units in the UK, including tank regiments which demanded a conversion programme prior to deploying. Over the next few years the size of UNFICYP gradually reduced, and this was exacerbated when some of its troops were redeployed to Egypt in the wake on the 1973 Yom Kippur War; by early 1974 UNFICYP was under 2,500 strong.

Having handed its unwelcome peacekeeping role over to the UN by mid-1964, the SBA armoured component came from another single RAC squadron, equipped with Saladins and Ferrets and based, from 1967, in an old RAF camp at Pergamos outside Dhekelia. This was an up to two-year accompanied posting and was to become one of the most popular 'sunshine' postings in the RAC, particularly as other locations east of Suez were closing down. This would remain so until summer 1974, when the situation suddenly changed.

In 1973 Archbishop Makarios was re-elected for his third term as president of the republic. He continued to survive assassination attempts, which demonstrated how fragile the political situation was. In Greece a *coup d'état* in late 1973 brought a new military junta to power which favoured the old idea of Enosis, the political unification of Cyprus with Greece. This ambition led to a coup in Cyprus in mid-July 1974, in which Makarios was toppled and replaced as president by the notorious EOKA terrorist from the 1950s, Nikos Sampson. Clearly the two new governments would be working to unite Cyprus with Greece, an intolerable situation for Turkey. It moved quickly. On 20 July 1974 the Turkish armed forces invaded the northern part of Cyprus, using all three services to conduct seaborne, heliborne and airborne landings, principally around the small northern post of Kyrenia. Amidst a real shooting war (between two supposed NATO allies), an immediate concern was for the 4,000 or so service wives and children, many of whom lived not within the SBAs but in hirings and quarters outside the wire, and whose menfolk found themselves in full battle gear and deployed on protection duties. At this time the RAC squadron on SBA duties was B Sqn 16/5L in Pergamos, with the RAC Parachute Squadron having arrived as the UNFICYP Force Reserve in early June, expecting a quiet, even routine tour following a number of deployments to Ulster over the previous few years.

The sudden emergency required urgent reinforcement of both the SBA troops and UNFICYP. The early warnings that a Turkish invasion was imminent led to 16th/5th Lancers in Tidworth being placed on 24 hours' notice to move. As B Squadron was already on the island, and C Squadron was in Hong Kong, only the HQ elements and A Squadron were available, therefore B Squadron RHG/D from Windsor and C Squadron 4/7DG (then operating as an independent RAC recce squadron) were placed under command. The force flew to Akrotiri, arriving on the 22nd. The Blues and Royals Squadron remained in Akrotiri with responsibility for the Western SBA, and A Sqn 16/5L deployed to the two most exposed camps at Pergamos and Ayios Nikolaos. As both of these squadrons were mainly equipped with Scorpions which were generally viewed as light tanks, it was decided that they should remain under UK control and

Guided Weapons on a UN deployment! C Sqn 4/7DG included a troop equipped with Ferret Mk 5 when they deployed to Cyprus during the Turkish invasion of 1974.

not deploy outside the SBAs unless absolutely necessary, once again to reduce the chances of mistaken identity. This left B Sqn 16/5L and C Sqn 4/7DG as wheeled armoured car squadrons, and as such they were able to be re-brigaded to UNFICYP command to serve alongside the Para Squadron, hastily marking up their vehicles with UN signs and flags, and painting them white as quickly as they could. C Squadron spent their first three days in Episkopi but on the 26th was sent to Nicosia airport – the UN HQ was adjacent to it – where 'en route the squadron were given blue berets and so became UN troops'.[3] The Swingfire-armed GW troop was left to 'guard' the airport, and the remainder sent up north to work with the Finns.[4] In the confused situation both food and water were in short supply, and the squadron lived off their vehicles.

An account of the activities of the RAC Para Squadron – probably penned by Captain David Churton, Royal Hussars – gives another glimpse into the period, starting with the unrest caused by the coup on 15 July:

> The UN went on increased vigilance … and confined itself to barracks. The presidential palace, the airport terminal, Kykko monastery and many police stations were involved in heavy fighting and a great many people lost their lives … Makarios sought refuge and had lunch with the UN in Paphos, donating AK47 rifles and field glasses to 1st Troop.[5]
>
> On Saturday, 20 July the Turkish Forces' landing took place with … heavy naval and air bombardment.[6] The Greek Cypriots fought with a tenacity and bravery hitherto unknown and inflicted very heavy casualties onto a casual [but] well equipped modern army. At this time the squadron was heavily involved in fighting between the Cypriots in the south of the island, arranging ceasefires, surrenders, and disarming the Turkish villages under siege by the Cyprus National Guard. In Limassol heavy fighting was taking place and one Ferret took a direct hit from an 81mm mortar. Fortunately the crew was unhurt and the Ferret was able to continue on its run flats [tyres]. By the evening of the 20th the squadron was fast deploying troops to Nicosia to aid the Canadians who were in the thick of the fighting. 2nd Troop, with great bravery, used an (open-topped) Mk 1 Ferret to rescue many wounded Canadians. During this period we gladly welcomed two squadrons and RHQ of the 16th/5th Lancers and one squadron and GW troop from the 4/7DG. The area then stabilised with the Turks holding a wedge of land some twelve miles wide from Kyrenia through to Nicosia.

After three days of genuinely heavy fighting the Turks had managed to secure Kyrenia and commence an armoured thrust towards Nicosia, as well as securing some territory in the northern (Turkish) part of the capital. At this point a ceasefire was brought into force, and the pause in fighting allowed the British families, largely controlled by announcements made on BFBS radio, to be convoyed into the SBAs as part of Operation Fallacy. B Sqn 16/5L was heavily involved and flew large Union Flags to reduce the chance of them being mistaken for combatants. This was a wise move as both sides seemed to be operating a 'shoot first ask questions later' policy. Both of the SBAs quickly became congested with not only service families but also those from other nations seeking sanctuary from the fighting, and the Happy Valley sports pitches in Episkopi became a refugee camp, housing over 5,000 Turkish Cypriots. Adding to the discomfort was the climate, as the fighting was taking place in the hottest part of the summer and daytime temperatures were frequently over 100 degrees.

However, on 14 August the talks between the two sides following the ceasefire collapsed without agreement, and the Turkish forces almost immediately launched the second phase of the war. This brought the fighting much closer to the SBAs, particularly Dhekelia and its surrounds, and on the 15th a number of Turkish tanks halted on a ridge overlooking the signals intelligence outstation at Ayios Nikolaos. In the afternoon these tanks shot at a BBC camera crew, and in a moment of pure farce, one of the tanks halted outside the main gate. It was quickly established that the commander was completely lost – poor Turkish map reading being the root cause of many incidents of both UN and SBA troops being engaged – and luckily was out of ammunition and had a jammed MG. He was shown where he was, given some jerrycans of fuel and 'sent on his way'.[7] Disaster was averted when a Turkish battlegroup appeared to be about to assault the camp, believing it to be a Greek position, and the British commander managed to persuade them of their error; they 'wheeled left and overran the [Greek] camp'.[8] The single road linking Dhekelia to 'Ay Nik' separated the Turkish forces in the north from the Greeks in the south, and fire was frequently exchanged across the road, making travel between the two locations very hazardous.

By the end of the 15th, after two days of very intense fighting and manoeuvre warfare, the victorious Turks had reached their objective, their planned 'Attila Line', thereby securing about 38 per cent of the island. This line became the de facto border in a now-divided island, with UNFICYP setting up a buffer zone between the two parties – in places, particularly the original green line through Nicosia, only the width of a street – and redeployed to try and keep the armies apart, placing multiple observation posts with platoon or smaller outposts along 'the line'. Greek refugees from the north flooded south, and likewise many Turks went north, although significant numbers of both groups remained misplaced as minorities; many who were on the 'right' side were still internally displaced.

The resumption of the fighting meant that the RAC units returned to working flat-out, and as such were both observers and actors in a short but violent war. Captain Churton continued his account of the activities of the Para Squadron:

All was quiet until Wednesday 14 August when the Turks broke out, and over the next three days captured the third of Cyprus they desired. It was now that the UN received a fair proportion of its casualties. It was also a time that is amusing in retrospect, but very unpleasant then, as the squadron was shelled, mortared, attacked by aircraft, and machine-gunned. Fortunately we suffered only one casualty [Sergeant Pole REME, hit by SA fire]. We had a grandstand view of the battle and it was a sight that will not be forgotten by those who saw it. The Turks on many occasions were casual in the extreme and took many casualties, they would carry out their attacks with Sandhurst precision … a sight not to be forgotten by many was the M47 and M48 tanks being used to ferry great piles of wounded on the back decks to the dressing stations.

The squadron completed its tour, noting that their final six weeks were something of an anti-climax.[9] The other RAC units had similar experiences and also took some casualties during the second phase of the war. Three members of 6 Troop B Squadron 16/5L were wounded on 14 August when they were attacked by a Turkish Super Sabre jet at Ayia Marina. In an incident at Ayios Nikolaos on 15 August an A Squadron 16/5L Ferret was engaged by a Turkish tank, luckily without being hit. In both instances the attacks were probably not deliberately targeting UN troops, but it proved the point made in the regimental journal that 'the UN flag is not bullet-proof'. During this second round of fighting, B Squadron 4/7DG on the northern coast realized that they had become largely irrelevant where they were, and they and the Finns they were supporting were withdrawn to Mia Milia, north of the capital, where they 'had a grandstand view of the Turkish forces advancing on Famagusta'. Their SHQ occupied the UN camp at Kykko, which was situated between the two armies, and whilst not deliberately targeted, was constantly hit by MG and rifle fire, and over twenty mortar rounds landed inside the perimeter. Two of the squadron personnel were seriously wounded by shrapnel, with many others receiving lesser wounds, and the camp had to be evacuated. The squadron was then moved to the west of Nicosia, assisting the Danes and, once the situation stabilized, was able to return home on 24 September; by Christmas they were all serving in Northern Ireland.

Quite rightly, the UN force commander managed to persuade New York that the usual qualification period for a UN medal, ninety days, should be halved over the period of the war.[10] However, this was, as is often the case, unfair on those who served in the SBAs over the period, as no British campaign medal was awarded. Creating a CYPRUS 1974 clasp to the General Service Medal would have been a simple solution, perhaps too simple as it runs contrary to the strange British aversion to awarding campaign medals and clasps in a timely manner, if at all.

The Turkish invasion changed the placement and role of the UN forces. They now became responsible for supervision of the 180km-long ceasefire line – the so-called Buffer Zone, including the already established green line running through

A CVR(T) from A Sqn 16/5L observing action in Famagusta during the war.

Nicosia. The buffer zone stretches from Kato Pyrgos in the west, through Nicosia, to Paralimni in the east.[11] Different national contingents became responsible for stretches of the line, known as sectors. For example, in 1978/79 when B Squadron 3RTR (including the author) was the resident unit, the Canadians were responsible for Nicosia and the original green line, with the Danes and the British to the west of the capital, and the Swedes and Austrians to the east. The RAC squadron forming Force Reserve continued to come from troops stationed in the UK, and was stationed in their own camp adjacent to both 'BBC' – Blue Beret Camp, housing HQ UNFICYP – and the old international airport, out of use and still bearing the scars of war including two destroyed Trident airliners. At any one time, Force Reserve deployed three of its six Ferret troops to outstations at Skouriotissa (Danes), Athienou (Swedes) and the 'Box Factory' (Austrians) for a month at a time. Two of the troops in Nicosia patrolled the British sector and the capital, and the sixth troop was on R&R. The end of the tour was marked with a formal medal parade, with the airport runway doubling as a huge parade ground, allowing an impressive drive-past of the immaculate Ferret troops.

Although widely referred to as the 'sunshine tour', there were times when tensions were raised, particularly in the 1970s when shots were frequently exchanged across the buffer zone, and life in Force Reserve became somewhat more exciting. In a unique incident, members of C Squadron 3RTR were on duty at Larnaca airport in February 1978, at the very end of their six-month tour, observing a Cyprus Airways DC8 airliner that had been taken by skyjackers. Egyptian special forces were landed in Larnaca from a C130 where they attempted to assault the airliner, but were then engaged by the Cypriot National Guard, with RPG7 and 106mm rockets being used. The British soldiers, up to that point bored and simply waiting for something to happen after hours of inactivity, found themselves diving for cover as small-arms fire was sprayed around the airfield. The Egyptian C130 was destroyed and fifteen of the assault force killed. (It later emerged that the hijackers had already surrendered before the assault force landed.) The final UNFICYP Force Reserve tour took place when A Sqn 16/5L, fittingly one of the sub-units so heavily involved in the 1974 war, completed the commitment over the winter and the unit was formally dissolved on 12 January 1993.

Additionally to Force Reserve, some RAC regiments also served in UNFICYP in an infantry battalion role, manning one of the 'line' sectors and mainly involving OP duty, although foot patrolling and internal security were two additional tasks that required brushing up pre-deployment. The first of these came immediately prior to the war, when 5DG – not allowed to serve in Northern Ireland at that time due to being an Irish regiment – was deployed until April 1974.[12] From the late 1980s RAC and RA regiments were routinely required to take over the task, with 4/7DG, reinforced by a squadron from 15/19H, taking over the role in June 1988. Since then, the following regiments have served in the role: 4RTR (twice), QOH, 15/19H, 2RTR, QRL (twice), 1RTR, QRH, SCOTS DG and RL; many of these included either troops or complete sub-units from other RAC regiments.

Separate to the UN commitment, another armoured car squadron from the RAC was still required within the SBA; this was a popular accompanied tour. Following the 1974 war, the squadron was relocated to Episkopi in mid-1975, although it maintained a troop at the each of the two outstations near Dhekelia, namely Pergamos and Ayios Nikolaos. The delights of serving on a holidaymaker's island, as Cyprus was to become from the late 1970s onwards, could sometimes be disturbed. In early August 1986 a Libyan-backed terror organization mortared and rocketed RAF Akrotiri and also fired at civilians on a beach, with two dependents wounded by shrapnel in their married quarters. As this happened A Squadron 15/19H was in the process of handing over to F Sqn 3RTR, who took over the responsibility for increased patrolling of both SBAs, including the Akrotiri base and perimeter. Asking the same question that 16/5L had in 1974, the Tankies often wondered why the RAF was incapable of protecting its own airbase, particularly with a Scorpion-equipped RAF Regiment squadron available. As it was the venerable Saladins and Ferrets took the duty. Although the SBA commitment came to an end in June 1993 with B Squadron QOH as the final sub-unit stationed in Episkopi, there was one more time when many RAC soldiers were to visit the island, although this time on a very temporary basis. This was when transit accommodation camps were used for troops returning from tours in Afghanistan, as a short stop for a few days to allow for 'decompression', prior to flying back to their families and post-tour leave.

Northern Ireland, 1969–2007

Following the independence of the southern twenty-six counties of Ireland in 1922, six largely rural counties were left to form Northern Ireland, still part of the United Kingdom and generally, although inaccurately, referred to as Ulster.[13] These are Antrim, Armagh, Down, Fermanagh, Londonderry and Tyrone. There were only two major towns, Belfast the capital and Londonderry. About 80 miles from north to south, and 120 miles from west to east, in 1969 the population was about 1.8 million, with a Protestant majority. This was to become the setting for what has often been described as the British army's longest continuous campaign, lasting thirty-eight years.

At the root of the problem was widespread discrimination practised against the minority Catholic population, with many of them being housed in what were in effect ghetto estates of rotting slums, and unemployment was widespread. The NICRA (Northern Ireland Civil Rights Association, modelled on the one formed to support Black rights in the US) was formed, and from 1968 began to march, in parody of and in opposition to the Unionist/Protestant Orange Order marches. Violence followed and the Royal Ulster Constabulary found itself increasingly unable to deal with the situation. Rioting became commonplace in the towns, with petrol bombs being the weapon of choice. By mid-August 1969 the RUC could no longer police much of Londonderry (and some areas of Belfast) effectively, and so an infantry battalion was called in to assist the police, using riot-control techniques and equipment that had been developed for use in the Middle and Far East. Op Banner was the code name given to the deployment of troops from BAOR to assist in policing the civil disturbances and terrorism from 1970; it later came to be used as the overarching codename for all tours in the Province, with the emergency, also known as the Troubles, officially lasting from 14 August 1969 until 31 July 2007.[14]

British forces were deployed on one of three types of tour: residential, a two-year long tour in which families accompanied the troops; roulement, an eighteen-week-long planned deployment into one of the many security force bases; and emergency, a short-notice 'move tomorrow' type of operation that generally only lasted a few weeks in order to support a specific need. Emergency tours were a necessary evil and a recurring feature of the first three years or so of the conflict, and the need for them was much reduced after 1973 or thereabouts. Tours were also broadly classified as urban or rural. From the RAC perspective, it is possible to divide the campaign into a number of parts, naturally with overlaps and grey areas. From 1969 until the mid-1970s, the RAC was mainly used in a mobile role, using Saladin Armoured Cars, Ferret Scout Cars and Saracens APCs. Although this was chiefly rural, they were also frequently used in the large urban areas of Belfast and Londonderry, where the armour was proof against small-arms fire.[15]

As so often, the Ferret Scout Car proved its worth in the rural areas of Northern Ireland; this is a patrol from 3RTR, 1974. Note the additional Makrolon transparent armour added around the top of the turret.

The first RAC unit to be deployed on an emergency tour was B Squadron Life Guards, arriving in the Province on 19 August 1969. Over the next couple of years many squadrons were sent from Great Britain, often at extremely short notice, for tours lasting from as short as ten days to several months, and equipped with armoured and scout cars. Some were sent in support of the resident RAC regiment in Omagh, 17th/21st Lancers, which at the outbreak of the emergency had two of its three sabre squadrons deployed in the Middle East. Others were sent to locations such as Gosford Castle and increasingly to Belfast, where rioting had become a daily occurrence and small arms were in frequent use. Second Lieutenant Horsfall of the Life Guards recorded his impressions of what became known as the Battle of the Lower Falls Road, on 3 July 1970:

> At 1930 I was summoned urgently to the ops room … it had been decided to impose a curfew and cordon off the whole Lower Falls area … just before 2300 the Company commander summoned me and his briefing went like this: 'Right, we have a shooting match on our hands. There are several hundred hardnuts in the cordoned area; many are believed to be carrying arms and explosives. The orders for opening fire are unchanged.' Perhaps I should add here that the orders to open fire were to shoot on sight anyone

carrying arms and explosives. Having conveyed my orders to the troop, carried out a radio check and loaded the Brownings, we moved to the Start Line.

The order to move came at 2340. It was fairly dark and most of the street lights had been put out ... The entrance to Leeson street had been blocked and therefore we were compelled to take the next turning into Leeson Street via McDonnell Street. We were confronted by about fifty youths ... [they] dived for the cover of the street corners and opened fire. We had closed down ... I sent a contact report. It was easy to distinguish the crack of rifles and pistols, the burst of automatics and the explosions of grenades and petrol bombs. Bullets were thumping the sides of our Ferrets incessantly. I was very hesitant to fire my Browning [machine gun] as it was very difficult to determine from whence the fire was coming ... I saw a flash on the corner of Plevna street and fired six rounds. I then selected another target ... firing upon the troop became less concentrated.

I ventured to peer over the turret, I had barely opened the turret lid when there was a terrific explosion in the engine decks of 34C (LCpl Dearden) ... By now the shooting had almost finished. I was informed by a corporal that there was a sniper in the house beside me and that they were going in to arrest him ... Seconds later a white-shirted man was dragged out, also a .303 rifle and a box of ammunition. I breathed a sigh of relief as I could well have been a sitting duck for that particular gunman. At about 0530 ... we reorganised and continued to take up positions covering street corners. Shortly afterwards my troop stood down and a breakfast of cold sausages and beans was brought up ... We were pretty thankful to receive orders to move out ... The bag was some one hundred firearms [and] 21,000 rounds of ammunition ... My troop had sustained some forty bullet scars, fortunately none had penetrated the armour but some of the bins were rendered useless and one tyre was shot through. In retrospect, a very memorable occasion.

Almost from the outset, the infantry was struggling to meet its commitments worldwide and many battalions found themselves being sent to Ulster for a tour almost every year, which was a strain on the individuals and families and bad for recruiting and retention, as well as preventing them from improving in their normal non-IS roles. By early 1972 eleven battalions were needed to police Belfast alone. This led to RAC regiments being deployed in an infantry role, which meant retraining and often taking on additional manpower – or even complete troops or squadrons – from other regiments to bring them up to the strength of a four-company infantry battalion. This necessitated ever more training pre-tour and the regiments required assistance from experienced infantry battalions. The exact nature of the pre-deployment training was dependant on whether the regiment was going on an urban or a rural tour. Those deploying to Belfast or

Londonderry would concentrate on street patrols, house searches and riot control, whereas those going 'into the cuds' along the 310-mile long border were trained in more traditional infantry work, including culvert drills to avoid improvised explosive devices, rural patrolling and both laying and avoiding ambushes.[16] Both tours extensively relied on personal and vehicle check points (P checks and VCPs). By 1972 the Northern Ireland Training Advisory Team or NITAT was in operation, allowing better and more up-to-date training to be delivered. Most units conducted the majority of the training inside their own barracks, and finished off by going through the 'Tin City' training locations, in Sennelager and Lydd, trying to control a vigorous CivPop (civilian population, formed from non-deploying servicemen), who enjoyed the opportunity to riot and generally cause as much mayhem as possible. Many soldiers found themselves injured and even hospitalized as a result of the 'vigorous' training package, and not a few commented that it was more intense than the actual tour.

That is not to say that some tours were not exciting, but simply that a lot of time was spent conducting routing patrolling (hopefully not so routine that patterns were set that could be exploited by the terrorists). Most reports submitted at the end of a tour noted that a lot of time was spent conducting routine activity and waiting for something to happen. Lieutenant John Potter of SCOTS DG

The QOH in Belfast conducting riot control, 1973. The soldier on the left carrying a baton is probably a member of a 'snatch squad', whose job was to arrest ringleaders by dashing into the crowd and grabbing them. Note how young the rioters are. (Courtesy QRH)

recalled the boredom of his tour as a watchkeeper in 1972 being punctuated with one major incident:

> We did have a major fire fight when there was a cross-border night battle which included us using our (Saladin) armoured cars, which had two Browning machine guns, one in the turret and one mounted on the hatch cover. They were also armed with a 76mm main gun but this was not for use in Ireland. So much ammunition was fired on this occasion that we had to re-supply some ammunition for the battle via helicopter. The final casualties the following day were found to be one cow which was caught in the crossfire.[17]

The living conditions for the first units deployed were far from salubrious. Because Northern Ireland lacked military barracks, the troops found themselves accommodated in church halls, bus depots – including sometime having to sleep in the buses – schools, even deserted houses. In the urban areas a number of out of use mills were pressed into service, but this meant that they were not necessarily in the right places and needed a lot of work to make them habitable, let alone defensible. Operation Windfall in 1972 somewhat belatedly provided funding for better amenities – washing machines, TVs, furniture and gym equipment. At the same time Op Fortress improved the security of often vulnerable sites, with towers ('sangars'), anti-RPG fencing and surveillance equipment, and Op Bulldoze cleared the slums around some sites, which removed the nearest cover for the terrorists, but which then inevitably left them standing in isolated spots, which the troops had to 'hard target' from whenever they started a patrol.

There was, however, one RAC permanent location already in Ulster, which was Lisanelly Barracks, Omagh, used for armoured car regiments for accompanied tours of about two years. From late 1959 this had become a dedicated RAC posting, initially for 11th Hussars, and the camp (which had been a Second World War infantry training centre) was in dire need of repair and improvement … but at least it was a camp. Between the start of the violence in 1969 and its handing over to an infantry battalion in late 1982, eight RAC regiments were stationed in Omagh as the resident RAC regiment. These were, in order: 17/21L, 16/5L, 1RTR, 15/19H, 9/12L, 13/18H, 2RTR and, finally, QDG.[18] The resident RAC regiment in Omagh had a huge chunk of the Province to patrol, amounting to about 1,500 square miles of counties Tyrone and Fermanagh, which included a lot of the border area known as 'bandit county', and over which fire might be exchanged, but which could not be crossed to conduct a hot pursuit, a fact well known to the IRA and frequently used to their advantage.

When 16th/5th Lancers was the resident regiment in Lisanelly Barracks from November 1971 to May 1973, at the very height of the campaign, troops would operate on a three-week cycle, generally spending two weeks on IS operations, with the third spent in camp, conducting not only rest but also administration, vehicle servicing, training and all the other tasks necessary to be completed even during an operational tour. Despite the Omagh tour sometimes appearing to lack the concentrated frenetic activity of a roulement tour conducted as infantry, the dangers were the same and the combat real enough: on 27 March 1973, Second Lieutenant Somervell 16/5L was killed when his Ferret was blown up by a 500lb explosive device placed under a culvert. During 1RTR's tour (from May 1973 to November 1974) the unit experienced eight rocket attacks, with thirty-three rockets fired; three mortar attacks with twenty-five bombs fired; thirty-seven shootings, an average of two per month. During the tour they found twenty-nine weapons, nearly 3 tons of explosives, and over 3,000 rounds of small-arms ammunition.[19] Because of the potential problems caused by such a long period spent on operations as well as the proximity to violence and the threat to the families, in 1972 the tour length at Lisanelly was reduced to eighteen months. The threat to the loved ones was real enough: in August 1973, the married quarters of 1RTR in the camp were deliberately targeted, with a bomb exploding on 'the patch' injuring wives and children but thankfully causing no fatalities.

By 1975 every single RAC unit (less the two Irish regiments) including the independent RAC Para Squadron had sent at least one squadron to serve in Ulster, and some had experienced multiple tours at both squadron and, increasingly, regimental level.[20] In June 1973 the Queens Own Hussars were the first RAC unit to be sent as a complete regiment operating in the purely infantry role on an urban tour, in south Belfast. Such urban tours tended to bring the soldiers into regular close contact with civilians on both sides of the sectarian divide. Sometimes this would include tea stops, cakes and friendly voices, on other occasions it might include full-blown riots with petrol bombers being 'snatched' and the extensive use of CS gas and baton charges; it is likely that most injuries sustained during Op Banner tours were of a minor variety and caused by missiles, especially bricks and bottles. Some tours were relatively – relatively – quiet, whilst others seemed to be non-stop action, including the worst type, when personnel were killed or seriously injured. Being in the Province when there were major disturbances, such as the building in 1971 of the 'Silver City' internment centre at the former RAF Long Kesh (from 1976 known as HMP Maze), or during the hunger strikes in 1981, was guaranteed to bring additional risk. From the early 1980s the situation had stabilized enough to end the seemingly unceasing round of RAC regimental and squadron tours in the Province, as the infantry could provide sufficient battalions for the reduced amount of tasks. The main role that remained, and which was shared with the RA, was the single squadron Prison Guard Force at the Maze Prison, which, on some tours, also included HMP Crumlin Road in Belfast; this commitment was in place between 1980 and 1998. Possibly the strangest tour by an RAC unit was when, under Op Bravado, 4/7DG sent Green Goddess fire-engine crews to Belfast over the winter on 1977/78, because of the nationwide firemen's strike.

Soldiers from QOH in Belfast, 1973. The regiment was the first from the RAC to be sent to Belfast in a purely infantry role. They would not be the last. (Courtesy QRH)

The units that were sent at short notice to the Province in 1969 and 1970 went with what they had, including riot-control equipment that had in some cases been designed for use in Singapore; troops unfurled banners giving instructions to disperse in Chinese or Malay, which caused much confusion and not a little hilarity. As time went on, additional and better items were procured, with RAC units hurriedly being issued the brand-new Disruptive Pattern Material (DPM) camouflage combat uniforms for tours starting in late 1972. US-made M1952 and M1969 'Flak Jackets' were issued to give some protection to the torso, although they were never meant to be bulletproof; these were replaced in the early 1980s by the INIBA vest which included small bulletproof plates front and back to protect the heart. Helmets were simply the issue steel helmets, although some were fitted with visors for use in riots; modified motorcycle helmets were also used in urban areas and new NP Aerospace combat helmets came into use to replace steel helmets in the 1980s. High-leg patrol boots (reputably made of compressed cardboard), privately bought Doc Marten boots and black leather 'paddy basher' gloves were popular items.[21] Military radios proved all but useless in urban areas and so civilian radio systems were used instead. In rural areas, an increased threat from radio-controlled bombs meant that patrols had to carry heavy electronic counter-measures equipment, such as Violet Joker and White or Brown Sifter. Before the development of the Wheelbarrow remote device to allow bomb disposal officers to investigate suspected vehicle bombs, the 84mm Carl Gustav anti-tank weapon was used to disrupt/explode potential vehicle bombs from a safe distance, although things did not always go to plan. Regimental journals of the early to mid-1970s abound with stories of unsuccessful attempts to hit a parked car from a couple of hundred yards away, the Charlie G crews almost invariably identified as two unfortunate corporals from the Quartermaster's department, hurriedly pressed into the role of anti-tank gunners.

From the late 1980s RAC units once more were used in an infantry role with, for example, 3RTR deploying to the bandit country along the border of South Armagh and Fermanagh from July 1990 to late January 1991, and other

Until the introduction of specialist body armour, the troops wore American 'flak jackets' of Korean and Vietnam war vintage. The 7.62mm Self-Loading Rifle was the main personal weapon until the 1990s.

regiments deployed to fill the Girdwood commitment in Belfast. After 1998 the RAC commitment to Northern Ireland was conducted at regimental strength only. There were two locations that the RAC would fill, alternating with the RA; one was the Urban Roulement Battalion (URB) with tour dates from January until July, and the other the Drumadd Roulement Battalion (DRB) from April until October (a summer tour, if indeed there was such a thing in the notoriously wet Province).

The deployments to the Province were a distraction from the real business of training as tank and recce crewmen; as pre-tour training became more sophisticated, the AFVs had to be put into storage earlier in order to allow the crews time to be fully trained. As a rule of thumb, a squadron or regiment going on an NI tour would be out of role for twice the length of the actual tour, due to training and post-tour leave. However, the chance to go on operations was welcomed by many (at least for their first tour), with a common view being expressed in the phrase, 'It's not much of a war, but it's the best war we've got.' The Commanding Officer of the Queen's Dragoon Guards summed up the positive aspects – and many of the typical frustrations – of an Op Banner tour when he wrote in 1974:

> We eventually ended up in Londonderry after having been told we were going to HMP Maze, Londonderry, Belfast City Centre and finally Londonderry again. There is absolutely no doubt that an operational tour as infantry is an excellent and beneficial role for an RAC regiment. The training is fun, and all in all the tour is a most effective way of bringing home the problems of the infantry; it is also a very valuable experience for the young officers and NCOs and certainly a four-months which those who took part in it will never forget.[22]

In the period 1969 to 2007, about ¼ million British soldiers served in Ulster, a lot of them conducting two or more tours. At its peak in summer 1972, the army had 28,000 soldiers deployed, and in that year (the worst in terms of casualties) had 102 soldiers killed in action, the worst since Korea and until the Falklands campaign of 1982. Overall, the Troubles claimed the lives of 1,441 serving British military personnel, of whom 722 were killed by paramilitaries, and 719 died from other causes, mainly accidents; 44 of these came from the RAC. The very first casualty, both RAC and army wide, was Trooper Hugh McCabe of the QRIH, shot and killed in the notorious Divis flats in Belfast on 15 August 1969, ironically both because he was home on leave at the time and also because his regiment was subsequently not allowed to be deployed to Ulster. Equally ironically, the final RAC casualty did not take place in the Province, but in Germany in July 1989; Corporal Steve Smith of 1RTR was murdered by a car bomb outside his home in Hannover.[23]

Rhodesia, 1979–80

In late 1979 a Commonwealth Monitoring Force was set up to control the disarmament of well over 20,000 guerrillas who had been fighting in Rhodesia – the country that was to become Zimbabwe, and to keep the peace before elections could be held early the following year. Included in the force were numbers of RAC officers and soldiers. As an example, the CO of the QRIH was despatched to join the force with three of his officers and twenty-one men to act as monitors. Suddenly summoned to see the Tidworth Garrison Commander, Lieutenant Colonel Robin Rhoderick Jones was told that he was to be sent to Rhodesia 'within a week'. As is common with these things, the force did not deploy until a week before Christmas, and soon found themselves 'busy. Busier soldiering than I can ever remember because we are never off duty'. R-J and his 350-man team found themselves responsible for the largest of the Joint Operational Centres, called Hurricane, and the most northerly area. As he later wrote, 'There were no text books, no manuals, no precedents' – it had to be made up on the spot using experience, military judgement and, not least, common sense and humour. The QRIH force returned home in April 1980 without loss to their numbers. However, such operations are not without risk, as another member of the RAC deployed was to discover; Corporal Andy Drewery 13/18H was seriously injured on New Year's Day when the Land Rover he was driving for a ZIPRA liaison officer hit a mine, resulting in him losing his right leg.

The Falklands Campaign, 1982

Operation Corporate was the name given to the campaign to liberate the Falkland Islands after they had been invaded and occupied by Argentina on 2 April 1982. As a Task Force was rapidly put together, the inclusion of armoured vehicles was not initially at the forefront of anyone's minds, but as B Squadron The Blues and Royals reported, a decision was made and time was tight:

> During the Easter leave, the squadron, on rear party again, had two troops and SHQ loaded on containers for another Warminster exercise when the news broke of the Argentine invasion … at 3PM on Sunday 4 April the squadron was ordered to produce two sabre troops and a fitter section totalling 9 vehicles and 28 all ranks. The vehicles, many of whom [*sic*] were in a BRS depot at Bournemouth, had to be collected, thoroughly checked, equipped for war and reloaded onto containers for transit to MV Elk by early Tuesday 6 April.[24]

3 and 4 Troops commanded by Lieutenant Lord Robin Innes Ker and Lieutenant Mark Coreth respectively were the two involved, in mixed troops of two Scorpion

and two Scimitar each, plus two officer watchkeepers at brigade, and a small REME fitter section of four men with a Samson ARV.[25]

The ships sailed on 9 April from Portsmouth with all the vehicles and a party of three on the *Elk*, the remainder of the crews were on SS *Canberra* which sailed via Sierra Leone to Ascension Island where some practice firing (out to sea) was allowed, as well as the feasibility of firing from Landing Craft Utility in case that should become necessary against an opposed landing. At Ascension cross-decking the vehicles to the assault ship HMS *Fearless* took place, and bombing-up and final preparations made for an amphibious landing, the first since Suez in 1956. The Task Force arrived at San Carlos Water early on 21 May 1982, with a Scorpion and a Scimitar 'parked' immediately behind the ramp of each LCU for fire support, with a company of marines crammed in behind – in the event, the landing was unopposed. An anxious moment occurred when the leading LCU grounded about 200m from the beach, necessitating LCoH Klaus Fisher in callsign 23C to have to drive off the craft into water of unknown depth – luckily it was shallow enough and the landings were made, although the presence of previously unidentified 5ft-deep sandbanks on the beaches made life very difficult for the crews, necessitating the commanders having to dismount and walk their vehicles forward. At daylight 3 Troop managed to commandeer a couple of sheds in which to conceal their vehicles from air observation, with defensive fire positions dug-in to the terrain outside by an RE JCB digger, ready for the inevitable air attacks.[26]

The story continued as related by Coreth:

> The air raids began and became a daily feature of life. [Lieutenant Coreth from 4 Troop] replaced CoH Stretton at Windy Gap (where a half troop was providing flank protection). On the way there we proved our point for the first of many times. 'Inexperts' had said that CVR(T) could not move on the Falkland's terrain, we said they could … For the remainder, by day we shot at aircraft which we enjoyed, and by night we froze.
>
> We then hit a logistical problem that was to dog us throughout the campaign – fuel. There were not enough jerrycans for our fuel. Ordered to stay behind [on 26 May] we went on a hunt. The vehicles rolled at 1400hrs and the engineers discovered they were missing 28 jerrycans.[27] It was this move that proved to commanders that CVR(T) could cope with the terrain, given good driving and common sense.[28]

After starting the slow advance westwards towards Port Stanley, 4 Troop were annoyed to be 'denied' their first action at Estancia which had been abandoned by the enemy, and instead were employed in classic Armoured Reconnaissance work, putting in an OP 'from where we could observe Stanley with its famous nightlife, discos, bars and hundreds of pretty girls'. At this point the two troops joined up for the first time since the landings, after moving in some atrocious weather, with frequent mist and driving rain and sleet; it was often extremely cold, and ration resupply was uncertain. When 3 Para decided to mount what was euphemistically described as a 'battalion sized patrol' to Mount Longdon, both troops were allocated the ask of providing a fire base. Coreth again:

> I and 3 Troop moved forward to join 24A and 24C who had gone on a recce. We found them singing 'Always look on the bright side of life' as the mortar bombs rained down around them. LCoH Ward moved positions by 20m to find a mortar bomb took up his old position. CoH Paul Stretton and Tpr Taff Flynn saw the Mortar Fire Controllers on a hill so gave them some HESH to keep them quiet. We pressed on, now under artillery fire, only to have the operation stopped by the Brigadier.
>
> We were then ordered to Fitzroy ... this meant we had to cross the 'impassable' central mountains. This was truly CVR(T)'s most gruelling test. We learnt that to move in the Falklands one must always make one's own tracks, never to follow someone else's ... The 'experts' thought it would take 48 hours, we made it in 6.[29]

Both troops were lucky enough to find some barns where maintenance and hygiene could be attended to, and alcohol taken on board, leading to one trooper having a single sideburn shaved off for the crime of owning a pair deemed to be too long, and Trooper Voyce's exuberant 'tour 'tache' reduced to resemble that of a well-known German dictator. On 7 June the war resumed, with 4 Troop moving to Bluff Cove to support the Welsh Guards. Under attack by Skyhawks initially mis-identified as Harriers, 3 Troop enthusiastically returned fire including two magazines of 9mm fired from an SMG. This action included the incredible feat of a Scimitar shooting one down, more by luck than judgment, as explained by the gunner of 23B, Trooper Harry Ford:

> During the afternoon of 8 June 1982 the Sir Galahad was bombed by Argentinian warplanes.[30] There were two attacks and the following happened after the Skyhawks have completed the second run.
>
> We were staying in an open sided barn with the vehicles facing the water where the war ships were berthed. As the troop went to leave 23B broke down with a gear box failure and had to remain behind while the rest of the troop deployed to another location. There was an air raid warning signalling that there were several Argentinian Skyhawks approaching and that everyone should go to their action positions.
>
> My commander, LCoH Gary Dunkley, ordered the vehicle and crew to action and he loaded both the 7.62 mm GPMG and the Main Armament 30mm. We had made a modification to the 7.62 ammunition. We replaced

the standard 200 box with an empty 30mm box placed on the turret floor. This meant that the weight of the much longer belt was going to be an issue so Gary had to support the belt to prevent it breaking once the weapon started to fire. The 30mm was loaded with the standard 6 rounds (I cannot remember what type).

Sure enough the Skyhawks appeared, deployed their bombs and after their bombing raid one of the Skyhawks turned directly towards us. We had watched all that had happened and Gary was constantly talking and instructing me on what he thought might happen and what he wanted me to do. He said that if any of the warplanes came our way I should aim as best as I could taking into account how fast it was travelling. He would manually operate and fire the GPMG from his seat and I would fire the main armament on automatic from mine.

As the Skyhawk headed in our direction Gary gave the order to fire, he fired the GPMG and many tracer rounds headed towards the Skyhawk. I fired the main armament and those rounds headed towards the oncoming Skyhawk. I will never know what went through the pilot's mind but I suspect all of the tracer rounds startled him. The first four missed, but then the pilot banked slightly to his left which caused the fifth to strike – a hit! This round had done the damage and the Skyhawk lost control and crashed in a ball of flames in the distance. Within seconds of this happening, surrounding British troops who had been watching jumped onto the vehicle rubbing our heads and congratulating us on shooting down an aircraft.

This was by total luck more than any skill, those aircraft were travelling at such speeds that if they were travelling horizontal you could not have tracked them, they were out of your sight picture before you could react. If this one had not been heading straight towards us, we would not have been able to engage.[31]

Further forward and closing-in on Stanley, 3 Troop used their vehicles to extricate casualties from a Scots Guards observation post, despite LCoH Fisher's vehicle shedding them all – temporarily – when it drove headlong into a deep ditch at speed, during the night.

For the final assault on the range of named hills and ridges surrounding Stanley, 3 Troop were attached to 2 Para, with 4 Troop still with the Guards. As there was little chance of an ammunition resupply once in action, the troops carried all the spare ammo they could forward with them, in order to dump it as far forward as they could. Coreth again narrated the events:

On the night of 13th June 2 Para, supported by 3 Troop, attacked Wireless ridge. CVR(T) was really able to show its colours in the direct fire role. 23 threw a track in the middle of an attack, there followed the quickest CVR track

Scimitar 23B dug-in, with commander Lance Corporal of Horse 'Rocky' Dunkley and Trooper Harry Ford. It was this crew that shot down a Skyhawk jet on 8 June 1982. (Courtesy Harry Ford)

repair in history … on the third bound they came across heavier resistance and considerable return fire. They satisfactorily filled their game books for the season. 23C, with LCoH Fisher and Tpr Hastings, even managed to fire at Stanley on the last bound, hitting a POL or ammo dump with spectacular effect. They pressed on in the dawn and when the white flag went up, they, with 2 Para sitting on the vehicles, were among the first into Stanley.

4 Troop was also to have an exciting time … [The] incessant mortar fire falling around did help concentrate the mind … Bad communications meant that we could not talk direct to Maj Bethell [the Scots Guards recce platoon commander] but the sounds of a fire fight meant that they were in trouble. We moved forward to give support … there followed the most incredible explosion – we had hit a mine. The wagon flew into the air and LCpl Farmer failed his flying test for he crashed on landing. Shaken but not stirred, we all had roaring headaches for the next few days. The smell of smoke and burning cordite helped speed up the evacuation of the vehicle [which] was a shambles; the driver's hatch was blown off, as were the sprockets and some road wheels, the hull was buckled and the turret a mess.

We began to fire as best we could onto the enemy positions. This involved the invention of new techniques, taught at the Gunnery School. LCoH Ward and LCoH Meiklejohn used the previously unheard of '30mm HE at 4000m technique', and CoH Stretton the '76mm indirect night shoot'. I corrected fall of shot from the outside of the vehicles and awarded A grades to all.

We pushed on past endless articles of abandoned enemy equipment, artillery pieces, and dead ... The war was really over ... News came that we were to move to Stanley and board Fearless. That we did, taking along with us two captured Panhard armoured cars. On 24 June we kissed the Falklands goodbye, we had all our vehicles with us, but most importantly, we had not lost any men.[32]

There is little doubt that the performance of the small force proved the detractors wrong; not only were the vehicles able to cope with the treacherous and boggy conditions, but their flexibility and, not least, firepower, added much to the success of the campaign. Had this been known before selecting the units for the Task Force, it is very likely that more armour would have been taken. As 2 Para recorded after the infantry battle at Goose Green, 'Major Keeble [who took over the battalion when the CO was killed] could not help wishing that the Scorpion and Scimitar tanks of the Blues and Royals, which he had been most anxious to have for the operation, were available now...'.

Chris Keeble was to have his wish granted at the end, when the battalion attacked Wireless Ridge. In reporting the infantry's perspective, the battalion made the case not only for the use of light armoured vehicles in the Falklands, but, more widely, on other (past and future) operations that might initially be thought of as not needing them:

> Fire support was to be lavish in comparison to Goose Green. The [2 Para] MG platoon had been flown forward with six guns. (The single troop of CVR(T) mounted four GPMG in addition to the two 76mm and two 30mm guns.) The light tanks of the Blues and Royals would be there, and equipped with very high-quality night-vision equipment ... As D Company moved forward, the tanks of the Blues and Royals and the machine-guns provided fire support ... the fire support was immaculate. The tanks used their powerful image intensifier night sights to pinpoint targets, once enemy positions were identified, they fired. As soon as the battalion's machine gunners saw the strike, they too opened up ... Fundamentally, the battle was won by supporting arms, the infantry being free to do their own job ...
>
> It was strange that use was not made earlier of the support available from the weapons of the two troops of the Blues and Royals, for their effect during the battle of Wireless Ridge was considerable. Maj Keeble had tried to get them for the Goose Green venture but had been told that they were not available, although they were not used for anything else ... It seems they were added to the Task Force as an afterthought, and that no-one further

up the chain of command appears to have appreciated their cross-country capability, or the skill and tenacity of their crews. It is to be hoped that all the hard-won lessons of the Second World War about infantry tank cooperation have not been forgotten.[33]

Lebanon, 1983

Lebanon had seen years of bitter fighting since a civil war broke out in 1975. In 1981 the US managed to broker a ceasefire between Israel and the Palestinian Liberation Organization elements sheltering inside the country that were using it as a sanctuary and training ground from which to attack Israel. In June 1982 Israel invaded the country and besieged the capital Beirut for nearly two months, eventually forcing the PLO to agree to withdrawal, with a Multi-National Force (MNF) formed to supervise the withdrawal. Troops came mainly from the US, France and Italy. However, despite her misgivings and against her better judgement, Prime Minister Margaret Thatcher agreed in December 1982 to send a small British force to join the MNF, mostly in response to an American request and in order to be seen to be backing the UK/US 'special' relationship. Under the title of Operation Hyperion, BRITFORLEB (British Forces Lebanon) was formed, based on an armoured reconnaissance squadron of Ferret Scout Cars.

It was very difficult for the army to force generate this squadron, with other commitments worldwide, and so it was decided that C Squadron QDG, due to deploy to Cyprus for a routine UNFICYP tour starting in March 1983, would be made responsible for both commitments concurrently. This led to the whole UNFICYP task, normally involving 6 troops, being taken on by only 2, with a 5-troop squadron of some 115 men deploying to Beirut as part of the MNF.[34] The short-notice nature of the commitment meant that the Wimbish-based squadron was recalled from Christmas leave early, and issued with twenty-two mine-protected Ferrets and twelve Land Rovers (unusually, fitted with roll over bars) for use in Lebanon, which after some rapid preparation were despatched aboard MV *Fenchurch* to Cyprus.[35] After only sixteen days of training and equipment issue, on 23 January 1983 the main body departed for Cyprus. On arrival a small SHQ and forty-eight men formed the UNFICYP contingent, the remainder carrying on their training whilst awaiting the arrival of the ship.[36] Many of the vehicles, which had been in long-term storage at Ludgershall vehicle depot, broke down during a range day and needed urgent repair before they could be deployed.

The force was deployed in a chartered Greek cargo ship and arrived in Beirut on the morning of 6 February 1983. The arrival was marked by a short formal parade, during which the tyres of one of the logistic lorries were shot out by an over-enthusiastic Lebanese soldier as it had 'failed to stop'; fortunately the squadron was briefed to expect such antagonism and responded

C Sqn QDG was the first of three RAC squadrons to deploy to Lebanon. These Ferrets are on patrol in Martyrs' Square, Beirut. (Courtesy QDG)

with humour, defusing the situation. Taking residence in the Regie Hadith area of East Beirut, the conditions were not very salubrious and their new four-storey base, an old tobacco factory, required a lot of RE attention to make it habitable and defensible. Within 48 hours of arrival the first Ferret patrols were despatched; over the next six months 'not one day passed without a patrol going out'. At first, the environment was benign and during rest days the troops could sunbathe on the Byblos beach and even ski at Farayah, as well as indulge in sports competitions against the other contingents, and from May a week's R&R was allowed. C Squadron's tour was largely more peaceful than they had expected, although there were frequent firefights in the city and an Israeli position 150m away from the base attracted a lot of sniper fire at night; one lasting recollection was of 'joy in the eyes of the war-weary Lebanese when they spot the Union Jack'.[37] C Squadron departed on 9 August 1983, handing over to A Squadron the previous day.

However, only two days after the replacement squadron arrived, the situation rapidly deteriorated and the airport was closed and artillery shelling of the city took place, causing the first MNF casualties. The violent reaction by the US Marines (a large component of the MNF) came to be viewed by the belligerents as partisan and therefore made them a possible target. A Squadron improved their defensive preparations in response, and wondered what the imminent Israeli withdrawal might bring; 'it was a strange feeling to have a grandstand view of the fighting and yet not be involved'. The base was hit many times by shrapnel and small-arms fire, although not deliberately targeted – yet. On 30 August a Ferret patrol by 2 Troop escorting the British force commander came under deliberate MG attack, and the following day the squadron clerk was targeted by a sniper. When the nearby Israelis withdrew on 4 September their base was occupied for a time by the QDG; known as the 'Alamo', it was evacuated a fortnight later. The Israeli withdrawal was the signal for inter-factional fighting to resume at full intensity. RPG7 attacks started and a nearby Italian ammunition dump was blown up, fortunately without any casualties. Despite a local ceasefire, on 23 October a US Marine base was targeted by 2 suicide bombers driving truck bombs, and 241 Americans and 58 French military personnel were killed. As a precaution, accommodation in the British base was moved into the lower floors, and an 'almost unlimited budget' allowed more defensive improvements to be put in place. Even as the squadron was in the process of handing over to A Sqn

A Ferret patrol from QDG leaving their HQ. As time went on, the small British force found themselves increasingly the target of attack. The deployment was notable for the being the sole RAC-only campaign conducted after the Second World War. (Courtesy QDG)

16/5L in early December, fighting resumed and a trooper was wounded in the head by shrapnel.[38]

In typical British (some might say RAC) fashion, the Lancers were originally due to take over the commitment earlier but had a major Guidon parade scheduled for July, and so QDG 'sportingly' agreed to delay the handover. The 16/5L noted that there was no suitable training package in place for the task, and standard training for operations in NI or Cyprus was not appropriate, 'Nothing in Belfast nor County Armagh resembled conditions in Beirut, where men went about armed to the teeth and needed no encouragement to fire their weapons whenever the fancy took them … It was virtually impossible to distinguish friend from foe'.[39] From late January 1984 'heavy fighting made street patrolling both irrelevant and dangerous'.[40] On 7 February the decision was made to remove BRITFORLEB from the MNF, and after some amazingly fast work, the squadron was withdrawn the following day, ending the sole example of an RAC-only campaign conducted since the Second World War.

Other, less glamorous commitments also frequently involved army manpower, including the national firemen's strike of 1977/78. 3RTR Green Goddess crews tackle a large warehouse fire in Edinburgh.

Chapter 7

RAC Development Part Two

Canada

Even before the RAC was ejected from Libya in early 1970 and forced to look for another large area for manoeuvre training, some armoured training had already been conducted in Canada. This came about in 1964 when a composite squadron known as Hale Force was formed from members of 3rd Carabiniers, Scots Greys, 11th Hussars, 9/12th Lancers, 13th/18th Hussars and 1st and 5th Royal Tank Regiments, with a squadron headquarters from 17th/21st Lancers. A brief period of training in Sennelager revealed that there were a number of differences between the regiment's style and approach to warfare, but in late June the squadron flew from Germany to Edmonton in Canada, bound for Camp Wainwright and an attachment to Lord Strathcona's Horse. As the Canadian unit operated Centurion tanks, the squadron (labelled as C Sqn LSH) was able to take over the vehicles with few problems. One aspect that amazed the crews from Britain was the standard of the food, 'It was excellent at all times – not just when there were visitors around. We did not once have anything cold that was supposed to be hot. Everything was laid on – even paper serviettes on the tables.'[1] On 3 July the unit moved out onto the training area, and quickly found out that the Centurion Mk 3 tanks, which had been taken out of long-term storage, had up to 9,000 miles on the clock and thus were prone to frequent breakdowns.

Four exercises, each three day's long, were named Beaver's Pelt 1, 2, 3 and 4, with the final one being called Lash Back. Each exercise used force-on-force training, including exercising against Canadian infantry units such as the PPCLI, the Princess Patricia's Canadian Light Infantry, known irreverently to the Brits as the 'Ping Pong Champions of Long Island'. A period of R&R followed, including a visit to the Calgary Stampede followed by a week off to travel across Canada and the US, with the party arriving back in Germany in mid–August. Unbeknown to them, a pattern had been set, and would be re-used when the British army returned to Canada seeking a new, more permanent training area post-Libya.

BATUS

During 1970 a small party of RAC officers and senior NCOs (including the author's father) was sent to Alberta in Canada, in order to work out how to make best use of a large training area that looked like becoming the replacement for the desert training grounds in Libya, and which would allow not only manoeuvre at the battlegroup level, but also was remote enough for live-firing of tank and artillery weapons. The following year a ten-year lease was agreed, allowing the newly named Canadian Forces Base Suffield to be used for armoured training.[2] In January 1972 a new unit, the British Army Training Unit Suffield (BATUS) was founded, and in June, the first field exercise took place. The unit chosen to be the guinea pigs was 4th Royal Tank Regiment, with a single Chieftain squadron, C, under Major Coombes having the privilege of being the first ones to train there; they were to be followed by countless others.

With an area of around 2,690km², twice the size of the Isle of Wight, it was immense. It would be possible to fit the training areas of Bergen-Hohne, Otterburn, Drawsko Pomorskie, Salisbury Plain, Münster South, Hohenfels and Grafenwöhr inside its boundaries with room to spare. The area (often referred to as 'the block') was divided into smaller named areas which were allocated to different users; many of these were named after Canadian battles, such as Kap Yong, Dieppe, Hochwald and Coriano. Some extremities were not much used for military training, being set aside for oil commercial exploration, but still leaving about 1,700km² as the main military manoeuvre area.[3] Features and routes such as the Rattlesnake Road, Long Eagle Butte, Easy Lake, the OK Corral, Dragoon Trail and Reid Coulee became familiar to generations of British soldiers, although navigating around the area was often far from easy. In fact, it is fair to say that problems of navigation were often the most difficult obstacle to be overcome on the block. Even crew commanders who were experienced navigators found difficulties with the featureless terrain, in which there were so few trees that they were marked individually on the map. Although the transit routes – for use by wheeled vehicles only – were helpful, large parts of the area were barren prairie and required navigation using the contours of the map. Such difficulties were compounded at night, or when closed down. Stories of horrendous problems with map-reading abounded, with vehicles, troops and even whole squadrons going off in the wrong direction. In order to prevent such problems, in the late 1980s a series of distinctive towers (made of oil drums and other bits of scrap metal) were erected on prominent high ground across the area and marked on the maps, which made life a lot easier. From the mid-1990s crew commanders started to be able to afford commercial GPS receivers that could be purchased in the nearby town of Medicine Hat for a couple of hundred dollars, and later still (with the advent of Bowman) all vehicles carried GPS.

In order to allow six or seven battlegroups to exercise there every summer season, a permanent staff of about 200 was required, with the combat arms to the forefront and an RAC Colonel always the commander. As well as the headquarters and range safety staff, there was a large RE range targetry contingent and a full workshop and maintenance facilities to look after the substantial training fleet. A popular posting, the families of those posted there lived in the nearby military village of Ralston, not that they saw much of their menfolk when the exercises were live, as the safety staff on the prairie worked exceptionally long hours. During the season additional augmentees were necessary to increase the size of the staff, and this could require up to 1,000 additional officers and men per year – another demand on all the RAC regiments, as everyone had to supply their quota, and only experienced personnel would do.

From the outset, close attention was given to the needs of safety, as there were many hazards caused by the terrain, the nature of the exercise and not least during the live-fire phases when everything from 9mm up to 155mm artillery was in regular use. From 1972 the safety vehicles were painted in fluorescent orange/red, in order to make them clearly visible at long distances; over the years, different colours were introduced to allow different groups (arms) to be identified, including blue, white and yellow. Nonetheless, due to the original colour they were invariably referred to as 'red tops'. Despite their best attention, accidents were unavoidable and over the course of its use, tragedy was not a stranger to BATUS; forty-two soldiers were killed in training accidents over the decades.

The duration of the exercise and size of the training area allowed all elements of a combined arms battle group – infantry, armour, artillery, engineers, air defence, logistics and equipment support – to conduct realistic live-firing training at all levels, and to practise sustaining this activity over a long period of time. Typically, in the 1970s the troops would be on the block for about three weeks, which was broken down into increasingly complex live-fire training in fire and movement, followed by a 'dry' battlegroup exercise. Over the years, more time was needed to conduct all the elements that could only be rehearsed in BATUS, and so by the 2000s it would be more typical for exercising troops to be deployed on the

Chieftain conducting live firing at BATUS. The huge size of the training area offered unparalleled opportunities to carry our realistic training.

prairie for four weeks. The names of the exercises also changed. The initial name given to the prescribed, pre-formatted series of exercises was Exercise Medicine Man, with each numbered from 1 to 7 throughout the season, and allocated to a battlegroup HQ and its elements; Med Man 7 was the final exercise of the season and, as the bitter winter approached, could sometimes be little more than an exercise in trying to stay warm with inadequate clothing. After years of suffering for the troops involved – I can testify to its misery – it was decided to cancel it leaving Med Man 1–6. (It may be that the shrinking size of the manoeuvre force due to defence cuts had more to do with this, rather than concerns over troops welfare …) Later, as other elements beyond battlegroups started to use the area for training before deploying to Iraq and Afghanistan, exercise names such as Prairie Storm, Prairie Brave and Prairie Fire came into use.

Every ten years the lease for the use of the facilities at BATUS was extended. However, on 3 July 1998, a new financial agreement came into place, granting the continued use of BATUS in part-payment for the purchase by the Canadians of four ex-Royal Navy submarines. In 2006, on the expiration of this lease, the British and Canadian governments concluded another agreement that would allow British forces to maintain their training practices in Canada indefinitely. From training season 1995 a live enemy in the shape of OPFOR (Opposing Forces) was introduced, with 2RTR becoming the first regiment to take the role, using surplus CVR(T) vehicles with some VisMods (visual modifications) made to allow them to represent a generic enemy, using Eastern-bloc tactics.[4] Rather than the two forces being umpired in the traditional manner, with all the inherent problems of situational awareness and accusations of bias, the use of OPFOR was made viable by the use of Training Engagement Simulation (TES).[5]

Once the exercise phase had finished, the ammunition removed and the vehicles serviced and handed over, R&R and AT could begin, allowing troops to visit Calgary, the Rockies and the US, although for some the dubious delights of Medicine Hat (aka The Hat) were all that were required to deprive them of their attention and their money. Many local establishments entered into British army folklore, but probably none more so that the Assiniboia Inn, known to one and all as the Sin Bin. For many of its regular visitors, they never saw it during the hours of daylight, and probably had little idea of what it looked like from the outside …

At the time of writing, there have been numerous press reports that BATUS was going to be closed, and that the army favoured a new desert training area in Oman. This caused major alarm in Medicine Hat because of the potential effects on the small town's economy, after five decades of British army money, which had been estimated at $100 million. However, in late 2021 the defence secretary denied this, stating that the use of BATUS would change but that it would not close, so it may be that future generations of RAC soldiers will get to visit The Hat and The Bin, as well as conduct valuable training on the Albertan prairie.

RAC Organization in the 1980s

BAOR remained the centre of mass of the RAC units during the 1980s, with thirteen regiments stationed in the major garrisons of Wolfenbüttel, Fallingbostel, Hohne, Herford, Detmold, Paderborn/Sennelager, Münster and Osnabrück, as well as the detached squadron in Berlin. Some of these units found themselves having to provide a troop of six Scorpions located in Holdfast Camp, Belize, for a six-month tour as part of a response to aggressive moves made by the neighbouring Guatemalans. This was a popular posting as it allowed access to AT and R&R opportunities in Florida, Mexico and the Caribbean, but for the majority Germany meant the usual round of training, ranges, site guards, border patrols and training in Canada.

The unreliable though potentially battle-winning Chieftain tank continued to be worked on and improved, with much effort expended in trying to increase its reliability, particularly because of problems with the L60 engine, which made an excellent defensive tank something of a joke; by the mid-1980s things were much improved, and crews had much more confidence in the tank. Fire-control improvements followed on from the introduction of a laser range-finder which came into service in the late 1970s, and the Improved Fire Control System (IFCS) of the early 1980s finally made use of more modern technology to introduce a ballistic fire-control computer, making the gunner's job much easier and improving the chances of a first-round hit against both static and moving targets.[6]

But Chieftain needed to be replaced; the emergency Stillbrew additional armour added in the mid-1980s brought the levels of protection up significantly, but the tank remained unreliable; it was assessed as only having a 55 per cent chance of completing a battlefield day – 60km of mixed road and cross-country – without breaking down. As a short-term fix, a design intended for service with the Iranian army was amended slightly and introduced into service as the Challenger. During August 1984 the Royal Hussars in Fallingbostel took over the last of its complement of fifty-seven Challenger tanks, becoming the first regiment to be so equipped. More Challengers (later renamed Challenger 1 when Challenger 2 was developed) followed, and became the standard MBT in BAOR, although the three armoured units based in the UK and the squadron in Berlin remained equipped with Chieftains. The later marks of Chieftain, and Challenger (almost from its introduction), were fitted with TOGS, the Thermal Observation Gunnery Sight, which revolutionized the ability to fight at night and in conditions of poor visibility, and which was to have such an impact during the 1991 Gulf War.

Tactically, the RAC became much more professional over the course of the decade, with crews taking personal camouflage and low-level infantry skills much more seriously, in part coming from increased exposure to them during Northern Ireland tours. Some of this was reflected in appearances – the wearing of 'denims' (coveralls) on exercise became rare, with units insisting on the wearing of DPM combat uniforms, mainly to allow compatibility with NBC suits and drills. Tactical movement became better and commanders had to remain 'head and shoulders' only in turrets – no more the sight of tank commanders virtually standing on the top of their turrets on exercise. New helmets, hi-leg boots, camouflage parkas, two-piece waterproof oversuits, a new respirator (the S10) and other enhancements made life in the field more bearable. In a reversal of policy, from the end of the decade two members of each tank crew were issued 9mm L9A1 Browning pistols, replacing the 9mm L2 SMG which had been the standard personal weapon for many years.[7] On the logistic front, issues started to be made of the Bedford TM, an 8-ton 4x4 truck which increased the capacity of the echelon.

In 1974 the trade structure was amended. A Class III crewman was one who held one of the two main trades (gunnery or D&M) plus Phase One signals. These trades would be acquired at Catterick or at Bovington, the Junior Leader having the advantage as both Phase One and Two signals were taught there. To become a Class II crewman, the soldier needed to complete the other main trade course, plus Phase Two signals; this was normally done at regimental duty, and within the first two years of regimental service – the sooner the better, as it made the soldier a 'full crewman' and thus more employable, and a pay rise came with it. Acquiring one of the BI trades – gunner mechanic, driver mechanic, control signaller or GW controller – would result in a Class I crewman, again with extra money; these courses were usually run at the RAC Centre.

One of the things that definitely improved during the decade was the military salary, with (in particular) corporals qualified as crew commanders being recognized as being particularly well off. Local Overseas Allowance made a big difference for those posted outside the UK, and the allowances for married soldiers made them comfortable. The table below is taken from the pay statements of WO1 Michael Everton 1RTR, and which show his daily rates of pay as he progressed through the ranks during his twenty-two-year career, as well as the LOA he received, mostly when stationed in BAOR:

Table 7: Example Rates of Pay Over a Twenty-Two-Year Career

Year	Rank	Trade	Pay (£)	LOA (£)
1976	Trooper	Band 1 Class 2	5.70	2.23
1978	Lance Corporal	Band 1 Class 1	9.13	3.13
1979	Corporal	Band 2 Class 1	15.02	4.65
1980	Corporal	Band 3 Class 1	18.73	2.94
1982	Corporal	Band 3 Class 1	22.37	5.35[8]
1983	Corporal	Band 3 Class 1	24.04	4.98 (Cyprus)
1984	Corporal	Band 6 Class 1	27.54	Nil (UK)
1985	Sergeant	Band 6 Class 1	30.92	Nil (UK)

Year	Rank	Trade	Pay (£)	LOA (£)
1987	Sergeant	Band 6 Class 1	35.66	7.63
1989	Staff Sergeant	Band 6 Class 1	42.63	9.17
1991	Warrant Officer Class 2	Band 6 Class 1	55.09	10.21
1993	Warrant Officer Class 2	Band 6 Class 1	60.89	28.86 (US)
1995	Warrant Officer Class 1	Band 7 Class 1	74.73	Nil (UK)
1997	Warrant Officer Class 1	Band 7 Class 1	79.15	Nil (UK)

The Arms Plot

As mentioned briefly earlier, the Arms Plot was the name given to the routing rotation of regiments between the UK and elsewhere; for the RAC, by the mid-1980s this meant mainly BAOR and Berlin. An amended NATO Northern Army Group (NORTHAG) plan called the General Deployment Plan 86 required Britain to field twelve armoured regiments in BAOR, meaning that an additional operational regiment – and all its equipment – needed to be found. Until March 1988 the length of time that each regiment could on average expect to spend stationed in Germany was dependent on the role. Armoured regiments had an average BAOR tour length of somewhere between six and eight years, as opposed to two to three years spent in the UK. For armoured reconnaissance regiments, their tours were four to six years, in both countries. The two regiments of Household Cavalry, with their unique system negotiated in 1971, did approximately six years in each, alternating between Windsor (Reconnaissance) and Detmold (Armoured).[9] They had also negotiated an agreement that on no account would they have to serve as either the RAC Centre or Training regiments, which limited flexibility overall. Once the necessary details had been worked out, BAOR would find itself with nine Type 57 armoured regiments (each of four sabre squadrons) and two Type 43, with only three squadrons. The two smaller regiments were structured like this not for operational reasons in BAOR but because they would be responsible for supplying their fourth squadron for two independent roles: the tank squadron in Berlin, and the armoured car squadron in Cyprus,

Finding the additional regiment of tanks for BAOR – which was to be formed by 3RTR stationed in a new RAC barracks in Hemer – caused significant administrative pain. The until then separate roles of manning the RAC Centre in Bovington and Lulworth, and the RAC Training Regiment in Catterick, had to be combined, so that when QRIH moved back to the UK in March 1988 they were responsible for manning three separate locations that until then had been the responsibility of two complete regiments. The biggest negative impact however was to be felt in tour lengths. It became necessary to increase the average expected tour length for an armoured regiment in BAOR to eleven years; to put it another way, a regular career soldier in a tank-equipped regiment could now expect to be stationed in Germany for eighteen of his twenty-two-year engagement. It was recognized that this could prove to have a great impact on both recruiting and retention, but there were no alternatives. For the reconnaissance units, things were not quite so bleak; in fact, the units in the two locations in Germany (Herford and Wolfenbüttel) would alternate with the two in the UK (Tidworth and Wimbish) for tours that were shorter than before, at four years in each. The only real change for the Household Cavalry was a move from Detmold to Sennelager, which had already happened, in November 1986.[10]

The End of the Cold War

Late in the evening on 9 November 1989 a totally unexpected – for many unimaginable – event occurred: the fall of the Berlin Wall. The Wall, erected overnight in August 1961 and then substantially improved and extended, had come to symbolize the stark division between East and West. From June of the following year, 1990, the Wall (and the much longer inner German border fence) started to be formally demolished, and on 1 July the East Germans officially adopted the West German Deutschmark, and all border controls were abolished. The unification of the single German state occurred on 3 October. Although the Warsaw Pact continued to exist de jure until February 1991, the Cold War enemy no longer existed, and the USSR disestablished itself as a Communist state in December 1991.

These events called into question the rationale for the British Army of the Rhine. Stationed in Germany in case of Communist aggression, with no enemy left in place, why were they there? And a much larger question was being asked in Westminster: what to do with large and expensive armed forces that had been structured, trained and equipped for war in Europe against the Warsaw Pact? Were they now needed? As the 1990s beckoned, there was a definite feeling of uncertainty hanging over the Ministry of Defence. As is so often the way with such things, within months a large part of the British army would find itself fighting a major war 3,000 miles away.

Chapter 8

The End of the Cold War and Unexpected Commitments, 1989–2003

The Gulf War, 1991

When the Berlin Wall suddenly came down in November 1989, the certainty of the Cold War, the binding force that had kept British troops stationed in Germany for decades, disappeared, to be replaced by ambiguity, and what happened within a year of that momentous event took everyone by surprise. When Iraq invaded Kuwait during the early hours of 2 August 1990, most spectators in the West, including the majority of the members of the RAC still stationed in Germany, assumed that this had nothing to do with them. Their governments generally disagreed with this assumption, and on the 8th, President Bush announced that the US would be sending substantial forces to the region, primarily in order to offer a protective shield to Saudi Arabia in case Saddam Hussein contemplated attacking that country as well. Later that day the UK confirmed that it would take part in the 'coalition of the willing' that the US was assembling. On 14 September it was confirmed that part of that contribution, to be codenamed Operation Granby, would include the deployment of a much-enhanced 7th Armoured Brigade from Germany. As the brigade Chief of Staff remarked ruefully to his commander, Brigadier Patrick Cordingley:

> No Staff College exercise author could have written such a fanciful scenario. 'Your brigade has been stationed in northern Germany for forty years, training and operating within the tactically cosy matrix of the General Deployment Plan. During the next twenty-six days your establishment is to treble in size. You are to move your strategically immobile main battle tanks to Saudi Arabia in order to counter Iraqi aggression. You will be operating under the tactical control of the United States Marine Corps. Oh, and by the way, the first ships leave in fourteen days!'

It was not fanciful; it was real and it had to be done. Because of the nature of the terrain and the enemy, and the distances involved, it was clear that if there was going to be fighting on the ground, armoured forces would be required. 7th Armoured Brigade Group was formed from the usual units under command plus others, including a much larger logistical tail than normal, and included, from the RAC, two regiments of Challenger, SCOTS DG and QRIH, with the addition of A Squadron QDG as the armoured reconnaissance sub-unit for the formation.

As well as vehicle preparation, dealing with a sudden flood of spare parts, training took priority in the time available.[1] Although the troops considered themselves well-trained in general terms, there was a need to get all of the tanks on to ranges to conduct live-firing; SCOTS DG were well into their normal training cycle including exercising in BATUS, but QRIH had only just arrived back in Germany in April following a two-year stint in a non-operational role at Bovington and Catterick, and were somewhat behind the curve, having only just become a Challenger-equipped unit and they were not meant to achieve full operational readiness until April 1991. In the short time left before deploying, low-level training concentrated on what were seen to be the most important areas for the coming campaign: gunnery, radio, NBC, first aid and vehicle recognition. The huge Iraqi army had just finished an eight-year campaign against Iran, and was assessed to be battle-hardened and under such tight command that it would be willing to take casualties; there was also great concern about its willingness to use chemical or even biological weapons. There were particular concerns about the much-vaunted Republican Guard, Saddam's supposedly elite formations equipped with the best weapons, including T72 tanks.

Another problem that needed to be solved urgently was how to bring the deploying regiments up to strength. All personnel on courses were returned to unit, but there were still many gaps, in part caused by the sudden increase in each unit's establishment. Therefore, all of the other RAC regiments in Germany were asked to provide different amounts of men, with certain trades and skills. For example, the 17/21L in Münster, probably the most experienced armoured regiment in BAOR, supplied about 100 officers and men, all volunteers, making up 15 complete tank crews plus others for both command and reconnaissance troops. Their band joined with the band of The Skins to become medics within B Squadron of 1st Armoured Field Ambulance RAMC, and around eighty crewmen from 15/19H were trained as individuals to become Battle Casualty Replacements, or BCR, with members of their band joining A Sqn 1AFA. 9/12L supplied one complete armoured reconnaissance squadron, GW troops and all of their assault troops. And so it went on …

And it was not just manpower that was causing problems. The perception of the threat from the Iraqi army, and the Republican Guard in particular, led to the need to amend organizations and structures, and to modify equipment. With the former, some of this was related to the initial deployment of a single brigade, without much in the way of a level of command (or logistics) above that, meaning that 7th Armoured Brigade became a much larger 'group', as it had to take responsibilities for many areas that normally would have been the concern of someone else; at its largest it had 12,000 personnel under command, more than double the normal war establishment. This led to each unit being given a much larger logistic tail than was normal, including, for example, receiving US-loaned M548 tracked vehicles. Equipment modifications included the requirement to up-armour the Challenger fleet with additional modular packs to enhance protection against both tank guns and rocket-propelled grenades, which could only be done once the tanks were in Saudi Arabia. Another decision was that only the very newest Mk 3 tanks with the latest armoured charge bins were to be used; however, there were not enough of these to go around, so not only were all Mk 3 tanks quickly 'robbed' from other RAC regiments, but an emergency programme to develop an armoured charge bin system for older Mk 2 tanks had to be implemented.[2] And not least, in order to deal with the increasingly worrying threat of the Republican Guard T72M1 tanks, a complete new ammunition nature was rushed into service. This was the L26 Depleted Uranium APFSDS round, which caused much concern in the media at the time.

It was then decided on 22 November to increase the size of the British army contribution to a full armoured division of two brigades, stretching the personnel and equipment support to the limit.[3] HQ 1st Armoured Division was mobilized for deployment, with 4th Armoured Brigade under Brigadier Christopher Hammerbeck as its second manoeuvre brigade.[4] Unlike 7th (which had been declared operational on the 16th), this brigade only included a single Challenger regiment, 14/20H. The previous RAC actions to support 7th Armoured Brigade then influenced the deployment: 14/20H had already detached a complete tank troop to join B Sqn SCOTS DG, B Squadron had only just returned from Northern Ireland, and the regiment's C Squadron was stationed in Berlin on Chieftains, meaning that A Sqn LG (who had handed over the majority of their tanks to SCOTS DG in September) had to be attached to the Hussars. As the CO of 14/20H, Lieutenant Colonel Mike Vickery, explained:

> While 7th Armoured Brigade were preparing to depart for Op GRANBY in September 1990, the Challengers of 14/20H were being stripped of not only of their stocks of spares but also parts taken from tanks in order to give them to the two tank regiments deploying, SCOTS DG and QRIH. At that time, the plan was that 4th Armoured Brigade which included 14/20H, would not be going to Saudi Arabia until sometime in the second quarter of 1991 to take over from 7 Bde once they had been there for 6 months. The first complete equipments to be taken from us were all our latest Mark 3 Challengers, so we were very busy preparing those, in order that

we could hand them over in top condition to their new owners. But in short order we were then required to strip our remaining tanks to provide additional spares for 7 Bde. We removed powerpacks, final drives [gunnery fire-control computers] and the like, in a depressing series of depredations which eventually left us, by the end of October, with only one working tank. This, I insisted, remained in working order so that we could at least do some in-barracks training despite the lack of equipment.

In the third week of November 1990 at the Corps Commander's Conference, we received the orders that would send us to Saudi Arabia by Christmas, as the single brigade there was to be reinforced to become a two-brigade armoured division. Our first squadron had to be ready for embarkation on 9 December. Replacement tanks, powerpacks, final drives, track, fire control computers, and the multitude of missing items of equipment then began to flow into the barracks at an unprecedented rate. It was clear that normal working practices and hours were not going to be enough to get us off in time. We split the regiment into work parties and shifts which worked around the clock for some six weeks. Since replacing powerpacks and final drives were both REME tasks, and we did not have enough REME to tackle all that work on their own, we used our own soldiers to do the work, overseen by REME. This certainly paid dividends later in terms of the level of knowledge and mechanical capability of our crewmen, and of the very strong bonding achieved between our crews and our quite excellent attached REME soldiers.

The first squadron was rapidly rebuilt and transported across northern Germany to the Hohne ranges, where we undertook a very painstaking Confirmation of Accuracy By Firing (CABF) – essentially a zeroing of all weaponry and all sights. We also achieved a high standard of complex gunnery tasks including conducting battle runs at night. The tanks were repainted in desert colours and were delivered to the docks just in time for departure on 9 December. It has to be said that the standard of availability and accuracy achieved by Challenger once in theatre was remarkably high, particularly considering the problems faced before deploying, the rapidity of the rebuild, and the demands of gunnery preparation.[5]

Also deployed from the RAC was 16/5L, an armoured reconnaissance regiment. On arrival in Saudi Arabia by early January 1991 it was given command of A Squadron QDG which had been initially deployed with 7th Brigade, and also received a complete assault troop from 9/12L. This allowed the regiment to field four sabre squadrons, each comprising three recce troops on CVR(T), one GW troop with Striker and an assault troop on Spartan, in order to carry out a function labelled 'recce strike' – using the firepower and mobility of the regiment in order to strike the enemy depth and reserves. In order to do this, unusually, the regiment was put under command of the theatre artillery group, tasked with fighting the depth battle, rather than using them as a conventional reconnaissance force.[6] All of the additional units deploying had the same equipment and manpower problems to solve that 7th Armoured Brigade had already faced, but with a similar lack of time. 16/5L were also tasked on arrival – in addition to conducting their own preparation and training – with providing an operational flank screen to protect the rest of the division whilst it assembled, trained and then moved forwards. An additional and very unusual asset manned by the RAC came in the form of a troop of QDG – 'Canary troop' – quickly trained to use German Fuchs NBC recce vehicles and placed under command of 32 Armoured Engineer Regiment, which also operated a fleet of ancient Centurion AVREs nicknamed 'The Antiques Road Show'. Additionally, an Armoured Delivery Group was formed in early February in order to 'hold, train and deploy the majority of in-theatre reserves'. This included the spare tanks and other AFVs, and this component was controlled by an ad hoc armoured delivery squadron based on 2RTR from Catterick.

On arrival in Saudi Arabia, 1st Armoured Division was tasked with supporting the US VII Corps in a wide flanking manoeuvre into southern Iraq, designed to surprise the Iraqis and destroy their combat power, rather than simply retaking the territory of Kuwait. The divisional commander, Major General Smith, decided to use a system of echeloning his two armoured brigades, making each one the main effort in turn, and allowing them to deal with a number of 'easily digestible objectives'. These were given codenames of metals, with the softer ones giving way to harder ones – from Copper and Bronze in the west, through Zinc and Steel, to Tungsten in the east. This required a change in mindset and to some degree in operational art, from the defensive/controlled withdrawal perceptions of BAOR, to an aggressive, mobile, attacking campaign.

The war-fighting campaign can be broken down into four phases. The strategic air campaign against depth targets, especially command and control, which started on 17 January 1991; the establishment of air supremacy over Kuwait and southern Iraq; specific attacks to degrade the Republican Guard; and the ground offensive to retake Kuwait, codenamed by the Americans Desert Sword; the British would call their contribution Desert Sabre.

Even with the air campaign five weeks old, General Smith deliberately delayed issuing his final orders as he wanted to avoid the confusion that he knew would be caused with numerous changes to the plan, which was, of course, an American conception. The divisional O Group only took place on the morning of 24 February, giving the British contingent the mission of attacking through the breach created by the US 1st Infantry Division in order to defeat the Iraqi reserves, and thereby protecting the right flank of the US VII Corps as it swept into southern Iraq. The GOC's objective was to create enough space for the division to be able to manoeuvre and use all its combat power to good effect. Despite all the preparation, discussion and thought, the late delivery of orders meant that there was a rush to complete battle procedure within the brigades and units; Brigadier Cordingley only had a sketchy idea of the actual enemy strengths and locations, did not yet know the order of march through the breach and had less than an hour to prepare his orders to his brigade. And early success enabled the Americans to bring their whole plan forward by some 15 hours, accelerating the process even more.

16/5L led the British advance into Iraq on 25 February, operating on a narrow (2km wide) single-axis frontage; by midnight it was 50 miles inside Iraq without any significant contacts. It was then ordered onto Objective Lead, with B Sqn and A Sqn QDG in position by first light on 26 February to overlook the enemy positions, and to observe MLRS strikes onto them, as well as American A10 Warthog air strikes. The battle became very confused and during the morning all four squadrons were in action; one Scimitar crew was lucky to escape when it was hit by a T59, and a REME crew was killed when their M548 was engaged by another Iraqi tank.[7] A column of tanks attempting to reinforce Lead was engaged and destroyed, with Striker knocking some out at 3,000m, causing the tanks to retire. The regiment's actions, controlling both direct and indirect fire were successful, and it was then ordered to withdraw in preparation for a subsequent advance. As an official history narrated, '16/5L's action on Lead had been a significant success ... In many respects the success of the action was a turning point in the overall operation. Prior to Lead there was every danger of a concerted counter-attack by the Iraqi tactical reserves; after lead the chances of a counter-attack were much reduced.'[8] Following this, the depth fire group artillery assets were split up and apportioned between the two armoured brigades, to be employed by whichever one was the main effort. When this happened 16/5L were deployed forward to clear enemy depth positions along the Iraq/Kuwait border to allow 7th Armoured Brigade to advance rapidly eastwards. Its final task was to drop back into Iraq to provide rear area security for the enormous divisional logistical area.

For the two armoured brigades, the contact battle commenced during the afternoon of 25 February. The infantry heavy 4th Armoured Brigade was originally slated to lead through the breach, but the unexpected and welcome early success meant that 7th Brigade were given the task of conducting a rapid break-out, with the two Challenger regiments and 1 Staffords in their Warriors conducting a complex operation called a Forward Passage of Lines, through the American infantry division at the breach. It was terribly complicated: to move the whole of the 1st Armoured Division through the breach, on four-tracked and four-wheeled routes, even with all vehicles moving nose-to-tail rather than tactically spaced, took 6 hours. The provision of GPS equipment in some key vehicles was a game-changer for the rapidly moving armoured forces: Brigadier Cordingley even going so far as to state that 'for the first time in the history of the British Army, we were likely to know where we were when we fought a battle'.[9]

Despite the problems caused in deploying so quickly into theatre and as explained earlier, other in-service equipment proved to be a real battle-winner, and none more so that the TOGS gunnery system. Colonel Vickery again:

> Challenger was equipped with the excellent TOGS Thermal Imaging (TI) night sight. We were able to see 'hot spots' created by armoured vehicles at over 10kms in pitch darkness. As we approached, vehicles, trenches, equipment and people became recognisable at ranges which enabled us to shoot at them. The TOGS sight was zeroed to the main armament such that we could fire accurately in the dark. Its output was fed to the gunner and the commander of the tank.
>
> This gave us a real technological superiority over the Iraqis, whose only night vision devices were active infra-red lights and sights. Challenger was equipped with IR detectors, so if we were illuminated by IR searchlights, we knew where they were and could engage them. Using GPS and TI together at night meant that we could move at a good speed at night, and were capable of accurate gunfire against point targets in total darkness.
>
> There was a problem, however, as neither our supporting Warriors, nor our Recce Troop were fitted with TI. They had Image Intensifying (II) sights which depend on a certain amount of ambient light which the sight multiplies to reveal targets. Starlight is sufficient for this, but in the cloudy weather we experienced, and the fact that clouds from burning oilfields were often obscuring the stars, II was of considerably less use than TI. This difference in night vision tended to split the Challengers from the Warriors in a night attack, the very time when infantry and tanks need to work intimately together. This was further exacerbated when the infantry dismounted as they then had no night vision at all and depended on artillery, mortar and Scorpions to provide illumination for them. This light was too bright for II sights, however, causing them to white-out completely. The moral of this tale is that all AFVs need to be provided with the same technology for night viewing if they are to work properly together.[10]

TOGS was key for the success of the Challenger regiments, as the official account explained:

Initial contact was nearly always made by Challenger and often came in the form of an ill-defined hot spot on TOGS. Once the contact had been identified as enemy, the main aim was to bring as many guns to bear and this often entailed manoeuvring a squadron (and sometimes more) into line … Once the firefight was won, the next problem was to convince the Iraqis that the squadron wanted to accept their surrender and then move on quickly. This was achieved by switching on the Challenger headlights and moving slowly onto the objective…. There were few examples of genuine meeting engagements although enemy armour was often engaged while moving around on positions. QRIH conducted an engagement which appeared to be against an enemy counter-attack during the early hours of 26 February; many hot spots were identified on TOGS at extended ranges, although accurate identification was difficult. 97 main armament rounds were fired mostly using estimated ranges, and the counter-attack was successfully halted … The marrying up of Warrior to Challenger sometimes did not occur until the Line of Departure was being crossed, and there were also occasions when the tanks were too far ahead or had already overrun the enemy position.

Captain Tim Purbrick 17/21L commanded 4 Troop D Sqn QRIH and recorded his crew's conversations in the turret of his tank during the ground war, which allowed him to produce an unusually accurate record of events, some of which were as follows:

I had been scanning for ten or fifteen minutes. Suddenly in the distance I started picking up hot spots in the thermal sight. I couldn't tell what they were. But they were targets. Most likely Iraqis bugging out in their tanks and trucks to a fallback position. We were cleared to engage, there were no friendlies to our front. We picked targets and started firing. We had Fin loaded but the targets were too far away. 'Stop loading, load HESH' I ordered when we fired off the Fin. 'Fire' from me. 'Firing now!' The turret rocked as the heavy shell left the barrel. There was a huge explosion about 100 meters in front of the tank. 'What the f*** was that?' Crest clearance. The round had slammed into a ridge in front of our tank and exploded. We moved up onto the ridge and started the engagement again. It was difficult to tell but we claimed a number of hits.

As the sun came up, we began to pick up targets on both thermal and visual. Tanks. They were ensconced behind sand walls or berms. We picked one. We had HESH loaded from the night before. 'HESH tank on'. 'Firing now!' 'Stop loading, load Fin.' It was going like clockwork on the ranges, but the target was not falling when hit. I glanced at the commander's range readout. 3600m to the target. Three times the battle range of the

Challenger, which was 1200m. Through the smoke and obscuration came a small lightning flash. 'Target!' This third round ... had entered through the front glacis plate and exited vertically through the gearbox, igniting the tank's bomb load and removing its turret. 'Target Stop!' Other tanks in the squadron were picking off T55s across our front. We were probably too far away for them to see us, let alone to shoot at us and hit us.

'Fire!' I ordered and looked at the range readout. 4700m. The fin round rent the air as it tore across the battlefield. At 1500m per second, it took just over three seconds to reach the target. By that time, the smoke and obscuration had cleared, carried off by the light wind. There was a blinding flash from the target and, a millisecond later, a massive fireball of boiling black and red smoke lifted off the target. It was a vast explosion. Underneath the mushrooming ball of smoke were hundreds of matchstick men running for their lives.[11]

4Tp B Sqn QRIH led by Lt Buxton – another of the 17th/21st Lancer troops – reported an interesting engagement during the ground offensive:

We advanced towards Objective PLATINUM 1, a regimental-sized enemy position, with our Lynx helicopters firing missiles over our heads. A vicious wind was whipping the sand up to about the level of the gunner's sight, making the visibility quite poor. Sgt Griffin in Callsign 41 observed a seething mass of men running from the position in front of him into the swirling sand. He pushed a further 200m forward, to about 1200m short of the objective. His gunner then saw a scene straight out of Lawrence of Arabia – out of the sand clouds came three camels complete with gun-toting Arabs and soldiers on foot charging towards them. The crew burst out laughing, but because the enemy had RPGs they had to be dealt with. A short burst [of coax] was used as a warning, but 1000 rounds later, they gave up – we think that they surrendered due to the fatigue as much as anything else![12]

The operations, at all levels, succeeded in a way that even the most optimistic could not have prophesied. By the early hours of 28 February a temporary ceasefire was imposed, bringing to an end about 100 hours of frantic combat, in which the armoured crews had been pushed to their limits, with little sleep and near-constant movement. For a time it looked as though further military action might be required, and the exhausted crews took the opportunity to catch up on much-needed rest. It then became clear that Iraq had been resoundingly defeated, Kuwait had been liberated and that there was no appetite to resume fighting. In short order the formations and regiments fell back into Saudi Arabia from where they flew back to their peacetime locations, the vehicles following on board ships. Almost as quickly as it had started it was all over, although unbeknown to anyone many of them would be returning to the region twelve years later.

What had happened demonstrated an amazing ability to cobble together an effective fighting force from often disparate parts, and weld them together quickly. This reflected well on the British army's training and leadership, not to mention grit and determination, although much less well on the size of the force or its logistic support arrangements in peacetime. In the most armoured campaign that the British army had fought since the invention of the tank, the Royal Armoured Corps had demonstrated its professionalism throughout the period of deployment, training and operations. This however would not be enough to save it from a more durable enemy than the Iraqi army – the Treasury.[13]

Options for Change, 1991

The Options for Change restructuring and cuts that were announced following the break-up of the Warsaw Pact hit the RAC hard; fundamental to the logic behind it was the fall of the traditional enemy, the Soviet Union, with its massed tank armies. When the package was announced at 1330 hours on 23 July 1991, there was widespread disbelief that such swingeing cuts could be contemplated only months after the successful conclusion of an armour-based expeditionary campaign. To many observers, the world was if anything less stable and therefore more dangerous and unpredictable than it had been in the days of the Cold War, but the Treasury had the last word and the phrase frequently heard was that this was a 'peace dividend'. Within the RAC, the nineteen regiments were ordered to be reduced to eleven, leaving only three unaffected. The new regiments formed were, in date order:

> The Royal Dragoon Guards (RDG – from 4/7DG and 5DG) 1 August 1992
> The Second Royal Tank Regiment (2RTR – from 2nd and 3rd RTR) 5 August 1992
> The Household Cavalry Regiment (HCR – from the LG and the RHG/D) 19 October 1992
> The King's Royal Hussars (KRH – from the RH and 14/20H) 1 December 1992
> The Light Dragoons (LD – from 13/18H and 15/19H) 1 December 1992
> The Queen's Royal Lancers (QRL – from 16/5L and 17/21L) 25 June 1993
> The First Royal Tank Regiment (1RTR – from 1st and 4th RTR) 3 August 1993
> The Queen's Royal Hussars (QRH – from the QOH and QRIH) 1 September 1993

The amalgamations ordered by Options for Change in 1991 created eight new regiments, including six new cap badges, shown here in seniority order, from left to right: HCR, RDG, QRH, KRH, LD, QRL. It reduced the size of the RAC by about 40 per cent.

Although rumours beforehand had been rife, the actual announcement of this round of cuts still came as a shock – possibly more so as it directly affected two of the three armoured regiments that had recently been fighting a short but intense war in Iraq; clearly, such things did not make one invulnerable from political decisions. As a result, the overall manpower for the Household Cavalry and RAC combined was reduced by 3,500 posts, from 9,100 to 5,600, a reduction of nearly 40 per cent. The Household Cavalry manpower was reduced by 24 per cent, but the RTR again lost proportionally more, around 50 per cent. Because of the reduced numbers, there was a variety of different mechanisms to deal with the personnel not immediately required for the new regiments or within the ERE establishment. The most popular of these proved to be a programme of generous redundancy packages, but only for those in the ranks of corporal to Class One warrant officer, and with between thirteen and twenty years' service. The less fortunate were compulsorily transferred to other parts of the army or, in some cases, made redundant.

The impact on the affected regiments was of course profound. By way of example, an officer in the Royal Dragoon Guards looked back on the 'Options' process twenty-five years later, and his following recollections reflected the shock felt by the announcement, quickly followed by the actions taken to ensure that the amalgamation was a success, at least in terms of those two hardy perennials – uniforms and dress:

> Five of us appropriated a couple of offices in the Skins RHQ and, despite not even knowing for certain the new name, duly put an RDG sign on the door. At that stage we had no cap badge, no motto, and no idea. However, we did know that we were about as welcome as a cuckoo in the well-feathered nest of Barker Barracks. Meanwhile, whenever I returned to Detmold, the 4th/7th treated me with a certain suspicion.
>
> There were two key elements to be considered: the manning plot, and the uniforms and traditions. [There were] a few provisos: the badge was to be based on the 4th Royal Irish Dragoon Guards star and the Inniskilling castle, but the castle was not to dominate. The green trousers of the 5th Dragoon Guards were a non-negotiable given … A Dress Committee was formed … the D-Day flash [of 4/7DG] was considered significant by the Skins and the green trousers likewise by the 4th/7th … one result was that all ranks would wear the coloured cap badge as opposed to plain silver … Especially when it came to Mess Dress the differing attitudes of the regiments became apparent; it is safe to say the Skins wanted lots of gold, and the 4th/7th somewhat less.[14]
>
> The first samples of uniform and accoutrements were ordered and tailors and hat-makers came touting for business … the gold buttons were approved before it was realised how much they would cost, but by then the pattern had been approved and could not be altered. Sadly, when we asked for cross-belts for all ranks we were told we would have to pay for them ourselves.
>
> The noisiest objectors were the Skins subalterns, reflecting the approach taken by their CO. The Skins NCOs were much more supportive, whereas the 4th/7th NCOs were much bolshier. But once they realised that we were so overmanned no-one would be particularly upset if they left the army, they soon came round …

The story of the so-called 'union' of the two regiments of Household Cavalry on 19 October 1992 is also worth relating. The Blues and Royals rightly felt aggrieved that they were being called upon to amalgamate again, only twenty-two years – the length of a soldier's full career – after the last time it had happened, whereas 'older' regiments were left untouched, notably the Queen's Dragoon Guards (1959) and 9th/12th Royal Lancers (1960).

Her Majesty made it clear that she required two distinct units of Household Cavalry to be retained for ceremonial duties, which indicated that somehow, the separate identities of the two had to be retained. The difficulty was that although the Household Cavalry Mounted Regiment had always existed together (although as two semi-independent parts) sharing the same barracks, the armoured regiments had not, merely swapping postings between Windsor (as an armoured recce regiment) and Detmold (as a tank regiment) every few years, a terribly inefficient arrangement. At some point, before the official 'Options' announcement was made, efforts had been made behind the scenes to find two heavy cavalry partners that the Life Guards and The Blues and Royals could each amalgamate with – in effect that they could absorb and therefore retain much of their identity. However, this failed, largely because the Life Guards had deliberately 'made themselves unappealing as a partner'. As a result, the CGS came up with the compromise solution of bringing the two operational regiments together, although he employed the term 'union' rather than 'amalgamation'; in hindsight, at least one CO of The Blues and Royals subsequently believed this to be a mistake and would have preferred the certainty of a full-blown amalgamation. Problems were many, including a remarkably different outlook from the members of both regiments, regardless of rank. The Life Guards called the CO 'Colonel Sir', whereas to The Blues he was simply 'Colonel'. The Blues would salute without headgear, whereas the 'Tins' would not. These can be written off as minor eccentricities, but other problems ran deeper. For instance, A and B Squadrons in the new Household Cavalry Regiment (armoured reconnaissance) were badged as Life Guards, C and D were Blues and Royals. However, the Headquarters Squadron had to be made up from personnel from both regiments; some posts were rotational, but others were tied to a specific regiment, meaning that the other could not fill a vacancy, even if a suitable person existed, simply because they wore the 'wrong' cap badge.

The link between the Household Cavalry Regiment, serving on armour, and the ceremonial Household Cavalry Mounted Regiment has an advantage in that it allows for a much-larger regiment overall, but as these are in two entirely different and non-complimentary roles, there is little experience that can be transferred from one to the other when making the switch. A pre-union report stated that:

> Service in the HCMR is not universally popular within [the Household Cavalry]. The majority of recruits join the regiment intending to become armoured soldiers, and seventy one per cent of the regiment is employed on either tanks or armoured reconnaissance. Many soldiers have a genuine dislike of horses, and view the long hours of kit cleaning and stable duties with dismay.[15]

The bands of the regular regiments were also affected, and in 1993 a somewhat tardy decision was made to remove individual regimental bands, and reduce them to four larger bands of thirty-five bandsmen each: these would be known as the Bands of the Dragoon Guards, the Hussars, the Lancers and the Cambrai Band of the Royal Tank Regiment.[16] These bands formed up in their new identities the following year, breaking hundreds of years of tradition that each regiment had its 'own' band. Inevitably, as a result of the Future Army Structure changes a decade later, in 2006 this was changed once more to amalgamate again in order to create only two RAC bands, the Light Cavalry Band at Bovington and the Heavy Cavalry and Cambrai Band based in Catterick.

Within the Yeomanry, Options meant that the Royal Mercian & Lancastrian Yeomanry (RMLY) was formed in November 1992 by the amalgamation of the QOMY and the DLOY, and in 1999 it became a four-squadron regiment by absorbing a squadron from the QOY, which itself had been formed in 1971. At the same time, the Scottish Yeomanry was formed in 1992 as a newly titled unit, although with many historical antecedents. The spare equipment made available from the amalgamations of regular units did mean that some of the Yeomanry regiments were able to say goodbye to the Fox Armoured Cars and become tracked for the first time in decades, operating CVR(T).

As the decade went on, there were other, often less public changes within the RAC. There was much less tolerance of alcohol and offences related to its misuse, including a reduction in the amounts that might be drunk on exercises. 1958 pattern webbing was replaced by a new nylon pattern, initially green and then camouflaged. A new DPM combat kit came into service in mid-1990s with rank worn on the chest, and the wearing of body armour – even inside AFVs – became common place on operations. Hearing protection, not only on ranges but also on the tank park, became mandatory. Much more attention was paid to the environment on exercises, with the use of 'live' cam cut from trees

The formation of the RMLY in 1992 was yet another in a series of Yeomanry amalgamations that continued to reduce the size of the RAC territorial units.

and shrubs banned, and care taken to collect or contain oil spills; all vehicles were required to carry a drip tray, even on operations.

On the equipment front the introduction of Challenger 2 (leading to the original tank being renamed as Challenger 1, CR1 for short) was the major change. As the Berlin Wall was being dismantled in 1990 the British army was still operating a reasonably large fleet of Main Battle Tanks (MBT), with no less than 1,072 in service within 13 tank regiments and including those in the training fleet and repair pool. The most obvious problem with this was that two different types of tanks were in service: 646 of the older Chieftains, plus 426 of the newer Challengers. Although there was some commonality between the two, particularly with turret systems, it is never a good idea to operate a mixed fleet, as it causes both logistic and training burdens. However, the real issue went beyond the types of tanks, in that both were based on 1950/60s technologies and they were no longer capable of defeating the latest generation of Soviet battle tanks, let alone anything that might be faced in the future – the Soviets were fielding a new tank roughly every seven years, and the British army needed to find a way to regain at least technical parity, if not superiority. A new tank was needed, and fast.

In December 1986, the Master General of the Ordnance, responsible for army equipment, visited the offices of Vickers Defence Systems (VDS) in order to deliver a briefing on the options under consideration for a replacement tank – initially for the Chieftain fleet only. On 30 March 1987 VDS formally presented the Minister of Defence Procurement and the Chief of the General Staff with a solution that the company hoped would be attractive, having only started work on the design at the very end of the previous year. VDS described the new tank thus:

> Challenger 2 will be a vehicle which is a considerable advance on other vehicles in service, including the German Leopard 2 and the US Abrams. It employs 'new recipe' Chobham armour [and a] new suite of sights to provide reduced target acquisition and engagement times. The inclusion of the new CHARM 120mm gun will ensure that the vehicle's firing power has growth capability. A great deal of effort is also being expended in providing the best ergonomic solution.

It was now critical to know how many tanks might be required – was the tank really only intended to replace Chieftain as the original discussions had indicated, or might it be used to replace the entire Chieftain and Challenger fleet? This was key, as costs would rise if fewer tanks were built, and economies of scale were a sensible way of forcing the overall price down, which of course was attractive to the Treasury. The existing operational tank fleet of 685 tanks looked like this:

Chieftain
1 x Type 43 Regiments = 43 tanks
5 x Type 57 Regiments = 285 tanks
Total 328

Challenger
3 x Type 43 Regiments = 129 tanks
4 x Type 57 Regiments = 228 tanks
Total 357

Arguments raged about numbers, but eventually only 386 Challenger 2s were built, replacing both Chieftain and Challenger – which had to be renamed Challenger 1 (CR1) once Challenger 2 entered the lexicon – giving the RAC a brand-new but much smaller fleet of MBTs. This allowed six regiments of forty-four tanks each plus a small reserve.[17] Although it was meant to enter service in 1994, problems with the build standard of production tanks caused delays and the first regiment to receive them, SCOTS DG, did not take over the last of their operational tanks until June 1998.[18] When the last regiment received its fleet of Challenger 2s, it was the first time that the RAC had been equipped with only one type of MBT since the introduction of Challenger 1 in 1985.

Within the CVR(T) fleet, Scorpion left service suddenly and prematurely in 1992 due to excessive toxic fumes being discovered coming from the 76mm gun, leaving the 30mm armed Scimitar and Sabre as the main reconnaissance platforms. An Urgent Operational Requirement (UOR) in Bosnia in 1996 led to the limited introduction of the SPIRE thermal imaging sight on Scimitar/Sabre to replace the in-service image intensifier, with an improved version, E-SPIRE, later coming into service. The whole remaining in-service CVR(T) family – over 1,200 vehicles – went through a 'life extension' upgrading programme starting at the end of the 1990s, which saw the Jaguar petrol engine replaced with a Cummings diesel; by the end of 2000 all of the regular Formation Recce regiments had their vehicles upgraded to the new standard.[19]

The Balkans, 1992–2003

Bosnia and Croatia

The reasons behind the racial and religious conflict that arose in the Balkans in 1992 go back many centuries, but the immediate cause was the breakup of Yugoslavia, the subsequent declaration of independence by Bosnia-Herzegovina (hereafter Bosnia) in March 1992, and the civil war that immediately followed it. A major humanitarian crisis in Europe complete with massacres of civilians and – a new phrase – ethnic-cleansing was not part of the so-called peace dividend, but warranted action by the international community. UN Resolution 743 (aka the Vance-Owen Plan) created the idea of buffer zones between the warring Serb and Croat forces in Bosnia and neighbouring Croatia, and was followed in September by Resolution 776, establishing a UN Protection Force (UNPROFOR), mandated to protect the humanitarian agencies working in the country.

A British Field Ambulance had deployed to the region in spring 1992, but the British contribution to UNPROFOR, known as Operation Grapple, included an armoured infantry battalion (1 Cheshire) mounted in Warriors that deployed in October. After being on stand-by for an extended period, B Sqn 9/12L was ordered to join the battalion group at very short notice – as always – and after hurried preparation left Herford, arriving in Split, Croatia on 10 November 1992. They can tell their own story:

> The preceding two months had been full of indecision, uncertainty and hard work. The squadron was recalled from leave on 22 August and was placed on seven days' notice to move for deployment on 7 September … It soon became apparent that there were many problems to overcome before a force could deploy and so the squadron continued to train, prepare the vehicles and most of all, wait.
>
> The advance party left on 29 October as did the squadron vehicles, by boat … The squadron moved out of Spilt to Tomislavgrad before deploying on its first task to regulate the move of the Battlegroup along Route Triangle. Few will forget the next six days. The term 'route' was generous for what was no more than a winter logging track over hills … It was bitterly cold. A Company managed just 10 kms in five hours and had to camp out on the route. Snow chains were still awaiting purchase. Our arctic clothing had still not arrived … after three more long days the last convoy was cleared and the squadron moved up to Vitez, the main base for the next 6 months.
>
> It was extremely difficult for the [battalion] Warriors to get about. Most of the main roads were closed due to fighting and mines and so movement was confined to the mountain tracks. This proved ideal for CVR(T) as they could recce new routes, escort aid and confirm the front lines, but this did not make for an easy relationship with the Battlegroup.
>
> 4 Tp, attached to A Coy, led the first convoy into the northern town of Tuzla … Later the convoy came under fire from Serb mortars as it passed along the road to Kladanj through an area that was soon to become nicknamed 'Bomb Alley' … After a further week of local convoys and patrols the squadron was finally able to break out from the main camp to a new base in an old fibre-glass factory at Kladanj, 100 kms away. During the

new year the temperature was regularly below -20 C at night and the snow-
blocked roads made driving treacherous ... the locally procured fuel often
froze due to its high water content.

The Christmas festivities ended very quickly at 0640 hours on Boxing
Day when 1 Tp came under fire at Kalesija while waiting to cross the Serb/
Bosnia front line. Three rounds landed to the rear of Lt Freeland's Scimitar;
he was hit in the upper arm but luckily the many layers of clothing he was
wearing helped reduce the damage. Tpr Godfrey, his gunner, had shrapnel
bounce off his helmet and survived unmarked.

3 Tp came under repeated mortar fire in 'Bomb Alley'. The troop had
a section picqueting the route and despite the range and failing light
successfully engaged the mortar baseplate; Lt Wooley was Mentioned in
Despatches ... 1 Tp and SHQ had a narrow escape in Tarcin when three
artillery shells landed 20 meters in front of them, destroying a car and its
three passengers.

In February the squadron moved up to Tuzla, which had replaced Kladanj
as the forward operating base ... Our ability to move was restricted and the
troops were often frustrated whilst SHQ were involved in lengthy and often
pointless negotiations ... The Bosnian army moved two Hip helicopters
onto the airfield where we were based, making it an attractive target for
Serb artillery ... Our final week in Tuzla saw the evacuation of several
large convoys of refugees from Srebrenica by truck. It was a pitiful sight,
2000 frightened women, children and old people crammed into 18 open
trucks for the 14 hour journey.

Tpr James in Support Troop had a lucky escape whilst escorting a
UNHCR team investigating war crimes when a sniper's bullet passed
through the top of his flak jacket as he took cover ... The arrival of B Sqn
the Light Dragoons was a welcome sight at the beginning of May [but] few
will forget the misery of the return journey back down Route Triangle in
8 Tonners with no seats for ten hours.

Op Grapple broke new ground for the army and the UN, the requirement
to operate and communicate over long distances, act and think independently
and simply to get where others did not want you to go were ideally suited
to the recce soldier.[20]

The experience of the first squadron to be deployed on Grapple was to be
the experience of all. Their main task was to provide escorts for convoys of
humanitarian aid, and they found to their delight that their small, 10-ton
Scimitars could move along routes that the infantry's 30-ton Warriors could not;
this gave them exceptional utility.[21] They found themselves in very austere living
conditions, often in old, disused and unhygienic factory buildings that required
considerable effort to make them both habitable and defensible. They had to

operate in fierce weather and inaccessible terrain, and they were often under fire, although others were mostly the intended target. Indirect fire and mine strikes remained the most common threats, although small arms fire, snipers and even occasional fire from tanks were all common enough. Possibly more than anything else, they hated the rules of engagement that prevented them being able to fight unless directly attacked themselves, or indeed being able to help the victims of the war more directly, and the necessity of having to negotiate with war criminals to obtain permission to do their job was immensely frustrating.

The second squadron to deploy was, as noted, B Squadron the Light Dragoons, one of the newly formed units that was created following Options for Change. Over the next few years the regiment would come to regard Bosnia as its own theatre of operations, as each sabre squadron, and then RHQ, operating as a battlegroup headquarters, was deployed in turn.[22] The small size of a reconnaissance regiment at peace establishment meant that many of them would have to return for second tours. The main party of B Squadron deployed on 4 May 1993:

> Even on amalgamation day 1 December 1992, the buzz was already going around the regiment that one of the squadrons would soon be warned off to go on Op Grapple 2 … When [the CO] announced that B Squadron had been selected to deploy with 1 PWO, a resounding cheer went up from the squadron.
>
> Having taken over the vehicles from 9/12L in Vitez the squadron headed on to Tuzla in the northern part of Bosnia … the airfield at Tuzla was to be our base for the next three months … [The Serb] engagement of squadron vehicles with artillery, mortar or tank fire became increasingly frequent. Sgt Gavican had a particularly hair-raising experience when a Serb M84 tank fired 14 main armament rounds at his patrol.
>
> Freedom of movement was very restricted in central Bosnia because of the fighting between Muslim and Croat forces, and also distrust of UNPROFOR … The squadron made its third and final move in early October down to Tomislavgrad. The squadron reorganised into the pure squadron Orbat, losing our infantry attachments and regaining our two detached troops from 1PWO … Our main task was to ensure that the main supply route from the Croatian border to south of Gornji Vakuf was kept open … having literally done Bosnia top to bottom, B Squadron were more than ready to leave on 4/5 November [handing over to C Sqn].[23]

In March 1994 the British contribution was reinforced with the so-called Augmentation Force, including an additional infantry battalion (1DWR) and D Sqn LD, with RHQ LD deploying at the end of July to form BRITCAVBAT, the 'British Cavalry Battalion' – a horrible mis-mash of terms – based at Zepce.

In part this was due to the increasing demands for convoy protection, but also to allow heavy weapon monitoring to begin and to police a buffer zone that in central Bosnia was 125 miles long through difficult country. In yet another example of rapid movement, the LD squadron drove from its base in Hohne to Hannover airport from where it was flown by C130 into Split airport, allowing it to begin operations in Bosnia less than one week after being notified of the deployment. This meant that with A Sqn LD taking over from C Sqn as scheduled at the end of April 1994, unless the regiment was to start recycling its squadrons through the commitment once again, another unit had to take on the role. With 9/12L having only recently completed a six-month tour in Belfast, there was only one option: the Household Cavalry Regiment, based in Windsor. B Sqn HCR, officially a Life Guards squadron, deployed at the end of August 1994. It described itself as 'a true child of the Union', as about one-third of its manpower came from the two Blues and Royals squadrons.[24] It was stationed in Gornji Vakuf, working for the British infantry battalion there, where it would remain until succeeded by A Sqn for Grapple 6 in early March 1995. Only one month after B Sqn deployed, RHQ and D Sqn HCR also moved to Bosnia to take over the BRITCAVBAT role.[25]

With a ceasefire taking effect in in October 1995, and following the Dayton Peace Accords which were signed on 14 December 1995, a 'General Framework Agreement for Peace (GFAP) in Bosnia' was agreed which included military annexes, and a new, non-UN force was needed to implement those annexes and ensure compliance from the warring factions. This force was called IFOR, the Implementation Force, or IFOR, and was a NATO-led undertaking, although non-NATO nations did contribute forces and assistance. The force came into being on 20 December, and the British took responsibility for one of three divisional areas, the Multi-National Division South West (MND-SW), based in Banja Luka. The HQ element was supplied by 3(UK) Division, and then 1 (UK) Armoured Division; the operation was called Op Resolute.

The switch from UN to NATO was more than just a change in the colour of the vehicles, although it was observed that the mere fact that the peace-enforcement vehicles were now painted in war-fighting camouflage rather than in white reinforced the more robust rules of engagement; having achieved a peace, there was determination that it was going to be kept.[26] This was reflected in the types of forces deployed. During UNPROFOR, Britain had only deployed Warrior and CVR(T) vehicles. It now deployed an armoured regiment in Challenger.

The first unit to deploy was the Queens' Royal Hussars, arriving in early January 1996. The regiment had already conducted pre-Bosnia training during 1995, as it was intended to convert them to CVR(T) in order to take over the BRITCAVBAT role, but was then stood down, much to the disappointment of the whole unit. It was an obvious choice therefore to be given the new role, and they were delighted to have two squadrons of tanks as their main combat vehicle; they were based in Bosanski Petrovac, known to all as Boz P. Also deployed was C Squadron Light Dragoons, still on CVR(T) but now in more familiar green; they were based at a new location at Glamoc, once unkindly described to the author as 'Castle Anthrax'. A Squadron LD also deployed in February to the 'Wood Factory' in Banja Luka. Tragedy occurred on 28th January 1996 when a Spartan of the Light Dragoons drove over an anti-tank mine, killing all three of the crew: Lieutenant Richard Madden and Troopers John Kelly and Andrew Ovington; these were to be the only RAC soldiers killed in action during the Bosnia campaign.[27] After six months, the RAC units were replaced by QDG (on Challenger), and HCR squadrons took on the CVR(T) armoured reconnaissance roles. After a visit by a parliamentary committee in the first half of the year, their report included that:

> The Committee was impressed with how soldiers of the Queen's Royal Hussars had deployed with their Challenger 1 tanks to a disused factory ... both to deter anyone tempted to resort to military force and to reassure people seeking to rebuild their homes and lives. That increased military capability is a key feature of IFOR— tread softly, but carry a big stick.[28]

This was, of course, the big difference from the days of UNPROFOR. After one year, the mandate for IFOR ran out in December 1996 and was replaced with one for a new force called SFOR, the Stabilization Force. Still NATO-led and more a change of title that anything else, the British operational name became Lodestar.[29] For the next six years almost all RAC units, as well as a number of detached squadrons, deployed to Bosnia, and the peace was kept. Not all were on armour, with some units and individuals deployed as infantry or on specialist observation tasks. In April 2000 the first operational deployment of Challenger 2 took place, when C Sqn 2RTR deployed with the new tank. SFOR remained in being until 2 December 2004, when it was replaced by a European Union force (EUFOR) under the operational title of Op Althea, with Major General David Leakey (ex-RTR) as the first commander.

Macedonia and Kosovo

Even as the situation in Bosnia was settling down somewhat, and there was a peace to keep, further south in the Balkans another area that few had even heard of was starting to simmer: Kosovo. Another former part of Yugoslavia, Kosovo had initially escaped the violence that engulfed other provinces.[30] However, that would not last. In large part, this was due to the ethnic make-up of the region, with around 90 per cent of the population being ethnic Albanians, and most of the remainder Serbs. During the early 1980s increasing Albanian nationalism within Kosovo led to demands to establish it as a province in its own right, meaning much more independence from Serbia. This was firmly resisted by Belgrade, with violent clampdowns on protests and subsequently a restriction in the level of autonomy; it was clear that the Serbs would not countenance Kosovo gaining more independence.

In 1990, the Kosovo Albanians unilaterally declared their independence under the banner of the Republic of Kosova, although it failed to gain recognition from the international community. Hope that the Dayton Accords might grant independence to Kosovo was dashed, and by 1996 largely non-violent opposition to Serbian control had been eclipsed by the actions of the Kosovo Liberation Army (KLA). Massacres almost inevitably followed, and in late 1998 the Organization for Security and Co-operation in Europe (OSCE) deployed observers, including a few British military personnel, into Kosovo in order to monitor a very fragile ceasefire. Simultaneously, under Operation Upminster, a French-led multi-national response force (the Kosovo Extraction Force) was positioned in northern Macedonia in order to be able to rescue the monitors if the situation deteriorated; this also included British military personnel and a Warrior-mounted company of the King's Own Royal Border Regiment.[31] Macedonia also became temporary home to large numbers of Albanian Kosovars who fled the violence being inflicted on them by the Serbian army and paramilitary forces. By the start of 1999 it was clear that the Serbs would not allow a restoration of Kosovo's autonomy, let alone independence, that the state-sponsored violence would continue, and Belgrade also refused demands to allow a NATO peacekeeping force into the country. It was decided that NATO would deploy a large multinational armoured and heliborne force into Macedonia, in part to put pressure on Belgrade but also in readiness for, if necessary, an invasion of Kosovo. The HQ element was from the Allied Rapid Reaction Corps, and the main British land component of this operation, known as Agricola, was 4th Armoured Brigade commanded by Brigadier Bill Rollo, ex-HCR, including two squadrons of Challenger tanks and the Battlegroup HQ from the King's Royal Hussars.

Following an intensive NATO bombing campaign of Serbia from late March until mid-June, NATO forces entered Kosovo on 12 June 1999 through the Kacanik defile and secured the country. With the Kosovans welcoming the NATO troops as liberators, a lot of the work over the next weeks was directed at preventing revenge attacks on the small Serbian population, many of whom fled into Serbia.[32] After the initial entry phase, the RAC armoured regiment subsequently committed to Kosovo was usually tasked to provide not only one tank but also two dismounted squadrons to be used in the peacekeeping role. In order to meet something like an infantry company orbat, these had to be increased in strength by about 50 per cent, requiring not only personnel from elsewhere in the regiment, but often reinforcement from other RAC units, both regular and reserve. Fortunately, there was no shortage of volunteers for such tasks, but of course this meant depleting the other regiments which, although not operationally deployed, were equally busy.[33] Over the years, the following RAC regiments deployed in whole or part to Kosovo: HCR, QDG, SCOTS DG, QRH, QRL, 2RTR, including many in the light-vehicle or infantry roles.

Strategic Defence Review, 1998

The Strategic Defence Review of 1998 had a major impact on the RAC, and required restructuring of the existing regiments. Until the review, the eight armoured regiments were a mix of Type 50 and Type 44; they were now all required to operate as Type 58. This required each of them to 'grow' a fourth sabre squadron, which could not be done overnight, and DRAC estimated that it would take up to four years to implement.[34] Two of the existing armoured regiments were to change roles, with QDG reverting to formation reconnaissance and 1RTR becoming the basis of a new Joint NBC Regiment – see below. At least this meant no loss of cap badges, although the 1RTR soldiers took some persuading of the merits of this consolation. On the larger stage, the UK would operate only two warfighting divisions, each to contain three brigades.[35] These would become part of the new formation readiness cycle, in which units would rotate around a schedule of annual tasks, dependent on which brigade they were part of.

The review also reduced the overall size of the TA from 57,000 to about 40,000, and this of course affected the Yeomanry. It also changed the (somewhat unpopular roles of the RY, RWxY and RMLY from home defence to the provision of individual reinforcements for the CR2-equipped armoured regiments, with the QOY doing the same job but with CVR(T) for the armoured recce regiments; two of the RY squadrons had the role of providing IR for the Joint NBC Regiment. This led to the following laydown with effect from 1 July 1999:

Table 8: RAC Yeomanry Regiments from July 1999

Unit	Squadrons	Location
Royal Yeomanry (RY) (RHQ London)	A (RWY) Sqn	Swindon
	B (L&DY) Sqn	Leicester
	C (K&SY) Sqn	Croydon
	S (SRY) Sqn	Nottingham
	W (WD) Sqn	London
Royal Wessex Yeomanry (RWxY) (RHQ Bovington)	A (DY) Sqn	Bovington
	B (RWY) Sqn	Old Sarum
	C (RGH) Sqn	Cirencester
	D (RDY) Sqn	Barnstaple

Unit	Squadrons	Location
Royal Mercian and Lancastrian Yeomanry (RMLY) (RHQ Telford)	A (S,W&WY) Sqn	Dudley
	B (Shropshire Y) Sqn	Telford
	C (CY) Sqn	Chester
	D (DLOY) Sqn	Wigan
Queen's Own Yeomanry (QOY) (RHQ Newcastle)	Y (QOYY) Sqn	York
	A (AY) Sqn	Ayr
	B (NIH) Sqn	Belfast
	C (F&FY) Sqn	Cupar
	D (NH) Sqn	Newcastle

Many yeomen rejoiced in the new roles, and there was another upside: overall the authorized strength of the RAC Yeomanry would increase from 1,319 posts of all cap badges, up to 1,770. In 2002 the four regiments of RAC Yeomanry were configured as follows:

RY   2 x NBC Defence Sqns (A & W), 3 x Armd Reserve sqns (S, B, C). Supporting SCOTS DG, QRL, 1RTR

RWxY   1 x Armd Replacement sqn (A), 3 x Armd Reserve sqns (B, C, D). Supporting RDG, KRH

RMLY   4 x Armd Reserve sqns (A, B, C, D). Supporting QRH, 2RTR

QOY   4 x Formation Recce sqns (Y, A, D, C), 1 x Formation Recce support sqn (B). Supporting HCR, QDG, 9/12L, LD[36]

Apart from the almost constant restructuring, the introduction of Whole Fleet Management (WFM) system was an unpopular imposition on the regular RAC; it had first been trialled by the Royal Dragoon Guards in Germany in 2002 before being brought into widespread use. Rather than holding their full stocks of vehicles, regiments were reduced to holding only a small number of vehicles, known as the basic unit fleet; this was assessed by the powers that be to be sufficient to run internal training courses and for the crews to maintain proficiency. This would be about the size of a single squadron. When deploying on exercises, ranges or operations, the units would draw the additional vehicles necessary to bring them up to full strength, with such training fleets created and passed between regiments in the manner of the BATUS vehicle fleet, and with all the problems and complaints that come from such frequent handovers. Those vehicles not required for immediate use would be stored in low-maintenance Controlled Humidity Environment, or CHE, conditions. Regiments objected strongly to WFM as it prevented crews developing the pride in, and bond with, 'their' vehicle that had proved to be so valuable in the past, and the standard of the vehicles in service declined as the mileage increased and caused the traditional inter-unit squabbles – reading regimental journals, it is clear that every RAC unit invariably hands over its vehicles (and barracks etc.) in the most exemplary condition, yet at the same time the incoming unit always manages to inherit the most badly maintained broken-down heaps of metal imaginable …

The Joint Nuclear Biological and Chemical Regiment

1RTR became the main component of a new Joint NBC Regiment, forming up on 1 April 1999 and becoming operational on 1 August; the unit was based in RAF Honington under No. 2 Group of RAF Strike Command. This was a completely new role for an RAC regiment, and included personnel No. 27 Squadron of the RAF Regiment under command, giving a roughly 80 : 20 split in manpower.[37] A Squadron of the regiment remained on Challengers and CVR(T), in the role of RAC Demonstration Squadron, based in Warminster. The regiment found itself on operations almost immediately, as it took over the biological monitoring role on Op Bolton at the Ali Al Salem airbase in Kuwait from the Royal Yeomanry on 19 July 1999.[38] The equipment used in the role was the Prototype Biological Detection System, or PBDS, in essence a multi-functional laboratory mounted in a box container on the back of a 4-ton lorry; PBDS was operated by G Squadron. The regiment's D Squadron used the eleven Fuchs chemical reconnaissance and survey vehicles gifted during the 1990/91 Gulf War in the ground manoeuvre support role, and H Squadron was the support squadron, primarily operating the Multi-Purpose Decontamination System, MPDS.

Concurrently with the Kuwait role, the regiment deployed teams in support of NATO involvement in Afghanistan from early 2001, the first RAC contribution to the country, but not the last. It also deployed as a complete unit on Operation Telic from January 2003, providing the British contribution to the coalition force for a war that was being fought, at least according to the political spin, to prevent Saddam Hussein from acquiring or using such 'weapons of mass destruction'.[39] Extremely busy throughout the war and based across the whole region in at least six countries, the regiment acquitted itself well, including by changing role for a couple of months after the end of the war as an infantry battlegroup, based in Al Qurnah, Iraq. Concurrently, the search for WMD continued within Iraq, and it continued to deploy twelve-man teams over the subsequent years of operations, finally leaving in March 2008 after a commitment that lasted for nearly five years. From July 2005 the name of the regiment was altered to reflect updated NATO terminology (although not in fact a change in role or capability), becoming the Joint Chemical, Biological, Radiological and Nuclear Regiment.

   The experience in Afghanistan had led to the creation of Light Role Teams (also called Specialist Monitoring Teams, LRT/SMT), able to deploy on a whole range of rapid-reaction operations, particularly in support of airborne and commando forces and Special Forces, and these proved their utility in Iraq. At that stage, the regiment was attracting much favourable comment and was looking to expand. However, as a result of the inevitable cost-saving measures that always accompany a Defence Review, most of the capabilities were transferred to direct RAF control during 2011, with the unit disbanding on 14 December 2011 and 1RTR reforming as a purely army regiment, almost immediately sending two of its squadrons to Afghanistan. This was not quite the end of the NBC story within the RAC, as in July 2014 the semi-independent Falcon Squadron RTR was created in Warminster, operating the original (but now much upgraded) Fuchs vehicles that had been in storage since 2011, and coming under Royal Engineer control for operational purposes.

Chapter 9

Further Unexpected Commitments, 2003–14

Iraq, 2003–9

The Royal Armoured Corps was not totally new to Iraq when it was heavily involved in the invasion of 2003. It had led the advance into the southern part of Iraq as part of the liberation of Kuwait in 1991, and indeed had earlier deployed a tank training team to Iraq at the end of 1951 to assist the (then friendly) Iraqi army. However, by the early part of the new millennium it was increasingly looking like the British army would, once more, have to go to war there.

In October 1998 the US government foreign policy was amended to include the removal of Saddam Hussein's Ba'ath Party regime as a policy objective. This followed the apparent expulsion of UN NBC weapon inspectors after a period of limited cooperation. In mid-December 1998 a series of air attacks against Iraqi targets, named Operation Desert Fox, was launched; RAF Tornados participated in the operation. In a period of three days, air and cruise-missile attacks hit multiple targets inside Iraq. Because of concerns that the Iraqis might retaliate by launching biological weapon SCUD missile attacks against the RAF airbase in Kuwait, volunteer part-time members of the Royal Yeomanry found themselves crewing hastily created biological detector systems in Ali Al Salem, an extraordinary operational deployment of yeomen.

Despite the paucity of clear links to Iraq, the 9/11 attacks in the US significantly upped the ante, and gave the hawks in the American administration additional leverage in mounting an invasion of Iraq with the intention of toppling the regime. On 20 September 2001 President Bush declared his 'war on terror', justifying the US willingness to take pre-emptive action against 'rogue states', and some officers in the RAC started taking bets amongst themselves as to when a war against Iraq would take place. A year later, Bush started making a case to the UN General assembly for a full-scale military invasion of Iraq, and although many countries, including other NATO members, were extremely dubious of the legality of the proposed action – and indeed the veracity of the intelligence that purported to demonstrate Saddam's continued attempts to build the infamous 'weapons of mass destruction' (WMD) – Prime Minister Blair supported Bush and British forces were committed to the upcoming war.[1] However, although the government was increasingly set on war, attempts had to be seen to be made politically and diplomatically to allow Saddam to accept unacceptable terms, and so officially the forces required were not allowed to begin any overt preparations that might signal British determination to go to war – the reverse in many ways of the situation in Suez in 1956. It was not until January 2003 that it was clear that deployment – if not actual war – would soon be taking place, and the usual frantic round of preparations for a deployment to a faraway land began.

The initial assumption was that the invasion would be launched both from Kuwait and from southern Turkey, and planning began on that basis. JNBCR was on a routine regimental Command Post Exercise when instructions were received to begin planning for an early deployment of the entire regiment, hardly a surprise if the reason for going to war was centred on the existence of WMD. Initial activity was hampered by a lack of clarity, and indeed the first assessment of where the regiment might deploy (Turkey) was conducted using the Adjutant Captain John Craddock's world atlas, after he had hurriedly cycled home to retrieve it from his married quarter. As it was, Turkey refused to participate and denied the American-led coalition forces permission to deploy, so the plan had to be changed for an invasion delivered solely from Kuwait. The armoured and armoured reconnaissance regiments of the RAC earmarked for the operation probably had it even worse; JNBCR had been operating in the Middle East since it was formed, had recently conducted major desert exercises in Egypt and it was obvious that the unit would be first on the list of capabilities needed.[2] For all the others, they had to wait for confirmation that they were going, before conducting as much training and vehicle preparation as they could in the time available and then shipping their vehicles and associated equipment out to Kuwait.

The first RAC reconnaissance parties started to deploy to Kuwait in late January 2003; for example, the author (as the echelon commander of JNBCR) deployed with four other members of the unit in a British Airways aircraft that was full of military personnel dressed in civilian clothes, all comically doing their best to look inconspicuous to each other. By the end of February the tempo had increased, and Kuwait was filling up with US, UK and other contributing nations' troops and equipment, by now completely overt; the country had become one large military camp.[3] The British named the operation Telic and deployed 1st Armoured Division (albeit with a single armoured brigade) as well as 3 Commando and 16 Air Assault Brigades, both of which had RAC units attached. The RAC troops deployed on Op Telic 1, as the war-fighting campaign was subsequently named, were as follows:

- Theatre Troops: Joint NBC Regt (1RTR)
- Divisional Troops: QDG
- 3 Commando Brigade: C Sqn QDG
- 7 Armoured Brigade: SCOTS DG, 2RTR, B and C Sqns QRL, A Sqn QDG
- 16 Air Assault Brigade: D Sqn HCR

Of course, this was not how the units fought, as the Challengers were embedded within the Warrior-equipped infantry battalions (1st Bn Royal Regiment of Fusiliers and 1st Bn Black Watch) in the armoured brigade to provide mixed battlegroups, so that the initial redeployments looked like this:

- Scots DG BG   30 x CR2 (RHQ, B and C Squadrons)
- 2RTR BG   30 x CR2 (RHQ, Cyclops and Falcon Sqns)
- 1RRF BG   28 x CR2 (B and C Sqns QRL)
- 1BW BG   28 x CR2 (A Sqn Scots DG, Egypt Sqn 2RTR)

Some of these troops only arrived in Kuwait shortly before hostilities commenced, limiting the amount of time available for gunnery and tactical training. The Iraqi army (as well as the better trained and equipped Republican Guard) was still extremely large and, naturally, had the advantage of fighting on its own territory. It was believed to be over ⅓ million strong, with 10 mechanized or armoured divisions; it also possessed over 5,000 armoured fighting vehicles, including T72 tanks, and had plenty of time to create obstacles and construct defensive positions.[4]

Since Desert Fox in 1998, American and RAF aircraft had continued to strike at selected Iraqi targets, ostensibly in support of enforcing the northern and southern no-fly zones but in retrospect, probably also to degrade Iraqi air defence and command and control facilities in preparation for the invasion. On 17 March 2003, President Bush delivered a public ultimatum to Saddam Hussein, telling him and his sons to leave Iraq within 48 hours or face war. He did not comply, and in the early hours of 19 March, the war started with an attempt to kill Hussein and the senior Iraqi leadership by using an air strike on one of his palaces near Baghdad, following intelligence reports of a conference there. Many in the region and elsewhere now anticipated a lengthy air campaign to 'soften' up the Iraqi forces before a ground invasion was attempted, as had happened in 1991. The US instead favoured a more concurrent if not quite simultaneous approach, called 'shock and awe', using overwhelming firepower to destroy military objectives, whilst avoiding where possible the main Iraqi cities. This was intended not only to minimise civilian casualties but to avoid being dragged into urban fighting and also to speed up manoeuvre. It was also expected that the overwhelming displays of military might and firepower would convince many of the Iraqis to surrender without fighting.

The British forces were given the mission to secure southern Iraq (and particularly the country's second largest city, Basra) in order to free up the much larger American forces to rapidly advance and capture the capital, Baghdad; this also meant that less direct coordination was required, as the two armies were, in large part, fighting two separate operations. 7th Armoured Brigade crossed the border into Iraq on 20 March 2003, concurrently with 3 Commando Brigade

Ex Saif Sareea II, a desert training exercise, took place in Oman in autumn 2001. Over sixty Challenger 2s from RDG were deployed, but very few of the RAC soldiers who took part in the exercise were – initially at least – deployed to Kuwait. (Courtesy MoD)

Challenger crews from Egypt squadron 2RTR 'bombing up' with service ammunition prior to the invasion. (Courtesy RTR)

Troops snatching some last-minute sleep immediately before the start of the ground invasion, March 2002. (Courtesy RTR)

A QRL Challenger 2 on Operation Telic. Two soldiers from the unit were killed in a blue-on-blue incident near Basra in late March. (Courtesy QRL)

A CVR(T) commander from 7th Armoured Brigade – with a hand-held GPS attached to his vehicle – during the advance into Iraq, March 2003.

RPG damage on a Cyclops 2RTR Challenger; the tank was able to withstand such attacks, despite the often suicidal heroism of the firers. (Courtesy RTR)

A tank commander's view of the often terrible terrain that made up southern Iraq. It was not classic desert country, with irrigation ditches and oil pipelines making manoeuvre difficult.

Burning Iraqi armour in the desert. As had happened in 1991, many Iraqi vehicles were abandoned by their crews, although some tank-versus-tank engagements did take place. (Courtesy RTR)

A Fuchs vehicle of the Joint NBC Regiment, manned by D Sqn 1RTR. The vehicles, gifted in 1990, remain in service at the time of writing. (Courtesy RTR)

A Challenger 2 from Badger squadron, 2RTR on the outskirts of Basra, Iraq's second largest city. During the war-fighting phase, tanks were used with infantry to conduct night-time raids into the city, to avoid getting bogged down in urban warfare. (Courtesy RTR)

A convoy of QRL WMIK stop for a short halt in a muddy Maysan province. The lack of protection in these vehicles was a serious limiting factor in their use. (Courtesy QRL)

The repatriation ceremony for Lance Corporal Alan 'Bracks' Brackenbury KRH, killed by an IED in Iraq in May 2005. (Courtesy KRH)

It wasn't always hot and dusty in Iraq – when it rained, it really rained, as Captain James Lance the Ops Officer QRL demonstrates. (Courtesy QRL)

In 2005 QRL converted from tanks to formation reconnaissance, leaving the RAC with only five MBT regiments, despite their success of only two years previously. (Courtesy QRL)

Panther, brought into service to replace the already departed Ferret as a battlefield liaison vehicle, was found to be ill-protected for the threats it would face on a modern asymmetric battlefield. Additionally, once it was fitted out with the Bowman communication system, there was hardly any room left for the crew.

CVR(T) would remain the mainstay of the RAC in Afghanistan, and received many modifications during the course of the campaign. A great deal of effort was expended in improving the protection of the troops, both on the man and in vehicles, including the introduction of Scimitar II, using modified Spartan hulls to improve survivability. This Scimitar is in Forward Operating Base Condor, one of well over a hundred operating locations used throughout Helmand province.

An HCR soldier aims his GPMG along a compound wall in the green zone. RAC troops frequently operated on foot, as well as in the more familiar vehicle role. (Courtesy HCR)

Mastiff was a large, 6x6 protected patrol vehicle made in the US and specially designed to maximize crew survivability. RAC crewmen found themselves converting to this and other vehicles in order to operate in theatre.

Embarrassing? A Danish Leopard 2A5 MBT provides overwatch for a British Jackal in Helmand.
(Courtesy RAC)

C Sqn QDG sharpshooters were part of the Brigade Reconnaissance Force (BRF) on Herrick 15 in 2011. They are using a small 'murder hole' in the compound wall to sight and shoot through.
(Courtesy QDG)

Right: *Here the Light Dragoons are removing ammunition and critical equipment prior to denial of the vehicle following a mine strike. Sights and other items would be manually damaged, fuel lines opened and then, in all likelihood, a Hellfire missile would be used to complete the destruction.* (Courtesy LD)

Below: *A Scimitar II of the QRL, 2012. Although not a new vehicle, it offered much greater survivability for the crew members.* (Courtesy QRL)

A soldier from QRL using the German-made Vallon metal detector to search for tell-tale signs of an IED. The job of leading a foot patrol with the Vallon was an unhealthy one, but the detector, along with carefully designed tactics and procedures, saved many lives. (Courtesy QRL)

B Sqn HCR soldiers operating on foot as the Brigade Reconnaissance Force on Herrick 18. The Chinook is preparing to extract them from a hasty landing zone; Chinooks were also used to provide the lifesaving MERT (Medical Emergency Response Team) function. (Courtesy HCR)

The number of MBT operated by the British army continued to fall, as a series of defence reviews reduced the size of the army, both regular and reserve. Challenger 2 can be expected to still be in service in the late 2020s, after thirty years of service. (Courtesy Andy Brend)

The experience in Afghanistan led to the creation of the light cavalry role, mounted on wheeled high-mobility vehicles; here a soldier from QDG is on exercise using a quad bike. (Courtesy QDG)

Left: *Second Lieutenant (currently Captain) Sarah Batts was the first RAC female troop leader, joining the RTR in 2016.*

Below: *What Challenger 3 may look like; 148 Challenger 2 hulls are expected to be re-used as the basis for this evolutionary tank, armed with a smoothbore 120mm gun.* (Courtesy MoD)

The troubled Ajax vehicle in prototype form. (Courtesy RAC)

Working as a team – soldiers of the Queen's Royal Hussars engaged in pre-deployment training.
(Courtesy QRH)

In all weathers, and wherever required: Light Cavalry troops from QDG deployed on the UN MINUSMA operation in Mali. (Courtesy QDG)

In all weathers, and wherever required: QRH Challenger 2 tanks deployed on Operation Cabrit in Estonia. (Courtesy QRH) assaulting the Al Fawr peninsula in order to secure the port of Umm Qasr which would allow better logistic support for the operation. Fighting around the port was unexpectedly fierce, and took several days to subdue the enemy. Further to the north and west, 7th Armoured Brigade, once more revelling in their title of the Desert Rats, manoeuvred to isolate Basra, again with the intention of minimising casualties on both sides. In a tragic fratricide incident on 25 March, two members of C Sqn QRL were killed, and two others seriously wounded, when their Challenger 2 was misidentified and hit with a HESH round fired by another British tank at night outside Basra.

16th Air Assault Brigade – known to the rest of the Division as 'chairborne rather than airborne' as they were moved around in lorries – was heavily involved in the operations around Basra, ably supported by D Sqn HCR who were able to provide much needed firepower and mobility, as well as engaging in what amounted to independent, long-range missions. Their OC, Major Richard Taylor (not me – the other Richard Taylor in the army list at the time!), related the story, beginning with the crossing into Iraq:

> That night Lieutenant Jules Speer's 1 Troop was pushed forward to establish contact with 1/5 Marines, whom he found terribly unsavoury! At first light the squadron moved north through the GOSPs (Gas/Oil Separation plants). We spent an eerie few hours driving up through a landscape scarred by bombing, although the infrastructure was largely intact – a couple of oil heads had been set alight to add a dramatic background to photographs. With the squadron stretched over 60km, communications were maintained by troop rebroadcast on the squadron net … All around odd groups of men kept popping out of bunkers in civilian clothes leaving weapon caches and piles of military uniforms.
>
> We bided our time in the Rumaylah oilfields setting up VCPs and detaching flying columns to assist the BGs. One morning, having chosen a tactical dip in the ground to conceal SHQ, it started to rain – and boy did it rain! I realized we were sitting in a wadi … within twenty minutes it was ten feet deep in water. We [extracted the vehicle and] spent the next three hours sitting in the Sultan in our boxer shorts and body armour, praying that the Brigade Commander would not choose this moment to visit.
>
> [There was then] a courageous counter-attack by five enemy pick-ups firing RPGs and small arms. As Lt Speers destroyed the first pick-up with 30mm, he left the pressel down on his radio so that the squadron could hear the automatic fire and whoops of 'target!' Thirty minutes later all five pick-ups had been destroyed – CoH Heaton destroyed one with Swingfire at great cost to the taxpayer …
>
> Later that afternoon 2 Tp were engaged out of the blue by American A10 aircraft. LCoH Hull was killed and LCpl Tudball, LCoH Gerrard and

Lt MacEwan were injured. Tpr Finney dragged Tudball out of the turret, placed him in safety and bandaged his wounds. He then went back into the vehicle to send a sitrep on the casualties … Just as Finney was carrying Tudball towards the Spartan the second A10 came in injuring Finney, Tudball again, and Sindall.

At exactly the same time LCoH Flynn sighted two T55s, a BMP and a D30 howitzer. Only his Scimitar and LCoH Telling's Striker were in position to fight off the Iraqi armour from interfering with the Casevac. Coming under intense tank and artillery fire, Telling withdrew to set up a separate sight position for his Swingfire. For thirty minutes Flynn endured accurate artillery and tank fire and suppressed the Iraqi armour with 140 rounds of 30mm to protect the extraction of casualties. Telling then destroyed the first T55 and Flynn's firing forced the second T55s crew to dismount and withdraw. The AAC arrived and with tracer indication from Flynn, destroyed the BMP and the D30.[5]

D Sqn later reported that the 30mm APDS round was capable of disabling a T55 tank even at 1,500m range, and that HE was useful against soft vehicles as well as infantry, and could also be used as a means of indicating targets. They also noted that about 30 per cent of their engagements had been against moving targets – many of them doing their best to leave the battlefield. But even as the Iraqi army was melting away, the appearance of Fedayeen, a fanatical paramilitary militia group that was prepared to fight and die in support of the Ba'ath Party and Saddam, became a serious concern. Operating on foot, using pick-up trucks and lightly armed, they nonetheless presented a serious threat to the stretched British forces, who had to take great care not to assume that there was such a thing as a front line in the campaign. They intimidated the local populations and were particularly supported by the Shiite population, and were quite prepared to die during their operations, which made them a difficult enemy to deal with.

Major Andy Britton commanded Cyclops Squadron 2RTR during the war and recalled his memories of the time in *Tank Journal*:

Cyclops had the distinction within 2RTR of being the squadron that would complete not just the war-fighting phase but then remain in theatre until mid-July completing peace support operations … The advance party flew to Kuwait on 5 March [and] the panzers arrived on the ninth … The in-theatre training package comprised DU (Depleted Uranium APFSDS) commissioning and a challenging combined arms live firing exercise. Of particular note was the accuracy of the tank with the new round [and] the closeness of the border with Iraq – only some 5km away … The squadron was bombed-up on 18 March and on the

19th received orders, marked up maps, and carried out final checks. The war started early on 20 March ...

Thar day was to be a flavour of warfare at its most unpleasant; the strident call of 'gas gas gas' rang out over the assembly area fourteen times that day ... we learned of several Iraqi missile launches ... and generally the threat of WMD was more a matter of 'when' rather than 'if' ... 1RRF and 1BW were the lead battlegroups within 7 Armoured Brigade and so 2RTR was to follow up. We crossed the border into Iraq on the morning of 22 March ... I received hasty orders from the CO to lead the battlegroup in the clearance of Route Topeka, a 20km stretch of highway that had been bypassed by the advancing [US Marines]. This was achieved by nightfall with no live enemy encountered, merely an abandoned company position, complete with vehicles.

The squadron was given orders to take over the south west sector of Al Zubayr from A Squadron SCOTS DG. Having received an excellent brief from Major Tim Brown (delivered in memorable fashion with his feet soaking in a bowl of warm water in the back of his Sultan), Cyclops conducted a relief in place of the Scottish Cavalry. This marked the start of the most intensive period of operations for the squadron.... Just after dawn an Iraqi with a white-painted face attacked Sgt Steve Roberts in the 8 Tp vehicle check point [that] led to the death of this great man, who is still sorely missed by the squadron.[6]

Despite this, the squadron had a job to do and they did it ... A team of Fedayeen deployed, running out and firing accurate small arms fire, and an RPG7 round which span and shot out sparks as it raced lazily towards my tank, fortunately impacting on a sand wall just in front. A heavy machine gun and mortar opened up. 31 and 0B deployed forward, engaging the militia with coax and then the Fedayeen HQ with HESH, with some success ... Later that day [the squadron] came under heavy fire. The enemy had apparently set an RPG ambush for us. With quite incredible bravery they took on our tanks at virtually point-blank range. 7 Troop were caught in the thick of it taking seven direct hits for no damage and causing many enemy casualties.... we had no infantry and therefore should have been very vulnerable. Seven MBTs faced and defeated an estimated fifty militia with hand held anti-tank weapons.

On the 6 April the battlegroup was ordered at very short notice to assault the centre of Basra. Cyclops was to lead the assault, and quickly crashed out of our barracks, [I] gave orders on the move, and moved at full speed to link up with the CO ... We expected [the enemy] to make a final stand in the centre of Basra ... We were amazed to find no real resistance [just] some sporadic shooting. That evening we cleared a Ba'ath party HQ which had only just been evacuated, the inhabitants had left their dinner on the stove in their haste to escape! Cyclops then moved again to conduct peace support operations, including raiding suspected militia cells at home, [and] having the odd firefight/contact …

I would like to restate that the tank is alive and well – it is as hugely relevant today on the 21st Century battlefield as it has ever been … an armoured squadron retains a unique range of capabilities that every CO in theatre wished to have in his battlegroup. Challenger 2 itself surpassed all of our own high expectations and was a source of great confidence to the crews.[7]

Operation Panzer, also known as the '14–0' engagement, was in many ways the ultimate demonstration of what Challenger 2 was capable of when handled by determined and professional soldiers. On 27 March 2003 the fourteen CR2s of C Sqn SCOTS DG, operating as two half-squadron groups, intercepted a similar number of Iraqi T55 tanks and other AFVs south of Basra moving towards the Al-Fawr peninsula, and destroyed them all without loss. Colin Macintyre had been heavily involved in the trials of CR2 was then the squadron sergeant major of C Sqn, and he recalled the difficulties that the tanks faced in getting into action. He noted how the squadron were given brief orders to move as quickly as possible about 50 miles to join up with 40 Commando Royal Marines, in order to give them much-needed firepower as intelligence indicated that a large Iraqi armoured assault upon them was likely. The squadron had never worked with the Commandos before.

The move out was done at night, made much more difficult by the lack of maps, as only the squadron leader and his second in command had one, and they each led their respective half squadrons, the rest of the commanders moving 'blind'. Crossing the major water obstacle of the Khawr Abd Allah, a wide estuary of the Shatt Al-Arab River, was a hugely difficult task, the tanks having to drive down what felt like vertical slippery banks in order to cross the water using M3 ferries operated by 23 Amphibious Engineer Squadron RE. Led by recce cars from the Queen's Dragoon Guards, the tanks moved into the city using the best routes they could find in the marshy ground – it was realized that the sand-covered oil pipelines were clear of obstructions and were thus used as a makeshift road, although whether the pipes could bear the weight of a CR2 was the cause of some uncertainty … they did, but probably only just. 3rd Troop made the initial contact with the force of enemy tanks, and C Squadron let the APFSDS and HESH do their talking for them. Avoiding (but also using coax MG fire to engage and clear) a surface-laid minefield, the tanks of C Sqn manoeuvred and engaged the enemy T55 tanks and MTLB personnel carriers, as well as dismounted infantry, RPG teams and bunker positions. In only a few minutes the final tally was seven tanks, six APCs, two fortified bunkers and any number of infantry – leading one to question where the media-inspired 14–0 tally came from; someone in the media clearly could not count. What was not in doubt was the performance of the crews and their tanks.

Another demonstration, this time of the survivability of Challenger 2, came outside Basra on 6 April involving B Sqn SCOTS DG and in particular callsign 30 belonging to the troop leader. As the regimental journal recounted, 'Captain De Silva's crew were taken aback to discover that a previously abandoned T55 fired a [100mm] round which hit them squarely on the nose. A good shot from the T55 but sadly its last as some stunned seconds later the whole troop responded by firing back and destroying the enemy tank.' Other incidents were recalled:

The enemy still proved determined and one man, on a suicide mission, emerged from a bunker to throw a grenade into Cpl Smith's tank; he was promptly cut down by machine gun fire from the rest of the forward tanks ... We came under fire from heavy machine guns mounted on the bridge of a boat that had been held in dry dock. It was hit with main armament HESH ... USMC Super Cobra attack helicopters flew in front of our arcs whilst we were firing in order to engage and destroy two enemy AFVs ... The infantry investigated some bodies at the entrance to a complex; the 'dead' miraculously rose up and fired RPGs at the armoured congregation! One unfortunate met his end as a result of a 25 meter range HESH engagement, and another was crushed under a wall as he rose to fire his RPG ... Most of them were foreign nationals who had come to fight for Saddam; none were able to use the return portion of their airline tickets.[8]

Attacks against the extensive Iraqi oil infrastructure were widely expected, and care was taken to prevent unnecessary damage during combat, as well as having to protect them from insurgent attacks subsequently. Concurrently, JNBCR were deployed in a manoeuvre support role to the British formations, equipped with their Fuchs reconnaissance and survey vehicles and a single troop of six MPDS decontamination vehicles. The regiment's few PBDS biological vehicles, supplemented with a rapidly designed and procured unmanned sample collection system, attempted to provide a comprehensive detection matrix over the whole theatre, including beyond Iraq and Kuwait. As is invariably the case, it became clear that not having capabilities that were needed in wartime ready and available on the shelf brought increased risk in war. Other elements of the regiment based on H Squadron were moved up to Baghdad with the American forces, in part to assist the US Exploitation Task Force in the search for evidence of WMD, which of course would justify the war; in the event, none were found.

However, overall success – or so it appeared at the time – was rapid, with the collapse of the regime and Iraqi armed forces in about three weeks and the fall of

Baghdad on 9 April; the end of 'major combat operations' – thought at the time to herald the end of hostilities – was announced as being 1 May. Once the war was won, it was hoped that the majority of units could be withdrawn and replaced by a new but much smaller force, and by mid–May many had already moved back to their home locations; 2RTR left a single armoured squadron (Cyclops) behind, and then had to rapidly reorganize another, Badger, to return and take over from them in July. With 85 per cent of that squadron having just fought in the war, they then found themselves back in the same theatre for a second tour, only two months after departing.

As the operation morphed from war into a kind of peace, the RAC troops found themselves not only operating in Challenger 2 but also from Land Rovers, on foot and even in boats. Helmets were removed and the wearing of berets on patrol became the order of the day, in an attempt to try to normalize a situation that was anything but normal. It had also been hoped that the brutally repressive nature of Saddam's regime over decades would lead to active support from the Iraqi population, but it was not to be so; rather, a sullen silence fell over the country, punctuated by incidents of violent resistance from Fedayeen units. The Iraqi army had been defeated in battle, but what would happen next?

By June, increased activity made it clear that an organized insurgency was underway, which in most respects was to prove more of a challenge to the occupying forces than the Iraqi army had. The desire to withdraw the majority of British forces became a distant memory, as it was clear than the army was going to be committed to a counter-insurgency campaign for many years. By 2007 every single regiment in the RAC had deployed to Iraq at least once, and all six of the Telic 1 regiments had returned to that theatre for subsequent tours. The operation was brought to an end on 15 May 2009 (Telic 13) with QRH being the final RAC unit to be deployed. In that time, the multitude of tasks that the RAC units had to fill were enormous: they ranged from counter-insurgency operations (patrols, raids, VCPs, ambushes, searches etc.) to boat and helicopter operations, mentoring and training Iraqi soldiers and policemen, to assisting with reconstruction and conducting hearts and minds operations amongst the local population. They were not welcome there: the people of Iraq were surprisingly ambivalent about the removal of the Saddam regime, and many factions subsequently appeared, all with one intent – to kill coalition soldiers and to force them to leave the country. The frequent use of large and increasingly sophisticated Improvised Explosive Devices (IED) became a major problem, and a lot of time was spent trying to maximize the protection of the troops – the term 'survivability' rather than protection became the order of the day, with the focus on saving lives and limbs, even if that meant that the vehicle was written-off. Specially protected vehicles such as Ridgback and Mastiff came into service under the Urgent Operational Requirement system, and were frequently crewed by RAC squadrons working out of role. The lack of a large enough training fleet in the UK often necessitated rushed training before deployments, with stories of the precious vehicles being handed over from one unit to the next at motorway service stations in the middle of the night. Challenger 2 continued to be deployed, in a specially modified form (known as the Theatre Entry Standard, or TES) albeit in smaller numbers, and as well as using the forty-year old CVRTs, they also operated in the Bulldog (the up-armoured version of the even older FV432, now in its Mk 3 form), in Warriors and in Land Rover Snatch and WMIK vehicles, as well as on foot.[9]

At the end of 2004 the Royal Dragoon Guards deployed on Op Telic 5. On Sunday, 2 January 2005 5 Troop B Squadron were conducting Operation Carriage, a replenishment in support of the Welsh Guards battlegroup, outside Al Amarah. Their convoy consisted of sixteen logistic vehicles, escorted by four Snatch Land Rovers. An ambush occurred, initiated when two DROPS vehicles were struck by IEDs, later assessed to be 155mm artillery shells. Following the explosions, a concerted attack followed using RPGs and small-arms fire. The RDG crews dismounted and fought off the attack, sustaining no casualties. The ambush was remarkable for two reasons. Firstly, it was the first time that the RDG had fired their weapons in anger since their formation. Secondly, of the twenty-one British personnel involved, no less than fifteen were volunteer Yeoman, eight from RWxY and seven from the QOY, including the patrol commander, Lieutenant Greenwell.[10]

A flavour of the sort of tour a typical RAC regiment might find itself conducting was that of the KRH in 2005, on Op Telic 6.[11] A Squadron with seven Challengers were deployed to Al Amarah where they worked under the 1 Staffords battlegroup. The squadron was located near the border with Iran and tasks included the new role of 'mentoring', for both the Iraqi police and the border agencies. B Squadron, with nine Challengers, came under command of a Danish infantry battalion in Shaiba, north of Basra; during the six-month tour their vehicles covered in excess of ¼ million miles. RHQ and HQ Sqn were located close to Al Nasiriyah in Tallil airbase, responsible for running a basic training centre for recruits joining the newly reformed Iraqi army, under the title of SSR: Security Sector Reform. As the regimental journal recorded:

A Squadron's tour proved to be testing and dangerous. Their duties included providing the usual camp [guard] commitments as well as patrolling large swathes of Maysan province. On 29 May a roadside IED detonated killing LCpl Alan Brackenbury and injuring Lt Bishop, LCpl Rawlinson, LCpl Simcock and Tpr Smiles. Two days later the squadron Leader's rover group was attacked by another IED that detonated twenty five meters behind the last vehicle … As the threat rose, rendering the Snatch Landrovers too vulnerable, the squadron was frequently employed as dismounts from the [infantry's] Warriors ... The squadron was tasked with patrolling the Iran/Iraq border and with training the Iraqi Border Enforcement Agency. To reach the border their Landrovers had to be underslung beneath helicopters. The patrol areas often included the marshes and as a result riverine operations were conducted using boats.[12]

Although many such tours produced casualties, both killed and injured, there were lighter moments: during Telic 5 in 2005 B (The Black Horse) Squadron RDG produced a hugely – nationally – popular version of 'Show Me the Way to Amarillo'. It was originally made for an in-theatre version of Comic Relief, which, on being played once back in Germany, led to enormous demand and which crashed the MoD IT system; it even led to sending of the three soldiers responsible for the production back to the UK to appear on national television.

The need for RAC units on the enduring Op Telic created a sudden surge in demand. Within a twelve-month period between 2002 and 2003, of the thirty-six sabre squadrons nominally available within the RAC order of battle, no fewer than twenty were deployed on operations: thirteen in Iraq, four in Northern Ireland and three in the Balkans. Not included in this was the whole of the Joint NBC Regiment (1RTR) supported by many members of the RY, who were also deployed to Iraq. The non-deployed squadrons elsewhere were not off the hook – as well as many having to prepare themselves for service in one of the three main operational theatres, they were all required to undertake training of a different sort for potential service on Op Fresco, the military response to the firemen's strike in the UK that commenced in October 2002.[13]

Serving in Iraq was rarely enjoyable: the climate, the spartan living conditions and not least the antipathy of a largely hostile local population made for a challenging tour for all concerned, and which was only made more poignant when, inevitably, casualties occurred. The RAC Memorial wall at Bovington records the names of seventeen RAC soldiers killed on operations there, and many more were injured. What the RAC did get out of the campaign was, once again, the chance to prove that armour, both heavy and light, still had a major role to play in land warfare. It also demonstrated the inherent flexibility of the RAC, particularly when required to take on unfamiliar roles at short notice.

More Changes

In 2002 the HCav and RAC had comprised 815 officers and 4,915 ORs, representing about 6 per cent of the overall strength of the regular army. The Defence White Paper of 2004 reorganized the infantry into fewer, larger regiments, but on the face of it left the RAC alone, certainly in terms of numbers of regiments. However, in December 2004 it was announced that the RAC structure and some roles within it would change, and would be amended so that it would look like this:

- 5 x Armoured Regiments: SCOTS DG, RDG, QRH, KRH, 2RTR
- 5 x Formation Recce (FR) Regiments: HCR, QDG, 9/12L, LD, QRL
- 1 x Joint NBC Regt: 1RTR (less A Sqn in Warminster in the armoured demonstration role)[14]

That seemed simple enough, but in fact was only scratching the surface of the latest reorganization; each of the regiments would soon find themselves with different manpower ceilings and numbers of squadrons, and so they were not exactly like for like. It was also notable that the balance between MBT and armoured reconnaissance – now increasingly being referred to as FR, or Formation Reconnaissance – was shifting in the favour of lighter armour. Only fourteen years previously, the RAC had comprised twelve armoured regiments and five recce regiments.

By autumn 2005 QRL had completed their conversion from tanks into FR, to become the fifth RAC recce regiment. The composition of the FR regiments were then amended once again, with the welcome formation of a Command and Support (C&S) squadron, splitting out some of the elements from an otherwise over-large and unwieldy HQ squadron. Within the Yeomanry, many roles would also change. RY lost their CR2 role, and was tasked with supporting both JNBCR and the FR regts. RMLY was to provide mainly CR2 support, but with some FR support responsibilities. RWxY also supported the armoured units, with RHQ and A Squadron (Dorset Yeomanry) tasked with the armoured replacement role, and QOY remained in the role of supporting the FR regiments.[15]

In 2002 adult recruits for the RAC completed twelve weeks of basic training, generally referred to as Phase One training, at A Squadron of the Army Training Regiment Winchester, using the Common Military Syllabus (Recruit). Each intake would consist of about forty recruits, supervised by an RAC squadron headquarters, broken into troops. Allowable wastage figures varied: in the training year 2000/01 up to 31 per cent of each intake might be allowed to fail due to being unsuitable or through failing to pass mandatory tests, but the following year this was reduced to 16 per cent, putting pressure on the instructors to pass some recruits who the previous year would probably have not made the grade.

From 2004 the ancient FV432 was upgraded somewhat with a rebuild programme including the replacement of the powerpack with a new diesel engine and braking system in order to modernize about 500 vehicles, thereby extending their in-service life; at the time of writing the vehicle is still in widespread use and has been in service for sixty years. The upgraded vehicles were designated as

Mk 3, and with a full fit of defensive armour were known as Bulldog, although the name is in widespread use to refer to the Mk 3 variant as a whole. Elsewhere, the Panther (formerly FCLV, the Future Command and Liaison Vehicle) was brought into service in 2008 to – finally – replace the 'run-around' scout-car type of vehicle that had been lost when the Ferret went out of service in the early 1990s, although it was not well-protected enough to be used in operational theatres with an IED threat. New logistic vehicles in the shape of a new family of German MAN trucks were issued from 2008, replacing the old MK, DAF and TM types.

The Javelin ATGW was brought into RAC service in about 2005 in order to 'bridge the gap' between Striker (with Swingfire) going out of service and the hoped-for FRES ATGW 'Overwatch' capability coming into service – at some unspecified date in the future; see below. Javelin proved to be an excellent weapon system in Afghanistan, although of course it was not used there against enemy armour. Rather, it was used as a precision attack munition, able to deliver its 8.4kg warhead with great accuracy out to a maximum of 4km, giving the soldiers a long-range direct-fire capability that was most welcome, even being used against individual enemy soldiers on occasion.[16] On the small-arms front, in October 2005 a shortened (L22 carbine) version of the L85 rifle, the so-called SA80K, was introduced into service, with all crew members on Challengers and CVR(T) receiving the weapons. It was fitted with an optical sight as standard and although classified as a self-defence (rather than assault) rifle, it had an accurate range of 200m. The deployments to Iraq and then Afghanistan had a positive effect on the personal equipment that the soldiers received, with much better footwear, body armour and helmets, personal equipment, camp cots and countless other items. These were packaged up as the so-called 'black bag' deployment issue, and older soldiers were amazed to find themselves being properly sized to ensure a good fit of their personal protective equipment, and even being offered a choice of three or four different types of boots. In 2010 a new CBRN respirator, the GSR, was introduced; in the same year a new pattern of camouflage called Multi-Terrain Pattern (MTP) was introduced to replace DPM, and was instantly found to be much more effective when operating in the 'green zone' in Helmand Province.[17]

In 2005 the Future Army Structure (FAS) doctrine and organization required three Challenger-equipped regiments to experiment with something called Medium Armour, MA. Squadrons selected for this role from RDG, KRH and 2RTR used CVR(T) as surrogates in order to conduct tactical experimentation to prepare the ground for the equipment fleet changes that were assumed to be in the offing.[18] Once in service, the MA concept was meant to field three RAC regiments operating the Direct Fire variant of the proposed Future Rapid Effects System, starting in 2015. FRES was an ambitious – probably unrealistically so – vehicle programme that was expected to deliver a fleet of seventeen different capabilities, all based on a common vehicle chassis. This was the utopia of all vehicle programmes that the army had attempted to attain since the Second World War, and which had only really been successful in two instances: CVR(T) and FV432. The expected 3,500 FRES vehicles were broken down into four groups, with Group 1 being those required to equip an infantry battalion, Group 2 recce, ATGW and artillery fire-control vehicles, Group 3 communications and electronic warfare types, and Group 4 CBRN vehicles. The programme was beset by difficulties, as will be recounted shortly.

Afghanistan, 2001–14

The campaign in Afghanistan was directly linked to the US global war on terror, and resulted from the 9/11 attacks on the American mainland. The Americans saw themselves as being at war, and with Osama Bin Laden in particular. Bin Laden had viewed the Soviet invasion of Afghanistan in 1979 as an attack on Islam, and was involved in fighting, organization and in raising funds. He formed a militant network that he called al-Qaeda (the base), which became redundant when the Russians withdrew from Afghanistan, having been forced to withdraw, and having taken many thousands of casualties during their decade there. Bin Laden then focused his group's efforts on fighting the US, which included carrying out attacks on American embassies and even on an American warship. He was the mastermind behind the 9/11 attacks of 2001, and was known to be in refuge in Afghanistan, under the protection of the Taliban government, a group that had come to prominence during the civil war that followed the Soviet withdrawal. Fiercely anti-Western, by the turn of the century the Taliban was in control of much of the country, ran the opium drug trade and the US saw them as a threat not only in their own right, but was also – and this was probably the primary reason – the regime harbouring the US' number one international enemy.

In late 2001 the International Security Assistance Force, ISAF, came into being in order to oust the Taliban and stabilize Afghanistan as a democracy, with Britain as one of many dozens of troop-contributing nations. The swift occupation of the capital, Kabul, by ISAF with the help of the so-called Northern Alliance of warlords opposed to the Taliban, led many to believe that the war had been won at little cost and that the desire to stabilize Afghanistan and promote democracy would be achieved. But this was a false hope; as would happen in Iraq, a short war would be followed by a lull, and then an extremely violent insurgency that did not follow the rules of warfare would plunge the country into even more violence than it had seen in the previous decades. The first deployment of RAC troops was when an eight-man team from the Joint NBC Regiment at RAF Honington was deployed in a matter of days shortly after Christmas 2001 to Kabul, to support and protect the British troops that had just deployed into northern Afghanistan on Op Veritas. There was a genuine concern that there were myriad chemical, radiological and even potentially biological threats in the country, and after quickly equipping the team with whatever lightweight (and hugely expensive) technology could be purchased off the shelf, the team deployed, allowing the quartermaster responsible – the author – to retrospectively sort out the payments and support mechanisms and develop a logistic system that stretched over many thousands of miles.[19]

Op Herrick came into being as the new over-arching UK name for operations in Afghanistan in late 2002, although the focus at that stage was on consolidating the situation in the capital, Kabul, having ousted the Taliban. A few RAC officers and soldiers deployed to ISAF over the next couple of years in an individual capacity, including Major General Peter Gilchrist ex-RTR as the deputy commander of the Combined Force Command, Afghanistan from December 2004, on a twelve-month tour. However, it was not until April 2006 when the remit of British forces suddenly expanded into taking responsibility for the whole of Helmand province in southern Afghanistan that the first complete sub-unit from the RAC deployed. This was D Sqn HCR, mounted – as so often for early entry forces – in CVR(T), now entering its fourth decade in service. Unlike Operation Telic, when the RAC led the armoured attack into Iraq, the campaign that ensued from that point until late 2014 saw the RAC firmly in a supporting role, and often in low numbers compared with the overall total of forces deployed, which was usually about a brigade employed directly on combat operations, backed-up by a huge number of others in support and specialist roles. Helmand would quickly become the most violent province in the whole of the war-torn country, sucking in resources and rarely seeming winnable to the soldiers on the ground.

Helmand province is the largest of the thirty-four that make up the country, being slightly larger in area than Latvia. Helmand was chosen as it was thought that it was there that the small British force could do the most good, replacing the existing American forces and engaged primarily on mentoring Afghan forces and delivering reconstruction and development projects, but not, hopefully, having to take a direct-combat role.[20] With Lashkar Gah as the capital (which came to be known by the troops as Lash Vegas), the province is dominated by the river of the same name that flows north–east to south–west and provides irrigation water for the agriculture of the area, as well as its most important product: opium poppies. Nearly two-fifths of the world's supply was estimated to come from Helmand, making it important not only to the inhabitants, but also to the enemy, in the shape of the recently ousted but now returning Taliban who derived a large part of their income from the crop.[21] The southern part of the province is largely desert, with a 'green-zone' of towns and villages mostly located around the river in the more mountainous north, punctuated by irrigation ditches and abundant flora, providing useful cover and routes for infiltration. Most villages were nothing more than a collection of individual compounds, self-contained family dwellings that were surrounded by high walls of adobe-style construction, with a single entrance, ideal for defence if the defenders were prepared to die – which they were – and allowing the emplacement of IEDs and other booby traps. A porous border with Pakistan allowed easy movement of Taliban to and from safe havens in Pakistan.

D Squadron HCR recorded their impressions of being the first RAC unit to be sent to Helmand, commencing with the usual 'are-we-aren't-we' scenario marking the start of their six-month tour:

> The squadron returned from leave eagerly awaiting news of its upcoming Afghanistan deployment. Were we going on exercise with the regiment or were we training with 16 Air Assault Brigade? Preparations began in earnest … the OPTAG staff seemed somewhat stumped as to how CVR(T) may operate. We gave them a few pointers and cracked on … The squadron completed its training and conducted field firing. Fighting withdrawals from CVR(T), which seemed great fun at the time, sadly proved to be pertinent months later in Musa Qaleh. Our vehicles finally arrived in early March, less than two weeks before their departure date … [they] were loaded into containers and shipped to Karachi…. The squadron eventually found itself complete, in a staggering 115 degree heat, [in] Camp Bastion…. [we fitted] bar armour … the already stretched brigade needed us to be operational.
>
> As operations intensified through their frequency and enemy resistance, the CVR(T) started to prove its worth, both through the protection afforded to the crews and the firepower that could be delivered from it … Often recce soldiering as we knew it would be adapted, in order to provide the much needed weight of fire that the vehicles could provide in support of the infantry … this also meant that the static locations were crying out for permanent support from CVR(T) and it was not long before the squadron found itself split between two outstations and Camp Bastion. The squadron remained broken up for the entire tour.
>
> The squadron was pushed forward to support the Danish recce sqn experiencing problems in Musa Qaleh. CoH Moses and his crew were lucky enough to survive an anti-tank mine strike en route and his vehicle was subsequently denied to the enemy using Apache Hellfire missiles. The following day [1 August] … 3 and 4 Troops were ambushed … by coordinated and opportunistic Taliban in numbers, resulting in the deaths of 2Lt Ralph Johnson and LCpl Ross Nicholls, and seriously injuring Tpr Martin Compton … Tpr Compton was casevaced to Bastion whilst others ensured the recovery of those killed.
>
> Restrictions on the resupply of parts had a huge effect on the squadron's ability to deploy, often causing embarrassment and a huge amount of frustration. Although the REME worked tirelessly in conjunction with

vehicle crews … it was sometimes necessary to 'cross service' through the fleet. September saw the squadron deployed on more battlegroup operations but also on Manoeuvre Outreach Group (MOG) operations between Now Zad and Musa Qaleh, designed to dominate the ground … the squadron and 3 Para patrols platoon suffered six mine strikes between them.[22]

As a result of D Squadron's deployment, CoH Mick 'Taff' Flynn was awarded an MC to join the CGC that he had won in Iraq in 2003, making the Falklands' veteran the most decorated soldier in the RAC. His own account included the following:

> We had to go forward and provide an overwatch on the district centre at Musa Qaleh so that the Danish could come out of their camp. I was in the lead vehicle and the vehicle directly behind me got blown up. I had driven over the IED, they let me past and blew up the vehicle behind me. I was then trapped and they fired numerous rockets at us. Three RPGs [rocket-propelled grenades] hit us and one went over the top. We took out the machinegun posts to the front of us and killed them. The Taliban's main killing group was probably about ten meters away. There was about twenty or thirty of them. I made a decision to go on through the ambush and I looked behind and saw that there was a lot of smoke coming from the vehicle behind. We turned round and went through the ambush firing phosphorous grenades at them. The bar armour which protected the vehicle had been hit so we had to dismount. The Taliban were coming down the lane towards us. We killed three of them, but the rest kept firing. We had to fight our way along then jump in a ditch … I could only account for three bodies. I couldn't see the other body. I talked to the Paras and they sent a company to give us support and to get the bodies out. Because I knew where the positions of the bodies were I was asked if I could lead the Paras back in. We still had one body unaccounted for. You have to go back for him. You can't just leave somebody there. There was no question about us not going back. The Paras then formed up and brought in lots of fire and artillery. We pushed forward and cleared their positions with grenades. This is our job. It is what we do for a living.[23]

Exactly as had happened in Iraq on Operation Telic, every regiment in the RAC deployed to Afghanistan, often at least twice, with some crewmen – frequently although not always volunteers – completing three (or more) tours. Roles for the squadrons included providing the BRF (Brigade Reconnaissance Force – by far and away the most popular role and allocated to the AR regiments), crewing Mastiff, Viking and Warthog (and other) protected patrol vehicles, operating as OMLT (Operational Monitoring and Liaison Teams) with the Afghan National

Army, becoming Afghan police advisors and mentors, and operating the RSOI (Reception, Staging, Onward Movement and Integration) training and support package at Camp Bastion, the extensive British HQ and logistic hub.[24] In addition, many other RAC personnel served on the staff of various HQs and as individual augmentees to a whole range of other units, as everything from UAV operators to dog handlers. As had happened so often in previous decades, the inherent flexibility of the RAC meant that the units found themselves, probably uniquely in the army, subject to frequent short-notice changes of role, equipment, mission and even theatre of operations. In early 2008 D Sqn KRH recorded that:

> In December 2006 we were exercising our skills in Challenger 2 MBTs on Salisbury Plain [but by] October 2007, however, our journey was complete. In that time the squadron had been reformed as a Bulldog squadron [but] then converted to Warrior, had been united with 1st Mechanised Brigade from 12th Mechanised Brigade, planned its deployment with the Irish Guards battlegroup, fought in Basra as a sub-unit of the 2 Royal Welsh battlegroup, and been cut back to the KRH battlegroup for counter-smuggling border operations …

In the same year and the same regiment, B Squadron KRH related their experience of the traditional 'on-the-bus-off-the-bus':

> From January to mid-March the squadron was training to deploy to Iraq with 1st Mechanised Brigade. However, the squadron was stood down days before the mission rehearsal exercise; shortly afterwards [the OC] was warned off that we would be heading to Afghanistan as part of UK's Helmand Task Force with 52 Infantry Brigade, operating the army's new Mastiff armoured vehicle.[25]

Operating in new vehicles brought a variety of challenges, including the training burden and the need to alter the mindset of the officers and soldiers. Conducting active 'strike operations' came easy to the troops, that was what they were trained for. But commanding and driving Mastiff and other protected patrol vehicles in order to carry troops around the battlefield required a different approach. There is little doubt that despite the outwardly unglamorous nature of such roles, the squadrons who found themselves completing such tasks did so with as much verve and aggression as could be hoped for, and did much more than just make the best of a bad job. B Squadron KRH again:

> Mastiff is a new vehicle that was procured to protect logistic convoys against the threat of roadside bombs, and there is no manual that tells us how to conduct combat operations across the mountains and the close country

of Helmand's notorious 'Green Zone'… But it is in this situation that the soldiers of the RAC excel. Whilst the vehicle has wheels rather than tracks and machine guns rather than a 120mm main armament, the principles of manoeuvre warfare remain the same … Falling back on our training on the Canadian prairie, the squadron has been able to push Mastiff to its limits and achieve far more than many thought was possible.

On entering the village [of Regay] we were ambushed by the enemy who were waiting in large numbers. With Taliban engaging us at ranges from 100 meters to as little as five meters, and firing RPGs and small arms with armour piercing ammunition, the squadron spent two hours clearing a route through the village, only to discover that the bridge at the north was too narrow for our vehicles. You could hear the tension on the radio net as I ordered the squadron to turn around and drive back into the heart of the enemy…. engagement ranges being too short for our 40mm grenades to arm, the squadron had to clear the enemy from doorways and alleyways using carbines, pistols, and hand grenades.[26]

The comment about not deploying with the familiar comfort of a 120mm gun is a pertinent one; Britain did not deploy any of its fleet of Challenger 2 tanks to Afghanistan. When the US became involved in supporting the British effort in Helmand in late 2010, it immediately deployed a company of M1A1 MBTs in order to support their troops, stating that, 'The deployment of a company of M1 Abrams tanks, which will be fielded by the [USMC] in the country's south-west, will allow ground forces to target insurgents from a greater distance – and with more of a lethal punch – than is possible from any other US military vehicle'.[27] Seventeen tanks arrived in the country, flown in by Globemaster aircraft, arriving on 25 November and marking the first use by the US of tanks in the campaign. An American spokesperson stated on their arrival that:

We're conducting full-spectrum combat operations [in Afghanistan], we'll be doing it tomorrow, we'll be doing it next month, [and] until the Afghan security forces are ready to take over lead for security … we will continue to do combat operations to defeat the enemy. Whether we use tanks, or infantry on the ground, these are all tactics we use to defeat the enemy.[28]

Both the Canadians and the Danes also fielded numbers of Leopard II tanks in the country, with the Danish tanks on occasion directly supporting British army units.[29] But why didn't the British army come to the same conclusion? It cannot have been a question of utility, as there was plenty of terrain in which the firepower from a 120mm gun could have been used to great effect, both to provide overwatch and in response to combat. The Danes reported that the Taliban failed to recognize the range at which their tanks could deliver munitions – they had been modified pre-deployment to use a specially developed airburst anti-personnel round – and as a result often moved around in the open, not understanding that the tank could accurately engage them at ranges of 2 miles or more. The answer must surely lie in an unwillingness to pick up the bill for the support necessary to maintain even a small number of tanks in the field, despite the enormous overall cost of the campaign. It is of course true that the Challenger 2, even with its Dorchester 2 base armour and additional add-on packages, would not be invulnerable to some of the threats found in Helmand, especially the ever-increasing size of Taliban IEDs when exploded under the vehicle. In particular, the underbelly armour of the tank was relatively weak; the Danes had expended much effort (and within a period of only fourteen months) in up-armouring this area as well as re-designing the driver's station extensively to provide him with more protection in the event of an IED strike at the front of the tank. But the real point is that no vehicle can be made truly invulnerable from all threats, and the deployment of (even a squadron of) tanks would have added a unique form of mobile direct-fire capability that was much less weather/availability dependent than that from air and aviation, and which had far more punch and reach than could be delivered by the 30mm cannons on CVR(T).

When the Queen's Dragoon Guards deployed on Herrick 15 in September and October 2011, it had just been announced that the withdrawal of the majority of British combat forces was to take place by the end of 2014, leaving a much-reduced presence in the country which would focus on developing and supporting the Afghan National Army – one of the tasks envisaged in 2006. When they arrived, the American forces had about 20,000 troops in Helmand, which allowed the British brigade to concentrate on three 'key' central districts in the province. The regiment, like all of its predecessors, had to be completely reconfigured for the operation, with each of the three sabre squadrons being allocated different tasks. As the CO reported with obvious pride:

QDG formed the nucleus of the Intelligence, Surveillance, Target Acquisition and Reconnaissance (ISTAR) group, made up of over 900 men and women from eleven different cap badges. With RHQ based in Lashkar Gar ... QDG remained very much insurgent focussed, primarily in the contested battlespace and in the insurgent safe havens. The ability of the ISTAR group to generate tempo – for example four air assaults in one twenty four hour period – had never been achieved before. The performance of C Squadron, the Brigade Reconnaissance Force (BRF), as the primary strike force in the brigade was one of our key achievements.

The commitment of our cavalry troopers and attached arms during eighteen months of arduous training was sensational. Taking over the role in theatre from the Pathfinders and 3 Commando Brigade patrols company was a challenge that many of our detractors thought was destined for failure.

The reality was the formation of an exceptional force that outperformed all expectations and claimed new records for the number of operations conducted, weapons seized, and insurgents killed.[30] A Squadron mentored and trained an Afghan infantry kandak (battalion) in Nad e Ali. Meanwhile B Squadron was the only RAC squadron to be in their primary role and ensured the [security of] key routes.[31]

The CVR(T) fleet struggled as Herrick progressed; the vehicles in theatre were handed over from unit to unit and thrashed mercilessly, putting on large amounts of track mileage and with insufficient time between missions to conduct the necessary servicing and preventative maintenance. Dust ingression into components was found to be a serious issue. Some vehicles were later found to have been constantly on active operations for over eighteen months, and consequently – and not surprisingly – poor availability was the result, often unreasonably blamed by the staff on the crews and units. In mid-2008 half of the operational fleet had to be withdrawn into Camp Bastion, so two troops had to be converted to Jackal wheeled vehicles, a 'more reliable and stealthy vehicle, albeit one with less protection and only limited ISTAR capability'.[32] A couple of years later, after some rapid re-engineering, the (sort of) new Scimitar 2 and Spartan 2 appeared, with better protection for the crew including new hulls, a blast attenuating seat for the driver and a turret roll-over bar. It proved itself almost immediately, as the Light Dragoons on Herrick 16 were able to report:

> [A Sqn] started operations on H16 with three sabre troops on Scimitar 2, one support troop on Spartan 2 and SHQ was based mainly on Jackal and Husky … No sooner had we got into the swing of the operations being thrown at us by [the CO], than we started to suffer the tides of change. 2nd, support, and GW troops were re-roled into Afghan police advisor teams (PATs). They were sent away to Bastion for another period of training, where they would learn the necessary skills to become mentors/advisors as well as some vehicle conversion courses and extra weapons training … This change in ORBAT had left the Squadron looking markedly thinner, but still with the two sabre troops commanded by Capts Tod and Paske with Sgts Sampher and Newell … The squadron spent significant time in Combined Force Burma, with an almost permanent squadron presence until the end of July. It was here that Sgt Sampher and his crew really tested the integrity of the Scimitar 2 with rollover protection system in an IED strike, which all of the crew survived with [only] minor aches and pains.[33]

In autumn 2012 the Queen's Royal Lancers deployed on Operation Herrick 17, their second regimental tour within two years, with three of the four sabre squadrons under command; C Squadron was detached to under command of the Royal Dragoon Guards as part of the police-mentoring and advisory group. All four sabre squadrons were thus deployed at the same time – an unusual occurrence – and all in very different roles. Although no soldiers were killed during their tour, it still came at a high price: seventeen soldiers were wounded, some with life-changing injuries.

The final RAC presence in the country was in 2014 on Herrick 20, with troops from the QDG and QRH.[34] In the course of the campaign, the RAC suffered twenty-three personnel killed in action (not including the attached personnel who also lost their lives alongside their RAC friends), with dozens more wounded, often seriously, meaning with life-changing injuries, all too frequently the loss of two or more limbs. The Defence Medical Services provided outstanding cover for the injured throughout the campaign, ranging from individual RAMC medics attached to the troops, through the Medical Emergency Response Teams (MERT) which conducted life-saving surgery in the back of Chinook helicopters, to the world-class facilities at Bastion, the superb evacuation chain back to the UK, and, not least, to the fantastic rehabilitation staff and facilities at Headley Court.

Chapter 10

Returning to Normality? 2010–22

The end of the combat phases of the campaigns in Iraq (22 March 2011) and then Afghanistan (27 October 2014) were meant to be followed by a period of a few years in which the army would have time to re-set and in some ways recreate itself ready for the challenges of 2020 and beyond. The phrase 'end of campaigning and return to contingency' was intended to signal the end of a lengthy period in which the army, including the RAC, had been (over) committed to a series of overlapping commitments, from Northern Ireland, through the Gulf War of 1991, into the two Balkans commitments, followed swiftly by the Iraq War and subsequent insurgency, and then the seemingly open-ended trial of Afghanistan.

SDSR, 2010

The Strategic Defence & Security Review of 2010 was delivered even as the campaign in Afghanistan was ongoing, and announced the intention to restructure the army once again, in part to try to create a structure that would allow an interval of thirty months between operational tours for the combat arms. This was to be achieved by creating, in addition to the two rapid response (air assault and commando) brigades, five large and identical multi-role brigades, each of which would include one armoured and one armoured reconnaissance regiment along with one armoured infantry (Warrior) and one mechanized infantry battalion (Bulldog), plus two light-role battalions. But this was quickly changed: in June 2012, a further restructuring did away with three of the existing divisional HQs, rolling the old 2nd, 4th and 5th Divisions into a new organiatizon called Support Command. This left only two genuinely deployable divisions. 3rd (UK) Division was to be the basis of the new 'Reactive/Reaction Force', consisting of three Armoured Infantry Brigades, 1st, 12th and 20th. 1st (UK) Division – no longer armoured – was to be the HQ responsible for the 'Adaptive/Adaptable Force', based around seven large (and all different) infantry brigades which also had geographical responsibilities within the UK.

As part of SDSR 2010 another personnel reduction was announced, bringing total army strength down by about 7,000 soldiers to an initial 95,500, with a target of a further reduction to 82,000 by 2018, with an army reserve target of 30,000.[1] Key features of the review for the RAC included the closure of all remaining

The Royal Lancers, formed in 2015, have antecedents from no less than ten former cavalry regiments; at the time of amalgamation this added up to 1,262 years of service. Although looking very similar to the QRL design, the subtle difference is that the scroll is now attached to the lances, not the bones.

bases in Germany by 2020, and a reduction in the number of Challenger 2 tanks to 227; the 79 now surplus tanks had their special armour and any useful parts removed before being reduced to scrap.[2] Within the RAC, four regiments were directly affected by SDSR. Both 1RTR and 2RTR were in effect merged on 4 August 2014, becoming a single regiment of the RTR, formed out of the personnel from the two regiments and known simply as the Royal Tank Regiment. The 9/12L and QRL were amalgamated to become the Royal Lancers (Queen Elizabeth's Own) on 30 April 2015, the first regiment to operate in the new title of armoured cavalry – see below.[3]

In July 2013 the announcement was made that there would be further Yeomanry amalgamations, with a new regiment called the Scottish and North Irish Yeomanry (SNIY) formed from the rump of the RMLY – placed into suspended animation with effect from the announcement – and three of the squadrons from the QOY: those located in Ayrshire, Fife and Belfast, as well as a new headquarters and a command and support squadron based in Edinburgh. The official date of the new regiment entering the order of battle was 31 October 2014. This left the RAC in mid-2015 consisting of just nine regular operational regiments, four Yeomanry regiments, plus the HCMR in its traditional ceremonial role and sitting outside of the corps:

HCR	KRH
(HCMR)	LD
QDG	RTR
SCOTS DG	RY
RDG	RWxY
QRH	SNIY
RL	QOY

The reorganizations post-Iraq and especially Afghanistan led to three very different types of regiment being formed; armoured, armoured cavalry (FR in old money) and light cavalry. This meant that although there were some common elements that applied to each type, there were very different technical and tactical skills required from the crewmen and officers in each, making cross-postings between

By 2014 there were only four remaining
Yeomanry regiments in the RAC: RY, RWxY,
SNIY and QOY.

the different types of regiment more difficult. There was much more emphasis within the light cavalry and armoured cavalry regiments on dismounted skills than there was within tank units, and the size of the regiments also varied significantly. In 2009 the three armoured cavalry regiments had an authorized strength of only 335, whereas armoured regiments were capped at 419.[4] The Household Cavalry, including its mounted ceremonial regiment the HCMR, was 683 strong.[5] The QDG was the first RAC regiment to convert to the new role as (wheeled) light cavalry, completing the conversion in 2015, followed by the Royal Scots Dragoon Guards and the Light Dragoons. Only the QRH and the RTR remained on tanks with a Type 56 establishment, the remainder becoming armoured cavalry – still on CVR(T), and anxiously awaiting the outcome of the Ajax programme.

In 2018 an Armoured Cavalry Squadron consisted of: three sabre (sometimes called 'find') troops, each with four Scimitars; a GW troop with four Javelin-equipped Spartans; a support troop of four Spartans, which included sniper teams; and an SHQ/REME support element in two Panthers, two Sultans and two Samsons. A Light Cavalry Squadron at the same time would be: three sabre troops each with four Jackals; a support troop of four Coyote; a fitter troop of one Coyote and one Jackal; and an SHQ of one Panther and two Jackals. Firepower would total sixteen GPMG, eight .50in HMG, eight 40mm grenade machine guns, as well as 60mm mortars, underslung grenade launchers, sniper rifles, six LMG and Javelin anti-tank missiles, an exceptional amount of punch from such a lightweight force. This allows them to be used as a strike force in their own right, or to provide fire support to the infantry, as well as the more traditional role of reconnaissance.

SDSR, 2015

According to this review, the army would remain at the figure of 82,000 regulars noted in the 2010 report. Additional resources were promised for both the regular and reserve forces, and, critically for the RAC, 589 Ajax vehicles would be ordered to replace CVR(T). The main location for these would be in two new 'Strike' brigades, which would be formed by converting two of the armoured infantry brigades and which would operate solely using variants of the Ajax family. These brigades would not contain any MBTs, but would seek to provide a balance between light, readily deployable forces and the heavier, slower to deploy formations that had significantly more firepower but also much more of a logistical 'tail'. The Challengers themselves would be upgraded through a Life Extension Programme, or LEP, which would attempt to keep them competitive.

Women in Close Combat

On 25 October 2018 – Balaclava Day – the Defence Secretary Gavin Williamson announced that, following a review, all roles in close-combat units would henceforth be opened to women. This announcement made official a long-standing desire to include women in those roles that had historically been unavailable to them, although it must be noted that the RAC had led the way with this, introducing its first female officer, Second Lieutenant Sarah Batts, in November 2016; she was appointed as 11 troop leader in Cyclops, RTR, commanding a troop of Challenger 2 tanks. Heading off complaints from some of the old guard that women are not physically capable of such roles, the army now uses a gender-free Role Fitness Test (Soldier) or RFTS. This comprises a 4km 'tab' carrying 40kg in 1 hour, then, after a 10-minute breather, a 2km run carrying 25kg in under 15 minutes. Following another 10-minute break, a casualty drag, jerrycan carry and a fire and movement serial must all be completed. Numbers remain low, but the bar to women joining the RAC no longer exists.[6]

The 2021 Integrated Review

On 22 March 2021, the Defence Secretary informed the House of Commons of the results of the Integrated Review (IR) and issued the associated report, entitled 'Defence in a Competitive Age'. Included in this was an announcement that the army – despite what SDSR 2015 had stated – would shrink once again, from the nominal 82,000 (in reality nearer 76,000 due to manning shortfalls) to only 72,500 by 2025, making it the smallest British army since 1714 – the year before many of the antecedents of the current cavalry regiments were founded. At the time the review was published, there were 73,446 trained soldiers in the regular army, with 4,431 of them in the Household Cavalry and the Royal Armoured

Corps, representing 6 per cent of the overall strength of the army. It was also confirmed that the number of main battle tanks held would reduce again, from 227 to 148, enough to field only 2 regiments. These would be rebuilt with a new turret and other enhancements to become the upgraded but unimaginatively named Challenger 3.

Challenger 3

On 10 May 2021 it was announced that the British army had signed an agreement for £800 million for the acquisition of 148 Main Battle Tanks from RBSL – Rheinmetall BAE Systems (Land). The latest version of Britain's Challenger tank, first introduced in the mid–1980s, was expected to be introduced by 2027, although, if previous vehicle programme forecasts are anything to go by, this is unlikely to be met. The announcement stated that this would:

> … ensure the army has a revolutionary main battle tank which is designed to be deployed against near-peer adversaries and implement next generation digital applications. The tank will include a host of latest generation equipment including a 120mm smoothbore gun, designed by Rheinmetall, similar to those already in use by the United States M1 Abrams tank, and Leopard 2 … The tank is also set to receive enhanced digital sights for day and night targeting ability … Sources close to the program mention that the tank will have unparalleled survivability thanks to a newly designed modular 'Epsom' and 'Farnham' armour, which will be layered with a brand new Active Protection System. The hull and suspension is also being upgraded to include third generation hydrogas … Deputy Chief of the General Staff, Lieutenant General Chris Tickell CBE said: 'The Integrated Review described a transformed Army that will be more lethal, better protected, and better connected than any of its comparators. Challenger 3 is a manifestation of exactly that change and will sit at the heart of our warfighting capability. Its digital open architecture will ensure that it is integrated across the battlefield, its main armament will overmatch its adversaries and the crew will be afforded a unique level of protection. It is a battle winner.'[7]

Infantry Vehicles

The IR of 2021 stated that Warrior would not now be upgraded with a new turret/gun and other improvements as had long been hoped through the Warrior Capability Sustainment Plan, but would be retired once the 8x8 wheeled Boxer mechanized infantry vehicle (MIV) entered service to replace it – the MIV being described in the *Daily Telegraph* by a disgruntled ex-general as nothing more than a 'battlefield taxi without a turret', albeit an expensive one.[8] Boxer is based upon a design from a German-led consortium, intended for service not only in the UK but also by Germany, Netherlands, Lithuania and Australia. On 5 November 2019 a £2.3 billion deal for the purchase of 523 vehicles in 4 variants had been signed; this number was increased to 623 in April 2022. Boxer is thus the off-the-shelf (if there is such a thing anymore in the field of vehicle procurement) replacement for the Utility Vehicle (UV) conceived of under the FRES programme.

Ajax

At the time of writing, Ajax is the base vehicle intended to fulfil the roles allocated to what was called the Scout Specialist Vehicle or SV variant within the FRES programme. This would finally allow the retirement of the CVR(T) fleet introduced in the early 1970s. Ajax is described as an up-armoured and improved descendant from the in-service Spanish ASCOD AFV, but with 'improvements' which take it up to 38 tons, about 10 tons (30 per cent) heavier than the original ASCOD vehicle on which it was based and never a good start point for any vehicle programme. The turret is a completely new design, and is armed with a stabilized 40mm cased telescopic ammunition (CTA) cannon. In September 2014 589 vehicles were ordered in a firm-price contract, reportedly worth £5.5 billion. The breakdown of the expected buy was:

245 turreted Ajax variants:
- 198 Reconnaissance/Strike
- 23 Joint Fire Control
- 24 Ground Based Surveillance

256 Protected Mobility Recce Support (PMRS) variants:
- Ares APC
- Athena Command and Control
- Ares Formation Reconnaissance Overwatch
- Argus Engineer Reconnaissance

88 PMRS-based REME variants:
- Atlas Recovery
- Apollo Repair

The programme has been beset by difficulties, many of which stem from the questionable method of taking a so-called off-the-shelf vehicle and then extensively trying to remodel it to perfect it. As of December 2021 only twenty-six vehicles had been received, and the programme was running at least four years late. The media reported that the programme had identified twenty-seven major faults, including: excessive noise and vibration; the vehicle was unable to reverse over obstacles 20cm high; and unspecified problems had been discovered when shooting on the move. This led to trials restrictions such as limiting the amount of time troops could spend inside a moving vehicle to under 2 hours, and imposing a top speed of 20mph – the same as a 1921 Vickers medium tank. Ajax was originally planned to start to enter service in 2017, with an Interim Operating Capability (IOC) date in the Ajax-equipped formations of July 2020; this was subsequently pushed back to June 2021 and has still not been met at the time of writing.[9]

With a Full Operating Capability (FOC) date of April 2025 extremely unlikely to be achieved, in March 2022 an MOD spokesperson stated that: 'Ajax is a troubled programme, and we will not accept a vehicle that is not fit for purpose'. This meant that ancient vehicles such as CVR(T) and the FV432 continued to be used in-service, despite their obsolescence and an increasingly expensive maintenance bill. At the time of writing in late 2022, the plan was that CVR(T) less Stormer would go out of service in early 2023, with Warrior following shortly behind, by the end of that year. Both of these assumptions are now seriously in doubt.

The RAC in 2022

Released at the end of October 2021, the *Future Soldier Guide* outlined an update on the changes to the organization of the 'new look' army, detailing both the deployable and support formations, and where the regiments are/ would be located and in which roles. Some of the brigades were retitled – using terminology directly copied from the Americans and which caused many to question the direction the army was going – as Brigade Combat Teams (BCT). In the guide, the RAC elements, including the Yeomanry, in the new formations were described and deployed thus:

FORMATIONS
1st (UK Division):
    4th Light BCT (HQ Catterick):
    • Light Dragoons (Lt Cav) Catterick
    7th Light Mechanized BCT (HQ Cottesmore):
    • SCOTS DG (Lt Cav) Leuchars
    19th Brigade (HQ York):
    • SNIY (Lt Cav Res) Edinburgh
    • QOY (Lt Cav Res) Newcastle
3rd (UK) Division:
    1st Deep Strike Brigade Combat Team (BCT) (HQ Tidworth):
    • HCR (Armd Cav) Bulford
    • QDG (Lt Cav) Swanton Morley until at least 2027, then to moving to Caerwent

- RL (Armd Cav) Catterick until at least 2026, then moving to Tidworth
- RY (Lt Cav Res) Leicester

12th Armoured BCT (HQ Bulford):

- KRH (Armd Cav) Tidworth
- RTR (Armd) Tidworth
- RWxY (Armd Res) Bovington

20th Armoured BCT (HQ Bulford):

- RDG (Armd Cav) Warminster
- QRH (Armd) Tidworth

Notes:

1. Both Netheravon and Stanley Barracks Bovington were briefly considered as locations for two of the Armoured Cavalry regiments, but were discounted as being unsuitable.
2. There was no change announced in the *Future Soldier Guide* for the Household Cavalry Mounted Regiment, but the army bands were further amended, now becoming regionally based rather than representing specific corps.

In Conclusion

> The principal and proper work of history is to instruct and enable men, by the knowledge of actions past, to bear themselves prudently in the present and providently towards the future.
>
> *Thomas Hobbes*

Hobbes, writing 400 years ago, was undoubtedly right. But has the RAC – and the wider British army – learned from the lessons of history and changed for the better? Has the RAC been allowed to develop prudently and sensibly? How much of its 'learned experience' is repetitive – are we able to recognize similarities between, for example, the RTC armoured car operations in India between the wars, and the campaigns in Malaya, Northern Ireland, Iraq or Afghanistan? What of the policies regarding the frequent re-equipping and role-changing of the units? And probably most importantly, what of the selection and training of the optimum type of soldiers and officers needed to carry out the multitude of different tasks given to the corps? In a lecture to RUSI in December 1939, Colonel Sir Fred Pile of the RTC started with these words:

> About six years ago, Sir Edward Grigg [then Governor of Kenya] in a lecture given at the Staff College stated that the outstanding lesson of the wars of the British Empire was that we were always unprepared for war. He added that, in his opinion, the most skilled British general was he who could improvise best, and that as it was unlikely that we would be much better prepared in the future, the ability to improvise should be one of the principal characteristics of every British soldier.[1]

Like Hobbes, Pile was undoubtedly correct, and he raised the interesting point that improvisation in war is a critical – if not *the* critical – component of the character of the successful soldier and leader. In that respect, the RAC can hold its head up, as it breeds such men. In a more direct criticism published in the *Report on the Committee on the Lessons of the Great War*, presented by Lieutenant General Kirke in 1932, stated that:

> Our study has led us to one broad conclusion, which is that the British Army has always been inadequate to finish any serious war quickly, and

there appears to be nothing in the present situation to disprove the theory that a large expansion of the peacetime army will be required in any future emergency.

Kirke's conclusion still holds true in 2022. That the regular army is always too small and unready for the next conflict is a matter of historical fact. Being too small and ill-prepared not only makes a conflict more likely but also prolongs it when it happens – this inevitably leads to avoidable casualties. How the standing army should be equipped is always a matter of debate, but what is clear is that the more high-tech an item of equipment is, the longer it takes to manufacture, and the longer it takes to train (and often constantly retrain) personnel to use it. Therefore, such systems must be available 'off the shelf', complete with crews to use them. This means that they must be properly trained, and have a system of support to keep them available. Whether the RAC finds itself in that position in 2022 is another matter of debate, although this author contends that this is unlikely and that the army will, once again, be found wanting when another shooting war rears its unpredicted head. What is almost certain is that the men and women of the RAC will rise to the challenge as they have always done, with flexibility, determination, and a strength of character that stems directly from working as a team, as a cohesive unit – in other words, as a crew.

Throughout the three volumes that make up the *Find, Fix and Strike* trilogy, there are clearly identifiable 'golden threads' that link the conduct of campaigns in war. To conclude, it will be a useful exercise to identify what these are, and what they might mean for the future. Firstly, and probably most important, is the human factor. Recruiting and retaining the right men – and women – is critical to success. The right 'type' is not always easy to describe or codify, but for the RAC it encompasses someone who is not only a specialist in the various trades, but is also, at heart, a real combat soldier, someone who is prepared to go forward, under fire, to complete a mission – and then do it all over again, day after day. This implies an aggressive yet intelligent soldier, both technically and tactically adept, and one who is completely flexible in mind and spirit – Pile's soldier who is comfortable with a need to improvise.

Another noteworthy feature of almost all of the campaigns and other operations described in this work has been how often the so-called mounted soldier is required to operate on his (and her) feet. This will be for one of two main reasons. Firstly, because there are many tasks that require the mounted crewman to dismount from the comfort and security of the vehicle – from maintaining a secure location when conducting maintenance and replenishment, to engaging with other troops or with the local population. Secondly, there are the countless times when RAC soldiers have been, often at short notice, required to take on a genuinely infantry role – Northern Ireland is probably the most obvious example, but Iraq, Afghanistan, the Balkans, Cyprus, Aden and Palestine also spring to mind.

The RAC in all its different guises has always believed, quite rightly, in the necessity of breeding a culture of excellence in both the technical and tactical aspects of its roles. Mobility focused as the corps is, this has always meant becoming masters of the various vehicles, and other equipments, that the corps operates with. This means not only the 'bread and butter' of becoming technically expert on tanks and armoured cars, but also on other items, from amphibious vehicles, helicopters and light aircraft, to armoured personnel carriers and other patrol vehicles, guided missiles, surveillance radars, sniper rifles and mortars, and, not least, having the ability to operate on foot. However, mastery of the equipment comes with a caution: the modern, obsessional use of technology, often trumpeted as the panacea for all battlefield ills, comes at a high price – both in terms of unimaginable costs, but also ridiculously long development times and not least the burden on the individual soldier. The soldier must not become a slave to the complexity of the equipment, whether it be a communications system of a fire-control computer. Such technology must be made simple to use, by a tired and stressed operator, in the heat of the battle.

This means that there is a desperate need for simplicity, one which is not apparent to this observer. In 1979, in *The Tanks*, the third part of Kenneth Macksey's history of the RTR, he noted that, 'Like so many of the post-war vehicles, the specification of FV301 tended to embody too many facilities in an attempt to satisfy all the contingencies the fighting men's experience had suggested'.[2] Although this particular vehicle was a design from the late 1940s, the same criticism is true today, perhaps even more so. Specifications have become far too complex, leading to attempts to design vehicles that in an honest attempt to be a jack of all trades end up not being able to complete their primary one. This also leads to increased cost, development times measured in decades, and – if the vehicle ever sees service – technologically complex vehicles that make the crewman's attempt to master them an impossible job, with very long training courses and huge levels of skill fade.

Another strong point has always been the RAC's excellence in the twin aspects of command and control. The requirement to pass information rapidly and reliably on a battlefield is a real force multiplier, and understanding how to get the best out of complex communication systems is another skill that cannot be easily acquired overnight. Communications are at the heart of another key to mission success – with very few exceptions, working as part of an all-arms grouping is required in all aspects of modern warfare. Success comes from mutual trust and understanding, and this work is littered with examples of where this has been achieved, and also where it has gone wrong. In short: the chance to meet, discuss and train/rehearse the whole team before the operation adds immeasurably to the chance of success, whereas throwing units together in the heat of battle without preparation rarely if ever leads to the desired outcome.

Finally, it should be clear to the reader that, although a tank man at heart, I am also a huge fan of light armour. Armoured and scout cars, CVR(T) and the like have a utility that must not be discounted. They have proved their worth time and again, from Flanders in 1914 to Afghanistan a century later. This utility comes from having the three key attributes of firepower, protection and mobility but linked to the ability to deploy rapidly and with much less logistic 'tail' than heavier forces. This does not mean that the days of the MBT are over, but it is to be hoped that the new Strike Brigades, equipped with the Ajax family of vehicles, will not become too bulky and unwieldy to fulfil this role. It is also critical to accept that no military vehicle, from a 4-ton scout car to an 80-ton main battle tank, can be made invulnerable from all threats – but having an armoured skin in a highly mobile vehicle with sufficient firepower to defeat the enemy is a truly valuable commodity.

Size does matter. Since the Second World War Britain has never had a large enough RAC to complete all the many jobs it has been called on to do satisfactorily. Every single operational deployment has come as a surprise and has often involved cobbling together forces with what can be made available, rather than with what should be deployed to ensure mission success – witness the problems involved in sending troops to Malaya, Korea, Suez, Cyprus, Kuwait, both Gulf wars, the Balkans and Afghanistan. Every one of these deployments involved significant

CVR(T) continues in service, awaiting the arrival of the Ajax family of vehicles, and may yet see another operational deployment before finally being replaced after six decades of service. (Courtesy Andy Brend)

disruption to the entire corps, both manpower and equipment. This 'rob Peter to pay Paul' modus operandi is, but should not be, the hallmark of an army that is frequently heralded by politicians as the best in the world – the politicians who boast about this are the same ones who are not prepared to pay the price of maintaining sufficient forces, in terms of both quantity and quality. This inability to have sufficient forces causes needless casualties and risks mission success. As Bill Slim is reputed to have said, 'The more you use, the less you use'.

Overstretch of RAC units and manpower is nothing new, and has been another constant thread throughout this volume. At its peak in 2011, with the RAC heavily committed to both Iraq and Afghanistan, 83 per cent of the corps was committed to operations; this meant that they were either on operations, had returned within the previous six months, were due to deploy within six months or were directly supporting operations as their main activity. This almost certainly represents the post-war peak and reflected the continuing requirement for the RAC in a staggering number of roles, despite much being made in certain circles of the fact that no tanks were deployed in Afghanistan, and using this 'fact' to question the relevance of the RAC. Overstretch could also manifest in other, more insidious ways: two squadrons of QRL returned to Germany from Operation Telic in May 2003, and were immediately involved in a regimental move to Catterick; within four weeks of arrival there the regiment was in BATUS, training for the next operation; the effects on the families as well as the soldiers can be imagined.

In 2016 HQ DRAC had become somewhat concerned about the possible negative impact of a perception of individualism within the corps as a whole, and stated that, 'The RAC at present is not greater than the sum of its parts. The regiments have always been strong in their own context [but] the corps has not functioned as a strong, cohesive body.'[3] As a result of this, in about 2017 the RAC conducted an army wide study to summarize the strengths and weaknesses of the corps, as well as the perceptions of it from the rest of the army. This found that on the negative side of the balance sheet, that the corps (mainly meaning some of its officers, with some regiments more guilty than others) were viewed as unnecessarily elitist and aloof, perpetuating the attitudes and behaviours of their Victorian forefathers. They were also thought to lack the robustness of the average infantry soldier when engaged in dismounted close combat.[4] The small overall numbers of the RAC also meant that they were not well represented on the staff in divisions and brigades, and that the small size of the units meant that they lacked critical mass on operations, particularly when they were asked to take the place of an infantry unit with roughly twice the manpower.

On the positive side though, the RAC was assessed to be admired for its professional and technical competence, with the caveat that this competence was at danger of being lost – or at least damaged – by the lack of ability to train on increasingly complex equipment. The RAC soldier was seen to take a particular pride in their vehicles and equipment, and possessed a determination to 'fight

The strength of the RAC lies in its high-quality manpower. Lieutenant Tilman HCR on exercise with his crew on Salisbury Plain. (Courtesy HCR)

it', meaning the ability to keep going when some systems broke down or failed. They were thought of as (sensible) risk-takers on operations, being resourceful, ingenious, flexible and adaptable, and thus providing a utility on the battlefield that was almost unique. Regimental charisma and elan were seen to be positives provided they were managed sensibly; a good performance on the battlefields of Waterloo or Alamein, or possessing numerous VCs and a stylish mess dress, were not seen as being relevant unless backed up by current exploits and professionalism.

Since the report, the 'RAC First' initiative plus the increasingly clear need for a small and shrinking part of the army to stand together in order to prevent it being defeated in detail, has brought the corps – including the all-too-often-prepared-to-go-their-own-way Household Cavalry – closer together than it has ever been in its ninety-three-year existence. In 1946 Field Marshal Montgomery wrote that it was 'vital that the RAC becomes a unified and happy corps' – hopefully, his wish has come true. In the opinion of this author, the RAC in 2022 is greater than the sum of its parts. Despite an often overblown, and occasionally unhealthy, desire to be seen as both different from and better than the 'rest', each regiment and unit of the RAC has much more in common with the others than it publicly recognizes.

As this book goes to press, the RAC continues to be regularly deployed on operations worldwide, notably using thirty-year old Challenger 2 – and of course, fifty-year old CVR(T) – as part of the NATO Enhanced Forward Presence in Estonia, as well as Light Cavalry units mounted on Jackal forming part of the UN MINUSMA mission in Mali. The war in Ukraine is now ten months old, with much being made of the poor performance of the Russian armoured forces in the face of stubborn Ukrainian anti-tank defences; time will tell what impact this will have on the size, composition and equipment of the British army in general and the RAC in particular, but impact it must have. The RAC will need to ensure that the chain of command continues to recognize the unique capabilities that the RAC brings to the battlefield, and which, in all the three volumes of this work, I have attempted to identify and crystallize. In an uncertain world, such flexibility and reliability are priceless military assets, and must be both retained and enhanced. The final word can be left in the hands of Brigadier Simon Caraffi, the Director Royal Armoured Corps, speaking in 2010:

> [The RAC] are the mounted combat arm of the British Army; whatever else has been questioned during my times as DRAC I have never heard anyone challenge our expertise in this. This is what the RAC exists for; take that argument away and I could not provide an intellectually cogent argument for our preservation. But I see no indication that Defence intends to dispense with either mounted reconnaissance or platform-mounted direct fire ... We must maintain this expertise and let nobody think this is easy ... Let us not be seduced by the view (usually a justification for a savings measure and little more) that such skills are easily restored.[5]

Mechanization in Other Arms

The Mechanization and Armouring of the Infantry

In 1956 the RAC conference noted that the army command now had the ambition to put 'one standard infantry battalion in some form of APC'. This was in fact completely lacking in ambition; during the Second World War the way ahead had been made very clear, with extemporized APCs made from surplus tank chassis proving a real force multiplier, and the use of light 'carrier' vehicles had been extremely successful in a number of support roles. However, only ten years after the end of the war this experience had largely been squandered, and the only APCs in service were a few old Second World War Ram Kangaroos operated for demonstration purposes at Warminster – none of the front-line BAOR infantry regiments had access to such vehicles. It would not be until October 1957 that such a moderate ambition would be realized, and then only with the help of the RAC.[1]

At that point, the 14th/20th Hussars changed their role to become the first BAOR APC regiment, with two large squadrons operating Saracen APCs on behalf of infantry battalions; the intention was for this to be a temporary measure until the infantry could take over the role from the RAC. The six-wheeled Saracen had in fact been delayed from entering BAOR service by the need to send all vehicles coming off the production lines to Malaya, where they were needed for the ongoing campaign. Although not a tracked APC, the Saracen was a step in the right direction, giving the troops inside reasonable cross-country mobility and protection from small-arms fire and shell splinters, as well as some firepower from the commander's .30in MG in the turret. The RAC was only given the job of operating the vehicles because it was thought too difficult to train (mostly National Service) infantry soldiers, most of whom could not drive and who had no mechanical training, to take on the role themselves. This would remain the case for six years – with 4RTR taking over the APC role from the Hussars in late 1960 – until the infantry was ready take over responsibility for providing their own APC crews, from spring 1963; 4RTR spent most their last six months in the role training infantry personnel in their new responsibilities.

The development and then introduction of the FV432 APC in 1963 gave the infantry, for the first time, its own purpose-built tracked APC. It was decided that due to the numbers required, it was not feasible for the RAC to operate them on behalf of the PBI, and that they would have to learn to drive and maintain them themselves; the infantry found their new charges to be 'complex', something

The Saracen APC was introduced into service during the Malaya Emergency, and was the first purpose-designed APC used by the British army. Later replaced with the tracked FV432, it gave useful operational service in Northern Ireland.

the RAC no doubt laughed at but which reflected the realities of taking on a new role from scratch. Training was mainly conducted at the REME depot in Bordon, before moving to Bovington in 1977. As well as the basic 'box' variant capable of carrying an infantry section, the infantry also operated command, ambulance, anti-tank (mounting the Wombat recoilless gun), surveillance radar and mortar variants, and a few were adapted to carry surplus Fox turrets with a 30mm Rarden cannon. In order to give the vehicles some form of supporting fire in the assault, many 432s were fitted with the L37 turret, a small cast one-man turret with a single 7.62mm GPMG. With over 3,000 being produced, the 432 remained in service in many arms and corps for 60 years. Over the time it was incrementally improved, its original Mk 1 petrol-engined version being replaced by the 1980s with a fully diesel-engined fleet (the Mk 2), and then upgraded to the latest Mk 3 variant.[2]

The Mechanized Infantry Combat Vehicle for the 1980s (MICV-80) was a 1970s project to enhance the mobility and lethality of infantry battalions in armoured divisions, and was renamed as Warrior in 1985, entering service in 1987 as the main equipment in the newly designated Armoured Infantry (AI)

The FV432 has remained in service for over sixty years, and can be expected to do so for many years to come.

battalions, with 1st Battalion Grenadier Guards being the first unit to convert. Equipped with a 30mm (non-stabilized) Rarden cannon and the (initially at least) unpopular 7.62mm chain gun, it massively increased the capability of the infantry on the modern battlefield and not before time – the Bundeswehr had introduced its Infantry Fighting Vehicle, the Marder, as early as 1971. The main type of Warrior was the so-called section vehicle, the FV510, but five other variants were also built. These were the FV511 (infantry command), FV512 (REME repair), FV513 (REME recovery), FV514 (RA OP) and FV515 (RA AS90 Battery Command).[3] With its introduction the Warrior-equipped units were known as Armoured Infantry, and the FV432 'battlefield taxi' battalions were renamed as Mechanized Infantry.[4]

By the early 2000s it was recognized that the vehicle was becoming tired, difficult to support and lacking sufficient firepower. The proposed Warrior Capability Sustainment Programme or WCSP, designed to modernize the vehicle in order to extend its service life to at least 2040, included fitting a new turret mounting a stabilized 40mm cased telescopic ammunition (CTA) cannon. However, after many hundreds of million pounds (estimated at £595 million) had been spent on development, WCSP was cancelled in early 2021, in part due to problems being found with the armour on the old hulls de-laminating badly, making using them unviable. Instead, MoD placed all its hopes on the

The FV510 Warrior was introduced to give the infantry a true infantry fighting vehicle; armed with the 30mm Rarden cannon, it proved its worth in the 1991 Gulf War and in both Iraq and Afghanistan, as well as in the various Balkans deployments.

introduction of the Boxer 8x8 wheeled vehicle, described by its many detractors as nothing more than a glorified (if reasonably modern) battlefield taxi rather than a true fighting vehicle, and representing a step backwards in allowing the infantry to operate on an armoured battlefield.

The Royal Artillery

Despite the experience gained in operating self-propelled artillery systems during the Second World War, the dramatic reductions in manpower and spending following the end of the war meant that the Royal Artillery was unable to capitalize on it, returning to an organization that relied mainly on towed guns to support the armoured and infantry divisions in the field role – significantly cheaper and less complex than SPGs. For a time the main wartime SPG, the 25-pounder-armed Sexton, remained in service, only being replaced by relatively small numbers of the American 105mm M44 from 1956, and this saw operational service only in BAOR, with 1 and 4RHA. A fully turreted vehicle with an armoured roof, they remained in service until 1968.[5]

In the mid-1960s the FV433 Abbot started to come into service. This small SPG was based on the running gear of the FV432 APC and carried a new 105mm L13 gun/howitzer, with a range of about 17.4km in its improved Mk 2 form; forty rounds could be carried on board with a rate of fire of between six and eight rounds per minute.[6] Abbot was a simple and popular vehicle, and, whilst lacking the weight of fire of larger 155mm SPGs, was a successful design despite never being used in action, and remained in service until it was replaced by the much larger and more capable – and also complex – AS90.

During the 1960s, near concurrent with the introduction of Abbot, other American-designed self-propelled guns were brought into RA service, albeit in smaller numbers. The most important of these was the 155mm M109. Nearly 150 M109s of various marks were procured with the first entering service in RA medium regiments in BAOR from 1965. The range of the gun, with its much larger shell, incrementally increased with the use of improved ammunition and longer barrels, and by the time it was going out of service could reach about 23km. (When it left service the fleet was sold to Austria, where it was reported that the turrets were removed and emplaced in the mountains as a defensive measure.) Other American designs used by the heavy regiments included the M107 (175mm) and M110 (203mm) tracked vehicles –

The FV433 Abbot SPG was based upon the running gear of the ubiquitous FV432. It remained in service for over two decades before being replaced by the larger and better-armed AS90.

An American design, the M109 was a 155mm armed SPG that was able to be incrementally modified and upgraded over nearly thirty years of service; it too was replaced by the AS90.

only the M109 was fully turreted, the others having open gun platforms and based on a common chassis design. The M110 was capable of firing nuclear shells, and the M107 with its extremely long barrel could reach about 40km, although the very large calibres meant that the rate of fire was extremely slow on both vehicles. Both were used during the Gulf War of 1991 before being replaced with AS90 and MLRS.

The AS90 (Artillery System for the 1990s) was developed to replace both Abbot and M109, as it was believed by the 1980s that only 155mm artillery shells had sufficient lethality on the modern battlefield. Entering service in 1992, AS90 had a much-trumpeted burst-fire capacity of being able to fire a three-round salvo in 10 seconds, allowing it to quickly move to another position before counter-battery fire could locate and target it – a genuine use of 'shoot and scoot' tactics. This was able to be done at the cost of increasing complexity, and the high rate of fire meant that the forty-eight rounds stowed on board could be quickly expended. There were 179 of these procured, with about 90 remaining in service at the time of writing, although approximately 10 of these were reportedly sent to Ukraine as military aid – with training – in 2022.

The M270 Multiple Launch Rocket System (MLRS) was based upon a stretched version of the tracked chassis of the US Bradley IFV and was procured by the RA in the late 1980s, just in time for sixteen systems to be used in the Gulf War where they proved to be highly effective, being nicknamed the 'grid square removal system'. In 2022 a reported six systems were sent as military aid

An AS90 in Iraq, 2003. The burst-fire capability allowed it to carry out the so-called 'shoot and scoot' fire missions, firing three rounds in 10 seconds and moving before effective counter-battery fire could target it.

to Ukraine; the remaining systems can be expected to remain in service for the foreseeable future, with a report dated September 2022 indicating that the size of the fleet might be increased, even doubled.

Artillery fire is most effective when it is observed. During the Second World War some RA Forward Observation Officers (FOO) were mounted in carriers or even in specially modified tanks with additional radio sets (and often dummy guns), and the practice continued until the late 1980s using modified Centurion gun tanks, when specialist Warrior FV 514 OP vehicles began to be introduced into service. These were fitted with dummy 30mm guns – the amount of surveillance and communications systems carried means that as much volume as possible needs to be created inside the vehicle, and removing the breech of the Rarden cannon creates extra space; the 7.62mm chain gun was retained for protection. A few FV515 Battery Commanders vehicles were also developed for those BCs in command of AS90 batteries, in the manner of the so-called chargers of the Second World War, albeit at a much higher technical level.

The use of guided weapons by the RA came about as a result of the formation of RA anti-tank regiments during the Second World War. When the US M10 Tank Destroyer became available through Lend-Lease, the divisional anti-tank regiments in Infantry Divisions were equipped with the vehicle (and towards the end of the war with the Valentine Archer SPG as an alternative). In 1950 this role was handed over to the RAC, who unwillingly took the role for a number of years before passing it to the Yeomanry. From 1960 the RAC took its first tentative steps in fielding an anti-tank guided weapons (ATGW) capability with Malkara, then Vigilant and Swingfire. In 1976 it was decided that all ATGW capability would pass from the RAC to the Royal Artillery, where it remained until 1 April 1984 when it once more became an RAC responsibility. In this period the RA operated both Striker and FV438 tracked launchers. Although not ATGW, from 1976 50 Missile Regiment RA (nicknamed 50 Miserable Regiment by the rest of the RA) also operated the Lance tactical surface-to-surface missile, with twelve launchers on tracked M752 vehicles (again, a derivative of the M113 chassis). The regiment was disbanded in March 1993.

The final group of tracked vehicles operated by the RA post-war (other than the 432s etc. used in support roles) were those used for air defence. During the Second World War many RAC regiments included an anti-aircraft (AA) troop within the establishment, although these were mainly broken up in late 1944 when it was realized that the Luftwaffe posed little threat to armoured ground forces. The task of air defence on the manoeuvre battlefield was then taken up solely by the RA, operating both Tracked Rapier (from 1981, on the US M113 chassis) and also, from 1997, Starstreak high-velocity missiles on Stormer (a stretched CVR(T) chassis with an additional wheel station). Although Tracked Rapier was withdrawn from service in the early 1990s, HVM Stormer remains in service at the time of writing.

The Armoured Engineers

At the end of the Second World War 79th Armoured Division was disbanded, with most of its specialist equipment being passed to the RAC and put in a new unit called the Special Armour Establishment; only the Churchill AVREs remained within the RE establishment. The SAE was made an RTR responsibility, with both 3 and then 7RTR taking up the task during the 1940s, which included the Duplex Drive swimming tank role, based in Gosport. It was while they were responsible for the SAE that 7RTR despatched a single squadron of Crocodile flamethrowers to Korea in 1950. Until about 1962 each armoured regiment in the RAC owned and operated three bridge-layers; it was then decided, sensibly, that the specialist nature of these vehicles was more appropriate for the RE, and they were transferred into the armoured engineers. Interestingly, in 1968 serious consideration had been given to removing all the specialized armoured vehicles and the role from the RE, and giving it back to the RAC, the logic being that the main equipments were based on tank types used in support of and by the RAC, and thus training and cooperation would be simplified. However, the RE was strongly against this, pointing out that the crewmen were all trained combat engineers, capable of so much more that simply operating the vehicle. This was a persuasive argument and one which won the day, and, almost certainly correctly, the status quo remained.

During 1948 all the remaining RE assault squadrons had returned to the UK from BAOR, and 32 Assault Engineer Regiment was established at Perham Down, where it stayed until 1957 with 26, 59 and 81 Assault Squadrons under command. In this period some new equipment was trialled and entered service, including the 6.5in Petard demolition gun on Churchill AVRE, the Churchill Flail and the Churchill Linked Ark (armoured ramp carrier) bridging system. In 1957 the regiment was disbanded, and 26 Squadron alone was returned to BAOR to support the armoured units there, based in Hohne. In 1961 an independent training and trials troop from the squadron was established at the RAC Centre Bovington, and this was the genesis of what would become the armoured engineer wing of the RAC D&M School, with a small gunnery section based in Lulworth. At this point the Churchill remained the main vehicle, with the first RE Centurion not coming into service until December 1962. It became common practice to use Centurion gun tanks for basic D&M training, including driving, saving the few specialist vehicles for the role-specific training. 32 Armoured Engineer Regiment was reformed at Hohne in 1965, although in 1969 it was re-classified as a field engineer regiment before being disbanded for a second time in late 1977. In 1980 it was again resurrected, once more as an armoured engineer regiment, moving to Dennis Barracks in Münsterlager in 1981.

In about 1964 the Centurion AVRE with a 165mm demolition gun came into service, and the armoured engineers were then, for the first time in many years, mounted on the same basis tank type as the RAC they supported, although this did not last long as Chieftain was nearing service. As early as 1965, the Royal Engineers were pushing for new vehicles to be designed using the not-yet-in-service Chieftain hull; these were two types of Armoured Engineer Vehicle or AEV, one mounting a 165mm gun, the other a bridge-layer. However, lack of funding led to the project being cancelled in 1967, meaning that the petrol-engined Centurion-based RE vehicles would have to remain in service alongside the diesel-engined Chieftains. As it turned out, a Chieftain AVRE did not enter service until two decades later in 1987, when seventeen surplus Chieftain hulls were converted to become AVRE – concurrent with the RAC adopting the Challenger as its new MBT. Between 1968 (in prototype form) and 1986, another fifty-two Chieftain were either built as, or converted to, Armoured Vehicle Launched Bridge, or AVLB.

These tank-based armoured vehicles were primarily developed so that gaps could be crossed using the bridge-layers and by laying fascines, fortifications destroyed using the 165mm gun, trackway laid to improve mobility, and minefields both breached (with various mine plough devices plus the Viper series of explosive lane-clearing devices) and laid (with the Barmine and Ranger

The huge Trojan armoured engineer vehicle is not equipped with a gun, but can be configured for multiple missions, including minefield breaching and gap-crossing.

mine systems). These last two both used the FV432 vehicle; later, the Shielder Vehicle Launched Scatterable Mine System (VLSMS) came into service on the CVR(T) Stormer chassis. Unusually, a purpose-built armoured engineer vehicle was introduced in the mid-1970s in the shape of the FV180 Combat Engineer Tractor, or CET; it was replaced in service by another specialist design, the Terrier, from 2013.

It was not until the mid-2000s that the British army, for the first time since mid-Second World War, introduced specialist engineer vehicles based upon the same chassis as the in-service battle tank, rather than operating from converted tank chassis that were at least one, and often two, generations behind. The Titan bridge-layer was designed to replace the ageing Chieftain AVLBs that had been developed in 1968, and thirty-three were built, entering service in 2006. They are capable of carrying a number of bridges with different gap-crossing capabilities, using the scissors principle. The Trojan is the latest and in-service AVRE, although not a direct replacement for previous AVREs as it does not carry a demolition gun, only a self-defence MG. The turretless Trojan has a hydraulic excavation arm, can be fitted at the front with a variety of ploughing systems, carries fascines for filling tank ditches and other gaps, and can tow a stores trailer. Again, thirty-three were procured, and it entered service in 2007, with some subsequently deployed to Afghanistan. Both Titan and Trojan can expect to remain in service for decades to come.

The REME

The creation of a new Corps to form the REME was announced by Royal Warrant on 19 May 1942, with the new corps coming into existence on 1 October 1942. In order to bring together the personnel of the trades for which the REME would be responsible, the RAOC lost about 60 per cent of its manpower, the RASC 2 per cent and the RE 1 per cent. Some regimental personnel (for example, men badged RAC) were also transferred across. The remaining RAC unit personnel would not be transferred until the early 1950s; until then, to be a 'regimental 'fitter' was a great honour, signifying high technical expertise in a recognized trade whilst still wearing one's own cap badge. The REME are required not only to repair and recover all the various types of vehicles, including AFVs, operated by the army, but also to operate their own specialist types. These have mainly been a range of repair and recovery vehicles, which post-war have included variants based on the Churchill, Centurion, Chieftain and Challenger, the Samson CVR(T), the Warrior-based FV512 and FV513 vehicles, and currently, the Challenger Repair and Recovery Vehicle. From the 1960s until recently, trade training – not only on all the RAC (and other corps) vehicles but also on the REME specialist repair and recovery vehicles – took place at 10 Training Battalion REME in the School of Electrical and Mechanical Engineering (SEME) in Bordon, Hampshire; in 2015 most trade training was moved to a new location at Lyneham in Wiltshire, with tracked vehicle driver training moving to Bovington.

The FV434 was designed to support Chieftain, and the bay in the vehicle rear could carry either the L60 engine – much in demand due to its notoriously poor reliability – or a TN12 gearbox. When neither was carried the crew used the space to create a comfortable armoured caravan!

The FV513 was the REME recovery variant of the Warrior infantry fighting vehicle, and together with the repair variant, FV512, supported the armoured infantry battalions.

The REME LAD from QRL supporting the unit in the field on operations, repairing CVR(T).

The RAMC and the Royal Signals

Both of these corps used variants of the FV432 series, the former as a battlefield ambulance (American-supplied M548 tracked vehicles were also used by the RAMC armoured field ambulances deployed during the 1991 Gulf War), and the latter with the FV435/6/9 series of specialist communication vehicles. To the annoyance and contempt of the RAC, these vehicles were sometimes referred to by their users as tanks, which they most definitely were not![7]

Yet another common role for the FV432 was that of battlefield ambulance, used as such not only by the RAC and infantry battalions, but also by the RAMC Armoured Field Ambulances.

Bovvie: Continuing the History of Bovington Camp

As of 2020, the Bovington estate comprised 2,661 acres, and the Lulworth range area covered 7,338 acres.[1] In 1995 the main camp was formally re-named Allenby Barracks, although this title had been adopted as far back as 1936. This name had for some reason had fallen into disuse, the barracks generally being referred to as either the top or main camp. The smaller southern barracks at the bottom of the hill that had housed the Boys Squadron and its successor the Junior Leader's Regiment had always been known as Stanley Barracks.

Headquarters

On 11 September 1939 the RAC Depot Bovington was renamed, to become 52nd Training Regiment RAC; at about this time at least ten other RAC Training Regiments were formed around the country to cope with the sheer numbers needing to be trained. Also at Bovington but 'down the hill' in Stanley Barracks from November 1941 was 58th Training Regiment, dealing with all types of tanks as well as young soldiers (those too young to serve in an operational theatre) and also RAC Potential Officer Selection, although this unit later moved to Farnborough.

In 1943 a new appointment was created, that of Director Royal Armoured Corps; the first incumbent was Major General Raymond Briggs ex-RTR. On 1 October 1964 the Headquarters Director Royal Armoured Corps was formed in Bovington, as before then corps business was mainly based out of and conducted in London. As an interim measure DRAC was initially housed at Merlincourt House in Lulworth, and then in Hulldown House in Bovington. At the end of 1977 a brand new purpose-built HQ building was opened and remains in use – largely unchanged in some respects and with the narrowest toilet doors in the army – to this day, now housing HQ RAC and the Armour Centre HQ. Until 1995 the post of DRAC was filled by a major general, but after that it became a one-star post, the first brigadier to take it up was Andrew Gadsby ex-RTR, and the last Simon Levey ex-LD. In 2007, for the first time, the RAC appointed a Command Sergeant Major, Warrant Officer Class 1 Clive Towell of the King's Royal Hussars. HQ DRAC was renamed as HQ RAC on 24 October 2011, as a

Allenby Barracks, Bovington seen from the north, with Sandhurst Block dominating the centre of the estate. (Courtesy ARMCEN)

result of the amalgamation of the Directors RAC and Infantry into a new Combat Capability Directorate based at Andover; the following year the first Colonel RAC took the helm at Bovington, Colonel Stuart Cowen ex-HCav. The remit of the new HQ RAC was to look after the RAC regimental matters, including personnel and recruiting, as well as the corporate identity of the corps and the RAC 'brand'. As part of this, under the guidance of Colonel Guy Deacon ex-QDG, an initiative called RAC First was introduced, aimed at fostering and increasing the perspective that the individual regiments made up a cohesive whole, and that the Corps flourished better when its officers and soldiers identified as part of it. At the same time the old and divisive 'Household Cavalry and RAC' title was replaced by referring to just the RAC – although acknowledging that the Household Cavalry remained part of the Guards Division for ceremonial and similar purposes, and that the Mounted Regiment (and the regimental bands) was not part of the Corps.

The RAC Centre

Elsewhere in Bovington, on 17 January 1955, the RAC Depot became the RAC Centre, although this name was unofficially in use well before then.[2] At that time Bovington was still recognizable as the ancient camp dating mainly from the end of 1918, and despite some incremental improvements including the building of the dominating Sandhurst accommodation block and central cookhouse in 1939, a substantial modernization programme did not start until the early 1960s, when brick married quarters were finally built along with other parts of the technical accommodation and thus standards were much improved over the next decade.[3]

In 1962 a new Junior Rank's club – the NAAFI – was built, with a new Sergeants' Mess the following year.

The RAC Centre Regiment came into being in August 1968 when QRIH took over the role. One squadron was stationed at Lulworth, at least one at Bovington, and possibly, if the regiment was lucky, one at Warminster as the demonstration squadron.[4] This last role was the plum, as it functioned as a fairly normal if extremely busy sub-unit, and the role had the advantage that the squadron was able to maintain armoured skills. The other squadrons were employed in the thankless tasks of keeping a huge fleet of vehicles 'on the road', to allow them to be used for the multitude of training courses run throughout the year. In 1976, the editor of the *QOH Journal* described the task thus, 'I can think of no other role which an RAC regiment is called upon to perform which is more potentially damaging to morale and regimental expertise'. Assuming this was true – and it was – twelve regiments were unfortunate enough to become the Centre Regiment over the years, including the especially unlucky QRIH and 2RTR who both served there twice, for crimes unrecorded.

Table 9: The RAC Centre Regiments

From	Unit
August 1968	QRIH
August 1970	2RTR
August 1972	13/18H
August 1974	QOH
May 1976	14/20H
November 1977	17/21L
November 1980	16/5L
December 1982	1RTR
October 1984	15/19H
November 1986	3RTR
March 1988	QRIH
April 1990	2RTR
June 1992	SCOTS DG
April 1993	9/12L

The final regiment to fulfil the role was 9/12L; when they left in late March 1997 for Swanton Morley after what was in effect a double tour, the role was turned over to Extra-Regimentally Employed (ERE) personnel and, increasingly, civilian contractors.[5] When the 9/12L left and the RAC Centre became a completely ERE environment, there were 1,739 posts within the garrison: 721 civil service, 592 from the private sector, and only 426 military (24.5 per cent). This was because in the late 1990s under a CFQ (Competing for Quality) project, the contractorization of many of the support services took place, initially awarded to Hunting Contract Services on 1 April 1998. Officially, the CFQ project was meant to generate the manpower savings to release 9/12L to become the third recce regt, but many saw it as cost-cutting accompanied by an inevitable lowering of standards. Amongst the areas in which civilian staff – many of them ex-military – took over from military personnel and civil servants were the various stores, MT, armoury services, ammunition storage and vehicle servicing. Some training in the schools was also contracted out, under the auspices of a specialist training company called TQ; the majority of the instructors were ex-RAC schools' instructors, allowing standards to be maintained. As a result, about 300 military posts were removed from across the Garrison, including in Lulworth.

Despite the appearance of many other cap badges within the Bovington Garrison, the name RAC Centre remained until 1 October 1999 when it was replaced by the current title, the Armour Centre or ARMCEN, under the direction of Colonel Chris Day ex-RDG, the Commander; this post is always held by an RAC Colonel. A possibly apocryphal story has it that one reason for the name change – if not the main one – was to put the new unit at the top alphabetically of the list of all army wide establishments, only for it to be trumped by the AAC Centre!

The Training Establishments

From 1945 the main training schools in Bovington, Driving and Maintenance (D&M) and Wireless (soon to be re-named Signals), as well as the RAC Gunnery School at nearby Lulworth, still operated.

The D&M School had had a Royal Artillery Wing since January 1946, as it was required to train tracked drivers for the new SPG fleet. An Infantry Wing was added in April 1977 when the APC Wing at Bordon in Hampshire closed and moved all infantry AFV D&M instruction to Bovington; in 2001 both of these wings combined for administrative reasons to form a combined RA and Infantry Wing, lasting until February 2011. The RE Wing, looking after the range of specialist types operated by the armoured engineer units, opened in September 1961 and enjoyed its own largely independent existence within the School. However, from 2011 a Combat Support Wing was brought into being, combining these three corps in one; the needs of the RAC were met by the Combat Wing. Both wings look after tracked and wheeled vehicles.

Unlike the other two schools, the RAC Signals School was commanded by an outsider, in the shape of a Royal Signals Lieutenant Colonel, although in the late 1990s it became an RAC appointment. It remained largely corps-specific until 2017, when it became the Combat CIS School for both RAC and infantry personnel. As of early 2022, the initial Bowman course for Waterloo Squadron trainees – see below – lasts for four weeks, with an additional one week's training required on arrival at their regiments to convert them to the specific platform they will be working on. The Advanced Signals course requires later attendance back at the School, for another six-week course, and the Regimental Signals Instructor course also lasts six weeks.

As the war finished, the RAC Gunnery School at Lulworth still occupied the First World War-era wooden huts, with the less-than-salubrious Park Camp the location for units unfortunate enough to be sent there in transit; 16th/5th Lancers spent a miserable winter there before heading off for sunnier climes. As a result of the McCreery report, it became practice from the late 1940s for only selected, high-quality gunnery instructors to be sent to the three training schools as staff instructors, and nowhere was this more apparent than at Lulworth, where the 'Schools' tick in a sergeant's personal file was seen as a real career-enhancer.[6] More importantly, the upsurge in standards was in part responsible for more standardization of gunnery techniques and training methods across the corps, as well as better application of science to support – or disprove – the theories of fire.

The location of the School 'over the hill' and on the coast was advantageous, as not only could the School enjoy a somewhat separate existence from the RAC Centre just over 6 miles away, but the ranges within the camp and around Tyneham were convenient for the frequent firing practices, including at night. The Gunnery School was also the only one of the three to maintain a long-term presence in Germany, in the shape of the RAC Gunnery Wing in Hohne. During the 1980s the Gunnery School started to train students and receive staff from both the RAF Regiment and the Infantry, the latter mainly to cope with the demand for 30mm Warrior and CVR(T) instructors, forcing a name change to the AFV Gunnery School.

In 2017, a new 'Technical Training School' was founded under Lieutenant Colonel Ian Fake RTR, which encompassed the D&M and Gunnery Schools under a single commanding officer for the first time. In 2020 this was renamed to become the 'AFV Schools Regiment', still under a single commanding officer, and became responsible for overseeing the running of the two wings within the D&M School, the Gunnery School, and the Combat CIS School.

After the Second World War, the demise of the eleven wartime RAC training regiments meant that for a short time the responsibility for basic and initial trade training for RAC recruits either fell upon the regiments, on the RAC Depots overseas (BAOR, CMF, India) or on the rump of those training establishments stationed in the Catterick area. In 1951, due to the expansion of the National Service scheme after the start of the Korean War and in light of experience, an RAC Training Brigade controlling four new training regiments was formed, again in the Catterick area.[7] These four regiments, numbered 65 to 68, were then replaced by normal regiments 'shoe-horned' into the role in the mid-1950s, before June 1960 when a single regiment became responsible for both

RAC recruit and initial trade training for adults (known to all Junior Leader's as Catterick Commandos) and was known as the RAC Training Regiment. In 1993 the RAC Training Regiment at Catterick was closed down, along with its responsibilities for Phase 1 (recruit) training of all RAC recruits; this role was taken up by the newly created Army Training Regiments.

A new unit also named the RAC Training Regiment in Bovington was then founded in 1999 by replacing the RAC Centre Regiment and was – and is – a component part of ARMCEN. This is a very different beast from the unit(s) of the same name that had previously existed in Catterick. As at early 2022, the regiment had two squadrons. The first, Waterloo, looks after the recruits who arrive at Bovington for initial trade training following Ph 1 training at an ATR – either Pirbright or Winchester – or from the Army Foundation College at Harrogate.[8] This initial trade training takes around four to six months.[9] In broad terms, the sequence is B and, if necessary, C vehicle licence acquisition, CIS training and then platform-specific D&M training including H (tracked) licence if required. There is a lot of emphasis on gradual and varied PT, with an hour's session every evening. In a 'blast from the past', the recruits do not select which regiment (and therefore which platform) they wish to serve in until they are in Waterloo Squadron, and they wear the RAC beret and badge until near the end, with a Commanding Officer's beret parade taking place every Friday, at which point they go into regimental uniform just prior to being posted to their unit. In the Training Year 2021 415 trainees went through the squadron, and about 4 per cent of each group are female.[10]

The other squadron is Normandy, and covers subsequent trade training. A major element of this is the JCC – the Junior Commander's Course, introduced in 2008. This is the required tactical course to allow a lance corporal to promote to corporal, and takes four weeks.[11] It is a totally dismounted command course, and the first component is ten days of ALDP, the Army Leadership Development programme, introduced in October 2020. This is followed by completing the 'M Qual', allowing them to run dismounted battle exercises, and there is a final tactical exercise to confirm skills. During 2021 seven JCCs were run, with forty students per course.[12]

Over the years the size of the vehicle fleet supporting the training at Bovington has grown in numbers and complexity, from about 130 AFVs in 2000 to about 230 in 2016; this peak was caused by the operations in Iraq and Afghanistan.[13] Also growing has been the number of students trained at Bovington, with about 3,200 individuals completing courses in 2016/17, with a student population of about 500 at any one time. In terms of permanent staff, at the same time there were 605 military staff, with 135 civil servants and no less than 776 contractors – about half of the total staff. Phase 2 (corps-specific initial trade) training was conducted not only for RAC soldiers and officers, but also for substantial numbers of RE and REME.

Also located within the Bovington estate is the world-renowned Tank Museum. Originally the collection was started in about 1923 as a result of an appeal by no less a personage than Rudyard Kipling, and the collection of roughly fifty vehicles was used to support technical and trade training, being housed in the D&M Wing. Tragically, in the drive at the start of Second World War for scrap metal, many unique vehicles were broken up, including Mother. In 1946 the museum became an independent organization, officially the museum of both the whole RAC and of the RTR and also open to the public. By the mid-1960s it was attracting ¼ million visitors each year. It now has a collection of over 300 vehicles, many of them unique, and operates as a charity; despite the effects of COVID it goes from strength to strength, attracting many hundreds of thousands of visitors each year including to its flagship weekend, TankFest.

The Armour Trials and Development Unit

Until the formation of ATDU, the RAC Equipment Trials Wing was responsible for the trialling of RAC equipment. Until then, the RAC Centre Regiment provided the administration and most of the manpower for ETW; the Weapons Branch was at Lulworth, co-located with the Gunnery School and with access to the facilities, expertise and ranges. The new unit was formed in 1971, and has an illustrious history in supporting the development of specialist equipment, from complete vehicles down to clothing and small items such as torches, for AFVs.

The role of the Armoured Trials and Development Unit (ATDU) is to carry out user trials and development tasks on armoured vehicle equipment in order to provide cost-effective support to the MoD Equipment Programme. It is worth emphasizing that it is not limited to armoured vehicles – it is much more than that. It could include looking at fuel for armoured vehicles, clothing for their crews, or even the food that they eat. The remit is a broad one. At the time of writing, ATDU is one of a number of Trials and Development Units in the army and is the biggest by a considerable margin. At any one time there can be as many as sixty different trials and projects under way.

The Junior Leader's Regiment RAC

Boy soldiers had existed in the army for decades; the term referred to under-age soldiers, often but not always employed in some capacity in the regimental band. For example, forty under-15 boy soldiers were enlisted on 31 January 1920 in Bovington to be trained as mechanics in the Tank Corps Workshops Training Battalion, which must have been successful as they were followed by another 150 the following year; this Tank Corps-specific scheme ended in 1924 when army apprenticeship schools were opened for technical training, primarily the Boys Training School at Arborfield. Although widely used between the wars (at a period when regular recruiting was struggling to gather the required numbers of recruits annually), the practice of enlisting boys was held in abeyance in both world wars, but post-Second World War, it soon became clear that an organized unit for the training and development of all the boys destined for the RAC made administrative sense.

The first location suggested was Park Camp at Lulworth, which sounded a lot better than it was. Luckily, this horribly bleak location was deemed to be unsuitable, and an in-depth investigation on how best to organize the unit was conducted between 1949 and 1951. The report spoke of 'untapped sources of potential', and 'taking advantage of a youngster who wants a full career in the army from the outset, rather than someone who has already been in work'. As a result, the Boys Squadron RAC was founded, and the first intake of boys arrived on 10 January 1952 in Stanley Barracks, Bovington; the first commanding officer was Major H.B. 'Barry' O'Sullivan MC RTR, taking up the post in November 1951. It was organized as a single large squadron capable of holding about 100 boys in 4 troops, named Alamein, Balaclava, Cambrai and Dettingen, each of which was organized and run on a term system along the lines of 'a public-school house' – presumably meaning strict discipline, poor food and cold showers. An entrance examination had to be passed before enlistment, with the results determining which trades the boys would be trained in, in the traditional descending order of signals, gunnery and then D&M. The first intake was of just thirty-one boys.

The ages of the boys was to be between 15 and 17½, with the oldest age accepted 16½, so the minimum training period would be one year and the maximum a little over two years, with the majority expected to do a full twenty-four months of training before joining their regiments. Boys could only be posted to regiments serving in the UK at the age of 17½, to BAOR on reaching 18 years and to units in the Middle or Far East Commands at 18 years and 4 months which meant that leaving ages varied according to the destination regiment. On reaching the age of 18 the (now adult) soldiers could opt for either eight years with the colours and four in the reserve, or for a twelve-year regular engagement which naturally attracted a higher rate of pay. On arrival at Bovington a boy soldier was paid 2s. 6d. per day, rising to 3s. 6d. after one year, and he would receive 4s. per day after two years' service. On reaching the age of 17½, he would be paid 7s. per day, which was the lowest adult rate of pay. At the time of formation, it was hoped that three-quarters of the boys would eventually achieve non-commissioned rank, and this was so successful that later it became a strong part of the branding that the role of the unit was to select and train the future senior NCOs and warrant officers for the corps.[14] 4th/7th Dragoon Guards saw fit to record with a photograph their very first boy soldier in 1953, one Trooper Craig, who within a year of leaving became a lance corporal and then very quickly after that a corporal, proving the point.[15]

By the end of 1953, the squadron was at full strength, at that time some 210 boys. By 1958 this had risen to 380 boys, with the intention to increase it to 480 'in the near future' and 600 in due course. The unit became the Junior Leader's Squadron RAC in 1956 – the designation of all army boys' units was changed to Junior Leaders at this time - and in November the first RSM was appointed, Warrant Officer Class 1 M.M. O'Conner, QOH. This was ready for the next major change, as in early 1957 and due to the success in recruiting, the strength of the squadron enabled it to be enlarged and re-titled as a regiment. The boys were now referred to as Junior Leaders, and, inevitably and invariably, as Junior Bleeders.[16] The regiment itself and its products were invariably referred to by its initials as 'Jay Ell Arr', or the 'Brat's school'. In late 1956 the DRAC was able to report that so far, 303 'regimental boys' and thirty-two 'band boys' had joined their regiments from the unit.[17]

By 1958 the regiment had become a lieutenant colonel's command, and been re-organized; it now had one recruit squadron and two training squadrons. On arrival, the boy would undergo standard basic military training in the first term, with a lot of emphasis on fitness and education, and they were required to pass the Army Certificate of Education (ACE) Class III certificate.[18] In order to give them all some experience of leadership, at this time the boys would take it in

For a number of years following its formation in 1952, boy soldiers continued to wear the pre-Second World War version of Service Dress. The ages of these youngsters can only be guessed at, but they are probably fairly new entrants and therefore may only be 15 years old. The First World War-era 'spider' huts are in the background.

turns to act as JNCOs for a week at a time. Later on, he would be required to pass ACE II, and then change squadrons and move on to trade training where he would need to pass the B III trade courses for both gunnery and signals.[19] The final phase of his training would be a three-week 'outward-bound' course in Wales, a three-week crew commander's course and he would be taught to drive a wheeled vehicle.

Stanley Barracks was completely rebuilt between 1956 and 1965 in the form that it is today, with better accommodation (eight large accommodation blocks, mainly of eight-man rooms), RHQ, stores, cookhouse, education and training block, hobbies block, band block, NAAFI, gymnasium, swimming pool, messes, a 30m range and, of course, a very large drill square. However, overspill of numbers meant that even as late as the mid-1970s, some unfortunates had to be accommodated in the old pre-Second World War wooden 'Spider' blocks located on what is now the Tank Museum car park. In 1963 a semi-permanent adventure training camp was taken over at Renney Lentney, near Plymouth, allowing access to many facilities on the Devon coast and around Dartmoor, including some used by the Commando forces. Generations of boys became familiar with the names of Tregantle and Scraesdon Forts, the old Royal Navy de-gaussing harbour at Pier Cellars, and infamous activities such as the bridge jump and escalation.

By the early 1960s the format had changed so that there were three squadrons (plus the band), and the junior soldiers moved through the three squadrons as the training progressed.[20] New juniors went into C Sqn initially for BMT, then into B Sqn for trade training on gunnery and signals, and finally into the pass-out squadron, A Sqn. Here the training was focused on education, wheeled vehicle driving, adventure training and preparation for regimental life. By the 1970s the format had been amended once again so that the juniors stayed with one squadron throughout. From 1973 Royal Military Police juniors arrived followed swiftly by Army Air Corps in 1974, all being placed in troops in B Squadron alongside RAC soldiers.[21] The raising of the school leaving age meant that, from the September 1974 term, the length of the stay had to be reduced from two-and-a-half years (seven terms) to one-and-a-half years (four terms), with a consequent loss of time able to be devoted to trade training. On the positive side, however, this led to a huge increase in the size of each year's autumn intake, rising in the first year to about 450 and thus providing each regiment with many more soldiers who were destined for the higher ranks within the Sergeants' Mess. At its maximum capacity, the regiment could have 1,023 juniors under training at one time, with a permanent staff of both military and civilians.[22]

Additionally from 1974, all three squadrons accepted new juniors, and they stayed in that squadron throughout their time, progressing through the syllabus; their relative status was very much visible by their troop title. In September 1976, for example, when the author joined, he went into A1 troop, with the second intake troop in the squadron being A1A; for reasons of capacity there were never

Stanley Barracks, Bovington was the home of JLR RAC from 1952 until it was disbanded in August 1993. Part of the Tank Museum can just be seen in the bottom left corner. (Courtesy ARMCEN)

more than two troops per term per squadron. In the second term the troop became known as A2, and was when gunnery training was conducted, followed a term later by signals training, as A3 – for the 'Alpha' Troop this trade training was conducted in the reverse order. Finally, in the final term, the remaining juniors – in my case about thirty out of the original seventy – became A4 or 'pass-out troop', denoted by wearing a white stripe horizontally through the A Squadron red shoulder strap and which came with certain unofficial privileges, including 'pass-off push-in' – going straight to the front of the meal queue, a real bonus in such a large unit. There was a notable reduction in applied discipline during the final term, with training concentrating on Battle PT (a form of torture), basic Northern Ireland training and Land Rover driving. In the final two weeks of pass-out term and just before the big day arrived, regimental uniforms were worn for the first time, including No. 2 Dress for the pass-out parade itself. In terms of pay, in September 1978, 16-year-old Junior Trooper Zak Hutton-Mills (destined for 3RTR) earned £3.70 per day (a 17-year-old would earn £4.13), but he had to pay £2.10 per week for accommodation and £1.12 per day for food, leaving him with £28.56 a month take-home pay, of which the majority went into 'credits', with only about £7 a week able to be drawn in a good old-fashioned military pay parade.[23]

Over the years, despite the many changes to the form and format within the unit, it can be said that overall, the approximate breakdown of military training and education was as follows: about 40 per cent of time was spent on general military training, including a lot of emphasis on drill and military PT; about the same was used on education; and the remaining 20 per cent on adventure training, sports and similar activities. To serve as an adult instructor at JLR was considered to be something of an accolade, and over the years many ex-juniors returned to take their turn in 'dishing it out'. For reasons of short-sighted military parsimony, the decision was made in the early 1990s to close JLR RAC down, along with the other regiments serving other corps. The final passing-off parade took place on Waterloo Day, 18 June 1993, under the last CO, Lieutenant Colonel H.N. Fairman MBE KRH, and RSM Warrant Officer 1 Class R.J.H. Stephenson LG, the unit finally closing officially in August. However, the story does not quite end there, as the Army Foundation College Harrogate was opened in September 1998, again taking under-adult age recruits. Two intakes a year (March and September) join the AFC and those cap badged for the RAC undertake the Junior Entry (Long) course, a forty-nine-week training course for those juniors destined for the combat arms.[24] After passing-off the recruits move to Bovington for trade training alongside adult recruits who have come from one of the Army Training Regiments – where it has been noticed that the ex-juniors almost invariably do better during trade training than their older counterparts.

Regiments and Units

Cavalry Regiments After the Second World War

1947 (22 Regiments)
Household Cavalry:
   The Life Guards
   Royal Horse Guards – 'The Blues'
Heavy Cavalry of the Line:
   1st (King's) Dragoon Guards
   2nd Dragoon Guards (The Queen's Bays) – 'The Bays'
   3rd Carabiniers (Prince of Wales' Dragoon Guards) – 'The Carbs/Third Carbs'
   4th/7th Royal Dragoon Guards
   5th Royal Inniskilling Dragoon Guards – 'The Fifth Skins/The Skins'
   1st (Royal) Dragoons – 'The Royals'
   2nd Dragoons (Royal Scots Greys) – 'The Greys'
Light Cavalry of the Line:
   3rd (King's Own) Hussars
   4th (Queen's Own) Hussars
   7th (Queen's Own) Hussars
   8th (King's Royal Irish) Hussars
   9th (Queen's Royal) Lancers
   10th (Prince of Wales' Own Royal) Hussars
   11th (Prince Albert's Own) Hussars
   12th (Prince of Wales' Royal) Lancers
   13th/18th Royal Hussars (Queen Mary's Own)
   14th/20th King's Hussars
   15th/19th The King's Royal Hussars
   16th/5th The Queen's Royal Lancers
   17th/21st Lancers

1960 (17 Regiments)
Household Cavalry:
   The Life Guards
   Royal Horse Guards – 'The Blues'
Heavy Cavalry of the Line:
   1st The Queen's Dragoon Guards

3rd Carabiniers (Prince of Wales' Dragoon Guards) – 'The Carbs/Third Carbs'
4th/7th Royal Dragoon Guards
5th Royal Inniskilling Dragoon Guards – 'The Fifth Skins/The Skins'
1st (Royal) Dragoons – 'The Royals'
2nd Dragoons (Royal Scots Greys) – 'The Greys'
Light Cavalry of the Line:
 Queen's Own Hussars
 Queen's Royal Irish Hussars
 9th/12th Royal Lancers (Prince of Wales')
 Royal Hussars (Prince of Wales' Own)
 13th/18th Royal Hussars (Queen Mary's Own)
 14th/20th King's Hussars
 15th/19th The King's Royal Hussars
 16th/5th The Queen's Royal Lancers
 17th/21st Lancers

1971 (15 Regiments)
Household Cavalry:
 The Life Guards
 The Royal Horse Guards and 1st Dragoons – 'The Blues and Royals'
Heavy Cavalry of the Line:
 1st The Queen's Dragoon Guards
 The Royal Scots Dragoon Guards (Carabiniers and Greys)
 4th/7th Royal Dragoon Guards
 5th Royal Inniskilling Dragoon Guards – 'The Fifth Skins'
Light Cavalry of the Line:
 Queen's Own Hussars
 Queen's Royal Irish Hussars
 9th/12th Royal Lancers (Prince of Wales')
 Royal Hussars (Prince of Wales' Own)
 13th/18th Royal Hussars (Queen Mary's Own)
 14th/20th King's Hussars
 15th/19th The King's Royal Hussars
 16th/5th The Queen's Royal Lancers
 17th/21st Lancers

1993 (9 Regiments)
Household Cavalry:
 The Household Cavalry Regiment (and The Household Cavalry Mounted
  Regiment)
Heavy Cavalry of the Line:
 1st The Queen's Dragoon Guards

The Royal Scots Dragoon Guards (Carabiniers and Greys)
The Royal Dragoon Guards
Light Cavalry of the Line:
    The Queen's Royal Hussars
    9th/12th Royal Lancers (Prince of Wales')
    The King's Royal Hussars
    The Queen's Royal Lancers
    The Light Dragoons

2015 (8 Regiments)
Household Cavalry:
    The Household Cavalry Regiment (and The Household Cavalry Mounted
        Regiment on ceremonial duties)
Heavy Cavalry of the Line:
    1st The Queen's Dragoon Guards
    The Royal Scots Dragoon Guards (Carabiniers and Greys)
    The Royal Dragoon Guards
Light Cavalry of the Line:
    The Queen's Royal Hussars
    The Royal Lancers
    The King's Royal Hussars
    The Light Dragoons

The Royal Tank Regiment After the Second World War

1950: 8 regiments: 1 to 8RTR
1960: 5 regiments: 1 to 5RTR
1969: 4 regiments: 1 to 4RTR
1993: 2 regiments: 1RTR, 2RTR
2014: 1 regiment: RTR

In and Out of Aircraft – Airborne Armour

Parachuting

During the Second World War some RAC units were employed in specialist roles in support of the newly formed and expanding airborne formations. During 1941, three 'Special Service Squadrons RAC' were formed from volunteer personnel from various cavalry and RTR units. One of these, 'C' Special Service Squadron (Light) RAC, became the Airlanding Reconnaissance (later Airborne Light Tank) Squadron RAC in June 1942 and became part of 1st Airborne Division. When the division was sent to North Africa, the squadron remained and was then transferred to the newly formed 6th Airborne Division. The squadron was expanded into a full regiment and redesignated as 6th Airborne Armoured Reconnaissance Regiment in January 1944. The regiment comprised an RHQ, a Tetrarch light tank squadron, a reconnaissance squadron mounted in jeeps, a support squadron, a headquarters squadron and a REME LAD; not all of the personnel were required to be 'jump trained'. The regiment also had a separate harbour party team who were trained parachutists. Their role was to jump with the leading pathfinder units and find and secure a suitable landing zone into which the regiment could deploy by glider. The unit saw action in Normandy and during the Ardennes campaign, before taking part in the Rhine crossing operation and the remainder of the campaign in North West Europe. On 1 February 1946 6th Airborne Armoured Recce Regt RAC was disbanded.

3rd Hussars had fought in Italy during the second half of 1944, before being recovered to Egypt in early 1945. The regiment was sent to Palestine in October 1945. On 1 February 1946 the regiment was converted to become the solitary airborne armoured regiment, operating as the recce unit for 6th Airborne Division which had been sent to the region to deal with the increasing unrest. Based in Sarafand, the size of the unit was enlarged – extremely unusual for the time – by sending in soldiers from the two now-disbanded airborne divisional reconnaissance regiments as well as 21st and 22nd Independent Parachute Companies, and the first jump course for the regiment was held on 22 March, with the requirement to do eight parachute descents in order to qualify for the award of wings and pay. Over the next 2 years about 330 of the regiment qualified as military parachutists.

It was decided that each of the three sabre squadrons should have different roles. A Sqn became the divisional pathfinders, B the divisional recce and C was to operate in an SAS-type capacity, the SAS having been disbanded at the end of 1945. At the end of July 1947 B Squadron were posted on detachment to Cambrai Barracks, Perham Down, in order to become the recce unit for 2nd Airborne Brigade in the UK. After the end of the mandate in mid-1948 the rest of the regiment was posted back to England but reverted to a normal armoured regiment role in August, as 6th Airborne Division was disbanded.[1]

Although the only RAC airborne unit had been disbanded, some individual training was still allowed. From 1949 RAC personnel, and it appears that this mainly applied to officers, probably because they were easier to release from duties, were encouraged to attend qualification courses. These comprised two weeks of physical conditioning and tests at Aldershot before conducting the parachuting phase at No. 1 Parachute & Glider Training School, Upper Heyford, which meant two weeks of ground training and eight jumps, including two from a balloon – generally thought to be worse than from an aircraft – and one at night. Aside from this, no attempt was made to include RAC personnel or units into the airborne order of battle for nearly two decades, despite the RA, RE, Royal Signals and RAMC all being represented. This was mainly because at that point even the lightest AFVs were difficult to deploy by parachute and needed to be landed by cargo aircraft on proper runways; this need could be fulfilled by designating a number of squadrons from existing armoured car regiments as 'air portable', meaning that they consisted only of scout cars.

In June 1962 a Special Reconnaissance Squadron RAC was formed, based in Alanbrooke Barracks, Paderborn. The intention was to create a small unit of specialists, able to form up to twenty four-man patrols for stay-behind and special observation duties. Although it did not have a parachute capability, it was a tough unit to get into and operated a robust selection procedure, which had a 75 per cent failure rate. In many ways its mission was similar to some of the roles that the Special Air Service would later come to consider their own. This was to prove its undoing; it was disbanded in September 1963 when it was decided to hand the role over to 23 (TA) SAS.

With the imminent introduction into service of the Malkara long-range guided anti-tank missile, in July 1959 the Army Council authorized the creation of an RAC airborne squadron equipped with twelve launchers. It had been realized that an opportunity existed to fill a major capability gap in airborne operations, that of providing a parachute-deployed force with an anti-tank capability beyond that of short-range shoulder-launched munitions. Cyclops Squadron 2RTR was selected for the task, and whilst the rest of the regiment was stationed in Omagh, it was posted to Tidworth for conversion into the fully parachute role. Formed in July 1962 and tasked with supporting 16 Parachute Brigade, the squadron had three missile troops each of four Hornet vehicles plus a missile resupply vehicle and a Land Rover-mounted troop leader, as well as a trials troop, an echelon and a REME LAD, all commanded by a small SHQ. Selecting personnel who were capable of not only passing the tough P Company selection course (run by the Parachute Regiment) but who were also above-average soldiers and who had the skill and dexterity required to be trained as missile controllers was not easy, and the whole of the regiment had to be trawled for suitable volunteers. Nonetheless the squadron enjoyed an exciting existence for nearly three years, and proved that the concept of parachute-deployed vehicles and crews was viable. On 1 February 1965 the squadron reverted to being a normal RAC armoured car squadron, as an independent – and pan-RAC squadron – was about to be formed to replace it.

The RAC Parachute Squadron formed on 3 February 1965, with sixty-four personnel from Cyclops as well as about thirty from the disbanded Special Reconnaissance Sqn providing most of the initial strength in order to get the now RAC-wide unit functioning as soon as possible. For the first time since the Second World War the airborne forces red beret was worn, with all members, regardless of parent cap badge, wearing the RAC badge (actually a collar dog on a scarlet backing) in order to bring the squadron together and make a statement of unit cohesion.[2] Initially at least, the squadron consisted of 108 personnel, with another 29 REME personnel in the workshops. The role remained ATGW

The Hornet was a modified Pig vehicle, able to carry two Malkara missiles ready to fire, and two as a reload. It was the British army's first operational ATGW.

A number of Cyclops Squadron 2RTR personnel in front of a Hornet on exercise; finding the right number of highly motivated personnel capable of passing the tough P Company selection tests proved to be a problem.

2RTR soldiers preparing for a jump: until the formation of the RAC Parachute Squadron in early 1965, 2RTR personnel continued to wear their favoured black berets.

support to airborne forces, initially using Malkara on Hornet vehicles, later replaced by Ferrets mounting Vigilant (Mk 2/6) and then Swingfire (Mk 5).

The squadron trained and operated in many parts of the world, including Libya, Bahrain, Radfan, Canada and Malaysia. The deployment of troops into Northern Ireland in autumn 1969 heralded the start of multiple tours to the Province, with the unit completing six tours there, beginning in November 1969. It also found itself stationed in Cyprus on what was meant to be a 'sunshine' UNFICYP tour in June 1974, only to find itself in the middle of the Turkish invasion, as related earlier. Defence cuts, as ever, led to the squadron being disbanded on 12 February 1976. During its 11-year life, 335 members of the RAC served in its ranks.[3]

The next unit to take up the parachuting mantle was the Household Cavalry. Until 1976 volunteer personnel from the two regiments were able to serve in No. 1 Guards Independent Parachute Company alongside their infantry brethren. Following the Falklands campaign of 1982, in which two troops of The Blues and Royals very successfully proved how RAC light armour could support rapid-deployment forces, from 1985 it was decided that the regiment serving in Windsor would be allowed to send volunteers through P Company (pre-selection course) and then the 'jumps' course at Brize Norton, in order to create a number of parachute-trained personnel, eventually with enough to form a troop (3 Tp A Sqn). Finally, from about 2005, the Joint NBC Regiment (1RTR) was authorized to allow volunteers to attempt Parachute or All Arms Commando selection in order to be able to support those formations with specialists, and new officers arriving at the unit from Sandhurst were interviewed by the CO and given a stark choice: 'Red or green?'[4]

Aircraft and Aviation

During the Second World War the Army Air Corps had existed as the overarching administrative HQ for both glider and parachute troops. Independently of this, the RA operated a number of light fixed-wing aircraft in the AOP role – Air Observation Posts. The AAC was disbanded in 1949. In 1957 the Glider Pilot Regiment and the Parachute Regiment were separated, with the battalions of the Parachute Regiment gaining independence and becoming a specialist role within the infantry, whilst the rump of the Glider Pilot Regiment was merged with the Air Observation Squadrons of the Royal Artillery into a new unit, once more known as the Army Air Corps; the obsolete glider operational capability ceased the same year. As well as operating light aircraft, the new AAC was looking to the future and taking the lead from experimentation in the US, desired to operate lightweight helicopters as observation/reconnaissance platforms. In 1958 the DRAC pushed for a helicopter flight to be created within each RAC reconnaissance regiment, and this was initially rejected by the War Office, only for the decision to be reversed two years later with the RAC authorized to create and man four reconnaissance flights within selected regiments by the end of 1961.

Different regiments were authorized and able to form their flights, known as air troops, at different times. For example, the newly amalgamated 9th/12th Lancers officially formed theirs as early as 8 March 1962, but only received their first aircraft, three Skeeter helicopters, three years later; in that time, however, they were able to qualify eight pilots, both officers and SNCOs. During 1965 5th Royal Inniskilling Dragoon Guards (in Aden), 4th/7th Royal Dragoon Guards and 10th Hussars all formed their air troops with varying types and numbers of aircraft.[5] Having a small number of aircraft directly under regimental control was enormously popular within the regiments, as the CO (especially) and other more senior officers made use of them to avoid long boring journeys by road; operationally, they were used for reconnaissance and liaison duties. The burden that came with them, in terms of aircrew training and, most importantly, repair and maintenance, was difficult to justify and the expanding AAC wanted to take back control of all army aviation.

Despite the valid arguments to retain the capability, the writing was on the wall and the air troops were gradually disbanded. The capability however lasted into the mid-1970s. 1RTR received six Sioux in order to form an 'Air Squadron' in Northern Ireland in 1973, with additional pilots coming from the AAC. And in 1975, just before it was disbanded, the 16/5L Air Squadron converted onto the new Gazelle airframe, but they were lost when the unit was disbanded in May 1976 and became an AAC Flight.[6] Since the loss of the integral capability, many RAC officers and NCOs have successfully trained as pilots and aircrew, some electing to return to their units after a flying tour, but (probably) the majority transferring to the AAC in order to pursue a full-time flying career (with all the incentives that came with it including, of course, flying pay).

Annex E

Gunnery

When the Second World War ended the RAC Gunnery Wing was still located on the Dorset coast at Lulworth, using a number of sea ranges included the newly developed Tyneham extension; the Wing, later School, would remain there until the time of writing. The majority of the old, hutted camp at Lulworth was largely demolished during the early 1950s, with two new instructional blocks, messes and guardroom – the ones that still stand there to this day – completed in 1954. However, many of the old wooden huts were kept well into the 1990s, providing accommodation for the medical centre and the camp headquarters amongst other purposes. Additional buildings in the shape of new vehicle instructional sheds and a new structure commissioned to house the suite of simulators bought to support the introduction of CR2 were opened in about 1993. The School trained student NCO instructors and

A typical cadre crew, with the author as the sergeant instructor – always known as 'Staff'. Standards were extremely high as were failure rates; only five of these students passed the course.

regimental gunnery officers, crew commanders, and the B1 trade, usually known as Gunner Mechanics. The premium course was the four-month long cadre, for qualifying selected NCO and officer instructors to teach at the Gunnery School.

In Germany, the RAC Training Centre BAOR was established in 1945 to replicate some of the training activities of Bovington and Lulworth, which was sensible as a large proportion of the RAC were now based in Europe, mostly in northern Germany. Post-war, all RAC training had initially been centred at Probsten near Fallingbostel but in April 1946 the training centre took up residence in Durham Barracks, Belsen Camp – it was still known by that name, although the name Hohne was adopted as the less-emotionally charged title for the camp within a couple of years. The new centre included Tactics, Gunnery, Wireless and D&M Wings, with the nearby ranges operating separately. Supporting gunnery training was the RAC Gunnery Training Establishment BAOR, and later renamed as the RAC Gunnery Wing Hohne.

At the end of the war, the RAC was operating a huge fleet of many different types. The most effective tank gun was the excellent 17-pounder, introduced on the Sherman Firefly in mid-1944 and still a potent weapon. Other types in use included the 77mm gun on Comet as well as both British and American versions of the medium velocity 75mm gun; both were able to use the same ammunition. Armoured cars and light tanks used the British 2-pounder – the gun that had been the main gun on front-line tanks in 1940 – and the American 37mm. Specialist close-support tanks were equipped with the 95mm howitzer, and flamethrower Crocodile tanks were also in the inventory. Very quickly the American fleet was (mostly) disposed of, with the intention to standardize using a Universal tank. Due to the failure to bring the FV200 series into production, the 1943-designed Centurion became, by default, the main tank in service, although this did not happen overnight; the Comet, Cromwell and Churchill all continued well into the 1950s. The biggest challenge for the gunnery world was trying to decide on the correct techniques to be used when firing the new Armour Piercing Discarding Sabot (APDS) ammunition.

APDS had been introduced in the second half of the war, and was known to be an excellent 'hole-puncher', able to penetrate the heavier armour thicknesses coming into service. Its high muzzle velocity (about a mile a second) meant that it had a flattened trajectory, in turn meaning that errors in estimating the range to the target were to a degree less important – an under-estimation of the range could still result in a hit low on the target, and an over-estimation a strike on the top; on average errors of about 200m either side of the true range could still bring a hit. But the biggest problem related to the inability to observe the flight to, or indeed a strike on, the target. Due to the short time of flight and also to the increased obscuration (flash, blast, smoke etc.) produced by the firing tank, at short to medium ranges it was nigh-on impossible for the gunner to spot where the shot had gone. This meant that techniques of firing involving making corrections (changing the point of aim having noted the fall of shot) were unable to be used. The problem was made worse as gun sizes increased; in 1949 the 20-pounder (83.4mm) started to replace the 17-pounder on Centurion, which was in turn replaced by the 105mm L7 gun from the early 1960s. Both Conqueror and Chieftain/Challenger mounted (different) 120mm guns, and the calibre was retained, again on a different gun, when Challenger 2 came into service.

Various techniques to deal with the APDS obscuration problem were tried, finding favour at different times. These included relying on flank observation, in other words one tank firing and a second, flanking tank doing the observation, but this was not satisfactory nor reliably practical in battle. Another involved engaging the target with HE or HESH (see below) and then, once a hit had been obtained, switching to APDS, but this took time, used a lot of ammunition and again was not really practical. Another method was to fire three rounds of APDS, each at a different range, typically 1,000m, 800m and then 1,400m. If a hit was not obtained the crew would switch to using HE/HESH which could be observed, In fact, two main problems needed to be solved: a better method of ensuring that the gun and sights were properly aligned, and also some form of range-finding device – it was well known that allowing commanders (irrespective of how well trained or experienced) to estimate the range led to inaccuracies of up to 50 per cent. The first issue was largely solved with the introduction of the Muzzle Boresight, developed during the 1950s by Major Wieland RTR. This was an optical device inserted into the muzzle of the gun.[1] The latter problem was initially resolved with the introduction in 1966, on Centurion, of the Ranging Gun. This was a modified .50in Browning heavy machine gun, adapted to fire bursts of three rounds of special flashing-tip ammunition. Each burst was fired at an increased range, and once a hit on target was achieved, the range of that burst was used to fire the main armament. This remained in service until a more accurate, faster and silent range-finder was brought into service in the late 1970s – the laser.

Laser range finding, although initially not well regarded due to the unreliability of the early ruby rod system used and frequent overheating, made a huge impact on the chances of a first-round hit to the extent that many gunnery experts (the so-called gunnery 'gods' or 'gurus') unreasonably expected every shot fired with APDS – and DS/T, its training equivalent – to hit the target; if not, it was the gunner's fault. This was simply not correct, but generations of gunners and commanders were excoriated for missing the target when, in fact, the real culprit was simply that the 'spread' of the ammunition was larger than the surface area of the target (especially as range increased). It was not until a better understanding of the mathematical statistical-based concept of consistency was explained that a more reasonable approach was taken.[2] What was needed was more consistent (although still mass-produced) ammunition, and better fire-control systems,

Above and below: *The Muzzle Boresight was a British design, and allowed a much more precise method of aligning the sights with the bore of the gun at the muzzle end, leading to better consistency and accuracy.*

with finer tolerances. In the early 1980s the second of these was forthcoming, in the shape of the Improved Fire Control System, IFCS.[3]

IFCS used, for the first time, a ballistic fire-control computer, the CIU, to assist the crew by taking into account some of the multitude of variables that could affect the chances of a first-round hit. The most important of these was still the range, but others now could be used, including trunnion tilt, meteorological data, barrel wear, charge temperature and the tracking rate of lateral moving targets. In fact, IFCS was initially conceived to improve the chances of a hit against a moving target, but the computer was found to greatly improve the ability of the average (or below average) gunner to hit static targets as well.[4] Shooting from a moving tank had fallen from favour during the Second World War as the fire-control equipment on tanks was not sophisticated enough to assist the gunner, the technique requiring masses of skill and training time which was simply not available during wartime. Post-war, it became a practical technique once more following the design and introduction of the electrical Gun Control Equipment used with Centurion, and subsequently improved and refined on Chieftain and Challenger 1. Battle runs, involving a single tank, a troop of tanks or, if range space was available, more than one troop concurrently, became the norm on ranges with a mix of firing from static positions and on the move, including at moving targets.[5]

IFCS produced an elliptical aiming mark, based on the size of a broadside Soviet T64/72 tank, which was injected into the sights. The electrical gun-control equipment used to power the turret and gun was then used to 'drive' the gun and turret to the right position; all things being equal, all that the gunner had to do was check that the aiming mark was correctly sized and positioned around the target before firing the gun.[6] The increasing accuracy and consistency made possible by IFCS meant that much more time had to be spent by the crew and REME in correctly 'setting up' the fire-control system, in order to remove, as far as possible, minor but multiple faults that overall would decrease the effectiveness of the system.

IFCS/CSS remained in service on Chieftain and Challenger 1 until they were replaced during the 1990s. With the introduction of Challenger 2, a much-improved system was brought into service, this time used with the new 120mm L30 gun. Still a computer-based system, the main improvement was the capability to conduct 'hunter/killer' engagements. To allow this, the commander used a fully rotating primary sight, allowing him to observe all around the tank. To engage a target, the commander would use his (and, from 2016, her) sight to lase the target which would not only establish the range but also designate the target, after which the engagement could be handed over to the gunner to complete, freeing the commander to concurrently acquire the next target; this technique allowed a succession of engagements to be conducted much faster, the relatively slow speed of loading being the main factor for slowing things up.[7]

Although night fighting was not much used during Second World War and during the decades that followed, much research was conducted behind the scenes in order to allow tanks to fight at night and in other conditions of poor visibility. Later marks of Centurion, from the early 1960s on, used a mantlet-mounted 22in searchlight that could be used as 'white light' with the normal

Above and below: *Challenger 2 in action on the ranges. The huge obscuration from firing armour-piercing ammunition increased as the calibres grew larger, making observation of the fall of shot very difficult for the crew.* (Courtesy Andy Brend)

gunner's sight or, with an Infra-Red (IR) filter fitted, with an IR swap sight for the gunner. Although relatively crude by modern standards, this was a step in the right direction; Chieftain included a similar 19in searchlight (now known as the Light Projector) but mounted in a lightly armoured box on the side of the turret. Engagement ranges were limited, but night fighting – and regular night firing on ranges – was here to stay. The need to swap sights over was an obvious disadvantage, with many associated difficulties such as maintaining the gun/sight relationship, as well as problems of stowage and vulnerability whilst making the change.[8] The introduction in the mid-1980s of TOGS (Thermal Observation and Gunnery Sight) to both Challenger and Chieftain removed these problems. TOGS used thermal imaging technology to 'see' at night (and in many other low-light or poor-visibility conditions) and was thus a genuine day/night sight, with both commander and gunner seeing exactly the same picture. The system was largely passive, and was used in parallel with the normal day sights; it proved to be a genuine battle-winner during the 1991 Gulf War and in improved form, is still used on CR2.

The British policy throughout the post-war period has been to use High Explosive Squash Head (HESH) as the secondary ammunition on MBTs.[9] Although not as effective as standard HE in an explosive role, HESH has a very useful ability to deal with lightly armoured secondary targets such as light tanks and APCs, thus saving APDS or APFSDS for use against tanks.[10] Unlike those types of ammunition, HESH is fired at a much lower muzzle velocity (c660m/s on Chieftain, for example) allowing corrections to be applied if the round misses. HESH has also featured as the main round on the 76mm guns used on Saladin and Scorpion.

On the reconnaissance side, the Daimler Armoured Car remained the main vehicle used by the recce regiments until the late 1950s. It was armed with the

CR2 firing at night. The introduction of increasingly sophisticated night-vision devices made engagements at night as simple as those by day – and in some ways easier, as thermal 'hot spots' could betray the presence of even well-camouflaged enemy vehicles. (Courtesy KRH)

A Chieftain loader, wearing an NBC suit, about to load a HESH projectile. Until the introduction of a properly designed crewman's helmet and headset in the 1990s, most crews wore berets in the vehicles. (Courtesy Andy Fisher)

2-pounder gun, and could be fitted with the 'Littlejohn' squeeze bore adapter to allow special high-velocity ammunition to be fired, although this prevented HE being used (which, because of the small calibre, was not much of a loss). With the introduction of the Saladin from 1958, the recce regiments found themselves with a medium-velocity 76mm gun capable of firing HESH and smoke, and able to deal with light armour quite comfortably, although not tanks. The same basic gun design was used in modified form on Saladin's replacement, Scorpion, although the gunner and commander's positions were switched over. More importantly, both CVR(T) Scorpion and Scimitar were equipped with an image-intensifier night sight, allowing observation and engagements to take place at ranges of about a mile. Scimitar was equipped with a 30mm Rarden cannon, originally designed to be an 'APC killer'; this could fire HE in addition to various AP natures, and had an automatic capability. This allowed the rounds, loaded in two clips of three, to be fired quickly, although some accuracy was lost, meaning its use was generally restricted to engaging area targets.

Finally, we must note that one or two machine guns have been mounted on all tanks and gun-armed recce vehicles as a secondary armament, and on all other AFVs (less ambulances) as a self-defence weapon. These have varied from the wartime 7.92mm BESA and .30in Browning, through the 7.62mm GPMG series and the L94 chain gun.

Anti-Tank Guided Weapons

In 1954 the War Office issued an Operational Requirement (OR) for a missile system to defeat the heavily armoured T10 tank. Only two years later, in 1956 the annual RAC Conference was told that an anti-tank missile was under development and expected to be introduced into service within the corps by 1962. The intention was to use the new missile technology in order to provide a credible means of anti-tank defence for the airborne forces, and not – as had been first intended – as a form of long-range precision AT weapon for BAOR. The Australian-made Malkara (Shield) system had been started earlier, in 1952, and was therefore tested in order to gain experience, as the British expected to introduce their own system made by Fairey Aviation and codenamed Orange William. When technical problems with it were unable to be solved, it was cancelled in mid-1958 and Malkara was fielded as a stop-gap. A Guided Weapons (GW) wing was formed at Lulworth around this time, with the instructors and staff involved quickly gaining a reputation for being involved in dark arts, bordering on magic. In 1960, both the QOH and 3rd Carbs formed temporary Malkara troops, but it would be the airborne troops from the RAC that would be equipped with them in an operational role. The missile used a HESH warhead and was large and heavy, and was mounted on the FV1620 Hornet. This launcher vehicle carried four missiles, two ready to fire and two stowed, and was based on the 1-ton 4x4 armoured truck (the 'Pig' of Northern Ireland fame), as the vehicle had to be small enough to be air portable by the Blackburn Beverley and, if required, air-dropped on a special six-parachute platform.[11] Although it had a good range, 4,000m, one of the biggest problems with the Malkara was that it tended to emit a lot of smoke from the moment of launch, which would be an easy way for the enemy to locate the launcher vehicle; this problem was exacerbated by the fact that the Malkara could not be fired remotely using a separated sight, and the controller had to remain in the Hornet. Despite its shortfalls, the system remained in service with the RAC Parachute Squadron until 1971. A much smaller missile with a HEAT warhead named Vigilant (made by Vickers, it stood for Visual Guided Infantry Light Anti-Tank) started trials in 1960. This had the advantage of being small enough to mount on a Ferret Scout Car, with one missile either side of the turret to produce the Mk 2/6, and it also had a separated sight capability. Although only short range (around 1 mile), it was easy to operate and was used within the armoured car regiments and the RAC Parachute Squadron as well as by the infantry.[12]

Concurrently, in 1960 an OR was issued for a replacement for Malkara, with the same range but with a separated sight capability. This was developed by BAC and became the Swingfire, which appeared on the FV438 launcher vehicle in late 1968, as well as (later) on the Ferret Mk 5 and the CVR(T) Striker. Regiments began to form GW troops of six FV438; for example, 15/19H, 1RTR and

The man-portable Vigilant ATGW could be mounted on the Ferret Scout Car to make it a Mk 2/6, giving this small two-man vehicle a lot of punch.

The FV438 carried fourteen Swingfire missiles, with two in ready-to-use launch bins and the remainder stowed under armour inside. Changes in organization meant that the Swingfire role was passed between the RAC and the RA.

4RTR all formed theirs in 1970, with QRIH following a year later.[13] Over the next few years the so-called 'Gobbly Wobbly' crews became extremely adept at the black art of ATGW, including spending many hours on the simulators in order to maintain the necessary skills to engage targets at both very close and extremely long (4,000m) range. However, in 1976 it was decided that all ATGW capability would pass to the Royal Artillery, where it remained until 1 April 1984 when it once more became an RAC responsibility.[14] The FV438 was used within armoured regiments, and Striker by the armoured reconnaissance units, the system seeing service in Cyprus in 1974, in the Gulf War of 1991 and then in the Balkans. As well as providing the armoured regiments with additional punch, it gave the reconnaissance units an integral anti-tank capability that was not provided by the guns and cannons on their main vehicle fleet. When Swingfire went out of service in 2005, it was replaced by the simpler man-portable Javelin system made in the United States, and which was successfully used as a precision means of applying direct fire out to about 4,000m, including on occasions against individual insurgents.

More Wiggly Amps: AFV Communications

Larkspur

The No. 19 set remained as the major equipment of the RAC until the late 1950s. The replacement, the C42 VHF FM radio, was on trials with 10th Armoured Division in Libya in 1956, where the users reported that it was a great improvement over the tired No. 19 wireless: it was easier to tune, it tended to say in tune and it was overall much simpler to use. By 1958 the 'front-line' regiments in BAOR had started to be converted, with most RAC AFVs being fitted with a C42 for regimental/squadron use, and a smaller short-range B47 for troop communications.[1] 10th Hussars recorded the much more reliable comms obtained with the new sets when they converted in 1957, and were delighted at how quickly a frequency change could be accomplished, with no need for the lengthy and insecure tuning and netting calls required for the No. 19. The C42 and B47, together with the HF sets C12, C13 and occasionally C11/R210 used by the recce regiments for longer-range comms, came to be known as the Larkspur range, although this was only retrospectively applied; the code name in the early 1960s was originally only intended to be used for the project to extend the issue of the new radios beyond the RAC and RA, the first two corps that had been issued them. Manpack sets were also introduced and were widely used by recce regiments, particularly by the assault troops and for communications with aircraft and helicopters. Secure communications to Brigade HQ was provided within RHQ by the BID 150 secure-speech system, allowing the transmission of orders in clear from Brigade Commander to unit CO – but only that far: communications downwards within the regiment had to be coded using the GRIDDLE, SLIDEX, MAPCO and later BATCO systems, a time-consuming procedure that was prone to user errors, especially when tired.

Until 1967 each regiment had a small contingent of Royal Signals soldiers, usually led by a sergeant or warrant officer, attached to them. The main role of these was to carry out the first-line repair of equipment as well as assisting in training; as they were not tank trained, they were not able to crew AFVs, although they certainly found themselves in armoured command vehicles from time to time and manned the formation rear-link radio net; for example, in 1956 3rd Hussars could boast a sergeant and nine others in their 'W troop', whereas the regiment itself provided a sergeant plus six ORs in what would later become known as Command Troop – the RHQ command vehicle crews. When they were withdrawn

The No. 19 radio set was largely obsolete by the 1950s, having given excellent service during the Second World War. It required constant attention to get the best out of it, and its main 'A' set operated in the HF range, not ideal for mobile communications.

BATCO was a reasonably simple paper-based code system used until the early 1980s. Practice made perfect in its use, but what was really required were secure communications systems for the army which allowed all radio users to speak in clear.

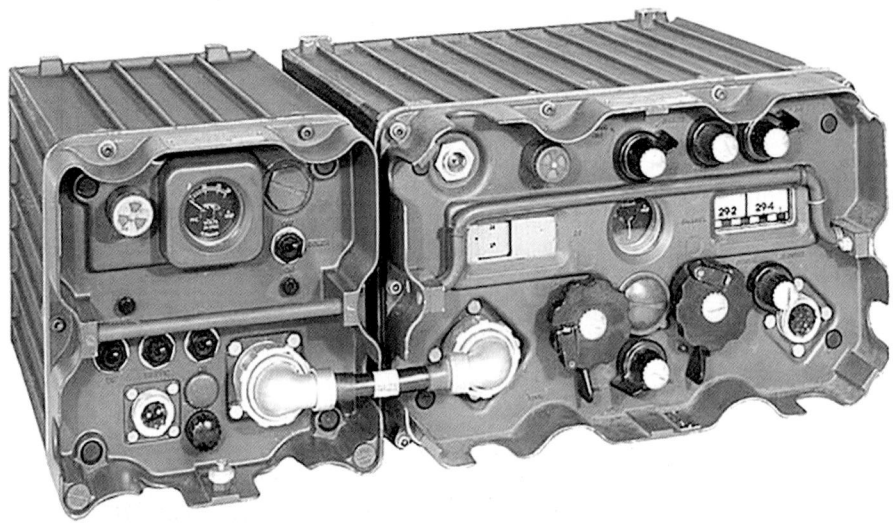

The C42 was the main radio set in the so-called Larkspur Range, and on tanks was used for regimental and squadron radio nets, with the smaller and shorter range B47 set reserved for troop nets.

the requirement for well-trained regimental signallers resulted in the BI trade signallers' course being modified to produce operators destined for RHQ and SHQs, and who were also trained to carry out basic fault finding and some low-level repairs; this was called the Control Signaller. There is no doubt that the standard of signalling and voice procedure within the RAC was the envy of other corps, and as such allowed the tank and recce units to be used to their maximum potential.[2]

Clansman Combat Net Radio

The replacement for the Larkspur range began to be introduced into service in the second half of the 1970s, the first units being equipped at the end of 1977 with BAOR having priority. The author clearly recalls returning to Tidworth from a UN tour of Cyprus in March 1979 to find that the radios and harnesses in the Chieftain tanks had been finally replaced during the tour with a new and frankly much more modern type – each tank now had the ability to carry two identical UK VRC 353 VHF radios, a huge advance.[3] The new feature that was possibly most appreciated was the provision of headsets incorporating boom microphones, which together with the new 'Live IC' part of the harness system allowed the whole crew to talk with each other hands-free. Other advantages included increased range, although there were strict limitations on the use of the 50W maximum power setting, and the ability to 'silent tune' the set without out-putting a signal that could be intercepted by the enemy. The CVR vehicles within the recce regiments usually mounted one 353 plus a 'clip-in' UK PRC 351/2

The Clansman equivalent of the C42 was the UK VRC 353, introduced in the late 1970s. Legend has it that it could have been made much smaller, but the manufacturers interpreted the maximum dimensions stated as being the required dimensions ...

manpack, designed to allow the recce soldiers to unclip it from the harness and use as a manpack for dismounted operations. HF and secure speech replacements for Larkspur were also issued, including the UK VRC 321 and PRC 320 HF radios, and a modified VRC 353Z set was used with the Digital Master Unit and BID 250 secure speech system. Clansman was first used in action during the Falklands campaign, and also during the 1991 Gulf War, where the lack of a secure-speech facility for all tank commanders and AFVs was deemed to be a major failing.

Bowman

The GS requirement for a replacement for Clansman was issued in 1989. The introduction into service took a very long time, as in 2000 the initial contractor, Archer, had the contract withdrawn due to persistent delivery failures, being replaced by a consortium headed up by CDC (later GD UK). This meant that the units deploying to the invasion of Iraq in 2003 were still using the same Clansman system that had been used twelve years previously, and still lacked secure speech at all levels. Bowman was finally introduced a few years later, officially entering service in March 2004, and was generally hugely unpopular because of its complexity and many faults; the crews scathingly referred to it as 'Better Off With Map And Nokia', and a frequent complaint from commanders at all levels amounted to, 'all we wanted was simple, reliable, secure VHF, and they gave us this!', referring to the ability of the system to transmit data, although it must be said that the integrated GPS was popular as an aid to navigation.

Another complaint was the reliance on virtual training methods; one RDG officer noted that he had attended three different and lengthy conversion courses, but had yet to see a real radio or other piece of hardware. And the size of the complex system was much larger and took up more space inside the vehicles than its predecessor: when the Panther FCLV was introduced into service, the inside of the supposedly four-man wheeled vehicle was so full of Bowman system boxes that the crew found it difficult to fit in the remaining space; another cynical comment often heard was that Panther had become the most expensive portable radio in the world. Unlike every other new system introduced since the 1930s, which had all been perceived as positive step-changes in technology, Bowman was extremely unpopular when it was introduced, although, as time has gone by, faults have been rectified, and especially as familiarity with a very complex system has been achieved, the complaints are now much less vocal.

In 2007 an MoD website described the system:

The Bowman family of digital radios, and the associated Combat Infrastructure Platform (CIP), are key to the plans of the Ministry of Defence to transform military communications and enable the armed forces to operate more effectively and at a quicker pace. The pressing need to replace the ageing Clansman radios used since the 1970s with reliable, secure voice communications has made Bowman one of the UK Army's top priorities.

By enabling transmission of large quantities of electronic data Bowman is intended to provide information on the position of UK forces, and forms the underlying network to carry the CIP. CIP is intended to replace and automate many existing manual processes for command and control on the battlefield. It is also key to plans for 'Network Enabled Capability', joining up military communications and electronic systems in a 'network of networks'. The ability to see the position of UK forces, on screens in vehicles and headquarters, should amongst other benefits, help to reduce the frequency of 'friendly fire' incidents. The secure radio capability provided by Bowman has only recently begun to enter service, later than originally intended, Though Bowman was declared in service in March 2004 and many useful new capabilities have since been delivered, conversion of vehicles and units has been slower than envisaged. The Bowman project covers all the VHF and HF radio configurations used as manpacks or installed in land, sea and air platforms. The outline Bowman conversion programme is as follows: 2004 – 2006: 12 Mechanised Brigade; 4 Armoured, and 7 Armoured Brigades; 1 Mechanised Brigade; 16 Air Assault Brigade and 3 Commando Brigade. 2007 – 2008: 19 Light Brigade and 20 Armoured Brigade. The programme involves conversion of up to 15,700 land vehicles … with training for some 75,000 service personnel. Contracts worth £2.4 billion were placed with General Dynamics UK, in 2001 for Bowman and in 2002 for the Combat Infrastructure Programme (CIP). Around 45,000 Personal Role Radios, 47,000 manpack and vehicle radios, and 26,000 computer terminals are being acquired.[4]

GD UK, the prime contractor, added more detail, which gives an idea of the complexity and ambition of the system:

In 2011, General Dynamics UK was awarded the contract to deliver Bowman, the tactical C4I system for the British armed forces. Bowman delivered a step change in capability over the Clansman family of radios through its security, data capability, reliability and resilience against Electronic Warfare (EW) attack. Bowman is a tactical communications system integrating digital voice and data technology to provide secure radio, telephone, intercom and tactical internet services in a modular and fully integrated system. The programme included the digitisation of more than 18,000 platforms, including vehicles, helicopters, naval vessels, landing craft and fixed HQ buildings.

ComBAT and P-BISA are the two main components in the battle management system which was procured as part of the UK's Bowman project. The system consists of:

- Common Battlefield Application Toolset (ComBAT)
- Infrastructure
- Armoured Platform Battlefield Information System Application (P-BISA) – known as Bowman ComBAT Infrastructure and Platform (BCIP). BCIP consists of three interrelated projects fielded together as a single system:

ComBAT provides situation awareness, instant messaging, mission planning, logistics, intelligence and a geographical information system; and has been optimised for use in armoured fighting vehicles, individual dismounted soldier systems and operational staff configurations.

The infrastructure part of BCIP includes the provision of a variety of hardware and software items, particularly to support the operation of Headquarters. Hardware included A1 plotters, large screen displays, printers, servers with RAID storage, projectors and smartboards. Software included an office automation suite, originally OpenOffice, now changed to Microsoft Office, centralised file and printer sharing, and network Quality of Service management supporting a Bulk File Transfer capability between headquarters.

The Platform Battlefield Information System Application (P-BISA) integrates ComBAT and the infrastructure software, together with existing and planned systems and sensors into armoured fighting vehicles. P-BISA introduces additional man machine interface (MMI) enhancements allowing for operations to be performed on-the-move in the form of crew station bezel function keys, commanders point device (CPD) and optimised ComBAT screen layout/functions.[5]

Clearly, the introduction of Bowman brought massive changes into the capabilities of AFV radio systems, but any thought that this meant simplicity of

Modern communication systems are not simple! This is the so-called Complex fit in a Land Rover, a typical configuration for a squadron leader's personal vehicle.

use for the user should be dashed. It is hugely complicated, as the accompanying photograph should illustrate. The 'fit' on an individual vehicle depends upon its role, for example, MBT and Ajax vehicles will usually carry 2 x VHF and 1 x HF, whereas some Jackal will only carry 1 x VHF; the main radios that are used in RAC vehicles at the time of writing are summarized below.

- PRC 325. HF manpack
- PRC 327. HF manpack in a vehicle installation kit (for example, clip-in)
- VRC 328. HF vehicle set
- VRC 329. HF vehicle set with power amplifier
- VRC 340. UHF high-capacity data-only radio
- PRC 354. VHF portable radio
- PRC 355. VHF manpack radio
- PRC 356. VHF manpack radio with additional battery
- PRC 357. VHF manpack in a vehicle installation kit (for example, clip-in)
- VRC 358. VHF vehicle set
- VRC 359. VHF vehicle set with power amplifier

Note: TacSat systems are used as required by the operation, for example, by Light Cavalry units operating over extended distances in Mali.

Annex G

RAC Calendar

Each regiment is rightly proud of the history not only of the existing regiment but also of its predecessors, and an understanding of the key dates is central to this. Like so much of this work, it may not be totally complete, but this calendar aims to show the main events in each RAC regiment's history, month by month.

January

1st   1938 Final mounted Parade 3rd Carbs, Sialkot. 1943 Disbandment of 8th Armoured Division. 1944 Absorption of Reconnaissance Corps into RAC. 1959 QDG amalgamation (KDG and Bays) Perham Down.

6th   1918 Tank Corps battalions numbered (i.e., no longer lettered).

10th   1952 Formation of Boys Squadron RAC.

14th   1941 Formation of Reconnaissance Corps.

28th   1846 Battle of Aliwal.

February

3rd   1965 RAC Para Sqn formed.

12th   1976 RAC Para Sqn Final Parade, Old Sarum.

16th   1916 Formation of Heavy Section MGC at Bisley. 1940 Mobile Division Egypt becomes 7th Armoured Division.

20th   1959 QDG Amalgamation Parade, Perham Down. 1969 Announcement of the amalgamation of 3rd Carbs and Scots Greys.

24th   1991 Start of Gulf War.

March

1st   1959 4RTR amalgamation (4 and 7RTR), Haig Barracks, Hohne.

2nd   1959 QDG Standard Parade, Clarence House.

9th   1941 Formation of 11th Armoured Division.

10th   1928 Announcement of mechanization of 11th Hussars and 12th Lancers.

17th   1912 Oates Day.

19th   1959 16/5L Guidon Parade, Buckingham Palace. 2003 Start of Iraq War.

20th   1959 QOH Guidon Parade, Tidworth.

23rd   1945 Rhine Crossing.

29th   1969 RHG/D amalgamation (RHG and The Royals), Detmold. (Parades held on 31st.)

April

1st   1933 6 Bn RTC formed.

3rd   1959 4RTR Amalgamation Parade, Hohne.

4th   1939 RAC formed.

5th   2017 RL Guidon Parade, Windsor.

10th   1928 12th Lancers final mounted Parade.

11th   1954 40RTR Standards Parade, Bootle.

13th   1944 Battle of Nunshigum.

17th   1937 7th (Army) Bn RTC formed Catterick.

24th   1918 First tank v tank action, Villers-Brettoneux.

27th   1954 The Royals Guidon Parade, Tidworth.

28th   1953 Household Cavalry Standards Parade, Windsor.

May

1st   1927 Experimental Mechanized Force forms up at Tidworth.

2nd   2015 Amalgamation Parade RL, Richmond Castle (9/12L and QRL).

4th   1979 9th/12th Lancers Guidon Parade, Tidworth.

10th   1941 Egypt disbandment of 2nd Armoured Division.

12th   1956 5DG Freedom of Enniskillen Parade. 1973 15/19H Freedom of Newcastle upon Tyne Parade.

15th   1959 17/21L Guidon Parade, Paderborn. 1960 NIH Guidon Parade, Belfast.

16th   1938 8th (Army) Bn RTC formed Perham Down.

19th   1983 LG and RHG/D Standard Parade, Horse Guards.

21st   1940 Battle of Arras. 2003 HCav Standards and Guidon Parade.

23rd   1958 4/7DG Standard Parade, Fallingbostel.

24th   1937 7th Bn RTC formed.

25th   1985 QRIH Tercentary and Guidon Parade, Münster.

27th   1962 RGH Guidon Parade, Badminton. 1993 HCR Standards Parade, Horse Guards, London.

28th   2014 HCR Standards Parade, Horse Guards, London.

30th   1973 LG and RHG/D Standard Parade, Horse Guards.

June

1st   1962 Special Reconnaissance Sqn RAC formed.

2nd   1953 HM Queen Elizabeth II becomes Colonel in Chief RTR.

6th   1944 D-Day.

8th   1958 QOW&WY Guidon Parade, Pembroke Castle.

10th	1961 14/20H Guidon Parade, Hohne.
11th	1961 RWY Guidon Parade, Tidworth.
12th	1982 14/20H Guidon Parade, Hohne. 1999 Entry into Kosovo.
13th	1997 QRH Guidon Parade. 2000 RTR statue unveiling, Whitehall Place.
15th	1944 Disbandment of 10th Armoured Division, Egypt.
17th	1941 Formation of Guards Armoured Division.
18th	1815 Battle of Waterloo. 1993 JLR RAC final passing out parade.
21st	1959 SY Guidon Parade, Shrewsbury.
24th	1961 Ayrshire Yeo Guidon Parade, Culzean Castle. 2000 KRH Guidon Parade, Tidworth.
25th	1993 QRL Amalgamation and Guidon Parade, Bulford (16/5L & 17/21L). 2008 1 & 2RTR Standards Parade, Buckingham Palace.
26th	1944 Start of Op EPSOM. 1998 RDG Standard Parade, Tidworth.
27th	1743 Battle of Dettingen. 1922 amalgamation of 17th and 21st Lancers, Tidworth.
30th	1961 10H Guidon Parade, Paderborn. 1990 RH Guidon Parade, Tidworth.

July

1st	1960 5RTR amalgamation, Wessex Barracks, Fallingbostel (5 and 8RTR).
2nd	1971 Scots DG amalgamation and Standard Parade, Holyrood Palace, Edinburgh (3rd Carbs and Greys).
3rd	1982 15/19H Guidon Parade, Paderborn.
5th	1956 Scots Greys Guidon Parade, Edinburgh. 2018 Scots DG Standard Parade, Leuchars.
7th	1944 Start of Op CHARNWOOD. 2018 Scots DG Standard Parade.
8th	1961 Cheshire Yeomanry Guidon Parade, Chester Castle.
12th	1985 RTR Standards Parade, Sennelager.
13th	1965 11H Guidon Parade, Hohne. 2018 Guidon Parade RWxY, Lulworth.
14th	1967 RTR 50th anniversary Parade, Hohne. 1972 Guidon Parade RHG/D, Windsor Great Park.
15th	1983 16/5L Guidon Parade, Tidworth.
18th	1944 Start of Op GOODWOOD.
19th	1958 QOY and FFY/SH Guidon Parades, Dundonald.
20th	1982 Hyde Park bombing.
21st	2000 9/12L Guidon Parade.
22nd	1812 Battle of Salamanca. 1961 13/18H Guidon Parade, Fallingbostel.
23rd	1960 9L Guidon Parade Busigny Barracks, Perham Down.
28th	1917 Formation of Tank Corps, battalions use letters.
29th	1987 13/18H Guidon Parade, Tidworth.
30th	1944 Start of Op BLUECOAT.
31st	1944 Disbandment of 9th Armoured Division.

August

1st   1941 Palestine Formation of 10th Armoured Division (from 1st Cavalry Division). 1944 Reconnaissance Corps absorbed into RAC. 1946 Reconnaissance Corps disbanded. 1992 RDG amalgamation, Paderborn (4/7DG and 5DG).

2nd   2014 RTR amalgamation, Tidworth (1RTR and 2RTR)

3rd   1993 1RTR amalgamation, Tidworth (1RTR and 4RTR). Formal amalgamation RDG.

4th   2014 2RTR disbanded, Bulford.

5th   1992 2RTR amalgamation, Fallingbostel (2RTR and 3RTR).

8th   1918 Battle of Amiens. 1944 Op TOTALIZE.

11th   1954 3H Consecration of Kettle Drums, Iserlohn.

13th   1704 Battle of Blenheim.

14th   1942 Formation of 79th Armoured Division. 1944 Op TRACTABLE.

15th   1916 First tank battle, Flers-Courcelette.

23rd   1914 Battle of Mons.

25th   1945 Formation of BAOR.

28th   1914 Battle of Moy.

September

1st   1923 Formation of the Tank Corps as a regular corps of the army. 1961 Standard Parade 5DG, Sennelager. 1993 QRH amalgamation (QOH and QRIH), Fallingbostel.

2nd   1898 Battle of Omdurman.

5th   1958 12th Lancers Guidon Parade, Wolfenbüttel.

11th   1960 9/12L amalgamation Tidworth (9L and 12L).

12th   1940 Formation of 6th Armoured Division.

15th   2018 SNIY Guidon Parade, Edinburgh.

17th   1966 B&WDgns Guidon Parade DoY HQ, London.

22nd   2007 QOY Guidon Parade, Alnwick. 2018 QOY Guidon Parade, Bramham Park, Wetherby.

23rd   1803 Battle of Assaye.

26th   1959 15/19H Guidon Parade, Barnard Castle.

October

1st   1993 Amalgamation Parade 1 and 4RTR, Tidworth.

2nd   1955 Fife & Forfar Yeomanry Guidon Parade, Culpar.

17th   1918 King George V becomes Colonel in Chief of the Tank Corps. 1943 Disbandment of 42nd Armoured Division.

18th   1923 Tank Corps becomes Royal Tank Corps. 1953 NY Guidon Parade, Althorp.

19th   1992 HCR Union, Windsor (LG & RHG/D).

23rd   1942 Start of 2nd Battle of El Alamein (Op LIGHTFOOT).

24th   1958 QRIH Amalgamation and Guidon Parade, Caen Barracks, Hohne (4H and 8H).

25th   1854 Battle of Balaclava. 1969 RH amalgamation and Guidon Parade, Perham Down (10H and 11H).

26th   1959 15/19H Bicentenary and Guidon Parade, Deerbolt Camp.

27th   1960 RTR Standards Parade, Buckingham Palace (1, 2, 3, 4 5RTR. Guidons presented to WD and NSY/44RTR).

31st   1956 40/41RTR amalgamation (40 and 41RTR). 1959 3RTR amalgamation, Sennelager (3 and 6RTR). 2014 SNIY formed.

November

1st   1941 Formation of 42nd Armoured Division. 1956 Formation of the Yorkshire Yeomanry. 1958 Queen's Bays Final Parade, Tidworth.

3rd   1958 QOH amalgamation, Tidworth (3H and 7H).

4th   1940 Formation of 8th Armoured Division.

6th   Start of Suez invasion by land forces.

16th   1916 HSMGC becomes HBMGC, companies become battalions. 1969 Laying up of 5RTR standard St Peter-upon-Cornhill.

20th   1917 Start of Battle of Cambrai. 1958 KDG Final Parade, Perham Down. 1969 5RTR Final Parade, Wolfenbüttel.

21st   1948 First RTR Cenotaph Parade, Whitehall.

22nd   1848 Battle of Ramnuggur.

December

1st   1940 Formation of 9th Armoured Division. 1992 KRH amalgamation, Münster (RH and 14/20H): LD amalgamation, Hohne (13/18H and 15/19H).

4th   1992 KRH Amalgamation Parade, Münster.

7th   1969 5RTR Disbandment

14th   2011 Disbandment of Joint NBC Regiment.

15th   1939 Formation of 2nd Armoured Division.

21st   1808 Battle of Sahagun.

Annex H

RAC Duty Stations and Barracks, Germany, 1945–2015

This is a summary of the locations used by RAC regiments in BAOR and Berlin since 1945. It is divided into two parts; the major barracks, meaning the main seventeen barracks in ten towns and cities, and the minor barracks, which are all the others used during the tumultuous period following the end of the Second World War, as temporary locations between moves, or the smaller barracks used less frequently to house the requirements of regiments operating fleets of AFVs and all the support required. It is almost certainly not complete, but probably represents about 90 per cent of the full story.

The dates used are largely based on those from the various regimental journals, but which, as a result, are not without their problems. Some regiments have been remarkably vague about the dates (and in some cases barracks) involved in the moves. Others seem to have recorded the date of the move of the first (advance parties) personnel from the regiment, rather than the date on which they adopted full responsibility for the camp. However, the majority of the dates used do represent that date, and which are now increasingly referred to as 'flag-changing ceremonies', a much more helpful method of diary-keeping for the historian!

Germany Major

Berlin – Smuts Bks – BFPO 45

4 July 1945–18 March 1946: 11H (in Von Seeckt Kaserne (later renamed) Wavell Bks)

7 July 1945–22 August 1945: 8H

30 August 1945–18 March 1946: 1RTR Kladow

18 March 1946–6 June 1947?: LG (Kladow (Blucher Kaserne, later renamed Montgomery Bks)

June 1946–mid-March 1947?: Det 13/18H

? –March 1947: D Sqn Inns of Court (in Mackenzie King Bks)

4 March 1947–1 June 1947: X Sqn Royals (Combined A and D Sqns) (in Mackenzie King Bks)

1 June 1947–early September 1947: A Sqn Royals (in Mackenzie King Bks)

Late 1947–spring 1948: C Sqn RHG

3 January 1948–May 1949: C Sqn 11H

16 November 1950–mid-January 1952: Det 3H (in Mackenzie King Bks)

May 1949– February/March 1950: A Sqn Royals

February/March 1950–February 1951: A Sqn RHG

February 1951–15 January 1952: Berlin Sqn 3H

15 January 1952–mid-October 1957: 1st Independent Sqn RTR (Mackenzie King Bks until July 1953, then Smuts)

17 October 1957–27 November 1960: B Sqn 14/20H (from BAOR APC Regt)

Mid-November 1960–3 May 1963: C Sqn 4RTR (from BAOR APC Regt)

May 1963–13 February 1965: The Independent Sqn RTR

14 February 1965–mid-February 1967: A Sqn QOH

Mid-February 1967–15 January 1969: A Sqn 1RTR

15 January 1969–6 December 1970: A Sqn 9/12L

7 December 1970–7 December 1972: A Sqn QDG

7 December 72–3 December 1974: A Sqn 4RTR

3 December 74–15 December 1976: B Sqn 5DG

16 December 76–April 1979: B Sqn SCOTS DG

April 1979–February 1981: D Sqn RH

February 1981–23 March 1983: D Sqn 4/7DG

24 March 1983–1 May 1985: D Sqn QOH

1 May 1985–24 March 1988: B Sqn 14/20H

25 March 1988–July 1992: C Sqn 14/20H (Tanks left 13 June 1992)

Detmold – Hobart – BFPO 15

15 July 1946–September 1952: 1RTR)

October 1952–25 July 1962: 3RTR

9 August 1962–9 February 1965: QOH

10 February 1965–29 March 1969: Royals (RHG from February 1969)

29 March 1969: Amalgamation RHG/D

29 March 1969–18 January 1971: RHG/D (Move to Lothian)

19 January 1971–mid-May 1976: 9/12L (A Sqn from December 1970)

Mid-May 1976–early April 1983: QOH

Mid-April 1983–31 July 1992: 4/7DG

Detmold – Lothian – BFPO 15

May 1946–August 1946: 7RTR

24 January 1951–15 June 1960: 9L

15 June 1960–early July 1962: Greys

Early July 1962–November 1967: 3rd Carbs (B Sqn from Warminster early February 1963)

October 1967–18 January 1971: QDG

18 January 1971–3 September 1971: RHG/D (15 March 1971 B Sqn LG vice A Sqn RHG/D)

10 September 1971–15 October 1975: LG
16 October 1975–2 March 1980: RHG/D
3 March 1980–February 1984: LG
February 1984–12 November 1986: RHG/D
12 November 1986–15 December 1992: 15/19H (Barracks closed)

Fallingbostel – Lumsden – BFPO 38
October 1951–13 June 1954: 7H
14 June 1954–7 October 1959: 4/7DG
18 November 1959–30 June 1960: 5RTR
1 July 1960–24 February 1965: 5RTR
24 February 1965–mid-January 1968: 3RTR
Mid-January 1968–September 1971: 16/5L
Mid-September 1971–27 October 1976: 3RTR
27 October 1976–March 1981: 4/7DG
April 1981–November 1988: RH
November 1988–June 1992: SCOTS DG
June 1992–August 2007: 2RTR (Barracks H/O to 1RRF)

Fallingbostel – Wessex Bks – BFPO 38
1949–31 August 1954: Bays
1 September 1954–22 January 1959: 4RTR
End October 1957– January 1959: 7RTR
22 January 1959–30 June 1960: 8RTR
12 February 1961–February 1964: 13/18H
February 1964–November 1969: Greys
November 1969–October 1974: 15/19H
November 1974–October 1977: 17/21L
November 1977–January 1984: Gap
January 1984–April 1990: 2RTR
April 1990–31 October 1993: QRIH
1 September 1993: QRH Amalgamation parade (QOH and QRIH)
1 September 1993–*c.* 20 July 1995: QRH
c. 20 July 1995–August 2015?: SCOTS DG

Herford – Harewood – BFPO 15
January 1955–March 1956: 12L
December 1957–September 1959: Royals
September 1959–November 1962: LG (One Sqn LG from September 1959,
   remainder January 1960)
29 November 1962–July 1966: RHG
July 1966–February 1969: 4RTR

March 1969–June 1970: 5DG
May 1970–1 July 1971: 3rd Carbs
6 July 1971–May 1973: SCOTS DG
1 May 1973–end April 1976: 14/20H (A Sqn ex HK from 1 August 1973)
Early May 1976–November 1982: 1RTR
November 1982–24 November 8196: 13/18H
24 November 1986–6 August 1991: 16/5L
7 August 1991–8 July 1994: 9/12L

Hohne – Caen Bks – BFPO 30
c. September 1948–3 September 1953: 5RTR
3 September 1953–23 October 1958: 4H
24 October 1958–19 June 1961: QRIH
Mid-November 1960–April 1963: RHQ 4RTR (BAOR APC Regt: A Sqn Stornoway Bks Lemgo, B Sqn Trenchard Bks Celle, C Sqn armoured sqn Berlin)
July 1961–December 1965: 1RTR
December 1965–end July 1970: 2RTR
5 August 1970–end August 1974: QOH
End August 1974–30 October 1977: 13/18H
30 October 1977–21 June 1985: 14/20H
21 June 1985–September 1993: QOH

Hohne – Haig Bks, Haig Bks North – BFPO 30
October 1957–28 February 1959: 7RTR
8 July 1957–27 November 1960: 14/20H (BAOR APC Regt from mid-October 1957–27 November 1960: RHQ Hohne, A Sqn Celle then Detmold, B Sqn Berlin, C Sqn Celle)
1 April 1959–mid-November 1960: 4RTR
28 November 1960–end July 1962: 14/20H
July 1962–March 1969: 11H
March 1969–December 1972: 4RTR
10 January 1973–22 January 1979: QDG – Move to Campbell Bks
Gap
1 December 1992: Amalgamation LD
1 December 1992–August 2000: LD
6 September 2000–? 2015: 9/12L

Hohne – Campbell Bks – BFPO 30
22 January 1979–November 1980: QDG – Move from Haig Barracks
November 1980–5 February 1984: 9/12L (To 1 Welsh Guards)

Münster – York Bks – BFPO 17

1946–November 1948: 5DG
October 1949–November 1950: 3H
Early December 1951–late September 1957: 17/21L
September 1957–October 1958: 3H
October 1958–30 June 1960: Greys
1 July 1960–8 August 1962: QOH
9 August 1962–August 1965: 4/7DG
Early November 1965–September 1969: 10H
September 1969–June 1970: 3rd Carbs AC
June 1970–December 1974: 5DG
Early December 1974–July 1982: 4RTR
July 1982–24 March 1988: QRIH
25 March 1988–November 1992: 14/20H (- one sqn in Berlin)
December 1992–21 February 2000: KRH
21 February 2000–September 2008: RDG

Münster – Swinton Bks – BFPO 17

15 February 1952–22 June 1959: 2RTR
22 June 1959–11 February 1960: 10H
July 1960–30 June 1961: 1RTR
4 November 1961–24 January 1968: 15/19H
25 January 1968–August 1972: 13/18H
21 August 1972–25 May 1979: 2RTR
26 May 1979–November 80: 9/12L (C Sqn re-join 26 June 1980)
November 1980–14 December 1990: 17/21L
14 December 1990–November 1992: RH

Münster – Portsmouth Bks – BFPO 17

7 December 1951–January 1952: 6RTR

Osnabrück – Imphal Bks – BFPO 36

February 1948–13 November 1950: 11H (Roberts Bks)
17 March 1952–9 June 1959: 3rd Carbs (Barracks renamed by 3rd Carbs)
9 June 1959–12 October 1963: 16/5L
1 November 1963–15 January 1969: 9/12L
15 January 1969–end May 1973: 1RTR
End May 1973–9 January 1977: SCOTS DG
10 January 1977–November 1984: 5DG
November 1984–24 June 1993: 4RTR
25 June 1993–21 July 2003: QRL

21 July 2003–7 December 2007: QDG (H/O to Brigade)

Paderborn – Alanbrooke Bks – BFPO 16
June 1962–September 1963: Special Recce Sqn RAC (disbanded)
Inf Bns
20 October 1977–October 1984: 15/19H

Paderborn – Barker – BFPO 16
December 1948–10 September 1951: 5DG
3 August 1951–15 February 1957: 8RTR
Late September 1957–2 February 1960: 17/21L
3 February 1960–March 64: 10H
March 1964–December 1966: 13/18H
December 1966–July 1970: 14/20H
24 August 1970–27 July 1979: QRIH
27 July 1979–4 November 1986: 3RTR
5 November 1986–1 August 1992: 5DG (1 August 1992 amalgamated with
    4/7DG)
1 August 1992–July 1996: RDG
August 1996–August 1999: 1RTR

Sennelager – Athlone Bks – BFPO 16
17 July 1953–14 December 1956: 16/5L (Built 1953–4)
December 1956–October 1959?: 6RTR
January 1957–December 1962: 5DG
December 1962–9 Aprril 1969: 17/21L
10 April 1969–14 June 1973: 4/7DG
15 June 1973–March 1979: RH
April 1979–12 November 1986: SCOTS DG
12 November 1986–5 February 1990: RHG/D (B Sqn 14/20H attached March
    1987–March 1988)
5 February 1990–23 September 1992: LG
23 September 1992–14 August 1998: QDG
14 August 1998–26 July 2019: QRH (H/O to Paderborn Garrison)

Wolfenbüttel – Northampton Bks – BFPO 101
1945–18 March 1946: LG
18 March 1946–17 April 1946: 11H
1 July 1946–mid-October 1947: 13/18H
23 October 1947–8 November 1950: Royals
12 November 1950–4 March 1952: RHG
4 March 1952–27 November 1953: LG

28 November 1953–March 1956: 13/18H (– B Sqn)
March 1956–9 March 1959: 12L
10 March 1959–18 November 1964: QDG
18 November 1964–January 1968: QRIH
January 1968–7 December 1969: 5RTR (Disbanded 7 December 1969)
8 December 1969–6 December 1971: 3RTR
6 December 1971–late November 1974: 17/21L
Late November 1974–November 1980: 16/5L
November 1980–January 1984: 2RTR
10 February 1984–8 April 1987: 9/12L
8 April 1987–14 May 1991: QDG
15 May 1991–1 December 1992: 13/18H (Amalgamated Hohne 1 December
   1992)

Germany Minor

Bielefeld – Ripon Bks
November 1950–July 1953: 3H

Brühl
July 1945–April 1946: RHG (Reconstituted from 1 and 2HCR wef 17 July 1945.
Camp H/O to Belgians)

Brunswick
18 October 1945–11 April 1946: 13/18H (RHQ Woltingrode, A and B Sqns
Vienenberg, C Sqn Bad Harzburg)

Celle – Taunton Bks – BFPO 23
?–March 1969: 5DG?

Deilinghofen/Hemer – Peninsular Bks – BFPO 24
February 1988–June 1992: 3RTR

Delmenhorst
2 April 1947–February 1948: 11H

Eutin
November 1945–June 1946: Royals

Flensburg (Hereford Bks)
11 February 1946–7 February 1948: 3RTR

Friedrichstadt
28 May 1945–28 August 1945: 3RTR

Gifhorn
June 1946–September 1946: Royals (Squadrons at Bodenteich)

Goslar
July 1945–March 1946: LG (Reconstituted from 1 and 2HCR)

Hamburg Area
May 1945–August 1945: 1RTR

Hamm – Newcastle Bks
6 July 1946–*c*. September 1948: 5RTR

Hannover
20 May 1945–18 October 1945: 13/18H

Hildesheim – Tofrek
November 1984–September 1993: 1RTR (from RA)

Immendorf
11 April 1946–1 July 1946: 13/18H

Iserlohn – Epsom Bks – BFPO 24
Autumn 1948–17 July 1953: 10H
17 July 1953–September 1957: 3H

Itzehoe
13 August 1945–30 August 1945: 8H
18 March 1946–23 July 1946: 1RTR
17 October 1945–22 July 1946: 8H

Jever – Cardigan
17 April 1946–1 April 1947: 11H

Kappeln
c. 15 May 1945–10 September 1945: 15/19H

Lingen am Ems
22 July 1946–14 February 1948: 8H

Lübeck – Knightsbridge, Waldersee Bks
December 1945–*c.* June 1948: 10H (Via Soest, Werl and Menden from September 1945)
End March 1947–19 December 1947: 4H
6 August 1948–October 1949: 3H (B Sqn from March 1948)
13 October 1949–12 April 1951: 15/19H
13 April 1951–May 1951: B Sqn 15/19H (Last occupant)

Lüneburg – Alma, Wyvern, Cavalry Bks
July 1946–22 March 1952: Greys (Wyvern)
February 1946–June 1946: 14/20H (BNK probably Alma)
Early June 1946–July 1946: LG (BNK probably Alma)
September 1946?–April 1948: 2RTR (Cavalry)
1949–October 1951: 7H (Alma)
22 March 1952–23 October 58: 8H (Wyvern)

Menden – Northumberland Bks
April 1946–late 1948: RHG

Münster – Portsmouth Bks
January 1952–January 1956: 6RTR
5 March 1956–8 July 1957: 14/20H

Neumünster – McLeod Bks
22 November 1951–March 1953: 15/19H
April 1953–March 1956: KDG
April 1956–14 April 1958: 13/18H (B Sqn to Aden via UK 15 August 1957)

Rahlstedt – Adams Bks
13 April 1951–20 November 1951: 15/19H
21 November 1951–April 1953: KDG

Rendsburg – Kingsway Bks
c. May 1948–July 1948: 3H

Schleswig-Holstein (Brunsbüttel, Orsdorf, St Margarethen, Tonning)
May 1945–12 June 1945: 11H

Schleswig – Kitchener, Cavalry Bks
February 1946–April 1946: 3/4CLY
April 1947–end October 1947: 16/5L

Sennelager – Dempsey Bks – BFPO 16
30 November 2007–20 July 1915: QDG (H/O to 1 Med Regt)

Soltau – Bournemouth Bks
7 October 1946–December 1947: 7H

Süchteln
28 August 1945–early February 1946: 3RTR

Wesendorf – Combermere Bks (Sometimes called Dedelstorf)
Late September 1946–October 1947: Royals (X then A Sqn in Berlin until early September 1947)
Late 1948–12 November 1950: RHG
13 November 1950–28 March 1953: 11H
1 April 1953–3 May 1954: 15/19H
4 May 1954–December 1957: Royals

Wilster
Mid-1945–5 July 1946: 5RTR

Wuppertal – Anglesey Bks
June 1946–13 November 1947: 14/20H

Notes: BNK = Barracks Not Known
? = Date or unit not known/confirmed

Notes

Chapter 1

1. Nigel Hamilton, *Monty: The Field Marshal 1944–1976*, Sceptre, 1986, p. 628.
2. The main equipment used by the armoured car units for the next fifteen years was the Daimler Armoured Car, although some AEC heavy armoured cars, as well as American Staghounds also remained in service. The Saladin armoured car began to replace them from 1958.
3. With the AVRE alone being retained by the RE. The first RTR unit to be equipped with armoured cars – through necessity – was 2RTR, in Libya in 1959.
4. The Arms Plot was the plan that rotated RAC (and Infantry and RA) units around the various stations and garrisons across the world. It was a complicated document, and a single emergency somewhere in the world could and did unhinge the plot. Regimental journals are awash with tales of cancelled postings and short-notice moves, often involving re-equipping with unfamiliar vehicles. In many cases units in Germany were made to move to the UK and into an invariably awful transit camp for a few weeks or months before proceeding to a posting in the east. The Royal Dragoons commented in 1960 that, 'The manoeuvre of introducing a double move (caused by the enforced transit time in the UK) into what would appear to be a comparatively simple direct move is one which is beyond the comprehension of the regimental officer.'
5. Martel was a dissenting voice, and despite having had no active part in the field since 1942, continued to argue into the 1950s for the provision of tanks designed for specific roles.
6. The three 'Wings' each became Schools in their own right in July 1948.
7. Although never a formal policy, many regiments for the next three decades operated a system whereby a newly qualified troop leader would be employed initially as a loader/operator, then as the troop corporal, before becoming the de facto troop leader. This was particularly useful during the period of National Service.
8. This was a strange proposal, and one wonders whether the RASC leadership was even consulted. It seems to have come about because of the existing role of the RASC in transporting the bulk of the infantry in their troop-carrying companies, using lorries. Why the RAC should think that giving

the RASC a tracked vehicle role was sensible is hard to explain, other than it was desperate to shift the role elsewhere. There does not seem to have been any suggestion that maybe the infantry themselves should operate their own APCs. However, an RASC platoon of nineteen Ram Kangaroos was operated as part of the demonstration squadron at Warminster after the war until mid-1948, when the RAC took over the vehicles.

9. The proposal reflected the ratio between the cavalry and the RTR, which was at this time 2.5 : 1.

10. In November 1959 the RTR introduced a change of policy designed to make young officers identify more closely with one regiment. This was known as the 'Thirteen Year Policy', as the majority of officers were meant to spend their first thirteen years of service with one specific regiment.

11. Possibly the strangest and most unlikely attachment came when Major R. Sullivan RTR was posted as OC B Sqn LG from October 1982 until August 1983, then becoming the regimental 2IC until January 1985. Such a cross-posting would have been unthinkable in McCreery's day. Sullivan took a 'Montgomery' approach and wore both badges on his beret!

12. Overseas tours would, in due course, frequently exceed these. And the point about recruiting was well made – the RAC units posted abroad really struggled to recruit, partly *because* they were overseas and far away, and partly because of the lack of presence in the UK.

13. Hamilton, *Monty*, p. 671.

14. Not everyone welcomed the change, as the RTR's predecessors had been known as battalions since 16 November 1916. The cavalry terminology of troops and squadrons, vice sections and companies, had been in use since May 1940 and the RTR had managed to adopt that without imploding.

15. The 16/5L recorded an extreme example of a soldier serving in Calais, whose route to get him home for Python involved moving him – slowly – across Europe so that he could embark at Naples, his designated embarkation point, before being shipped to the UK via Gibraltar.

16. In another example, in October 1945 8th Hussars received a sudden influx of replacements from no less than six regiments that were in the process of being disbanded: 23H, 9RTR, 1FFY, 2FFY, 49ACR and 107RAC.

17. *The KDG Journal*, 1948–9, p. 11.

18. And not always to the original unit; many returned from leave to discover that their regiment had been moved or disbanded, and were sent to wherever the need was greatest.

19. The twenty-two-year period was based on an assumption that the majority would join aged 18, and by 40 would no longer be physically fit enough for further active service in a front-line combat unit.

20. At this point, regiments still employed their own mechanics and other specialists who were part of the regiment in every way. In early 1952 under a scheme called REME Phase II, these soldiers were given the option of

transferring to REME (initially still serving with their former regiment) or reverting to the RAC crewman roll.

21. But loyalties ran deep. John Fisher was posted from 3/4CLY to 13/18H after the end of the war. On his way home to be demobbed, he took off his 'white lanyard and all my hussar insignia, beret and collar badges, and dropped them out of the carriage window onto the track. I had a battledress blouse with all the titles and badges of the Sharpshooters at home, so if I were to wear uniform again, I would appear as a Sharpshooter once more. That was the regiment to which I really belonged.' John Fisher, *Sharpshooter Snapshots* (Portway, 1996), p. 187.

22. Possibly uniquely, 14/20H had converted their band into a Mortar Troop in 1941. In August 1944 three cavalry bands, 7th Hussars, 11th Hussars and 16/5 Lancers, were suddenly ordered to reform, probably in order to have military bands available to perform at victory parades!

23. 6RTR was the last as in transit out of Austria; 4RTR was the last unit posted to Italy to leave.

24. In 1958 most of the remaining tank regiments were converted to armoured cars. There is no doubt that the TA units preferred being on armoured cars rather than tanks, not only because the equipment was simpler to teach and easier to maintain, but also because of the greater training opportunities across the country.

25. For example, Tilshead, Castlemartin. Some had been POW camps and had not even been cleaned when the last prisoners left.

26. Archer, Comet, Churchill, M10, Charioteer etc.

27. And they did not keep their new tanks very long; after only just over two years with them, the SRY had theirs taken away in January 1961 and they became a recce regiment using Ferrets and Landrovers.

28. Divisional Anti-Tank Regiments RAC were formed in 1950, when the RA passed the anti-tank role, complete with its M10 'tank destroyers' and Valentine Archer SPGs of Second World War vintage, to the RAC. 10th Hussars was one of the regiments affected by this change, as they changed roles and vehicle types rapidly during 1950, with the regiment crewing Comets, then Centurions and finally the totally obsolete Archer SPGs (which they referred to as Valentines). The Yeomanry subsequently inherited them later in the decade. It must have been galling for some of the cavalry regiments, who had just successfully argued that they should only crew tanks or armoured cars, and never 'Funnies', to be given such a role.

29. 1956 saw a major reorganization of the RAC TA, which left only three regiments in the armoured role.

30. Northern Ireland was excluded from the Act.

31. In Germany in the 1980s I was told that it stood for 'New in Germany', which was simply an attempt to explain the term.

32. The other factor leading to the extension was Montgomery's desire to set an example to France and the Benelux countries.

33. *5th Royal Inniskilling Dragoon Guards Journal*, 1950, p. 75.

34. National Servicemen could state up to three choices of unit, but these were not guaranteed. There was no ceiling to promotion, but, due to time constraints, very few RAC conscripts were able to rise above lance corporal.

35. Accommodation improved eventually; Alma and Cambrai barracks were modernized at the cost of £1.2 million and re-opened in 1967, becoming the home of the RAC Training Regiment. However, in the mid-1950s, as so often happened, once money was allocated for a future rebuild, the system became loathe to carry out any but the most urgent repairs, causing already dreadful barracks to deteriorate even further.

36. It is accepted that the lowest NS wage did not equate to the average civilian wage, as NS pay was based on unskilled labour; however, average figures for the lower end of the civilian market are difficult to obtain.

37. For the non-commissioned ranks, for pay purposes, soldiers were placed into different Groups and Classes dependent on their cap badge and trade qualifications. Additionally, the system was made horribly complicated by a 'star' proficiency system, with up to seven stars being awarded in each rank. For example, a corporal with one star received 91*s.* per week, whereas the same rank holding seven stars would get 126*s.* In Group B Class 1 a sergeant would be paid 143*s.* 6*d.* per week, a warrant officer Class 2 (non RQMS) 178*s.* 6*d.*, and a warrant officer Class 1 192*s.* 6*d.* Tax-free bounties for extending ones service were also available, ranging from £40 to £100.

38. One regiment remained responsible for armoured car recruits until 1961, when the 4/7DG became the sole training regiment and the first to be responsible for the training of all RAC recruits regardless of role. The HCav, both of which were armoured car units, obtained recruits via 67th Trg Regt from summer 1951 until 1955, when they opted to carry out their own basic training at the Guards Depot, Pirbright followed by trade training in Windsor. By the mid-1970s basic military training only was carried out at Pirbright, after which the trainees were sent to Catterick if they were going to the armoured regiment in Germany, or Windsor if destined for the UK unit. The depot closed in 1993.

39. Demand dropped steadily. In 1958 the four training units turned out just over 4,700 trained recruits between them, the majority NS. In 1961 the 2 remaining training regiments produced 2,700, of whom only one-third were NS.

40. When 12th Lancers sailed for Malaya in August 1951, 35 per cent of the soldiers were National Servicemen straight out of training and who would therefore be able to spend sufficient time overseas before they were 'demobbed'.

41. The main RAC paid trades were all B Class trades, graded as BI (the highest), BII and BIII. BIV was used for non-tradesman for pay purposes,

and they were sometimes referred to as General Duty (GD) men. They joined their regiments after completing GMT at the training units, although it appears that a small number was so unsoldierly as to be posted despite not actually passing-off.

42. This would be a perpetual complaint over the decades, that the training regiments took less care than they should in ensuring quality rather than quantity, but it was unfair for a number of reasons, including pressures from above, lack of time and resources, and unrealistic expectations.

43. By 1957 there were only three main trades: Signaller AFV (also trained as a loader), Driver AFV and Gunner AFV.

44. Catterick also trained the volunteer regular soldiers alongside the NS conscripts; roughly 20 per cent of each intake was regular.

45. *5RIDG Journal Christmas*, 1950, pp. 64–6.

46. Some had their service extended beyond the two-year period, as time spent in military detention did not count.

47. In mid-1958 5RTR reported with obvious glee that, 'It has finally happened! A recently joined recruit, one Trooper Sergeant, possesses the privilege of the army number 23456789!' Unfortunately, this did not last very long as he was swiftly given a medical discharge!

48. Until 1955 Household Cavalry training took place at the armoured car training unit in Carlisle; in 1955 they departed and conducted their own training, the regiment stationed in Windsor being responsible for the task. From 1966 the fourteen weeks of recruit (but not trade) training was conducted at the Guards Division at Pirbright, through the Household Cavalry Training Squadron. A Junior Guardsman's company was also operated at Pirbright from 1958 until 15 August 1982, which included HCav recruits.

49. *5 RIDG Journal*, 1956.

50. When 3rd Carbs departed Catterick in mid-1960, they handed over responsibility for all tank training to the 4/7DG, who subsequently also took over armoured car training from 15/19H at Barnard Castle, thereby becoming the sole RAC Training Regiment. On the positive side, money was allocated to rebuild Cambrai Barracks as the home of the regiment, replacing the decrepit and appalling Second World War (and earlier) buildings, as well as new Married Quarters.

51. This did not mean that the role was quiet: at the end of two years in the job in 1972, QDG recorded that they had trained 2,138 recruits. In 1976, The Skins recorded 1569 adult recruits in their time.

52. Initially tuition at RMAS consisted of 3 terms, each of 5 months. Each intake, of which there were 2 per year, in January and August, had about 300 cadets.

53. *5DG Regimental Journal*.

54. During the Second World War a number of locations were used for WOSB. In 1949, Victoria College (now Leighton House) was selected as the new

permanent home for the Regular Commissions Board, RCB, where it remains to this day.

55. Richard Vinen, *National Service 1945–1963* (Penguin, 2014), p. 203.

56. The alternative to a pass was deferment AKA 'watch', or worse still, the dreaded RTU – Return to Unit.

57. Towards the end of National Service, in 1960 Mons OCTU and the other OCTU at Eaton Hall combined to form the Mons Officer Cadet School. Mons OCS was responsible for training all Short Service Officer Cadets and for those regulars joining as graduates, with a six-month course compared with two years at Sandhurst. Mons OCS was closed in 1972.

58. The proper term is pass-out, not pass-off. A potential recruit passed tests, medicals etc. in order to commence training (pass-in), and if one completed training successfully, one passed-out (of the training unit).

59. As another example, between August 1960 and July 1961, 13/18H received four NS officers, possibly their last, four SSC officers from Mons and two regular officers from Sandhurst.

60. The Emergency Reserve replaced the pre-war Supplementary Reserve.

61. RARO officers with particular skills, for example, yacht skippers or mountain leaders, were frequently used solely in the adventure training capacity, which benefited them and the units, but not the army as a whole.

62. In March 1999 the name was changed from SSLC to Gap Year Commission. SSLC candidates undertook four weeks of training at RMAS before spending the best part of a year at RD as a probationary second lieutenant, with gentle – sometimes less than gentle – pressure applied on those thought by the regiment to be suitable material for a full career. About one-third subsequently converted the commission to become mainstream officers. SSC commissions were for three years, extendable up to a maximum of eight. The Intermediate, or IRC, gave a guaranteed ten years of service, which could be extended up to sixteen, at which point service became pensionable, an important point as it encouraged many to stay until this had been reached. The RegC commission was applied for after a minimum of two years as IRC, and if granted this gave employment of thirty-four years from the date of commission, or to the age of 60.

63. This meant that many outstanding officers who had been commissioned from the ranks during the war and who had proved their worth in the field found themselves immediately disadvantaged in the peacetime army.

64. For those commissioning from the ranks, and who were aged 30 or over, the Late Entry (LE) Commission replaced the QM commission, with the newly commissioned officer being given the lowly starting rank of lieutenant. This was unnecessarily parsimonious and, in order to better reflect the experience of the newly minted officer, from about 1998 was changed so that the entry rank was captain.

Chapter 2

1. POWs were those who had surrendered directly to the Allies either as individuals or in small units during the war, whereas SEPs were those who had surrendered en masse due to the German High Command capitulation.

2. The winter of 1947/48 was savage, and regimental journals all comment on how just getting through the winter was the major preoccupation.

3. A list of the various locations and barracks is in Annex H.

4. German POWs still provided a source of free labour for the British in North Africa and the Middle East for a couple of years. As late as mid-1947 in Camp 45, Egypt, 4RTR recorded that they had been entertained by a German POW band!

5. It is not clear if alcohol was involved, but in August 1952 3rd Hussars reported that the regiment held 'the doubtful distinction of the supplying the only soldier known to have escaped from the BAOR military prison – you can't keep a 3rd Hussar down … or out!'

6. Although by no means all involved drinking, but the RAC regimental journals in the whole post-1945 period invariably contain details of at least two or three soldiers killed in road traffic incidents, both on and off duty. Over the period the RAC must have lost hundreds of servicemen and some dependants in vehicle-related accidents.

7. This situation still applied in some cases decades later – the author occupied such a married quarter in Fallingbostel in the mid-1990s. To be fair, it was both convenient and spacious.

8. Over time, the numbers increased: when The Skins moved from Catterick to Osnabrück in 1977 they took 270 families with them.

9. In some places caravans were used until more permanent 'pads' could be made available.

10. Married soldiers and their families were often collectively known as 'the pads'. With less imagination, single soldiers were 'the singlies'. Married soldiers living in barracks paid no food or accommodation charges and were called 'bean stealers'.

11. The transition from Corporals' Clubs into Messes seems to have gained impetus with the advent of the all-regular army in the early 1960s, with a new, more formal structure being modelled on the Sergeants' Mess. By the 1970s many RAC Corporals' Messes encouraged the wearing of mess dress on formal occasions, although as it was privately purchased it could not be made compulsory. The author purchased his in 1980 as a new lance corporal and despite one or two 'scrapes' whilst wearing it, it lasted until commissioning in 2000.

12. In the 1980s renamed the Service Children's Education Authority.

13. Kevin Shannon, *Death or Glory The 17th/21st Lancers 1922–1993* (Fonthill, 2021), p. 222.

14. In 1959 a number of military-run local civilian organizations involved in low-level security, transportation, labour provision and the like were brought together into the Mixed Services Organization (MSO), known to generations of soldiers as MoJos. As far as RAC soldiers were concerned, the main role of these personnel, many of them Polish soldiers from the Second World War who were unable to return home, was to drive the fleet of tank transporters that were used to move tanks and other AFVs around Germany, and to and from the sea ports of entry in the Netherlands. They achieved legendary status, scaring the wits out of young tank drivers who had to accompany them in the cabs of the Scammels and Antars as they hurtled around Germany, often swapping over drivers at 40mph.
15. *17/21L Journal*, 1963.
16. Form 443 was the BAOR form used to requisition private landing for training purposes.
17. *3H Journal*, 1957.
18. Currywurst, a staple of German Schnell Imbiss fast-food counters to this day, was in fact invented by the NAAFI to suit British tastes; the sauce was made from a mixture of mayonnaise, Worcester sauce and curry powder.
19. For both professional and pride reasons, regiments tried their best to do things better – or differently – to the rest. In 1964 3rd Hussars went to Hohne ranges for their annual firing, and recorded that, 'We are glad to be able to report that the regiment achieved some excellent results, including a successful battle-run closed down, a feat which some had thought impossible.' Although this is clearly a boast, such attitudes did contribute to higher standards, and commanding officers took a great deal of interest in what the other regiments – their rivals – were up to. On the other side of the coin, it also led to a lot of unnecessary bullshit, such as painting all the vehicles just before ranges, and an abundance of signs and minetape …
20. No one seemed sure of what the C in CIV really stood for; some units called it Commanders, other Central/Centralized and others Civilian. Most just referred to it as CIV and put up with it.
21. *3H Journal*, 1956.
22. Later the main inspection was the FFR, or Fit For Role, inspection which encompassed all of the separate inspections into one, usually the responsibility of the Brigade Commander, and on which so much depended for the future career of the Commanding Officer.
23. Harald Jahner, *Aftermath: Life in the Fallout of the Third Reich* (Penguin (Kindle edn), 2021). In Dresden, the last of the rubble was not cleared until 1977.
24. Richard Brett-Smith, *Berlin '45* (Greensleeves, 1966).
25. The famous Berlin urban camouflage scheme in white, grey and brown rectangles was designed by Major Clendon Daukes, commanding D Sqn 4/7DG in 1982.

Chapter 3

1. Centurion left RAC service in July 1974, although some remained with both the RA (about twenty, as OP tanks) and the RE (about 60, in various roles).
2. The Mark system of denoting variants was changed from Roman (I, II etc.) to Arabic (1, 2 etc.) numerals during the 1950s.
3. An early attempt to solve this led to the Monotrailer, a 200-gallon armoured trailer with a single wheel, towed behind the tank on approach marches and then jettisoned. The crews hated it.
4. Over 4,400 Centurions were built (about 2,500 for export), a remarkable number for a peacetime tank.
5. In 1956 the establishment was authorized to be nine Conquerors for each BAOR armoured regiment (with thirty-nine Centurions) and three for each UK-based armoured regiment.
6. The regular armoured car regiments were fully converted by 1960, with the TA units 'promised' twelve each in due course.
7. The Saladin (FV601), Saracen (FV603) and Stalwart all belonged to the same family. Saracen was trialled by B and C Sqns 13/18H in Malaya during late 1952 and early 1953, in place of the old GMC APCs.
8. Series I from 1948, Series II from 1958, Series III from 1971, diesel 90/110 from 1983.
9. The Webley .38 revolver started to be replaced by the Browning 9mm automatic pistol in about 1956. The replacement of pistols by the 9mm Sterling SMG required a new ceremonial drill to be devised in autumn 1959 to allow the carriage of the weapons on formal parades.
10. In 1949 a new, smarter version of BD was produced, with an open collar designed to be worn with a shirt and tie – a first for non-officers. Photographs from the 1950s are testament to just how smart BD could be when worn by RAC soldiers.
11. Early versions of these came in a variety of brown colours, but also featured the common elements that defined this most-British of uniform items – the shoulder and elbow patches. Eventually by the early 1970s the colour had changed to green. RAC regiments from the 1960s, starting with the officers and then gradually extending to the SNCOs and then other ranks, began to adopt a whole variety of regimentally coloured and styled jumpers, usually only worn in Barrack Dress. The RTR officially adopted their black jerseys in December 1978 for sergeants and above, with the use by junior ranks 'at the CO's discretion'.
12. Since then some units have adopted coloured patches behind the cap badges, different coloured bands and in some cases a different coloured beret entirely – the grey of The Greys and later SCOTS DG, the green of the QRIH (from 1979) and the QRH. On formation both the Royal

Hussars and KRH adopted variations of the 11H brown beret. In 1950 all the RTR regiments wore black lanyards except for 1RTR, who wore red. In 1954 the RTR adopted black 1937 Pattern web equipment in place of the blancoed variety used in the cavalry, and the following year a black Sam Browne belt and leather gloves were adopted by officers. Black coveralls or 'denims' do not seem to have been widely worn until about 1958. The widely ridiculed RTR officers Astrakhan No. 1 dress beret (or 'poodle') came into use on 1 January 1962 and passed out of service in January 1977, after a groundswell of negative opinion. The less showy but equally disliked soldier's version with regimental hackle was withdrawn in August 1978.

13. During National Service, in most regiments, only the regular officers were required to have the complete range of expensive officers' uniforms, although there is a strong suspicion that in order to join an exclusive cavalry regiment, one had to 'play the game' and in all probability most NS officers were indistinguishable from their regular counterparts.

14. During the 1950s, when stationed in the Middle and Far East, SNCOs and WOs would have white mess dress jackets made locally, worn with a cummerbund and No. 1 dress trousers; these pre-dated the official adoption of mess dress when No. 1 Dress was withdrawn as standard issue for senior ranks.

15. The term Guidon comes from the French *guide hommes*. The average life of these expensive hand-made items is assessed to be twenty-five years, more, one suspects, to allow each generation a chance to take part in a big regimental parade than because they are worn out.

16. Other vehicles were much slower to be replaced – 11th Hussars REME was still operating Second World War-era US half-tracks in 1966 even as they were receiving deliveries of the first batch of production Chieftains.

17. Stalwart was brought into service due to the failure to get funding for a fully tracked logistic support vehicle based on the 432 chassis, the FV431.

18. It is my supposition that the issue of the new uniform was deliberately delayed until the end of National Service, for reasons of cost.

19. DMS stood for Direct Moulded Sole, but old sweats would swear that it stood for 'Dem's My Shoes'.

20. JLR RAC was still issuing black 1937 Pattern web equipment when the author served there between 1976 and 1977.

21. With the introduction of Service Dress (No. 2) for ORs, The Skins took the opportunity to put their soldiers into green trousers, and 11th Hussars did likewise with crimson. Following amalgamations, at the time of writing, the RDG wear green trousers and the KDG crimson. The dark-green polyester Barrack Dress trousers were not introduced until 1975.

22. Within the RTR, a new 'cavalry style' officer's mess dress was introduced in 1972, at which point the WOs and SNCOs adopted the previous officer's pattern as their own.

23. As CIGS from mid-1946, Field Marshal Montgomery had tried to improve the life of single soldiers in camps, and as a result fought a bitter battle with the WO financiers who were loath to spend money on quality of life initiatives. Monty argued that surely it was not right that adults had to switch their lights out in their barrack rooms at a certain time, and that they should be provided with an individual reading lamp. He eventually won, but it took many years for this to become widespread, as well as the issue of a personal locker, and a small scrap of carpet to act as a bedside mat in a soulless, linoleum-floored barrack room.

24. A great friend of mine, Charlie Wilde, when commanding Chieftain, always made his gunner wear the jacket, as he used the hood as a convenient receptacle for his chinagraph pencils, plus his cigarettes!

25. The final NS men with an obligation to join the TA as part of their service joined the territorials in 1965/66, after which the Yeomanry had to recruit all their manpower themselves.

26. The first production Scorpion was completed in January 1972. The Saladin (or 'Sally Can') remained in service with the TA – and with the regular armoured reconnaissance squadron in Cyprus – until the early 1990s before being finally withdrawn.

27. Scimitar was originally conceived as the vehicle to be used by armoured regiment (and mechanized infantry) reconnaissance troops. The Rarden cannon was mounted in order to allow them to deal with enemy light armoured vehicles, especially APCs. Spartan was designed for the Recce Regts' Assault Tps and was sometimes used to carry the ZB298 ground radar by Surveillance troops. Another variant with a lengthened chassis with a sixth roadwheel station, the Stormer, was later introduced but not within the RAC.

28. About 130 surplus Fox turrets were reused when the vehicle went out of service and matched with Scorpion hulls, as in 1992 it was decided to withdraw Scorpion from service due to armament toxicity problems. The resultant vehicle was introduced in about 1994 and renamed Sabre. Other Fox turrets were mounted on FV432 hulls to produce the so-called FV4330, used by some infantry battalions.

29. A turbo-diesel version, the Bedford MJ, was introduced from 1981, and about a decade later the Leyland DAF 4-tonner came into service.

30. During Op Burberry in 1977/78, RAC crews were deployed in ancient Green Goddess fire engines when the Fire Service went on strike. The crews were equipped with shiny black oilskin two-piece suits, wellington boots and RAC steel helmets painted in various colours denoting their status and role.

Chapter 4

1. 3rd Carbs had left in January bound for the UK, having spent the entire Second World War period in the Far East.

2. 17th/21st Lancers left Salonika in February 1947 where they operated a mix of vehicles: Sherman tanks, White scout cars and Staghound armoured cars. On arrival in Egypt they were reorganized as a Daimler armoured car regiment in order to be sent to Palestine. As the regimental journal recorded, 'It is with great pleasure we have received a complete refit of new or fully reconditioned vehicles – a great contrast to the junk we had in Greece.'

3. C Squadron 12th Lancers (and later B Squadron 17th/21st Lancers) had some of their old Marmon-Herrington vehicles joined back to back and adapted to run on the railway tracks; they were later replaced by Dingos. Terrorists would frequently try to derail these vehicles by placing stones or iron bars on the line, as well as mines and improvised explosive devices.

4. Jeremy Bastin, *The History of the 15th/19th The King's Royal Hussars 1945–1980* (Keats House, 1981), p. 28.

5. Ibid., p. 35.

6. Gregory Blaxland, *The Regiments Depart; History of the British Army 1945–1970* (Kimber, 1971), p. 43.

7. Ibid., p. 53.

8. Ibid., p. 56.

9. The Canal Zone was the name given to the British military area on the western bank of the Suze Canal, from Port Said in the north to Suez in the south.

10. The canal itself was the property of Egypt, but the company that operated it was multinational, mainly British and French. Under the 1954 Anglo-Egyptian Agreement the company would become Egyptian but not until 1968.

11. RAC Records made a major error in not realizing that the Centurion required 4 crewmen, not 5, and called up about 170 too many men. Rather than admit to the cock-up, all the reservists were deployed at the expense of trained regular and NS soldiers who had to remain in the UK.

12. As feared, King Idris forbade the use of troops from Libya to be used against an Arab neighbour.

13. The .30 in Browning was introduced to replace the outdated 7.92mm BESA in 1955, making the tank the Mk 5. B Sqn 1RTR, the demonstration squadron at Warminster, was the only sub-unit that had had issues with the Mk 5 when the Suez Crisis struck.

14. The Brigadier RAC in 3rd Infantry Division later commented that, 'In BAOR a whole year of concentrated training is required to train an

armoured regiment in an NS army, yet in the UK, where units are understrength, posted with ineligibles for overseas, and woefully short of stores and equipment, they are expected to spread themselves all over the countryside providing training facilities for the TA, and yet go to war, fit to fight, as part of the strategic Reserve at short notice. The whole system is nonsense!'

15. Why this change happened is a mystery. Everyone knew that 1RTR had priority, and when they were allocated range time, 6RTR took whatever spare time was available. There was also a requirement to train the crews on APDS ammunition, with which they were unfamiliar, in response to the perceived protection of the Russian-built JS3 tanks.

16. The original name was going to be Hamilcar, leading to large white letter Hs being painted onto vehicles as a recognition symbol.

17. One report states that some of the LVTs carried improvised armour in the form of track links or timber sleepers.

18. The small unit left Egypt at the very end of November, arriving back in the UK on 18 December. It then took Berry (soon to be awarded a Mention in Dispatches) and his men about ten weeks to hand their equipment back into 'the system', despite the fact that it had been able to be issued in the space of 12 hours in August.

19. 3PARA managed to capture some of the latter when they appeared, one of which is now a resident of the Bovington Tank Museum.

20. 1RTR never did make it, being disembarked in Malta where they waited until being returned to the UK. Back in the UK two other armoured regiments were in various stages of preparation but these were stood down. The Life Guards had an equally frustrating time, with, if the story is to be believed, their officer's mess truck being the only component of the regiment to be landed at Port Said, and this by mistake.

21. Kenneth Macksey, *The Tanks Volume 3 (RTR)* (Arms & Armour Press, 1979), p. 134.

22. Ibid., p. 136. For those who do not recognize the reference, look up the War of Jenkin's Ear. Jachnik's tank was also struck when he was strafed by aircraft in what was presumably a friendly-fire incident, with 20mm cannon shells penetrating the bazooka plates and lodging in the hull side armour.

23. Blaxland, *Regiments Depart*, pp. 254–7.

24. Much of the detail here comes from Captain Hugh Leach's unpublished and very detailed account deposited in the Tank Museum archives; he had been the troop leader in 11 Tp C sqn 6RTR.

25. In 1941 Malaya was producing 70 per cent of the world's rubber and 66 per cent of its tin.

26. Some RAC units were stationed in Singapore during the 1950s and 1960s, either as part of their acclimatisation before deploying 'up-country' into Malaya, or as an independent armoured car squadron. Some of these were used in Internal Security duties to deal with the sporadic outbreaks of violence in the city-state, linked to the Malayan Emergency. Singapore acquired independence in 1965.

27. Fortunately, a lack of weapons handicapped the terrorists throughout, becoming more acute as the Emergency went on and limiting the number and scale of attacks. As Communist China was immersed in the Korean War, none were forthcoming from there, and so the bandits relied upon the weapons that they had not handed in in 1945, and others that they could steal from the Security Forces.

28. Developed from the Otter Light Reconnaissance Car, the GMCs were originally built as armoured load carriers or ambulances. The 4x4 configuration gave adequate mobility for movement on roads and tracks, and although the vehicle only carried a maximum of 14mm of armour, this was sufficient to make it proof from small-arms fire – the bandits did not possess anti-tank weapons. It did however have an open-topped design, a major disadvantage in ambushes, as many roads ran through cuttings.

29. During the tour another four DCMs and an MM were also awarded. Robin Rhoderick-Jones, *In Peace & War (QRH)* (Pen & Sword, 2018), p. 78.

30. As C Squadron 12th Lancers had done in Palestine, some of the Hussars vehicles were modified to allow them to run on railway tracks, allowing the lines, a favourite target of the bandits, to be patrolled.

31. The ambush happened on the first day of 12th Lancers' deployment – probably a coincidence.

32. Another notable casualty was sustained by the Hussars when their RSM, 'Busty' Read MBE, was killed in an accident.

33. *4H Journal.*

34. From May 1957, the reduction in threat meant that the withdrawal of 15th/19th Hussars left the King's Dragoon Guards as the sole British armoured car regiment in Malaya, although the formation of the Federation Armoured Car Regiment lifted some of the burden from them. The RAC units did, however, have to train them first, another dissipation of scarce resources.

35. Although The Blues may run them close with their tour of Cyprus from February 1956 until May 1959.

36. In terms of soldiers, 108 were killed in 1951, 77 in 1952 and 34 in 1953.

37. *12th Lancers Journal,* 1952.

38. As impressive as this is, during an earlier tour 13th/18th Hussars claimed to have passed the 3 million mile mark at the end of January 1953.

39. At the end of the decade 1RTR managed, finally, to get permission to set up an AP and HE main armament range in Hong Kong, although through necessity the arcs of fire from left to right were very narrow – they reported it as being only five sighting screens wide!

40. Confirmed kills for RAC units were frustratingly rare. When Corporal Hearnden 12th Lancers killed a bandit with his Sten gun, the immediate reaction of RHQ was to discount it, and assumed that he had accidentally killed an innocent rubber tapper – thereafter, C Squadron referred to it as 'our bandit'.

41. In truth, the operation was very much a Commonwealth affair, with troops from Australia, New Zealand and Fiji amongst others.

42. Because of its longevity which matched almost exactly the use of National Service, the Malayan campaign was largely conducted by National Servicemen – in many ways it was 'their' campaign.

43. J.N.P. Watson, *The Story of the Blues & Royals* (Leo Cooper, 1993), p. 146.

44. One of the major reasons for denying tanks to the ROK was for fear that they might be used aggressively against the North; the possibility of using them defensively to counter North-Korean aggression seems to have escaped the planners.

45. Max Hastings, *The Korean War* (Pan, 1987), p. 47.

46. An 'infantry brigade minus' from 27th Infantry Brigade in Hong Kong was despatched at the end of August 1950, and the two battalions became the first British army forces to become engaged in Korea on 12 September. They lacked heavy firepower and had no British armour in support and consequently referred to themselves as the 'Woolworths Brigade'. In April 1951 it was renumbered to become 28th Commonwealth Infantry Brigade.

47. Hastings, *Korean War*, p. 94.

48. As an example, Michael Colston served with the 17/21L as a National Service second lieutenant, but was seconded to join 1RTR in Korea – almost certainly as a volunteer. In one notable incident he was hosting American guests and one of his crew was in the turret of the Centurion preparing breakfast. The tank was hit by an artillery shell and although no one was injured, the eggs were splattered all over the turret. With commendable sangfroid, the soldier calmly stated that the breakfast eggs would have to be served scrambled. *Daily Telegraph*, Obituary, 20 May 2021.

49. They generally kept one troop in reserve configured as Crocodiles, with the fuel trailers for the remainder kept in storage.

50. Hastings, *Korean War*, p. 95.

51. Blaxland, *Regiments Depart*, p. 157.

52. Such track problems were endemic in Korea, and a method was developed using plastic explosive to blow off thrown tracks. During 1952 an over-enthusiastic Corporal Peacocke of The Skins used too much and managed

to blow off his idler wheel which landed near the CO some distance away. He was 'reduced to the ranks within an hour'. C.J. Boardman, *Tracks in Korea (5DG)* (Shore Books, 2013), p. 78.

53. The Chinese seemed to know only two types of advance: the full-blown massed 'human-wave' attack, accompanied with bugles and gongs (designed to frighten the enemy), or a skilful infiltration using expert fieldcraft.

54. Typically for OP tanks, these had the 75mm guns removed and replaced by dummy wooden barrels, and thus were armed only with BESA machine guns.

55. There is a third option, which is that the tanks were used simply because they were all that were available, the Centurions being much further south.

56. Hastings, *Korean War*, pp. 200–1.

57. Sergeant Jack Cadman found that he had a Chinese soldier clinging to the outside of his tank; to rid himself of this dangerous distraction he ordered his driver to crash through a nearby house.

58. Blaxland, *Regiments Depart*, p. 177.

59. Ibid., pp. 179–80.

60. During 1951 realistic dummy Centurions were constructed by the RE in certain positions. *The 5DG Journal*, November 1953, p. 234.

61. The word comes from Assam in India, and means a shelter; although employed in Burma during the Second World War, its use seems to have become widespread during the Korean War and remains popular today.

62. C Sqn 7RTR was withdrawn, departing on 8 October 1951 and not replaced.

63. Blaxland, *Regiments Depart*, p. 196.

64. *The Crossbelts Journal*, 1951/52, Foreword.

65. The Skins Recce Troop operated three Daimler Armoured Cars and a number of Scout Cars, used to provide a courier and liaison service behind the front line. Later in the tour the DACs were replaced with additional Scout Cars.

66. *5DG Regimental Journal.*

67. Sergeant N. Wykes (5RTR), Lance Corporal D. Metcalfe (9th Lancers) and Troopers P. McFadyen and J. Cahill. The RAC Memorial in Bovington records Metcalfe twice.

68. In September 1951 the complete Sherman-equipped squadron of the Canadian Lord Strathcona's Horse was formally placed under the operational command of the regiment.

69. The fourth Skins operation, Maindy, took place on 23 June, and was an infantry operation requiring fire support from A Squadron.

70. The use of searchlights mounted on tanks had been considered before, but it was not until 1960 that a design was developed for Centurion, with a 22in light mounted onto the mantlet.

71. *5DG Regimental Journal.*
72. Despite the ceasefire there was no subsequent peace treaty and the South Korean president refused to sign; legally, the war has never been formally ended.
73. Cyprus is nestled close to the southern Turkish coast, which is only 50 miles away, and therefore despite being in the minority, the Turkish inhabitants looked to the mainland for support in their struggles with the Greek majority.
74. *Enosis*, meaning Union, was not unique to Cyprus, but was part of the larger 'Megali Idea', which strove for the unification of all of the historically linked Greek lands under foreign control. As a direct counter to the concept of Enosis, the Turkish community called for *Taksim*, the patronizing of the island to separate the warring communities.
75. Britain had in fact volunteered to cede the island to Greece in 1915 in return for Greek participation on the Serbian side against Turkey, but the offer was refused.
76. The National Organization for Cypriot Fighters.
77. Blaxland, *Regiments Depart*, p. 296.
78. EOKA only ever numbered a few hundred active terrorists, and struggled to make effective weapons to supplement the restricted supply it had of modern rifles and machine guns, forcing it to rely on pistols and stolen shotguns, plus weapons taken from raids on supply depots and armouries, and explosives and detonators from mining companies. It is fortunate indeed that many of its explosive devices failed to function correctly, otherwise casualties amongst service dependants would have been much higher.
79. 371 British servicemen died during the Emergency, of which an estimated 274 came from the army. Not all of these were killed 'in action', as the figures include those who died in accidents and from other causes.
80. EOKA used riots in major towns to pin down troops, giving them more freedom of action in rural areas. Riot control using tear gas, batons and shields – the original versions being dustbin lids – became the norm for the British soldiers, and presaged the Northern Ireland experience of a decade later.
81. There are some reports that 11 (Field) Sqn RAF Regiment rescued some Humber armoured cars from a firing range and used them in their patrols.
82. The island had been divided into three Brigade Group areas, and one squadron was deployed in each.
83. It is Household Cavalry tradition that their attached doctors are referred to as surgeons.
84. EOKA even came close to destroying a chartered Hermes airliner in early 1956; luckily take-off was delayed and the device exploded just as the passengers were about to board.

85. Watson, *Story of the Blues & Royals*, pp. 107–8.

86. Blaxland, *Regiments Depart*, p. 317.

87. Watson, *Story of the Blues & Royals*, pp. 109–11. A slightly different version has both casualties killed by accidental ricochets fired as warning shots, although The Blues believed the stone had fallen from a balcony hit by MG fire.

88. From July 1957 a squadron of Centurion tanks from 6RTR in Libya was detached to Dhekelia to form a strategic reserve based on the island, although invariably the soldiers became involved in the internal security operations, guarding vulnerable points and the like. Rotating through on a three-monthly basis, it was not a popular task. During their time on the island during autumn 1956, Warrant Officer Class 2 Martin of 6RTR was killed by a mine.

89. A number of 'retained sites' was also held, including the small RAF station on Mount Olympus, the Cape Greco site, and access to firing ranges at Pyla and Akamas.

90. 12th Lancers was required to move back to the UK for amalgamation, and the move could not be delayed.

91. Nick van der Bijl, *The Cyprus Emergency* (Pen & Sword, 2010), p. 214.

92. There are notable discrepancies between the names/spellings of the dead reported in the regimental journal and those names inscribed on the RAC Memorial at Bovington.

93. When the army took charge of Aden from the RAF in 1957, they were taken under command, and later, in November 1961, became the Federal Regular Army, or FRA.

94. At some points the amount of overstretch caused by sudden emergency deployments even threatened the Trooping of the Colour ceremony to mark the queen's official birthday.

95. Bastin, *History of the15th/19th*, p. 79.

96. For unclear political reasons, the Squadron Leader had to remain at Mukalla, hence Murray, a future CO of the regiment, getting all the interesting tasks.

97. Bastin, *History of the15th/19th*, pp. 77–83.

98. An airportable armoured car squadron consisted only of Ferrets, and had none of the heavier Saladins or Saracens.

99. Helicopter medevac was a lifesaver in the desert wastes. In the mid-1960s, 4th/7th Dragoon Guards was able to use one of their own Air Squadron's helicopters to transfer Lance Corporal Wilkinson and Trooper Kitching to hospital following a mine strike which destroyed their Ferret, a journey of 30 minutes by air but which would have taken about 5 hours over bumpy roads.

100. Eric Hunt, *The 13th/18th Royal Hussars* (Light Dragoons CT, 1996), pp. 111–25.

101. The TOS were routinely officered by RAC subalterns and majors, as well as NCOs, on detachment.
102. This point had been made at the 1958 RAC Conference – possibly following manoeuvring by certain cavalry regiments to secure for themselves armoured car roles – when it was stated in the minutes that 'over the years the cavalry have not all been light cavalry, nor must we forget that the Royal Tank Corps had armoured car companies before the war'.
103. The word 'Golly' came into use when the pejorative 'Wog' was banned; Golly shops were to be found in Cyprus and Northern Ireland over the next decades, referring to those private establishments, separate from NAAFI, that were set up within camps and generally run by West Asian traders.
104. Robin Brockbank, *A Short History of the 9th/12th Lancers 1960–1985* (9/12L, 1985), pp. 33–42. The British military has always been both slow and parsimonious in the issuing of campaign medals, and this is just one more instance of a bizarre policy which seemed to relish in not awarding justified medals.
105. The regiments were: QOH, 3rd Carabiniers, 17/21L, The Greys, 16/5L, 5DG, 1RTR. From late 1962 the tank regiment stationed in Aden had one of its squadrons detached in Hong Kong, and a second squadron was often maintained afloat in the Gulf or in Bahrain, as a strategic reserve force.
106. C Sqn replaced A at the end of August, in order to both spread the load in a 'hard and often very dull' deployment, as well as to make the most of the training opportunities.
107. A British Military Mission – training team – including a substantial RAC element was stationed in Kuwait and was still there when Saddam Hussein's forces invaded in 1990.
108. This is a microcosm of claims made in many regimental histories, in which units state that they 'have the most Second World War battle honours', 'completed more NI tours than anyone else' or are 'widely regarded as the best regiment in the RAC', and suchlike. Most claims do not stand up to rigorous historical investigation, and whilst they reflect pride in one's regiment, all too often become accepted at face value and prove divisive.
109. On 11 May 1964 HQ 39th Infantry Brigade was redeployed from Northern Ireland under command of Brigadier Cecil 'Monkey' Blacker of The Skins in order to command the Radfan operation.
110. James Lunt, *Scarlet Lancers (16/5L)* (Leo Cooper, 1993), pp. 189–98.
111. Over the years many immigrants had settled in Aden, and approximately one-third of the inhabitants of Aden were of Yemeni origin, with tribal links to their homeland.

112. Using an anti-tank mine designed to disable a battle tank against a 4-ton scout car would clearly have serious consequences for the crew. The driver in particular could be injured or killed not only by any blast penetration of the car's floor, but also by contact with the interior of the vehicle as it was violently accelerated into the air and then came back to earth. In this case both crewmen were injured, Sam Puckerin losing a leg.

113. Instructions to Servicemen employed on Guard Duties, Internal Security, and Duties in Aid of the Civil power in Aden State.

114. Blaxland described the town as affording 'easy access for infiltrators from the Yemen and a maze of shacks and closely huddled houses from which to toss grenades at the up-country traffic ... which had to pass through this ramshackle township', *Regiments Depart*, p. 448. It included a junction nicknamed 'Grenade corner'.

115. Bomb and grenade throwers, known as Cairo Grenadiers, were a particular threat and both rocket launchers and mortars were also extensively used. It was noted that the first attacks in the city were often amateurish, but over time the enemy became much more practiced and therefore deadly.

116. Michael Mann, *The Regimental History of the 1st The Queen's Dragoon Guards* (QDG, 1993), pp. 495–501.

117. During March 1961 a troop of five Centurions and an ARV of 17/21L was moved from Hong Kong to Kota Belud in Borneo, an epic journey of 1,200 miles by LST in order to set up a training area, where it remained for five months. This was the first RAC deployment to the island, albeit in a non-operational role.

118. *QRIH Journal.*

119. Ibid.

120. Consternation was caused when, despite the seriousness of the situation, orders were received not to fire 76mm and for machine guns to only fire single shots, an impossibility.

121. *Tank Journal.*

122. Macksey, *The Tanks Volume 3*, pp. 200–2.

123. Mann, *Regimental History of the 1st The Queen's Dragoon Guards*, pp. 493–4.

124. 1RTR was the final unit to serve on the fleet of venerable Comets, many of which had seen action in Germany in 1945, finally striking their last one off strength on 20 August 1959, receiving Centurions in their stead.

125. 17/21L was under the impression that they were going to be posted to Tidworth in 1960, until the QM starting receiving letters from Chinese and Pakistani traders in the colony, welcoming them and offering their services; shortly afterwards, the War Office confirmed that this was indeed so, and the regiment moved there in April.

126. The War Reserve of Centurion tanks was kept in the colony after the armoured squadron had departed, and a few lucky regiments had squadrons flown over there in the years to come, in order to bring the tanks out of storage, fire the guns on ranges, conduct a short exercise and then enjoy the mysteries of the East – many regimental journals record that most soldiers easily spent all their money – and more besides – but wisely chose to refrain from specifying exactly on what.

Chapter 5

1. The first RTR plan included the amalgamation of 4RTR with 7RTR, forming a unit called 4/7RTR, but it was realized that this might be confused with 4/7DG, and so it was decided that with RTR amalgamations, the senior regiment would retain its number, and the junior regiment would not be recognized in the unit title.
2. On receipt of the news, 16/5L send the Ninth a message offering 'their warmest sympathies'. The Ninth responded with thanks, and noted that they were now 'joining the select club of Her Majesty's Married Lancers'.
3. My father, 22549815 WOII DJ Taylor, was one of the younger 9th Lancers sergeants disadvantaged in this way. He had been in the top-ten sergeants within 9th, but found himself much further down in the new regiment, and probably lost a couple of years of seniority had the regiment not amalgamated. He always believed that the regiment was not fully amalgamated until the first RSM was appointed who had been a 9th/12th Lancer for his whole career; this was in 1978.
4. The Household Cavalry remained resolutely on armoured cars until 1970 when the Life Guards began to convert to Chieftain. Thereafter, the BAOR regiment was on tanks, the Windsor regiment on reconnaissance vehicles, which massively complicated training as the units swapped over every three years on average.
5. Officers did not use the term Local, instead the prefix Temporary was employed. Amongst ORs, Acting and Local ranks were indicated by the prefixes A/ and L/. This has led to confusion ever since: LCpl is the correct abbreviation for (a substantive) lance corporal, whereas L/Cpl is the abbreviation for local corporal.
6. During the period of NS, many observers commented that the educational standard of the average regular recruit was generally below that of the average National Serviceman.
7. *The Feather & Carbine (3rd Carbs)*, April 1966.
8. This gave certain – generally articulate and photogenic – young soldiers some extra leave, during which they would assist their local recruiting office.

9. There was no three-year engagement at this time. The system was known as the 'Notice engagement', whereby a soldier could announce his intention to leave by giving the required amount of notice. Alternatively, if desperate to leave quicker, he could opt to 'buy himself out' using the Premature Voluntary Relief system, or PVR. In 1990 this system was abolished, and replaced by soldiers joining on 'open' engagements, receiving committal bonuses not as part of their daily rate of pay based on the promise of future service, but by being given a lump sum when they passed the five- and eight-year points without giving notice to leave. In the mid-1990s the daily rate of Pay (DROP) system was replaced by annual salaries, allowing soldiers to receive the same amount each calendar month, rather than a variable amount caused by the number of days in each month.

10. If serving in the UK, thirty days' paid leave per year was allowed, increasing to forty-two days if serving in BAOR.

11. Analysis at the time indicated that each year, about 350,000 young men became eligible to join the army. Of these, it was thought that 300,000 would never join, between 15,000 and 30,000 would join anyway, so therefore the recruiting effort was targeted at the 20–35,000 'float', those who needed persuasion.

12. This followed the findings of the Goldsmid committee, which recommended the change.

13. During 1988 HQ DRAC imposed a recruiting ban on 15/19H as they were up to strength; by the following year they were thirty men understrength and desperate to re-start recruiting.

14. In the event, it went to 2 RTR.

15. Two types of recruiters were used: Special Recruiters were in effect controlled by the Home Headquarters of each regiment, and only recruited for their cap badge. Regular Recruiters were found in the Army Careers Information Offices, and recruited for the whole army.

16. In part this was due to the efforts of the Cadet Training Teams that worked with the Army Cadet Force and Combined Cadet Force, and the Army Youth Teams, that worked in the community with schools, youth clubs etc.

17. The two Irish regiments constantly struggled to get enough recruits from Ulster particularly after the troubles began in August 1969, and so the QRIH were allocated Sussex and The Skins received Cheshire in 1973.

18. It was initially suggested that the amalgamation should be a purely Household Cavalry affair between the Life Guards and The Blues, but this was quickly quashed, probably with assistance from the Palace. The abbreviated title that the new regiment used was RHG/D. Tantalisingly, it appears that this was the result of a clerical error, as someone misread the intended title of RHG1D and the rest is history. Because of the need to retain trained men for the mounted component, the make-up of the new regiment

was, overall, 58 per cent Blues and 42 per cent Royals. Within the operational tank regiment however, the split was exactly fifty-fifty. On amalgamation it was often possible to guess origins by height, as The Blues had to be a minimum of 5ft 10in, therefore all shorter men were probably Royals.

19. Similar to the Training Regiment role in Catterick, being the RAC Centre Regiment was a thankless task; on formation, C Sqn QRIH found themselves with 156 staff to look after 186 vehicles.

20. The Royals were told of their amalgamation on 23 November 1967.

21. At a meeting of the sixteen cavalry colonels in October 1968, a ballot was taken. Eight voted for the amalgamation to be with The Skins, but as this was not unanimous it was taken to be non-binding. Had one more member voted for, it is likely that the Army Council would have been advised to amalgamate The Skins with The Greys.

22. But only since 1959.

23. In 1967 yet another round of TA reorganizations meant that for a time, the RAC would only have one Yeomanry regiment, the Royal Yeomanry. This had two armoured car squadrons, the RWY and SRY, and two air portable squadrons, the KCLY (formed 1961) and the NIH.

24. *The RAC Journal*, April 1960, p. 73.

Chapter 6

1. Green was used to denote an obstacle, using the British army method of map marking in which enemy forces are Red, and friendlies Blue, hence the term Blue on Blue.

2. The troop-contributing nations would change over time, with some withdrawing and others joining, but Britain has been a constant presence.

3. *4/7DG Journal*.

4. 1 Troop were the stay-behind force, and they were tasked to guard the RAF married quarters, causing them to ask 'Where did the RAF go?' Although equipped with the Mk5 Ferret, their GW training had not been completed and the troop had not yet been able to fire any practice missiles!

5. He was crammed into a Ferret, *sans* hat, and driven to a safe location by Sergeant Paddy Pollin (REME).

6. Typically, the airborne soldiers of the squadron spent the time commenting on the quality of the airdrops!

7. Van der Bijl, *Cyprus Emergency*, pp. 209–10.

8. Ibid., p. 210.

9. In October they were replaced by C Squadron QRIH.

10. In 1964 the two Royals squadrons had experienced nearly three months of very active operations, but neither were deployed long enough to meet the medal criteria of ninety days.

11. Treated initially as a Turkish province, in November 1983 Ankara declared the unilateral formation of an independent – although mostly not recognized – Turkish Republic of Northern Cyprus, to widespread condemnation.

12. The author assumes that as the regiment was being referred to within the RAC as a 'non-operational regiment', giving The Skins a UN deployment was in part meant to counter such ill-judged criticism.

13. Historically, Ulster was made up of nine counties, but Cavan, Donegal and Monaghan all passed to the new republic in 1922.

14. The names used by the troops for the area were Northern Ireland, or Ulster or the Province; they were all used interchangeably and meant the same. Other, less-polite appellations were also in common parlance.

15. Humber Pig 1-ton armoured vehicles were also operated in the early days by the RAC, but as soon as could be arranged, the RCT took over the driving of fleets of these and Saracens, particularly in Belfast.

16. Sophisticated Improvised Explosive Devices (IED) were used a lot in Northern Ireland, and became a particular feature of the border war, requiring the use of technology to help defeat them, as well as tactics and procedures by the troops on the ground. They would return in both Iraq and Afghanistan, where the British experience in countering them from Northern Ireland gave the army a slight advantage, at least initially.

17. *The Eagle and Carbine*, 2021, p. 124. It was impossible to be certain about any casualties caused over the border, as follow-ups were not allowed and the IRA would not publicize their losses.

18. Lisanelly Barracks, just outside Omagh town, was initially occupied by an RAC regiment in January 1949, when the KDG took it over as a semi-derelict infantry training centre; an old RAF flying boat station at Castle Archdale was used as a satellite location housing one detached squadron. Although it was occasionally occupied by RA units, other RAC regiments stationed in the barracks before the start of the Troubles were 15/19H, 11H, 9/12L, 2RTR, QDG and 4/7DG. Four of these would return to the station during the Troubles. The camp was vacated in 2007 and redeveloped into a housing area.

19. Searches for weapons, explosives and ammunition became increasingly seen as a metric for measuring success, by denying the terrorists access to them and obtaining forensic evidence that could lead to convictions. Search teams were formed from specially trained personnel using the so-called Winthrop technique.

20. Because of their recruiting areas, it was decided not to deploy either 5th Royal Inniskilling Dragoon Guards or the Queen's Royal Irish Hussars to the Province – the same restriction applied to the Irish Guards and

the Royal Irish Rangers. However, the ban was later lifted and in 1981 The Skins conducted a six-month-long regimental tour of Fermanagh. In late 1983 D Sqn QRIH conducted the regiment's sole NI tour as the PGF squadron.

21. By the mid-1970s the image of the typical RAC soldier in NI included a blackened cap badge, a DPM combat jacket with cuffs rolled up a couple of turns over a pair of faded lightweight trousers, Doc Martens, and – one of the delights of a tour – over-long hair and sideburns, and often a 'tour 'tache'. The polyester lightweights were banned when they were found to be dangerous when petrol bombs were in use, forcing the soldiers into full DPM combat suits.

22. *QDG Journal*.

23. Four soldiers of The Blues and Royals Mounted Squadron were killed by an IRA bomb in London in July 1982.

24. *The Blue and Royal (RHG/D)*.

25. Only sending one REME vehicle was an error, as the two troops were generally tasked separately and it could not be in two places at once …

26. This led to a near-miss; LCoH Dunkley's shed was bombed and hit after he had vacated it.

27. Fuel remained a problem, with the headquarters staff seemingly unable to understand the vehicle's requirements; at one point petrol was 'borrowed' from local farmers.

28. Lieutenant M.R. Coreth, 'The Falklands', *The Blue and Royal (RHG/D)*, 1983, pp. 26–30.

29. Ibid.

30. Unknown to the British, Argentinian commandos on Mount Harriet had observed the ship's movements and called in the aircraft.

31. Email from Harry Ford to author, January 2023.

32. Lieutenant M.R. Coreth, 'The Falklands', *The Blue and Royal (RHG/D)*, 1983, pp. 26–30.

33. John Frost, *2 Para Falklands* (Buchan & Enright, 1983), pp. 97–159.

34. Four troops came from C Squadron, the 5th troop being formed from personnel from the rest of the regiment.

35. As part of the equipment issue, members of the squadron were all issued with the brand new high-leg and 'very resilient combat boots'.

36. There had not been time to fit the Clansman radio harnesses in the UK, and so this task was required to be completed in Cyprus, which took five days.

37. *QDG Journal*, 1983, pp. 1038–47.

38. *QDG Journal*, 1983, pp. 1020–5.

39. *16/5L Journal*.

40. Ibid.

Chapter 7

1. *17/21L Journal.*
2. Previously, from 1941 when it was established it had been used as a German POW camp, and was subsequently used for chemical and mock-nuclear testing.
3. The Experimental Proving Ground of 295km² near the base and the Oil Access Area of 139km² in the north-west corner were only used for transit. To the east along the South Saskatchewan River was a 458km² National Wildlife Area.
4. The two main types were Salamander (Scorpion, representing T80) and Sturgeon (Spartan, representing BMP).
5. The TES system identifies when vehicles have been fired at and damaged or destroyed and also informs soldiers when they are being fired at and if hit what injuries they have sustained.
6. A Sqn 14/20H, followed by the remainder of the regiment, introduced the system from early 1980.
7. When 3RTR formed up as 7th Challenger Regiment in Hemer in early 1988, the pistols were issued but no holsters were available, meaning that the crewmen had to buy their own – the author favoured a rather natty black shoulder holster.
8. Moved on to Married Rate of LOA.
9. From 1986 the Windsor regiment was responsible for assisting with Op Trustee, security operations at Heathrow airport.
10. Fortunately (?) for the armoured regiments, the problems inherent in the plan were never put to the test, as the reductions announced in Options for Change in 1991 made the whole plan redundant.

Chapter 8

1. The rest of the Challenger fleet was stripped of spare parts and other items in order to ensure that the two regiments deploying had tanks in the best possible condition. This was exacerbated when the third regiment was deployed.
2. In order to fully equip them with Mk 3 Challengers, SCOTS DG took forty-eight (90 per cent) of their tanks from other units. The ships with the tanks sailed on 30 September, just over two weeks after the announcement.
3. Of course, this indicates just how parlous was the real state of the supposedly 'operational' regiments in BAOR, which were meant to be able to deploy to their battle positions in Germany to resist a Soviet invasion with just a few hours' notice …

4. Officially, due to the coalition context, within the MOD the formation was called 1st (BR) Armoured Division, although on the ground it was usually called 1st (UK) Armoured Division.

5. Dick Taylor, *Challenger 1 Main Battle Tank* (Haynes, 2015), p. 119.

6. The speed and night-fighting capabilities of Challenger meant that it was likely to be able to move much faster across the open desert than the CVR(T)s in the reconnaissance units, and that the standard 'reconnaissance by stealth' tactics would be inappropriate.

7. The only RAC death during the war was Lieutenant Edward Whitehead, 16/5L.

8. Official, *AC71520 Operation Desert Sabre* (MOD, 1993), pp. 5–5.

9. Ibid., pp. 6–5.

10. Taylor, *Challenger 1*, p. 125.

11. Shannon, *Death or Glory*, pp. 364–6.

12. Taylor, *Challenger 1*, p. 124.

13. I have used *AC71520 Operation Desert Sabre* extensively in the preparation of this section.

14. The so-called 'D-Day flash' is a typical example of regiments not really knowing their own history. The emblem was designed by Captain Goldsmid in 1940, originally as a helmet badge.

15. Of course, there were others who wanted to join the regiment purely to undertake ceremonial duties on horseback and who hated armour, but the structure meant that, aside from a few specialists like farriers or riding masters, this was not an option. This then meant than in a twenty-two-year full career, soldiers would be expected to have become proficient in three separate career streams: mounted, tanks and reconnaissance.

16. Previously, the individual regimental bands had been smaller, with only around twenty-two personnel.

17. This configuration was known as Type 44, reflecting the number of MBTs held. Over the years many other organizations came in and out of favour, based on the number of tanks in RHQ plus those in the sabre squadrons. Others used or looked at over the years included Type 63 (RHQ 3 + 4 sqns of 15), Type 62 (RHQ 2 + 4 sqns of 15), Type 58 (RHQ 2 + 4 sqns of 14), Type 57 (RHQ 1 + 4 sqns of 14), Type 56 (RHQ 2 + 3 sqns of 18), Type 50 (RHQ 2 + 3 sqns of 16), Type 43 (RHQ 1 + 3 sqns of 14) and Type 38 (RHQ 1 + 3 sqns of 12). Whatever the type, SHQs usually had either 2 or 3 tanks, and there were 3 or 4 sabre troops either of 3 or 4 tanks per squadron. You do the maths!

18. Dick Taylor, *Challenger 2 Main Battle Tank* (Haynes, 2018), Chapters 1 and 4.

19. Subsequently, for service in Afghanistan the Scimitar Mk 2 was introduced in mid-2011, mating the turret to an upgraded Spartan hull with increased

mine protection, and various bar armour (RPG protection), underbelly protection and applique armour systems were also fielded.

20. *The Delhi Spearman (9L, 9/12L)*, 1999, pp. 68–75.

21. Escorting UNHCR aid convoys began in early 1993; by October 1993, the aid lifted into the besieged capital city of Sarajevo exceeded the total supplied during the Berlin airlift.

22. Eventually, between May 1993 and March 2003, the regiment conducted fourteen squadron deployments to the country.

23. *The Light Dragoon*, April 1994, pp. 18–21.

24. The requirement to send two of the four full sabre squadrons (B and D) to Bosnia, with a third (A) training for the next roulement, meant that at one point C Sqn HCR consisted of only seventeen men, of whom seven were on courses or awaiting discharge. The policy of robbing Peter to pay Paul once again had consequences that were entirely predictable ... See *The Household Cavalry Journal*, 1994/95.

25. The final iteration of BRITCAVBAT before UNPROPFOR ended was made up of a grouping of RAC sub-units: RHQ 9/12L, HQ Sqn HCR and C Sqn QRL (which included two troops from 9/12L).

26. An MP stated in the House of Commons on 18 July 1996, 'I think that it was with relief that our British troops in UNPROFOR took off their blue berets and put on brown helmets. It then became clear to everyone that they meant business.', Hansard, Vol. 281, cc1314–40.

27. Trooper Aled Jones QDG died in July 1996 but not as a result of enemy action.

28. Hansard, Vol. 281, cc1314–40.

29. From June 1998 it was renamed Palatine.

30. Kosovo was not one of the six provinces that made up Yugoslavia; rather, it was an autonomous province within Serbia.

31. The author was the Force RSM. At the time, due to Greek objections, what is now referred to as Northern Macedonia was called the Former Yugoslav Republic of Macedonia, or FYROM.

32. It was not a very civilized time. Now serving as the senior watchkeeper in HQ 4th Armoured Brigade, the author was shocked to hear reports of atrocities happening inside the city of Pristina, including one from the Irish Guards reporting the discovery of a severed penis ...

33. And of course such reinforcements were required not only for the six-month deployment, but also for the pre-tour training, and were non-effective and would not return to the parent unit until their post-operational tour leave (POTL) was taken.

34. Recruiting however remained fairly strong. In 2000 the RAC was 96 per cent manned, compared to the RA at 94 per cent and the infantry at 92 per cent. Such success could come at a price, however, as overall the army

could – and did – put brakes on the RAC recruiting efforts in favour of the infantry.

35. 1st Division would have 4th, 7th and 20th Armoured Brigades, and 3rd Division 1st, 12th and 19th Mechanized Brigades.

36. The support provided by the Yeomanry, even when not actively involved on operations, was considerable. For example, in Training Year 99/00, the 4 units provided 21,640 man-days of support to the regular army.

37. Initial manpower was 244 army and 55 RAF. A Sqn 1RTR remained at Warminster on CR2 and CVR(T), allowing armoured skills to be maintained on a rotational basis.

38. This role had been assigned to the RY in October 1997, in order to provide biological warning of the RAF Tornado base in Kuwait, enforcing the Southern No-Fly Zone over Iraq. The RY were in effect the forerunners of JNBCR, between 1996 and 1999.

39. Because of the size of the task, much reinforcement was necessary, and as well as IRs from mobilized reserves, the unit received many men and women from 'Y' Sqn RY, a composite squadron formed from volunteers.

Chapter 9

1. A key document was the 'September dossier', detailing Britain's intelligence that was meant to confirm Iraqi attempts to acquire WMD; much of it has been since shown to be false. The dossier was meant to create a *casus belli*, and seems to have been an intentional attempt to mislead the British public and generate support for the war. In September 2002, Blair stated in Parliament that, 'Regime change in Iraq would be a wonderful thing [but] that is not the purpose of our action; our purpose is to disarm Iraq of weapons of mass destruction …'.

2. Ex Saif Sareea II, a desert training exercise took place in Oman in autumn 2001. Over sixty Challenger 2s from RDG were deployed, and despite a comprehensive lessons learned process highlighting myriad defines in the army's ability to conduct desert fighting, few were addressed and the RAC deployed to Kuwait needing many urgent modifications to 'desertize' its equipment. Additionally, very few of the RAC soldiers who took part in the exercise were – initially at least – deployed to Kuwait.

3. By April 2003 the American forces alone had deployed nearly 150,000 personnel into Kuwait and, subsequently, Iraq. Britain sent about 45,000.

4. Although some missiles were fired into Kuwait, there was no serious attempt made by the Iraqis to disrupt the Coalition build-up. This was in hindsight a mistake – until only a few days before the start of the ground war, many British troops had no body armour or desert clothing, and had only been issued five rounds of ammunition.

5. *The Household Cavalry Journal*, 2003/04, pp. 17–22. Major Taylor received the DSO, Finney the GC and Flynn the CGC.
6. Sergeant 'TC' Roberts was the first British fatality of the war. He was not wearing the body armour that might well have saved him, as there was not enough to go around and he had been ordered to hand his over so that the infantry had enough.
7. Major A.M. Britton, *The Tank*, December 2003, pp. 26–9.
8. Taylor, *Challenger 2*, Chapter 4.
9. WMIK – Weapons Mount Installation Kit, a modification to the Land Rover allowing it to be fitted with a variety of light weapons (but not armour).
10. Volunteers from the Yeomanry regiments continued to be a small but significant part of the RAC contribution to the campaigns in both Iraq and Afghanistan. In addition to manning the Cortez base-protection systems on Op Herrick between January 2009 and mid-2010, during 2009, the four Yeomanry regiments deployed 258 soldiers on operations, representing an average of 15 per cent of their strength.
11. I have deliberately called the regiment 'typical', not the tour. There was no such thing as a 'typical tour' for any of the regiments deployed, as the tasks, locations and experiences varied so widely. What was constant was the level of professionalism.
12. *The King's Royal Hussars Regimental Journal*, 2005, pp. 3–6.
13. As an extreme example of what this meant, in 2003 RDG left their station in Münster in BAOR in order to serve as firemen in the north of England.
14. Under RAF control in Strike Command. In 2000 DRAC was given 'preponderancy' for NBC/CBRN defence operations within the army, with a small staff forming in Bovington in October.
15. From 2004 CVR(T) operating in Iraq were given Mine Blast Protection (MBP) and Ballistic Protection (BP) kits to enhance crew survivability. This meant that the Scimitar/Sabre fleet ended up at many different levels of modifications, with No. 52 sights, Battle Group Thermal Imager (BGTI) and E-SPIRE/TNTLS all in use at the same time, complicating support and training.
16. D Sqn HCR used Milan missiles mounted on Spartan in 2006 in order to increase their firepower, leading to PJHQ staff asking questions as to whether the crews were correctly trained, and therefore 'safe', to operate the system … They fired thirty-seven of them, and the only one who thought the missiles to be unsafe was the Taliban.
17. Operating in the Green Zone meant that neither the usual DPM nor desert camouflage were suitable, so many units took to wearing half and half in an attempt to improve the effect of the camouflage when dismounted. MTP solved the problem.

18. Such squadrons were referred to as IMA, Interim Medium Armour. They remained in being until 2011 when they were deleted.

19. The concept of the LRT (later renamed as Specialist Monitoring Team) was created to support the operation, and equipped with such equipment – including much state-of-the-art and very expensive technology bought from industry – as could be carried in a couple of Pinzgauer vehicles. This concept worked well and allowed the LRTs to be added to the order of battle officially, and used to support rapid deployment forces, including Commando, Airborne and Special Forces on Operations Telic and Herrick.

20. At this point, the total British troops in Helmand was capped at 3,300. It was to grow… in early 2007 an additional infantry battlegroup was added, bringing in another 1,400 soldiers, and by October 2009 the authorized total was 9,000. Over the campaign, British forces operated out of a total of 137 different bases, from the immense Camp Bastion down to the early and discredited use of 'platoon houses'.

21. Taliban literally means 'students', and originally referred to the ultraconservative Muslims from Afghanistan who, under this name, violently opposed the democratic government that the West was trying to establish in the country. The phrase the 'ten-dollar Taliban' came to be used to describe the less-fervent masses who fought for daily pay, and which was often many times what they could expect to earn as farmers etc.

22. *The Household Cavalry Journal*, 2006/07, pp. 19–25.

23. https://www.theguardian.com/world/2006/nov/18/afghanistan. military.

24. Viking originally saw operational service in Afghanistan with the Royal Marines Armoured Support Group. Because the group belonged to 3 Commando Brigade, some armoured squadrons from the RAC were converted to operate Viking on those tours where an army brigade was in command. From October 2010 Viking was replaced by the larger Warthog, with D Sqn RDG taking over the new vehicles mid-tour.

25. *King's Royal Hussars Regimental Journal*, 2007, pp. 35–45.

26. *King's Royal Hussars Regimental Journal*, 2007, pp. 45–7.

27. *Washington Post*, 19 November 2010.

28. https://www.618tacc.amc.af.mil/News/Article-Display/Article/453096/air-force-c-17s-deliver-abrams-tanks-to-afghanistan/.

29. The Canadian army committed a squadron of Leopard C2 tanks to Kandahar province as early as September 2006, and the Danes followed with a strengthened platoon of Leopard 2A5 in Helmand, where they were fighting under British command, the following year.

30. A focus on 'body counts' was sometimes an unattractive feature of the campaign, and one which, in any case, was never a true indicator of success.

31. The squadron operated both CVR(T) tracked AFVs and Jackal and Coyote wheeled patrol vehicles.
32. *The RAC Newsletter*, Autumn 2008, p. 5.
33. *The Light Dragoons Journal*, 2012, p. 11.
34. With the end of Herrick, combat operations officially ceased, although a follow-on mission called Op Toral required significant although smaller numbers of troops, mainly in training and mentoring roles around Kabul.

Chapter 10

1. The latter was upped slightly to 35,000 by the 2015 review, although critics claimed that the figure could not be relied upon as skulduggery would be used to make the reserve appear more effective than it was in reality.
2. A fleet of 227 gave Britain, the inventor of the tank, the fifty-sixth largest tank fleet in the world, operating fewer tanks than for instance Italy or Greece.
3. During 2014 RDG converted from being a CR2 regiment to Armoured Cavalry, but also found the time to send short-term training teams (STT) to support the UN in the Democratic Republic of Congo, and A Squadron provided support to the Commonwealth Games in Glasgow.
4. Overall, in 2009 the RAC at Regimental Duty, for example, not including those serving outside the regiments, was 4,437.
5. The strength of the HCMR is 303 soldiers and 280 horses. These are made up of a Life Guards squadron of three troops, an identical Blues and Royals squadron and HQ squadron.
6. The whole issue of women in combat roles had been looked at periodically, and then kicked into the long grass; this was most recently done in 2001.
7. https://www.defence-and-security.com/features/featureuk-army-set-to-receive-148-next-gen-challenger-3-mbts-8732290/.
8. To be fair, modern 8x8 vehicles have exceptional mobility in most terrains, and have 'operational reach' – range – that tracked vehicles cannot match. They are also less complex in terms of both training and maintenance.
9. In 2010 DRAC wrote, 'The time for debate on FRES is past. CVR(T) needs to be replaced.'

In Conclusion

1. *RUSI Journal*, May 1930, p. 378.
2. Macksey, *The Tanks Volume 3*, p. 161.
3. *The DRAC Newsletter*, 2016.

4. This observation immediately led to strenuous efforts to rectify this, particularly for the roles that could be expected to spend much of their time in that environment, for example, Light and Armoured Cavalry.

5. *The RAC Newsletter*, Spring 2011, p. 1.

Annex A

1. Various improved carrier types were developed, including the Oxford and Cambridge carriers.

2. Other variants (not operated by the infantry) include the FV434 REME vehicle with a crane, the FV438 Swingfire ATGW launcher, the FV436 Royal Signals-operated fleet of specialist communication vehicles and RA operated surveillance radars and command vehicles. Much of the concept came directly from the earlier FV420 family of vehicles, which was to include the FV421 load-carrying vehicle and FV422 APC; none of the family entered service. The FV431, the load-carrying variant, did not enter service as its place was taken by the cheaper Stalwart. The use from 1983 by the infantry of the wheeled AT105 Saxon, a so-called APC that was nothing more than an armoured lorry, will not be discussed further here …

3. At least six of the latter were subsequently disarmed and converted into armoured ambulances for use in Afghanistan.

4. The Reconnaissance Platoons in both Mech and Armoured Infantry battalions were equipped with eight CVR(T) Scimitar vehicles.

5. Using the 'ecclesiastical' naming convention that started with the Bishop, and continued with the Priest and Sexton, the M44 was occasionally referred to in British service as the Cardinal.

6. By way of comparison, the older 25-pounder had a maximum range of just over 12km.

7. Reconnaissance regiments used the Samaritan variant of the CVR(T) series for their armoured ambulances.

Annex B

1. In 1916 the camp area at Bovington was only half this size.

2. The wooden name boards in Bovington record the use of the title during the Second World War. In 1947 *Tank Magazine* noted that the RAC Schools in Bovington had just been renamed as the RAC Centre, but this announcement seems to have been both a little premature and a little late.

3. There is a persistent story that the famous RAC Officers' Mess, known to all as the Bovington Hilton, was an off-the-shelf design based on a mess that had previously been built at Mill Hill in London. The story has it that it was agreed without much oversight, and this led to the construction of the only

(at that time) multi-storey building in Dorset, visible for miles around and largely thought of as an eyesore. It was badly damaged in an avoidable fire – which is a story in itself – in July 2016 and at the time of writing the damaged building had just been razed to the ground. Another associated story is that the mess swimming pool was not part of the project but was funded through selling-off the contents of the mess vintage wine and port cellar …

4. During the 1970s: in 1977 the role of providing the demo sqn passed to the regiment stationed in Tidworth.

5. Personnel serving within their parent regiments were termed to be RD, or Regimental Duties. Those outside were ERE. Some others were employed in unauthorized posts, often becoming general's drivers or placed on the extremely nebulous 'gardening leave'. This was termed as the Black Economy, and strenuous efforts were made in the twenty-first century to eradicate such posts.

6. Each of the three Schools had its own foibles. The Gunnery School was thought to generate the most bullshit of the three, and the red and yellow Instructor 'tabs' worn on the epaulettes were both prized by the owner and much mocked by lesser mortals; they became known as 'Kit-Kat wrappers'.

7. Armoured Car training was conducted at both Barnard Castle and Carlisle. At this point the training schools in Bovington/Lulworth had nothing to do with the initial trade training for the RAC, concerning themselves mainly with subsequent trade training courses such as BI (mechanic), Instructor, Crew Commander and some officers' courses.

8. Previously, an independent RAC Training Squadron had existed to look after such trainees.

9. The time taken depends largely on: whether the recruit arrives with a driving licence, how long it takes to acquire the required licence(s), the platform on which the recruit will serve and the ability of the individual.

10. The numbers going through depends on the intakes into the corps, and the manpower requirements of the corps. Some example output figures: 2009/10: 644; 2010/11: 354; 2011/12: 361; 2012/13: 350; 2013/14: 490.

11. Regiments still run the JNCO Cadre Course, for selecting and promoting to lance corporal.

12. There is also a technical JCC which has gunnery and D&M phases and allows the NCO to act as an emergency crew commander in the place of a fully qualified NCO or officer commander.

13. As a result of the frequent introduction of new vehicles into the inventory for service in Iraq and then Afghanistan, on 23 May 2011 a separate Crew Training School (CTS) was formed as part of ARMCEN and separate to the 'steady-state' D&M School. Although it had a staff of only two officers and fifteen instructors, its outputs were truly phenomenal and took a load off the units that were trying to prepare themselves for imminent operations in those countries. It closed when the operational need diminished.

14. At one point in the mid-1980s every single regimental sergeant major in the corps was an ex-Junior Leader.
15. By 1956 he was a sergeant.
16. Until JLR RAC was created, a trainee's rank would be 'Boy'.
17. The JLR RAC Band remained as an integral part of the regiment until it was disbanded – pun intended – and became the Army Junior School of Music.
18. ACE was introduced in 1920; in 1923 passes were linked to promotion: no certificate, no promotion. ACE was replaced by the Education for Promotion Certificate (EPC) system in the early 1970s, designed to prepare soldiers for becoming SNCOs (EPC) and WOs – EPC (Advanced).
19. At various times, some boys were also taught to drive tanks but conducting D&M trade training was more time and resource intensive than gunnery, which tended to be preferred. Another factor was the oft-stated desire to get the youngster's 'into the turret as quickly as possible' in order to give them the opportunity to become effective tank commanders.
20. The JLR RAC band was initially a volunteer organization, formed as the 'Boys Band Sqn' on 23 April 1956 by Bandmaster Nobel 16/5L, but in September 1959 the first official Director of Music was appointed, Lieutenant Rodney Bashford, and band training was made official, effectively becoming a squadron in its own right. In 1985 the band was disbanded (!) and the training function taken over by the Army Junior School of Music.
21. In 1985 RAPC juniors were added, and in 1992 both RCT and RAOC, which changed to AGC and RLC following the creations of the large Corps in 1993.
22. Until 15 August 1982, Junior Soldiers, as opposed to Junior Leaders, were also trained under the Household Cavalry Squadron in the Guard's Depot, Pirbright.
23. The Juniors, as they progressed, took great delight in finding ways to 'buck the system'. The weekly pay parades involved marching up to a table occupied by the Troop Leader and one of the Troop Sergeants, who were responsible for dishing out the cash, which had to be signed for, swept it into the forage cap and then the Junior would replace his head dress (with cash inside), salute, about-turn and march off. Because the adults were heads-down and utterly absorbed in not making mistakes with the money or the paperwork, the members of my troop took it in turns to deliver the most outrageous salutes imaginable, worthy of a 'Japanese Admiral'.
24. At the time of writing (2022), the long course is for all combat arms less the AAC, plus drivers from the RLC. A shorter, twenty-three-week course is used for the remainder. In 2020 a junior soldier at Harrogate would earn around £14,000, whereas the lowest paid RAC adult soldier would receive about £21,000.

Annex D

1. The possible formation of an 'Independent Airborne Squadron RAC' was under serious discussion during 1948, but nothing came of it, probably due to the reduction in the size of the airborne forces and a lack of funding.
2. When on parade in No. 2 Dress, all other regimental accoutrements were worn, including the coloured trousers of The Skins and 11th Hussars.
3. Unsurprisingly, 2RTR supplied the most, with forty. No members of the Life Guards appear to have served in the squadron, as it seems they all went to the Guards Independent Parachute Company instead.
4. Because of the berets worn by those units, red for airborne, green for commando.
5. The Sioux, sometimes referred to as the 'clockwork mouse', replaced the smaller and less capable Skeeter from 1965.
6. This may have been unique, with most other RAC air troops and squadrons operating only Skeeters, Sioux and/or Scout. Some did, however, also occasionally operate fixed wing aircraft, mainly in the Middle and Far East theatres.

Annex E

1. In the early 1980s the introduction on the Muzzle Reference System (MRS) which allowed the gun to check and if required adjust the gun/sight relationship from inside the turret maximized this advance.
2. The introduction in the 1990s of the Live Fire Monitoring Equipment (LFME) allowing instructors to remotely monitor the commander's and gunner's actions assisted with this. Before then, the Second World War-era method of watching the crew from outside the turret and observing the fall of shot using binoculars, itself a near-miracle of multi-tasking and concurrent activity, was all that the instructor could do.
3. IFCS troop trials were conducted by 14/20H in 1981. On Challenger, the equivalent system was known as the Computerized Sighting System (CSS); as it was the system used *ab initio*, it could not be 'improved' hence the name change.
4. A familiar cry was that above-average gunners were slowed down by IFCS, but the reality was that most gunners improved as a result.
5. These were normally simple broadside movers, which did not replicate the 'head-on' mover expected to be the most likely moving target encountered in war. The introduction of (expensive and complex) multi-path railway systems on some ranges helped to alleviate this problem, but most training by the 1990s was being done using synthetic simulators.

6. Of course, this is a hugely abbreviated version of the IFCS technique, which included over a dozen variants and took many weeks of practice to learn properly.

7. Much criticized, the use of three-piece ammunition with 120mm guns from Chieftain onwards was a deliberate policy to improve the survivability of the tank if hit. Those in the know realized that the high rates of fire achieved by MBTs using one-piece ammunition might be spectacular on ranges, but were unlikely to feature much in a shooting war.

8. Some theorists thought that IR gunnery was a waste of effort, and preferred to rely on the use of white light, with all its obvious disadvantages. The phrase 'Go white, Go hard!' was used to summarize the aggressive use of white light.

9. Centurion was the last MBT to use HE ammunition rather than the dual-purpose HESH.

10. Armoured Piercing Fin Stabilized Discarding Sabot replaced APDS as the main ani-tank round from the mid-1980s.

11. The Beverley was replaced by the C130 Hercules in about 1967.

12. 3rd Carbs took over Vigilant-armed FSC Mk 2/6 from 5DG in June 1970 , describing it as 'sophisticated in concept and temperamental in operation'.

13. The introduction of GW into the armoured regiments came at a price: units equipped with six FV438 had to 'lose' the same amount of MBTs, in order to prevent an increase in regimental manpower of some twenty-four or so officers and soldiers, which the Treasury would not bear.

14. Despite intentions, the system was never used by the infantry, whose anti-tank weaponry included the 120mm BAT series of recoilless guns, the 84mm Carl Gustav 'Charlie Gee' shoulder-launched rocket, the 66mm LAW and then the Milan missile system.

Annex F

1. Initially the B45 set was developed for use in AFVs, but it was discarded as its frequency range was not compatible with the B47 and C42.

2. As late as the mid-1950s selected signallers could still attend the Long Range Comms course, and were taught Morse, but by the turn of the millennium this seems to have finally stopped being taught.

3. VRC stood for Vehicle Radio Communications, and PRC for Portable Radio Communications.

4. http://www.armedforces.co.uk/army/listings/l0102.html.

5. https://generaldynamics.uk.com/systems/mission-systems/land/bowman/.

Bibliography and Sources

A Note on Sources

A major component of the research for this work has involved the regimental journals; I have calculated that I have read over 700 of them. Whilst they are a particularly rich source of primary material, they are not without their problems.

General

Anon., *His Majesty's Regiments of the British Army*, Metro-Provincial, 1949

Anon., *Dinosaurs to Defence (BATUS)*, Purnell, *c.* 1985

Baker, Anthony, *The Genealogy of the Regiments of the British army: The Yeomanry*, BMH, 1999

Barker, Dennis, *Soldiering On*, Deutsch, 1981

Barzilay, David, *The British Army in Ulster*, Century, 1973

van der Bijl, Nick, *The Cyprus Emergency*, Pen & Sword, 2010

van der Bijl, Nick, *Operation Banner*, Pen & Sword, 2009

van der Bijl, Nick, *Nine Battles to Stanley*, Leo Cooper, 1999

Blaxland, Gregory, *The Regiments Depart; History of the British Army 1945–1970*, Kimber, 1971

Bodsworth, John, *Uniforms & Insignia of the RAC since 1946*, MLRS, 2006

Brett-Smith, Richard, *Berlin '45*, Greensleeves, 1966

Chrystal, Paul, *BAOR 1945–1993*, Pen & Sword, 2018

Clayton, Anthony, *The British Officer*, Routledge, 2013

Dawson, Malcolm, *Uniforms of the RAC*, Almark, 1974

Dunstan, Simon, *Centurion Main Battle Tank*, Haynes, 2017

Dunstan, Simon, *Armour of the Korean War 1950–1953*, Osprey, 2001

Fisher, John, *Sharpshooter Snapshots*, Portway, 1996

Fletcher, David, *British Military Transport 1929–1956*, The Stationery Office, 1998

French, E.G., *Goodbye to Boot and Saddle*, Hutchinson, 1951

Frost, John, *2 Para Falklands*, Buchan & Enright, 1983

Gorman, J.T., *The British Army*, Collins, 1940

Hallows, Ian, *Regiments & Corps of the British Army*, Arms & Armour, 1991

Hamilton, Nigel, *Monty: The Field Marshal 1944–1976*, Sceptre, 1986

Hastings, Max, *The Korean War*, Pan, 1987

Holmes, Richard, *Soldiers*, Harper, 2011

Jackson, Robert, *The Malayan Emergency & Indonesian Confrontation*, Pen & Sword, 2021

Jahner, Harald, *Aftermath: Life in the Fallout of the Third Reich*, Penguin (Kindle edn), 2021

Johnston, Peter, *British Forces in Germany: The Lived Experience*, Profile, 2019

Lister, David, *The Dark Age of Tanks: Britain's Lost Armour 1945–1970*, Pen & Sword, 2020

MacDonogh, Giles, *After the Reich*, John Murray, 2007

Murphy, Gerry, *Where did that Regiment Go?*, Spellmount, 2016

Pugh, Roger, *The Most Secret Place On Earth*, Larks Press, 2014

Robinson, M.P. and R. Griffin, *The RAC in the Cold War 1946–1990*, Pen & Sword, 2016

Strawson, John, *Hussars, Horses & History*, Pen & Sword, 2007

Tait, Janice and David Fletcher, *Tracing your Tank Ancestors*, Pen & Sword, 2011

Taylor, Dick, *Challenger 2 Main Battle Tank*, Haynes, 2018

Taylor, Dick, *Chieftain Main Battle Tank*, Haynes, 2016

Taylor, Dick, *Challenger 1 Main Battle Tank*, Haynes, 2015

Thompson, Graham N. and Teddy Nevill, *Territorial Army*, Ian Allan, 1989

Thorne, Tony, *Brasso, Blanco and Bull*, Robinson, 2000

Ventham, Philip and David Fletcher, *Moving the Guns*, HMSO, 1990

Verrier, Anthony, *An Army for the Sixties*, Secker & Warburg, 1966

Vinen, Richard, *National Service 1945–1963*, Penguin, 2014

Walker, Adrian, *Six Campaigns: National Servicemen at War 1948–1960*, Leo Cooper, 1993

Walker, Wallace Earl, *Reserve Forces & The British Territorial Army*, Tri-Service Press, 1990

Watson, Graham and Richard Rinaldi, *BAOR: An Organizational History 1947–2004*, Tiger Lily, 2005

White, Arthur, *A Bibliography of Regimental Histories of the British Army*, NMP, 1992

Corps and Regimental Histories

Anon., *1st The Queen's Dragoon Guards*, Gale & Polden, n.d.

Anon., *Short History of the Royal Dragoons*, Gale & Polden, n.d.

Anon., *Year of the Yeomanry*, Ogilby Trust, 1994

Anon., *Historical Record of the 9th Queen's Royal Lancers 1945–1960*, 9L, 1993

Anon., *A Short History of the Household Cavalry*, HCav Museum, *c.* 1986

Anon., *The Queen's Own Hussars*, Roundwood, 1985

Anon., *War in the Falklands*, BCA, 1982

Anon., *Regimental History 3rd Carabiniers*, 1957

Anon., *A Short History of the 12th Royal Lancers*, Gale & Polden, *c.* 1952

Anon., *A Short History of the 9th Queen's Royal Lancers 1715–1949*, Gale & Polden, 1949

Anon., *Short History of the 4th, 7th and 4th/7th Royal Dragoon Guards*, Gale & Polden, 1943

Barclay, C.N., *History of the 16th/5th Queen's Royal Lancers 1925–1961*, Gale & Polden, 1963

Bastin, Jeremy, *The History of the 15th/19th The King's Royal Hussars 1945–1980*, Keats House, 1981

Blacker, Cecil and Henry Woods, *5th Royal Inniskilling Dragoon Guards: Change & Challenge*, William Clowes, 1978

Blacklock, Michael, *The Royal Scots Greys*, Leo Cooper, 1971

Boardman, C.J., *Track in Korea (5DG)*, Shore Books, 2013

Bolitho, Hector, *The Galloping Third (3rd Hussars)*, Murray, 1963

Brace, Basher, *1st The Queen's Dragoon Guards: A Pictorial History 1959–2009*, QDG, 2009

Braddon, Russell, *All the Queen's Men (Household Cavalry)*, Hamish Hamilton, 1977

Brereton, J.M., History *of the 4th/7th Royal Dragoon Guards*, 4/7DG, 1982

Brereton, J.M., *The 7th Queen's Own Hussars*, Leo Cooper, 1975

Brett-Smith, Richard, *The 11th Hussars*, Leo Cooper, 1969

Brockbank, Robin, *A Short History of the 9th/12th Lancers 1960–1985*, 9/12L, 1985

Brockbank, R. and R.M. Collins, *A Short History of the XII Royal Lancers 1945–1960*, 9/12 Royal Lancers, n.d.

Fitzroy, Olivia, *Men of Valour (VIIIH, Vol. 3 1927–1958)*, Liverpool, 1961

ffrench Blake, R.L.V., *The 17th/21st Lancers*, Hamish Hamilton, 1968

ffrench Blake, R.L.V., *A History of the 17th/21st Lancers*, Macmillan, 1968

Hills, R.J.T., *The Royal Dragoons*, Leo Cooper, 1972

Hills, R.J.T., *The Life Guards*, Leo Cooper, 1971

Hills, R.J.T., *The Royal Horse Guards*, Leo Cooper, 1970

Hunt, Eric, *History of the 13th/18th Royal Hussars*, Light Dragoons CT, 1996

Keown-Boyd, Henry, *Remember with Advantages (10H, 11H, RH)*, Pen & Sword, 1994

Liddell Hart, B.H., *The Tanks Volume 2 (RTR)*, Cassell, 1959

Loyd, William, *Challengers and Chargers (LG)*, Leo Cooper, 1992

Lunt, James, *The Scarlet Lancers (16/5L)*, Leo Cooper, 1993

Lunt, James, *16th/5th Queen's Royal Lancers*, Leo Cooper, 1973

Macksey, Kenneth, *A History of the Royal Armoured Corps 1914–1975*, Newtown, 1983

Macksey, Kenneth, *The Tanks Volume 3 (RTR)*, Arms & Armour Press, 1979

Mallinson, Allan, *Light Dragoons*, Pen & Sword, 2012

Mann, Michael, *The Regimental History of the 1st The Queen's Dragoon Guards*, QDG, 1993

Manser, Roy, *The Household Cavalry Regiment*, Almark, 1975

Mileham, Patrick, *The Yeomanry Regiments*, Spellmount, 2003

Murland, J.R.W., *The Royal Armoured Corps*, Methuen, 1943

Murray, Major J.S.F., *A Short History of the 15th/19th The Kings Royal Hussars*, The Forces Press, 1954

Owen, Frank and H.W. Atkins, *The Royal Armoured Corps*, HMSO, 1945

Parkyn, H.G., *A Short History of the 16th/5th Lancers*, Gale & Polden, 1934

Rhoderick-Jones, Robin, *In Peace & War (QRH)*, Pen & Sword, 2018

Shannon, Kevin, *Death or Glory The 17th/21st Lancers 1922–1993*, Fonthill, 2021

Strawson, J.M. et al., *Irish Hussar (QRIH)*, QRIHA, 1986

Thompson, Ralph, *The 15th/19th The King's Royal Hussars: A Pictorial History*, Quoin, 1989

Watson, J.N.P., *Through Fifteen Reigns (Household Cavalry)*, Spellmount, 1997

Watson, J.N.P., *The Story of the Blues & Royals*, Leo Cooper, 1993

Wood, Stephen, In *the Finest Tradition (Scots DG)*, Mainstream, 1988

Journals

The 4th/7th Royal Dragoon Guards Regimental Magazine

The 5th Royal Inniskilling Dragoon Guards Journal

The X Royal Hussars Gazette

The XI Hussar Journal

The Acorn (LG)

Armour (RAC)

The Army Quarterly

The Blue (RHG)

The Blue and Royal (RHG/D)

British Army Journal

British Army Review

The Cavalry Journal

The Chapka (RL)

Combat (RAC, Infantry)

Conqueror (JLR RAC)

The Crossbelts (KRIH, QRIH, QRH)

The Delhi Spearman (9L, 9/12L)

The DRAC Newsletter

The Eagle (Royals)

The Eagle and Carbine (Scots DG)

The Feather and Carbine (3rd Carbs)

The Hawk (14/20H)

The Household Cavalry Journal
The Journal of the 4th Queens Own Hussars
The Journal of the 13th/18th Royal Hussars
The Journal of the Queens Own Hussars
The Journal of the Royal Dragoons
The KDG Journal
The King's Royal Hussars Regimental Journal
The Light Dragoon
The Queen's Own Yeoman
The RAC Centre Bulletin
The RAC Journal
The RAC Newsletter
The Reconnaissance Journal
The Red Lanyard (1RTR)
The Regiment Magazine
The Regimental Journal of the 3rd The King's Own Hussars
The Regimental Journal of the King's Dragoon Guards
The Regimental Journal of the Queen's Bays
The Royal Hussar Journal
The Scarlet & Green Journal (16/5L)
The Scots Grey Journal
Sharpshooters Gazette (3/4 CLY)
Soldier Magazine
The Tank/Tank Journal/Tank Magazine (TC/RTC/RTR)
The Twelfth Royal Lancers Journal
Vanguard (Inns of Court Yeo)
The Vedette (QRL)
The White Lancer & The Vedette (17/21L)
The Wolf (SNIY)

Official Publications

Mackintosh, Colonel H.W.B., *The Tank Factory: Seventy Years of Government Tank Design*, MVEE, 1984

Official, *Ballistics & Technical Aspects of Tank Gunnery*, RAC Gunnery School, 1996

Official, *AC71520 Operation Desert Sabre*, MOD, 1993

Official, *A Commission in the Royal Armoured Corps*, MOD, 1983

Official, *RAC Trg Pam 40 General Principles of Shooting from AFVs*, MOD, 1981

Official, *Royal Armoured Corps*, MOD, 1970

Official, *The Catterick Guide*, Littlebury, *c.* 1969

Official, *Regular Army. Why Drop Out?*, Fosh & Cross, 1946

Regimental Museums

Household Cavalry, The Household Cavalry Museum, Horse Guards, Whitehall, London SW1A 2AX, museum@householdcavalry.co.uk

King's Royal Hussars, Horsepower, Peninsula Barracks, Romsey Road, Winchester, SO23 8TS, assistant@horsepowermuneum.co.uk

Light Dragoons, Discovery Museum, Blandford Square, Newcastle upon Tyne, NE1 4JA, roberta.goldwater@twmuseums.org.uk

Queen's Dragoon Guards, Firing Line, Cardiff Castle, CF10 2RB, ast-curator2@cardiffcastlemuseum.org.uk

Queen's Royal Hussars, 1 Trinity Mews, Priory Rd, Warwick, CV34 4NA, info@qrhmuseum.uk

Royal Dragoon Guards, 3A Tower Street, York, YO1 9SB, hhq@rdgmuseum.org.uk

Royal Lancers, Derby Museum & Art Gallery, The Strand, Derby, DE1 1BS, angela@derbymuseums.org

Royal Lancers & Notts Yeomanry, RLNY Museum, Thorseby Park, Notts, NG2 29EP, mickholtby17@gmail.com

Royal Scots Dragoon Guards, New Barracks, Edinburgh Castle, EH1 2YT, info@scotsdgmuseum.com

Royal Tank Regiment/RAC, The Bovington Tank Museum, Dorset, BH20 6JG, info@tankmuseum.org

Index

Persons